Balkan Yearbook of European and International Law

Volume 2021

Balkans Yearbook of European and International Law publishes peer-reviewed scholarly articles, notes, comments and book reviews on private and public European and International Law. The yearbook contains summaries and analyses of recent decisions by national and international courts and arbitral or other tribunals. The yearbook has one section with a special hot topic or focus as well as sections about European and international law in each volume. Moreover, it presents book reviews to recent publications from the region or with a major impact for the region. The yearbook focuses on recent developments of European and International Law and presents a forum for scholarly discourse on European and International Law from the perspective of the region of South-East Europe. However, the publication is not exclusive in that regard: contributions from the perspective of the wider world are also strongly encouraged and welcomed.

More information about this series at https://link.springer.com/bookseries/16247

Dušan V. Popović • Ivana Kunda •
Zlatan Meškić • Enis Omerović
Editors

Balkan Yearbook of European and International Law 2021

Springer

Editors
Dušan V. Popović
Faculty of Law
University of Belgrade
Belgrade, Serbia

Ivana Kunda
Faculty of Law
University of Rijeka
Rijeka, Croatia

Zlatan Meškić
College of Law
Prince Sultan University
Riyadh, Saudi Arabia

Enis Omerović
College of Law
Prince Sultan University
Riyadh, Saudi Arabia

ISSN 2524-8715 ISSN 2524-8723 (electronic)
Balkan Yearbook of European and International Law
ISBN 978-3-030-97430-5 ISBN 978-3-030-97431-2 (eBook)
https://doi.org/10.1007/978-3-030-97431-2

This Springer imprint is published by the registered company Springer Nature Switzerland AG
The registered company address is: Gewerbestrasse 11, 6330 Cham, Switzerland

Preface

The legal systems of Southeast Europe are in transition for over three decades. Following the profound political and economic changes in the early 1990s, they took their own ways of development, sharing not only their legal history but also the continuous influences deriving from the European and international law. The intensity by which EU law affects the regional developments is very strong in all national legal systems of Southeast Europe, while the variances depend largely on the progress each country has made toward the EU membership. In addition, legal obligations under international law are continuous challenges for these countries.

The Balkan Yearbook of European and International Law (BYEIL) aims at providing insights into recent developments in European and international law and presents a forum for scholarly discourse on these areas of law from the perspective of Southeast Europe. While the BYEIL's focus is on the Southeast European region, its scope is not limited to that region and contributions concerning the issues in European or international law in general are welcomed as well. This policy is reflected in the contents of the BYEIL. Besides these two sections, each issue of the BYEIL is devoted to a particular topic.

The third issue of the BYEIL is devoted in particular to the specific legal challenges that the Southeast European countries are facing in the area of intellectual property law. In five papers, authors discuss topics in Serbian and Bosnian and Herzegovinian copyright, trademark, and patent laws, whose relevance extends beyond their national borders. The papers published in the permanent sections on European law and international law explore contemporary challenges in public and private law disciplines. They stretch across various legal fields, including consumer law, commercial law, company law, and criminal law, and tackle some of the fundamental theoretical matters as well as portray the most recent developments in legal practice.

Belgrade, Serbia Dušan V. Popović
Rijeka, Croatia Ivana Kunda
Riyadh, Saudi Arabia Zlatan Meškić
Riyadh, Saudi Arabia Enis Omerović

Contents

Part I
Intellectual Property Challenges in South-East Europe

The Referential Use of Another's Trademark in the Context of Comparative Advertising

Slobodan M. Marković

Contents

1 Introductory Remarks

This topic leads us in the field of trademark law and unfair competition law.

By the referential use of another's trademark, we mean the act of a person who is not the holder of the respective trademark, but who uses that mark in public communication for the purpose of identifying or indicating the goods/services (hereinafter: products) of the trademark holder. The term "nominative use" is

S. M. Marković (✉)
University of Belgrade, Faculty of Law, Belgrade, Serbia
e-mail: smm@ius.bg.ac.rs

D. V. Popović et al. (eds.), *Balkan Yearbook of European and International Law 2021*, Balkan Yearbook of European and International Law 2021,
https://doi.org/10.1007/978-3-030-97431-2_1

sometimes employed as a synonym.[1] In its broadest sense, the referential use includes all cases in which someone, through another's trademark, gives any public statement/information about the products of the trademark holder. This can be part of news reporting, creative expression, advertising, offering one's own products as compatible with the products of the trademark holder, etc. We shall limit our considerations to cases where referential use takes the form of information addressed to consumers for the purpose of influencing their market decisions. Sometimes, the sender of this information is an entity that is not a competitor of the trademark holder (e.g. the trader advertises which brands are represented in his shop).[2] Sometimes, on the other hand, the sender of the information is a competitor of the trademark holder.

The relevant legislation in the European Union (hereinafter: the EU), at the moment, consists of: the Directive on the harmonization of laws relating to trademarks[3] (hereinafter: the Directive on Trademarks), the EU Trademark Regulation,[4] the Unfair Commercial Practices Directive in the business-to-consumer relationship in the internal market[5] (hereinafter: the Unfair Competition Directive) and the Misleading and Comparative Advertising Directive[6] (hereinafter: the Advertising Directive).

In Serbia, as a country in the process of joining the EU, the relevant legislation, which is more or less harmonized with the mentioned EU legislation, consists of: the Law on Trademarks[7] (hereinafter: LOT), the Law on Trade[8] (hereinafter: LOTrade) and the Law on Advertising[9] (hereinafter: LOA).

The issue we shall deal with concerns the permissibility of referential use of another's trademark without the consent of the trademark holder. The answer to this question is not simple. The matter is challenging since certain legal norms require a deeper understanding of their meaning and purpose, so that the effect *summum ius summa iniuria* can be avoided. The problems we are talking about can only be

[1] *Max Planck Institute for Intellectual Property and Competition Law* (2011), p. 102.

[2] The trademark holder sold to the trader the labeled products for retail sale, and the exclusive right of the trademark holder to further market these products was exhausted.

[3] Directive (EU) 2015/2436 of the European parliament and of the Council of 16 December 2015 to approximate the laws of the Member States relating to trade marks (Official Journal of the European Union L 336/1).

[4] Regulation (EU) 2017/1001 of the European parliament and of the Council of 14 June 2017 on the European Union trade mark (Official Journal of the European Union L 154/1).

[5] Directive 2005/29/EC of the European parliament and of the Council of 11 May 2005 concerning unfair business-to-consumer commercial practices in the internal market (Official Journal of the European Union L 149/22).

[6] Directive 2006/114/EC of the European parliament and of the Council of 12 December 2006 concerning misleading and comparative advertising (Official Journal of the European Union L 376/21).

[7] Official Gazette of the Republic of Serbia, No. 6/2020.

[8] Official Gazette of the Republic of Serbia, No. 52/2019.

[9] Official Gazette of the Republic of Serbia, No. 6/2016 and 52/2019.

partially remedied by appropriate interventions in the legal text, while the rest is left to the ability of the judiciary to apply the law purposefully.

2 Critique of the Text of LOT from the Aspect of Its Harmonization with the EU Directive on Trademarks

The issue we are dealing with concerns the content and the limits of the trademark holder's right. In other words, we need to understand what prohibitive rights the trademark holder has in relation to third parties, how far they reach, and where the freedom of third parties to use someone else's trademark begins.

Our legislator incorrectly titled the provision of Article 49 of the LOT, which defines the exclusive rights of the trademark holder, with "Scope of the rights of the trademark holder".[10] This editorial flaw is harmless from the aspect of the interpretation and application of this legal norm. However, the matter becomes very problematic in the wording of paragraph 3 of the same article, which lists the exclusive rights of the trademark holder. This paragraph begins with the statement: "In terms of paragraph 2 of this Article, the trademark holder has the right to prohibit in particular:..." (the list of exclusive rights follows). The phrase "in particular" was translated into Serbian as "i sledeće" which means "and the following" or, more descriptively, "not only what is enumerated, but also something else." In this way, the legislator resorts to a formulation that makes this list of exclusive rights open, not closed.[11] It is not difficult to grasp the origin of this nomotechnical weakness: it is a failed translation of the beginning of paragraph 3, Article 10 of the EU Directive on Trademarks, which reads in English "The following, in particular, may be prohibited under paragraph 2". Quite specifically, the term "in particular" is translated to mean "especially". Indeed, this meaning of the term "in particular" exists in the English language, but there is also a meaning that only makes sense in this context, and that is "specifically" or "that and nothing else."[12] The whole problem can be solved by deleting the word "i" ("and") from the Serbian text. The fact that this oversight persisted despite several previous amendments to the LOT indicates that neither the legislator nor the professional public have any idea of the potential problem of too broad a linguistic definition of the rights conferred by trademark, thus leaving the door open for the trademark holder to prohibit certain cases of use of his trademark,

---

[10] The corresponding provision of Article 10 of the EU Directive on Trademarks is entitled "Rights conferred by a trademark". Obviously, content (rights conferred) and scope (outreach of the rights conferred, limitations etc.) are two different notions.

[11] The same mistake was made by the Croatian legislator when formulating Article 11, paragraph 3 of the Trademark Act (Official Gazette No. 14/2019). Such a mistake, however, was not made by the Montenegrin legislator. See Article 10 and Article 11 of the Law on Trademarks (Official Gazette of Montenegro No. 72/2010, 44/2012, 18/2014 and 40/2016).

[12] Cambridge Dictionary Online, https://dictionary.cambridge.org/dictionary/english/particular?q=in+particular.

although they cannot be subsumed under any of the points of paragraph 3, Article 49 of LOT.

There is another serious omission of the Serbian legislator in the harmonization of LOT with the EU Directive on Trademarks. Namely, the provision of Article 14, paragraph 1, point 3 of the Directive[13] has not been fully transposed in Article 54, paragraph 2, point 3 of the LOT. It omits that the trademark holder may not prohibit another person from using that mark in commercial transactions in accordance with good business practice for the purposes of identifying or referring to the goods or services of the trademark holder himself. Instead, our legislator has prescribed only one permitted form of referential use of someone else's trademark, and that is when its use is necessary to indicate the purpose of the goods or services, especially when it comes to spare parts or accessories. So, our legislator simply ignored the part of the text of the EU Directive on Trademarks, which is completely new in relation to the previous EU Directive on Trademarks from 2008.[14] There is one ironic moment in guessing what could be the reason for that. Namely, the general rule on the admissibility of referential use, on the one hand, and the example (that our legislator took over), on the other hand, the EU legislator connected with the words "in particular". This time, however, he had in mind the opposite possible meaning of those words: "especially", and not "that and nothing else". It turns out that our legislator, again completely ignoring the context, in this case also chose the wrong meaning of the English phrase "in particular".[15]

Although these issues will be dealt with in detail later, we shall present here only one example of the consequences of the mentioned legislative flaws. It is a common practice for traders to advertise by using trademarks of products they procured for retail purposes.[16] In respect to those products, of course, the exclusive right of the trademark holder to put them on the market is exhausted, but there is no exhaustion of the exclusive right to use the trademark for the purposes of advertising the products. According to the EU Directive on Trademarks, this practice unequivocally falls within the permitted forms of referential use, while according to the LOT it unequivocally represents a trademark infringement. Such a discrepancy between the EU Directive on Trademarks, and the "harmonized" LOT is simply not an acceptable situation.

---

[13] "A trade mark shall not entitle the proprietor to prohibit a third party from using, in the course of trade, the trade mark for the purpose of identifying or referring to goods or services as those of the proprietor of that trade mark, in particular, where the use of the trade mark is necessary to indicate the intended purpose of a product or service, in particular as accessories or spare parts."

[14] Directive 2008/95/EC of the European Parliament and of the Council of 22 October 2008 to approximate the laws of the Member States relating to trade marks (Official Journal of the European Union L 299).

[15] In this confusion, there is no need to absolve the EU legislator from responsibility for the use of linguistic phrases whose meaning is ambiguous. It is a great nomotechnical weakness.

[16] For example, INTERSPORT, a Serbian retail chain for sports shoes, clothes and gear of various brands, advertises by using the trademarks of the products on offer: "Adidas", "Puma", "Nike", etc.

3 Theoretical and Legislative Framework

3.1 *Trademark Functions*

The most difficult problems of the practical application of today's trademark law stem from the ambiguity of views on the purpose of trademark law, or more specifically, the functions of a trademark that are legally protected. Ample literature has been published on this subject. To save space and keep the reader's attention, we take the freedom to start with some commonplace statements,[17] and to take a step further from there. So, the following is indisputable.

(a) Since the historical beginnings of the legal protection of distinctive marks up to the present day, the dominant function of the trademark has been to protect/ ensure the credibility of information on the origin of the labeled product. The implied guaranty of the quality of the labeled product naturally relies upon this function. These two functions are the basis for the complementarity of the interests of trademark holders, on the one hand, and consumers, on the other. Namely, due to the reliability of the information on the origin of the labeled product, the consumer also believes in the consistency of its quality, on the basis of which he makes purchasing decisions. At the same time, the supplier of goods, i.e. the trademark holder thus has an incentive to maintain the quality of his product and to improve it, in order to ensure the loyalty of consumers. The cumulative effect of this interaction is to enable competition in the market.
(b) Since the third decade of the twentieth century, the idea that trademark law must provide immediate protection to an advertising function of a trademark has emerged.[18] This idea follows the evolution of marketing practices whose mission of building consumer awareness of the existence of a labeled product turns into a mission of persuading consumers to procure that product. The general term for the intangible value that trademark holders build and exploit in this way is REPUTATION of a trademark. In the last few decades, the trend of direct protection of reputation, completely independent of the protection of indicating the origin of products, has aggressively expanded in the trademark law.
(c) The correspondence between a particular legal good and a particular public interest in the cases under a) and b) is somewhat different. Thus, the trademark, as a form of legal protection of the credibility of information on the origin of products, serves the function of reducing transaction costs, which enhances the efficiency of the market. This is certainly in the public interest. However, with the trademark as a form of direct legal protection of the reputation of the mark,

[17] *Manifesta haud indigent probatione* (what is known requires no proof). This paper is addressed to trade mark specialists who don't need the meticulously sorted scientific references in order to take a position on accuracy of the statements under a), b) and c) above.

[18] The advertising function of a trademark has always existed, but not as an independent one and directly protected. It was indirectly protected since derived from the function of indicating the origin of the product.

the only public interest can be seen in the concept of abstractly understood property as one of the central social values from the arsenal of natural/human rights.[19] The logic of this view is that the trademark holder has INVESTED in the reputation of his mark, and that the protection of this investment must be covered by the functions of the trademark. In recent literature, this is increasingly referred to as the investment function of a trademark.[20]

Summarizing the presented views, we can state that today's trademark law has two focuses. The traditional one is the protection of the indication of origin of the labeled product; the modern one is the protection of the reputation of the mark as such (investment function of the trademark). The said dualism of focus is in fact a current reflex of the historical dualism of private law frameworks for the protection of distinctive marks: the trademark law and the unfair competition law.

3.2 *Interaction of Trademark Law and Unfair Competition Law*

It is common knowledge that distinctive marks have been used for more than 2500 years. The socio-historical conditions that have led to the need for a systematic legal regulation of their use can be roughly reduced to the following:

- the collapse of the medieval system of guilds, as a consequence of the industrial revolution, the abandonment of artisanal production and the establishment of a competitive market in early nineteenth century Europe;
- mass production and development of transport that increased the distance between the producer and the market for his products, as well as the time gap between production and consumption;
- the collapse of the traditional system of trust in producer-consumer relations, which existed only in the small local markets.[21]

These circumstances have led to the massive fraudulent labeling of products with other people's distinctive marks, and thus to the escalation of the asymmetry of

---

[19] Article 1, paragraph 1 of the Protocol No.1 to the Convention for the Protection of Human Rights and Fundamental Freedoms: "Every natural or legal person is entitled to the peaceful enjoyment of his possessions. No one shall be deprived of his possessions except in the public interest and subject to the conditions provided for by law and by the general principles of international law."

[20] The argument about reducing transaction costs and the consequent increase in market efficiency comes from the arsenal of so-called utilitarian doctrine, while the argument about investing comes from the spheres of natural law and law on human rights. This is a reflection of a deep theoretical dichotomy that permeates the law on trademarks, and which can be reduced to the fact that there is no single position on what is meant when it is said that a trademark is the "intellectual property" of its owner.

[21] Dornis (2017), pp. 10–12. The author refers to an abundance of sources that plastically depict the extent of fraud and confusion due to the use of other people's distinctive marks in the market.

information between suppliers and consumers. The first reaction of the legislator was the criminalization of such a practice and the threat of criminal sanctions. Obviously, the legislator put consumers in the center of protection against fraud, by protecting their interest in obtaining true information about the origin of products on the market.[22]

Although criminal protection of trademarks still exists today, it is the last one we think of when we talk about trademarks. The process of migration of protection of distinctive marks from the sphere of public (criminal) law to the sphere of private law is the result of the private nature of entrepreneurship as an expression of freedom of economic activity. This is where the bifurcation in the development of legal protection of distinctive marks begins: one stream represents the law on unfair competition, and the other the law on trademarks. The first established protection in the form of a tort lawsuit against the act of using someone else's distinctive mark contrary to good business practice; the other established protection in the form of an absolute exclusive right (trademark). The common private law denominator of both fields of law is empowering a legal person that uses a certain distinctive mark, to start a private lawsuit before a civil court in order to defend itself from third parties who use its mark without its consent, and thus compromise its market position.[23]

This, compared to criminal protection, has changed the emphasis in the protection mechanism. The public interest in preventing fraud and deception on the market was the goal in criminal law, and the protection of the interests of trademark holders was a consequential effect. In the private law protection regime, the matter is a bit more complicated. In the unfair competition law, the immediate goal remained the protection of the competitive market, but the interest of the holder of the trademark was instrumentalized for that purpose. In trademark law, on the other hand, the immediate goal becomes the interest of the trademark holder, and the prevention fraud and deception in the market becomes a consequential effect.

By focusing on the interests of the trademark owner, who has been given the legal authority to prohibit another (under certain conditions) from using his mark in commercial transactions, the basis of the idea of ownership over the mark has been formed. These "proprietary" powers originally arose from the fact that the mark really functions as a means of indicating the origin of the labeled product on the

[22] Prussian Criminal Code of 1851 (Art. 269), then the Criminal Code of the German Empire of 1871 (Art. 287). See details in Dornis (2017), p. 13, 14.

[23] For the sake of precision, we must draw attention to one nuance. Namely, according to the unfair competition law, consumers (through their associations) also have the right to sue. On this basis, one can understand the dichotomy "propertization vs. socialization", which some authors see in the relationship between trademark law and unfair competition law. See Dornis (2017), p. 50. Time has confirmed the appropriateness of this observation. It can be seen from Article 1 of the EU Directive on Unfair Competition, which states: "The purpose of this Directive is to contribute to the proper functioning of the internal market and achieve a high level of consumer protection by approximating the laws, regulations and administrative provisions of the Member States on unfair commercial practices harming consumers' economic interests." It is evident that there is no mention here of the rights of economic entities.

market.[24] In Germany and in a number of other European countries, soon after, the administrative proceedings for the registration of trademarks were introduced. The registration created a firm distinction between trademark law, on the basis of which the subject acquires the exclusive right to a registered trademark, and the unfair competition law as a form of protection for an unregistered trademark. At the same time, a hierarchical relationship was established between them, which provided stronger protection to the registered trademark than to the unregistered one.

In the United States, the development was different insofar as trademark registration was made possible only with the enactment of the federal Lanham Act in 1946. Until then, the protection of trademarks was based only on common law rules. More precisely, within the unfair competition law (being a part of common law), a corpus of rules that can be called common trademark law crystallized. The actual use of a certain mark to distinguish certain goods on the market was until 1946 the only way to acquire a trademark as an exclusive right; afterwards, it became an alternative to the registration of a trademark in administrative proceedings. This informality in acquiring a trademark has made the dichotomy between trademark law and the unfair competition law less pronounced in the United States than in Europe. Namely, the fact that the state creates a trademark as an exclusive right by its sovereign act, has become the main demarcation between trademark law and unfair competition law in Europe. In contrast, the prevailing view in the United States has always been that this is only a technical matter, and that the essence of both legal fields is the same: the protection of goodwill as an intangible asset owned by the trademark holder.

Until the middle of the twentieth century, the distinction between trademark law and unfair competition law in Europe resulted in legal practice reaching for trademark law in classic cases of infringement of a registered trademark because of confusion about the origin of products. At the same time, unfair competition law served for the protection against confusion caused by the use of unregistered marks, as well as against all other uses of registered and unregistered marks, in which an element of contradiction to good business practices could be detected (unfair/dishonest conduct in the market).

If we look at today's situation, we can notice a trend of intertwining of trademark law and unfair competition law. On the one hand, certain institutes of the unfair competition law spill over into the trademark law. The most striking example is the institute of the famous (renowned) trademark, whose protection against dilution was traditionally located in the unfair competition law, and now represents an integral part of the trademark law.[25] Another example concerns the criterion of fairness/unfairness as a measure of the permissibility/prohibition of a certain act. This

---

[24]This is the core of trademark's goodwill (German—*Verkehrsgeltung*).

[25]In the USA, this was done through the Federal Trademark Dilution Act of 1995. In Europe, see Article 10, paragraph 2, item c) of the EU Directive on Trademarks; Article 9, paragraph 2, item c) of the EU Trademark Regulation; Article 56, paragraph 2 of the LOT. At the international level, see Article 16 of TRIPS Agreement.

criterion is intrinsic to unfair competition law, but it is now integrated into trademark law as a criterion for trademark infringement.[26] On the other hand, confusion regarding trademarks has become one of the criteria for determining the act of unfair competition.[27] Conclusively, there is no longer an unambiguous prevalence of trademark law in relation to unfair competition law.

Based on these facts, the literature suggests that the protection of distinctive marks via unfair competition law and via trademark low shows a trend towards the consolidation of objectives, and, moreover, the unification of these two legal areas.[28]

3.3 *Consolidation of Goals*

Since the permissibility of comparative advertising as a form of referential use of another's trademark cannot be discussed without relying on both unfair competition law and trademark law, it is crucial to comprehend the consolidated goals of both branches of law. This is for the simple reason that all forms of use of another's trademark, which are compatible with these purposes, must be legally permitted, regardless of the discussions that are taking place about the functions of trademark. More specifically, these consolidated objectives must be reflected in the functions of trademark.

Let us start with the least controversial statement: labeling products with distinctive marks is a form of social communication. This statement calls for the need to look at this communication through the eyes of semiotics (the science of signs). The theory is dominated by the so-called triadic concept of a sign (mark), according to which a distinctive mark can be broken down into its three necessary components: (a) a verbal, graphic or three-dimensional signifier, (b) a specific commodity that is labeled and (c) information on the labeled commodity, such as goodwill (signified).[29] Therefore, when an economic entity labels its products and puts them on the market, it sends information to the consumer about its products. Since the consumer is a "referee" in market competition, competitors provide him with information through their trademarks, helping him to navigate the market and orient himself when deciding to enter a specific transaction. Hence, the correctness (which implies

[26] In the EU Directive on Trademarks, the term "unfair" is mentioned once in the preamble, and then in Article 5, paragraph 3, item a); in the EU Trademark Regulation it is mentioned in Article 9, paragraph 2, item 3; in LOT it is mentioned in Art. 6, para. 1, item 4 and Art. 56, para. 2.

[27] EU Unfair Competition Directive, Article 6, para.2, item a). At the same time, the EU Directive on Trademarks and the EU Trademark Regulation stipulate that the trademark owner has the authority to prohibit another from using his trademark, if such use violates the norms of unfair competition law, which regulate comparative advertising. These provisions have their counterpart in Serbian LOT and LOA.

[28] Dornis (2017), p. 239.

[29] Beebe (2004), p. 646. Inspired by the semiotic theory of Charles Sanders Pierce, the author discusses the fundamental issues of trademark law: the subject matter and scope of protection.

truthfulness in the first place) of information is the main condition for the functioning of the market based on consumer decisions. That is how the economic meaning of product labeling is established: information on the origin of the product (and indirectly on its quality) → reduction of transaction costs → market efficiency. Therefore, the trademark serves the function of economization of the process of informing the consumer about products on the market.[30]

Returning to the fields of trademark law and unfair competition law, we must conclude that their common (consolidated) goal is, first and foremost, to ensure the free flow of information to help the consumer make an economically rational (or at least informed) decision, that is, to prevent the flow of information that is not serving that function. That is why the prevention of consumer deception, i.e., the prevention of misleading labeling of products, has always been in the center of attention of both branches of law. A very pictorial way to define the information value of a trademark, which (value) is thus protected, is navigation information, or **navigation goodwill**.

But, as we have already indicated, trademarks are, due to various advertising techniques, carriers of additional information that can be generally tagged as reputation. Manipulating the will of the consumer through the reputation of the trademark is based on the scarcity of immaterial goods such as exclusivity, prestige, diversity, etc. The consumer's decision to obtain a trademarked product is thus attributed predominantly to his will to obtain the immaterial goods that the trademark symbolizes, rather than the product *per se*. In a word, by purchasing a product, the consumer appropriates the immaterial value of trademarks' symbolic meaning. This value, called BRAND in modern parlance, is an upgrade over navigation goodwill, and can be termed **surplus goodwill**.[31] The current issue of trademark law and the unfair competition law is to what extent and in what way it is possible and necessary to protect this surplus goodwill. In trademark law theory, those trademark functions that go beyond the scope of preventing confusion about the origin/quality of the product, in particular the investment function, are directly related to this issue.

To summarize, we can localize the issue of referential use of someone else's trademark in the field of relations between the legal policy that protects navigation goodwill and the legal policy that protects surplus goodwill. More precisely, the question is whether this second policy can limit or compromise the first one. If the answer is no, the referential use of another's trademark, which is in the function of

---

[30] Landes and Posner (1987), p. 269.

[31] We owe the terms 'navigation goodwill' and 'surplus goodwill' (which make up the information asset of the trademark holder), as well as a successful explanation of the concepts they denote to T. Doris: "Two different scenarios can thus be distinguished. The first consists of cases where the consumer is actually or potentially confused. In these situations, the consumer's referee function is impeded; damage will occur as a result of distorted decision making and transacting. What is affected in these cases is navigation goodwill. The second scenario, by contrast, comprises cases where the consumer's market transaction remains unmanipulated in terms of information correctness and the freedom of decision making. These cases may be characterized as protecting a different category of trademark goodwill—concretely, surplus goodwill. Protection then especially focuses on a trademark's prestige, association-creating capacity, or scarcity-signaling properties."See Dornis (2017), p. 358. We shall continue to use these pictorial terms in this paper.

correctly informing the consumer, cannot be prevented by reasons related to the protection of the reputation of that mark. If the answer, in turn, is positive, referential use can be prevented, although it would provide accurate information to consumers. As we shall see, the answer is not unambiguous, but it still allows the formulation of certain rules.

4 Comparative Advertising as the Most Legally Sensitive Form of Referential Use of a Trademark

The EU Advertising Directive defines comparative advertising as advertising that "explicitly or implicitly identifies a competitor or a good or service offered by a competitor".[32] Furthermore, noting that comparative advertising has the potential to harm competition but also to enhance it, the Directive sets as its goal the prescribing of conditions for the permissibility of comparative advertising. Liberalism or strictness of these conditions reflects different accents of competition policy, in different times and countries. The United States is characterized by a traditionally liberal attitude of legal practice towards comparative advertising.[33] Such a practice was also supported by the Federal Trade Commission in its Policy Statement on Comparative Advertising.[34] Moreover, the legislator took such a position when he explicitly excluded cases of using someone else's trademark in comparative advertising from the application of the rules on preventing the dilution of trademarks.[35] It is evident that the *ratio* of such attitudes is based on giving priority to the policy of freedom of

---

[32] The same formulation was provided by our LOA in Article 14, paragraph 1. Explicit identification exists e.g. in an advertising statement: "Ariel washes what is left behind Merix." An example of implicit identification could be: "TV Antena, as the second-ranked in terms of rating, has twice as many hours of cultural program as the first-ranked television." It is not superfluous to mention that the so-called superlative advertising (e.g. "Polly is the cheapest chicken hot dog on our market") is also a form of implicit identification of all other competitors.

[33] See Smith v. Chanel, Inc., 402 F.2d 562 (9th Cir. 1968) at https://casetext.com/case/smith-v-chanel-inc. This was a dispute between the holder of the "Chanel" perfume brand and the defendant who advertised his perfumes in a magazine by stating: "We dare you to try to detect any difference between Chanel #5 ($25.00) and Ta'Ron's 2nd Chance ($7.00)". The court sided with the defendant, assuming that the Chanel product itself was not patented and that the defendant had the right to copy it „for imitation is the life blood of competition. It is the unimpeded availability of substantially equivalent units that permits the normal operation of supply and demand to yield the fair price society must pay for a given commodity." Therefore, "a competitor's chief weapon is his ability to represent his product as being equivalent and cheaper."

[34] See Charlotte J. Romano (2005), p. 378.

[35] See §1125, (c)3 A 1) the Lanham Act: "The following shall not be actionable as dilution by blurring or dilution by tarnishment under this subsection:

(A) Any fair use, including a nominative or descriptive fair use, or facilitation of such fair use, of a famous mark by another person other than as a designation of source for the person's own goods or services, including use in connection with—

(i) advertising or promotion that permits consumers to compare goods or services..."

information for consumers. On the other hand, Europe is characterized by a more restrictive position of legal practice[36] and the legislator,[37] which carries out a kind of "censorship of true market information" in order to protect trademark holders.[38]

It is not difficult to assume that true information about a product is most easily communicated to consumers through comparative advertising, because the consumer experience with someone else's reference product is taken as a benchmark for consumer expectations regarding the product being advertised. Comparative advertising always aims to emphasize a certain superior characteristic of the advertised product, on the basis of which the consumer will choose that product and not the reference product. This practice has a positive effect on market efficiency due to the combination of the two consequences. The first is to eliminate the overestimation of the reference product, and alleviate the anticompetitive effect of the reference product trademark. The second is to eliminate the underestimation of the advertised product, which increases competition.

The only one who suffers here is the reference trademark holder. The question is whether trademark law and unfair competition law provide a basis for protecting his interest in such cases. As we shall see, the answer varies, depending on several factors that can be classified into two groups: factors related to the protection of navigation goodwill and factors related to the protection of surplus goodwill.

On the side of positive law, the criteria for this assessment are mostly contained in the unfair competition law, and the resulting assessment is unreservedly recognized by the trademark law.[39]

[36] One of the most striking examples is the L'Oréal case (C–487/07) before the European Court of Justice. There, the court took the position that the comparative advertising of the defendants' own perfumes through the use of Chanel's trademarks and the message that they smell the same, has elements of trademark infringement, although this does not cause any confusion.

[37] The EU Advertising Directive (Art. 4, para. 1, item g) explicitly prohibits comparative advertising of products that are presented as imitations or replicas of products labeled with someone else's trademark. The same provision is taken over in Article 14, paragraph 2, item 7 of the LOA of Serbia. That prohibition, through the appropriate blanket norm of trademark law, acquired the status of a basis for trademark infringement. For legal theory, this is, therefore, an example of the prevalence of unfair competition law over trademark law.

[38] Dornis and Wein (2016), p. 430.

[39] See Article 10, paragraph 2, item f of the EU Directive on Trademarks, i.e. Article 49, paragraph 2, item 5 of the LOT.

4.1 Comparative Advertising and Protection of Navigation Goodwill

To put it simply, this is an assessment of the permissibility of comparative advertising depending on whether it contributes informing consumers correctly or, on the contrary, misleads them, creating thereby confusion in the market.[40]

The referential use of another's trademark in permitted comparative advertising does not constitute a trademark infringement. If, on the other hand, the specific comparative advertising is misleading (and therefore not permissible) it constitutes a trademark infringement.

Our attention here is drawn to a special category of comparative advertising where the advertised product is presented as an imitation or replica of the reference product labeled with a registered trademark. From the aspect of consumer information and welfare, all the advantages of comparative advertising that have already been mentioned, are especially evident in the advertising of imitation or replica, because the consumer is suggested to have the same experience in consuming the reference and advertised product, with, as a rule, lower price or any other benefit that accompanies the advertised product.

In Europe, this method of comparative advertising is *a priori* not permissible and constitutes an infringement of the reference product trademark. How to explain this absolute ban from the aspect of market efficiency and consumer welfare? It is difficult to defend the hypothesis that this prohibition was based on the irrefutable presumption that any advertising of an imitation or replica is misleading. This is particularly in light of the statements in the preamble of the EU Advertising Directive: (a) for comparative advertising to be effective, it is sometimes indispensable to identify a competitor's products through his trademark, and (b) there is no trademark infringement if the intended target is solely to distinguish between the products and to highlight differences objectively.[41]

It is possible to speculate that this prohibition has to do with the protection of the reputation of the reference trademark i.e. of its surplus goodwill (which is our next topic). Namely, it is reasonable to assume that the reference trademark should already be renown, so that advertising a competing product as an imitation or replica would be effective.

Most probably, however, the ban is a consequence of the lobbying activities of the French cosmetics industry, which wanted to protect the trademarks of its powerful protagonists from competing advertisements of the type "X smells the

[40] See Article 4 of the EU Advertising Directive, i.e. Article 14 of the LOA. Without intending to present all these criteria in more detail, we can only state that the mere truthfulness of advertising information *per se* does not guarantee that it is not misleading. For instance, it will be misleading if it is used to compare different or irrelevant properties of the advertised and reference product.

[41] See items 14 and 15 of the preamble to the EU Advertising Directive.

same as Chanel 5, but is five times cheaper."[42] Thus, the legacy of the generally restrictive attitude of French law towards comparative advertising has gained some satisfaction in terms of EU law.[43]

Regardless of the genesis of this prohibition in EU law (as well as in the law of member/candidate states), let us try *ex post* to make some sense of it, if possible. Starting from the fact that it is basically a "perfume clause", we will examine what can be a problem with the practice of perfume advertising, such as "X smells the same as Y" or "if you like X, you will love Y". The problem may be the failure to meet one of the main conditions for the permissibility of comparative advertising, and that is the OBJECTIVITY of the information communicated to consumers. With the senses of smell, as well as with feelings of love, approval, enthusiasm, etc. there is no objective and verifiable comparison of the substantial, relevant and representative properties of two or more products. The statement "X smells the same as Y" must be interpreted as a suggestion of the same consumer experience, which does not necessarily mean the objective equivalence of product properties.[44]

Consequently, it seems that the mentioned format of comparative advertising of a product as an imitation or replica of another product would not be permitted, even if there was no explicit prohibition of such an advertising.[45]

However, the problem of prohibition remains in cases where the advertised product has objectively verifiable substantial, relevant and representative properties of the reference product (e.g. X drills are the same in quality and durability as Y drills, at half the price). Since it has no justification in the economic logic of protection of navigation goodwill, the prohibition in these cases must not completely prevent comparative advertising which conveys a message of the objective equivalence of the reference and imitated product. Therefore, it must be interpreted as narrowly and formalistically as possible. In particular, the solution lies in the skill of formulating an advertisement, where it is necessary to avoid the words "imitation" or "replica", and instead use Aesop's language, which will convey to consumers the

[42] Dornis and Wein (2016), p. 432. The authors refer to this as the "French signature in Brussels", recalling that this prohibition is referred to as a "perfume clause".

[43] For a detailed insight into French case law, see Romano (2005), p. 379 et seq.

[44] For example, a certain ice cream may taste and smell like raspberries because it is one of the ingredients of the ice cream. Other ice creams can have the same taste and smell, but thanks to the addition of artificial aromas. Thus, there is no objective equivalence between these two products despite the same smell and taste.

[45] In the second instance, the Federal Court of Germany decided on the permissibility of the use of "equivalence tables" (German - *Konkordanzliste*) of perfumes from well-known manufacturers and their imitations i.e. replicas (BGH, Urteil vom 5. 2. 2004 - I ZR 171/01 - Genealogie der Düfte; see https://lexetius.com/2004,846). The court's position is that using such a table in communication with consumers is not a permissible form of comparative advertising because it creates the illusion of equivalence of the reference product and imitation, based on the subjective impression of the consumer about them. It is interesting, however, that the court considers it permissible to use such a list in communication with product dealers, because that communication is not about advertising but about instruction.

message about product equivalence. This is view is accepted in German legal practice.[46]

There is one relic of French provenance in the trademark law of Serbia, which is difficult to fit into the last conclusion. It is a provision that explicitly prescribes that adding the words "type", "manner", "according to the process" to someone else's trademark is an infringement of the trademark.[47] These words are, as a rule, part of the statement in the comparative advertisement. The EU Directive on Trademarks and the EU Trademark Regulation do not have such a provision. This means that comparative advertising in Serbia is subject to an additional restrictive criterion that does not exist in the EU. Hence, we call on the domestic legislator to see the mentioned connection, and to eliminate this relic from LOT.

4.2 Comparative Advertising and Protection of Surplus Goodwill

Being a value *per se*, the reputation of the mark is today protected by unfair competition law and trademark law, independently of the occurrence of confusion about the origin of the product. Reputation is the *terminus technicus* that we use to denote the amalgam of fame, distinctiveness and labeling power in the market, making it a means of conveying to consumers not only information about the origin of products, but also other information aimed at promoting sales. So, it is about the "surplus" of information that forms the so-called **brand**.

While the legal protection of navigation goodwill deals with the issue of preventing market confusion, the legal protection of surplus goodwill deals with the issue of the external effect of using a reputable trademark. It consists in the attractiveness that the trademark has for consumers, and its ability to symbolically convey to them the reasons for buying any product that is labeled with it.

It is not difficult to understand why it is in the interest of the holder of a reputable trademark to internalize that external effect, i.e. to "appropriate" it economically by prohibiting others to use it. The argument for this thesis is the protection of investment in reputation building i.e. brand. In contrast, competitors are interested in freely enjoying the benefits of comparative advertising. The law has set certain rules by which it distinguishes the rights of the trademark holder from the freedom of competitors. However, the delicate task of purposeful application of that distinction is left to the courts.

---

[46] The Federal Court, deciding on the permissibility of comparative advertising of perfumes (Urteil vom 5. Mai 2011 - I ZR 157/09 - Creation Lamis; see https://openjur.de/u/228374.html, took the position that comparative advertising is not prohibited as long as it does not contain an understandable and clear statement that it is an imitation.

[47] Art. 90, para. 2 LOT.

What are the cases of comparative advertising in which harming the surplus goodwill, can lead to trademark infringement?

Firstly, it is an infringement of the so-called famous trademark on the reference product, if the product being advertised is neither identical nor similar to it, whereby the advertiser unfairly benefits from the reputation of the famous trademark or harms its distinctive character i.e. reputation.[48] In other words, the advertiser is not a competitor to the famous trademark holder, but wants to transfer to his product the attention and trust that consumers bestow on the famous trademark (e.g. X is a Rolls Royce among umbrellas).

Secondly, it is an infringement of any trademark with which the reference product is labeled, if the comparative advertisement discredits or denigrates that trademark.[49]

Thirdly, it is an infringement of any trademark of reference product, if the comparative advertiser unfairly benefits from the reputation of that trademark.[50]

Based on these three cases, we can conclude that the surplus goodwill of a trademark may, during comparative advertising, be harmed by: (a) dilution of the famous trademark (damage to distinctiveness), (b) harm to the trademark reputation and (c) unfair appropriation of the trademark reputation. The following is a commentary on each of these items.

Diluting a famous trademark is "overusing" its reputation by putting it in advertisements for various non-competitive products, with its role being to draw consumers' attention and transfer a part of its attractive power to the non-competitive product. The consequence of this practice can be the loosening of the connection that exists in the minds of consumers between the famous trademark and the products for which it is registered, the relativization of the uniqueness of that trademark on the market, and finally decrease in its advertising value. The economic explanation for the protection of the famous trademark from dilution is mostly indisputable, because it is based on the prevailing doctrine of the elementary purpose of the trademark, which is to reduce the transaction costs when choosing and procuring products on the market. This is, therefore, the case when there is no confusion about the origin of the product, but the use of the famous trademark by non-competitors creates "noise" on the information about the origin of the product. In this way, this form of protection of famous trademarks connects the issue of protection of navigation goodwill and surplus goodwill.

When it comes to defamation (discrediting or denigrating) a trademark, it is worth immediately pointing out that each comparative advertisement emphasizes the value

---

[48] See Article 56, paragraph 2 of the LOA, i.e. Article 10, paragraph 2, item c of the EU Directive on Trademarks. It is interesting that the Serbian legislator still uses the archaic term "famous trademark", even though the EU legislator does not.

[49] See Article 14, paragraph 2, item 4 of the LOA, i.e. Article 4, item d of the EU Advertising Directive.

[50] See Article 14, paragraph 2, item 6 of the LOA, i.e. Article 4, item f of the EU Advertising Directive. It is worth noting here that the Serbian legislator uses the vague and ambiguous term "reputation abuse" instead of sticking to the wording "unfair benefit from reputation" from EU legislation.

of the advertised product at the expense of the reference product. That is actually the point of comparative advertising. In order to be permitted, such advertising must not be misleading (which we talked about in connection with the protection of navigation goodwill), nor must it be defamatory. Defamatory advertising, explicitly or implicitly, verbally or graphically, attributes unworthy, devaluing properties to the reference product or entity from which it originates, even if this may or may not have any factual background.[51] This creates a negative impression on consumers, which they psychologically project on the trademark, more precisely, its reputation. The consequences of such an attack on the reputation of the trademark can be manifested in great economic damage for the trademark holder.

Unfair appropriation of the reputation of another's trademark is a type of comparative advertising, in which through the reputation of the reference trademark, consumers are suggested that the reference product and the competing advertised product belong to the same class of value. Regarding the permissibility of such a transfer of reputation, two questions arise. The first concerns the economic justification of this form of surplus goodwill protection, and the second concerns the condition of unfairness, which qualifies this transfer as impermissible.

At the beginning of the twentieth century, a school of thought was established in the United States, which sees the trademark reputation a value that its holder can legitimately protect from both competitors and non-competitors.[52] Inspired by this, Judge Frankfurter of the Supreme Court formulated the following thought in one verdict: "If another poaches upon the commercial magnetism of the symbol he has created, the owner can obtain legal redress."[53] The basis for this attitude is the understanding that where there is value (specifically, the reputation of the trademark), there must be protection against the appropriation of that value by persons

---

[51] For example, the historical fact is that Krupp, Siemens, Volkswagen are trademarks whose holders were very much associated with the Nazi regime of Hitler's Germany. Emphasizing this fact in modern comparative advertising would not be permissible, because it has nothing to do with comparing the properties of two products; its purpose would be only to morally disqualify one side and deter consumers from purchasing its products. This is all the more so if the defamation is based on untruth or on the subjective malice of the advertiser.

[52] The theoretical article that played a pioneering role in this process is Schechter (1927), pp. 813–833. It is a work that has become not only "the most cited legal article in the field of trademark law, of all time", but also which has had a huge impact on the theory and legislation in this field. See Beebe (2013), p. 2.

[53] See U.S. Supreme Court judgment in Mishawaka Rubber & Woolen Mfg. Co. v. S.S. Kresge Co. (316 U.S. 203) of 1949, the most quoted part of which reads: "The protection of trade-marks is the law's recognition of the psychological function of symbols. If it is true that we live by symbols, it is no less true that we purchase goods by them. A trade-mark is a merchandising short-cut which induces a purchaser to select what he wants, or what he has been led to believe he wants. The owner of a mark exploits this human propensity by making every effort to impregnate the atmosphere of the market with the drawing power of a congenial symbol. Whatever the means employed, the aim is the same—to convey through the mark, in the minds of potential customers, the desirability of the commodity upon which it appears. Once this is attained, the trade-mark owner has something of value. If another poaches upon the commercial magnetism of the symbol he has created, the owner can obtain legal redress." https://www.law.cornell.edu/supremecourt/text/316/203.

who did not create it.[54] Such protection prevents unjust enrichment, on the one hand, and unfair competition that undermines the incentive to invest in the reputation of the trademark, on the other hand. Somehow, at that time, a serious theoretical opposition to that doctrine appeared.[55] A very illustrative example of the case law in which this opposing viewpoint was applied is the first instance judgment of the British judge Lewison in the case of O2Holdings Ltd. and O2 (UK) Ltd. v Hutchison 3G Ltd. The point is that the right to a trademark protects the trademark, not the brand, and that the intangible value that makes the difference between a trademark and a brand does not enjoy legal protection.[56] One of the recent attempts to delegitimize the prevention of free reading on the reputation of another's trademark is based on the thesis that the trademark holder builds a brand with the unconscious cooperation of consumers, who position this brand not only in the market but also in the general public communication. An advertising technique that mobilizes consumers in this way is called anthropological marketing. Brands created in this way are the "co-ownership" of the trademark owner and the consumer audience.[57]

Bearing all this in mind, the question remains how a judge should understand the norm according to which "unfair extraction of benefits" from the reputation of another's trademark is prohibited.

In order to take a position on this issue, the difference between two cases must first be pointed out: (a) appropriation i.e. transfer of the reputation of another's trademark (free riding), without inflicting any harm to the reputation, and (b) the case when the reputation of another's trademark is thereby harmed.

In the first case, a lawyer can stick to the programmatic thought formulated in point 14 of the preamble of the EU Advertising Directive, which suggests that comparative advertising is allowed only if a reference to someone else's trademark is indispensable. If this were to be interpreted broadly, a comparative advertisement

---

[54] See f.n. 53.

[55] See, in particular, Cohen (1935), p. 809 et seq. Cohen on page 815 says: "The current legal argument runs: One who by ingenuity of his advertising or the quality of his product has induced consumer responsiveness to a particular name, symbol, form of packaging, etc., has thereby created a thing of value; a thing of value is property; the creator of property is entitled to protection against third parties who seek to deprive him of his property... The vicious circle inherent in this reasoning is plain. It purports to base legal protection upon economic value, when, as a matter of actual fact, the economic value of a sales device depends upon the extent to which it will legally be protected."

[56] O2 Holdings Ltd. and O2 (UK) Ltd. v Hutchison 3G Ltd., European Trademark Reports, 2006, 677, paragraph 7: "English law does not, however, protect brands as such. It will protect goodwill (via the law of passing off); trade marks (via trade mark infringement); the use of particular words, sounds and images (via the law of copyright); and configuration of articles (via the law of unregistered design right) and so on. But to the extent that a brand is greater than the sum of the parts that English law will protect, it is defenseless against the chill wind of competition."

[57] "Indeed, in such situations it is perfectly in line with the traditional doctrine of trade mark law to say that there are aspects of the brand that do not fall within trade mark protection, and that these aspects, despite their value, ought not to be owned by anyone. In other words, the courts should not be afraid to state the obvious: the purpose of trade mark law is to protect trade marks, not every single aspect of the wider brand, a point that seems especially evident in cases where no harm is caused to an underlying mark". McDonagh (2015), p. 635.

would be allowed only if the reference product was labeled with original equipment manufacturer (OEM) identification (without referential use of another's trademark),[58] or with another's trademark if it was impossible to use the OEM identification. This would automatically prohibit comparative advertising in which someone else's reference mark, for its own reputation, is used as a means to draw consumers' attention to the advertisement. Such a broad approach to trademark surplus goodwill protection would preclude the key economic benefits of comparative advertising—assisting the consumer to make an informed purchase decision (discussed above). Therefore, we consider that there is no place for the conclusion that the condition of "indispensability" from Art 14 of the preamble to the EU Advertising Directive is a disguised ban on any comparative advertising that results in a free riding of a competitor on the reputation of a reference trademark, without harming that reputation.

This view is consistent with the long-known economic insight that all positive and negative externalities cannot and should not be internalized.[59] Free riding is a popular economic term that means the freedom of people to learn and imitate, which is an elementary premise of development. On the other hand, freedom of competition certainly implies tolerance for some external effects of fair competition in the market.

We will now turn to another case where the free riding of a competitor harms the reputation of a reference trademark. When it comes to non-competitive products, most of these cases coincide with cases of dilution of the famous trademark. In these cases, a harmful effect of reducing trademark's distinctiveness is accompanied by the harmful effect on trademark's reputation.[60] Thus, harming the reputation of a famous trademark is certainly an unfair act that makes the referential use of another's famous trademark illegal. When it comes to competing products, it is worth looking at the theory that distinguishes pre-sale, point-of-sale and post-sale confusion. Confusions that occur before and at the time of purchase of the product are sanctioned by the rules of protection of navigation goodwill of the trademark (discussed above). However, post-sale confusion is a construction that has in mind the potential consumer of the reference product, who, looking at the advertised product bought by someone else as an imitation or replica of the reference product,

[58] The indisputability of using the OEM identification of the reference product in comparative advertising has been confirmed in the practice of the European Court of Justice. See Toshiba Europe GmbH in 2001 Katun Germany GmbH (C–112/99), E.C.R. I-07945, https://ipcuria.eu/case?reference=C-112/99; Siemens AG v VIPA Gesellschaft für Visualisierung und Prozessautomatisierung mbH of 2006 (C–59/05), E.C.R. I-02147, http://curia.europa.eu/juris/showPdf.jsf?text=&docid=56362&pageIndex=0&doclang=en&mode=lst&dir=&occ=first&part=1&cid=22894745.

[59] See the valuable article by Lemley (2005), p. 1031 et seq.

[60] An example might be the advertising statement "What a McDonalds meal is for you, it's an X for your pet." This is not only about connecting the famous trademark with a non-competitive product (dilution of distinctiveness), but the consumers make a mental association of McDonalds human food with dog or cat food. In short, the transfer of the reputation of a famous trademark to a non-competitive product is accompanied by a simultaneous damage to its reputation.

is disappointed with its quality, and transfers that disappointment to the reputation of the trademark. This is also a case of interaction between the navigation and surplus goodwill.[61] Criticism of the stated reasoning points to the fact that positive law sanctions confusion (misinformation) that exists at the moment of transaction. An act that was not illegal at that point in time (the consumer had all the necessary and accurate information at the time of purchase), cannot become illegal because the observer of the transaction gets confused about the properties of the product.[62] Our opinion, however, is that the point here is not in confusion, but in the harm to the reputation of the trademark, which can deter potential consumers from later buying the reference product.

Therefore, if free riding on the reputation of a reference trademark results in harm to that reputation, it has to be considered an unfair act that is sanctioned as a trademark infringement, because it harms the substance of value contained in trademark's surplus goodwill.

5 Conclusion

Modern regulation of distinctive signs is characterized by the process of merging of trademark law and unfair competition law. This is especially evident when regulating comparative advertising, as a type of referential use of a trademark. Since this matter in Serbia is regulated according to the EU model, we believe that for a start, Serbian LOT and LOA should be harmonized with the EU Directive on Trademarks and the EU Directive on Advertising. In particular, the following is needed.

(a) In Article 49, paragraph 3 of the LOT, the word "i" should be deleted before listing the exclusive rights of the trademark holder, because it erroneously suggests that these rights are listed as an example, and not as a closed list.
(b) Article 54, paragraph 2, item 3 of the LOT must be amended to read as follows: "the trademark for the purpose of identifying or referring to goods or services as those of the proprietor of that trademark, in particular, where the use of the

[61] A good example from US case law, which illustrates this situation, is the Ferrari S.P.A. v. Roberts of 1991 (944 F.2d 1235, 6th Cir. 1991). See https://www.lexisnexis.com/community/casebrief/p/casebrief-ferrari-s-p-a-esercizio-fabriche-automobili-e-corse-v-roberts. The defendant sold kits for assembling a car whose body is a replica of some old Ferrari models. This mechanical construction could then be mounted on the chassis of cars of other manufacturers, and certified for traffic. Anyone who bought that product could not be mistaken that it has nothing to do with a Ferrari, except for its appearance. However, the court found that a potential buyer of a Ferrari, disappointed with the easy availability of low-quality copies of that prestigious car, could give up the purchase. The reason for the withdrawal would lie in the changed perception of the prestige, rarity and superior social status that make up the reputation i.e. surplus goodwill of the trademark Ferrari.

[62] That is the thinking of Judge Kennedy, which he singled out in the Ferrari S.P.A. v. Roberts. See f.n. 61.

trademark is necessary to indicate the intended purpose of a product or service, in particular as accessories or spare parts."

(c) Article 90, paragraph 2 of the LOT should be deleted, because it contains an additional restriction on comparative advertising, which does not exist in the EU trademark law.

From the aspect of market efficiency and consumer welfare, comparative advertising is a rational way of economizing information on the basis of which a decision on a transaction is made. It is therefore permitted unless it is misleading or harms the reputation of the reference trademark in an unfair manner. By preventing misleading advertising, trademark law protects the credibility of information on the origin and the quality of the marked product. This can be vividly called protection of navigation goodwill of a trademark. Protecting the reputation of a trademark aims to protect the part of the information content that turns a trademark into a brand. This value can be vividly called surplus goodwill of a trademark.

Our analysis shows the following.

(a) The absolute prohibition of comparative advertising of imitations or replicas is incompatible with the economic justification of comparative advertising. There are indications that the EU has made a concession to the French perfume industry with this ban. As long as this prohibition exists in positive law, it must be interpreted as restrictively as possible in court proceedings. In other words, advertising that claims the objective equivalence of the advertised and the reference product must not be prohibited *per se*.

(b) Positive legal norms do not provide a basis for protection of a brand as a set of all meanings that the trademark conveys to consumers. There always remains one part of the surplus goodwill of the reference trademark, the transfer of which to the advertised product through comparative advertising must be tolerated as a natural consequence of competition. In other words, not every benefit from the reputation of someone else's reference trademark is unfair.

(c) It is certainly an unfair benefit from the reputation of another's trademark, if the act of comparative advertising has caused harm to that reputation.

(d) In all other cases, the impermissibility of comparative advertising (as a criterion for infringement of the reference trademark) should be interpreted as narrowly as possible, according to the principle *exceptionis sunt strictissimae interpretationis*.

References

Beebe B (2004) The semiotic analysis of trademark law. UCLA Law Rev 51:621–704

Beebe B (2013) The Suppressed Misappropriation Origins of Trademark Antidilution Law: The Landgericht Elberfeld's *Odol* Opinion and Frank Schechter's "The Rational Basis of Trademark Protection". New York University School of Law, Public Law & Legal Theory Research Paper Series, Working Paper No. 13–36 https://papers.ssrn.com/sol3/papers.cfm?abstract_id=2283391. Accessed Mar 2020

Cohen F (1935) Transcendental nonsense and the functional approach. Columbia Law Rev 35:809–849
Dornis TW (2017) Trademark and unfair competition conflicts. Cambridge University Press, Cambridge
Dornis TW, Wein T (2016) Trademarks, comparative advertising, and product imitations: an untold story of law and economics. Penn State Law Rev 121(2):421–470
Landes WM, Posner RA (1987) Trademark law: an economic perspective. J Law Econ 30:265–309
Lemley MA (2005) Property, intellectual property, and free riding. Texas Law Rev 83:1031–1089
Max Planck Institute for Intellectual Property and Competition Law (2011) Study on the Overall Functioning of the European Trade Mark System. Munich. https://www.ip.mpg.de/fileadmin/IP/pdf2/mpi_final_report_with_synopsis.pdf. Accessed Dec 2020
McDonagh L (2015) From brand performance to consumer performativity – European trade mark law after the rise of anthropological marketing. J Law Soc 42(4):611–636
Romano CJ (2005) Comparative advertising in the United States and in France. Northwest J Int Law Bus 25:371–413
Schechter F (1927) The rational basis of trademark protection. Harv Law Rev 40(6):813–833

Online Intermediary Liability in Serbian Law: Reconciling IP Protection and Freedom of Expression

Dušan V. Popović

Contents

1 Introduction

Online intermediaries play a neutral role on the Internet, consisting in enabling the flow of information between actors that create or post information, on the one hand, and recepients of the information, on the other hand. According to an OECD study, online intermediaries facilitate transactions between third parties on the Internet by giving access to, host, transmit and index content, products, and services originated by third parties online, or provide Internet-based services to third parties.[1] Over the time, different types of intermediaries have developed and include: access and

[1] OECD (2010), 'The Economic and Social Role of Internet Intermediaries', p. 9. Available at: https://www.oecd.org/internet/ieconomy/44949023.pdf.

D. V. Popović (✉)
University of Belgrade, Faculty of Law, Belgrade, Serbia
e-mail: dusan.popovic@ius.bg.ac.rs

D. V. Popović et al. (eds.), *Balkan Yearbook of European and International Law 2021*, Balkan Yearbook of European and International Law 2021,
https://doi.org/10.1007/978-3-030-97431-2_2

storage providers, marketplace exchanges, buy/sell fulfillment, demand collection systems, auction brokers, virtual marketplaces, as well as search-engines, advertising networks, web aggregators, news syndicators or social networking sites. In this paper, the notion of 'online intermediary' will be used to designate the providers of mere conduit, cashing or hosting services *stricto sensu*. In recent times, the role of online intermediaries has been met with criticism, which particularly include the lack of transparency in their management of online traffic and indirectly facilitating unlawful activities like intellectual property rights infringement on their platform by their end-users.

The infringement of intellectual property rights is very common on the Internet. The reason for it is the predominantly anonymous character of online interactions. Investigating the identity of an anonymous infringer is time-consuming and costly. One may even say it is a nearly impossible task for the IP right owners. Consequently, right owners started taking legal actions against online intermediaries, which are perceived as complice in the infringement. This has led to some concerns on how the online intermediaries are supposed to handle these IP right infringements or, more importantly, how they are supposed to prevent them from occurring. The role of online intermediaries is, beyond any doubt, very delicate, given that they need to balance the interests of IP right owners with that of freedom of expression and privacy.

Following the EU model, the Serbian legislator introduced a 'safe harbor' rule, securing an immunity regime for online intermediaries, under specific conditions. However, the recent reform of Serbian IP law allowed for an injunctive relief against online intermediaries. The purpose for the injunction can be to obtain the information on the primary infringer, so that an action can be directed against it, and/or to remove the infringing content from the intermediary's network (Sect. 2). The injunction mechanism needs to be used prudently, so as to avoid any possible abuse for the purpose of restricting the freedom of expression (Sect. 3). While enforcing these rules, the Serbian authorities should also consider the experience accumulated in other jurisdictions.

2 Legal Framework for Online Intermediary Liability in Serbia

The legal doctrine distinguishes between two main categories of liability for infringements of intellectual property rights: primary and secondary liability.[2] Primary liability refers to those who infringe on IP rights firsthand. End users are typical primary violators. On the other hand, secondary liability refers to those who provide a platform for a primary infringement to occur, for example, online intermediaries. Consequently, there must be a link between a primary and a secondary IP rights

[2]Dinwoodie et al. (2009), pp. 202–203.

infringer for a case of secondary liability to be established. One of the rationale for imposing secondary liability for IP rights infringement on online intermediaries is the fact that the latter control the 'gateway' through which the primary infringer accedes the IP-protected content on the Internet. Since most violators are anonymous, the online intermediaries are perceived by owners of IP rights as the only identifiable and solvent target for their lawsuits. Although the introduction of a blanket filtering obligation for user-generated content to online intermediaries may seem compelling, the national legislators, including in Serbia, did not impose such a duty, which is seen as an overwhelming burden for the online intermediaries and a possible breach of privacy rights of end-users.

The legal framework for online intermediary liability for IP rights infringements in Serbia is primarily determined by two sets of rules. First, the 'safe harbor' provisions which were modeled upon EU law. Second, the rules on injunction against intermediaries, such as online platforms, whose services are used by third parties to infringe IP rights. These provisions were introduced by the 2019 amendments to the Serbian Law on Copyright and Related Rights and the adoption of the new Law on Trademarks in 2020.

2.1 Safe Harbor Rule

The rules on online intermediary liability for infringements of IP rights were first articulated in US law. A specific 'notice and takedown' procedure related to copyrighted works was introduced by the Digital Millennium Copyright Act (DMCA).[3] This procedure allows for a copyright owner to request the removal of content posted online. The DMCA shields online service providers from monetary liability and limits other forms of liability for copyright infringement—referred to as safe harbors—in exchange for cooperating with copyright owners to expeditiously remove infringing content if the online service providers meet certain conditions. Specifically, Subsection 512(c)(1)(A) of the DMCA requires that the service provider: (1) does not have actual knowledge that the material or an activity using the material on the system or network is infringing; (2) in the absence of such actual knowledge, is not aware of facts or circumstances from which infringing activity is apparent; or (3) upon obtaining such knowledge or awareness, acts expeditiously to remove, or disable access to, the material. The DMCA has become a *de facto* global standard for addressing online copyright infringements, since the vast majority of removal requests are sent to global platforms that are US-based companies.[4]

---

[3]The DMCA safe harbors, codified at 17 U.S.C. § 512, are part of the Copyright Act.

[4]Popović (2021), p. 286.

The US DMCA legislation inspired the European Union to enact the Electronic Commerce Directive (ECD),[5] including safe harbors for mere conduits, caching, and hosting.[6] Although the EU rules were modeled on the DMCA, they differ from the US safe harbor in two ways. First and most importantly, the directive's hosting provision governs all claims related to user-generated content, not just copyright. These claims may be derived from private law, in the form of, e.g., copyright infringement or defamation, as well as from criminal law, in the form of, e.g., incitement to violence or hate speech. Second, the notice and takedown mechanism is prescribed by a directive that allows for certain flexibility within national legislators and has resulted in 27 harmonized, albeit not identical, national legal regimes in EU member states.[7] As an EU candidate country, the Republic of Serbia is required under Article 72 of the Stabilisation and Association Agreement (SAA)[8] to harmonise its legal system with that of the European Union. Serbia is not only obligated to ensure that its existing laws and future legislation is gradually made compatible with the EU *acquis*, but also to ensure that legislation is properly implemented and enforced. Specifically with respect to intellectual property rights, Serbia undertook an obligation to take the necessary measures in order to guarantee no later than 5 years after entry into force of the SAA[9] a level of protection of intellectual, industrial and commercial property rights similar to that existing in the Union, including effective means of enforcing such rights.[10]

The provisions of the EU Electronic Commerce Directive were implemented into the Serbian legal system by way of the Law on electronic commerce (LEC), adopted in 2009 and amended in 2013 and 2019.[11] Similarly to the EU Electronic Commerce Directive (ECD), LEC introduced a 'safe harbor' rule which is applicable to mere conduits, caching and hosting services. Instead of a more broader term 'intermediary', LEC refers to 'information society service providers' to which the said immunity applies. The notion of an information society service provider is defined broadly so as to comprise any natural or legal person engaged in the provision of infosoc. Services, which are normally provided for remuneration at a distance by electronic

---

[5] Directive 2000/31/EC of the European Parliament and of the Council on certain legal aspects of information society services, in particular electronic commerce, in the Internal Market, Official Journal of the European Community, No. L 178, 17.7.2000.

[6] See Arts. 12–14 of the EU Directive on electronic commerce.

[7] Before Brexit – 28.

[8] Stabilisation and Association Agreement between the European Communities and their Member States of the one part, and the Republic of Serbia, of the other part, Official Journal of the European Union, No. L 278, 18.10.2013.

[9] The SAA between the EU and the Republic of Serbia entered into force on September 1, 2013. However, the provisions relating to free movement of goods, customs, competition and state aid entered into force already in February 2010, as they were part of the Interim Agreement signed between the EU and Serbia.

[10] Art. 75, para. 3 of the SAA.

[11] Law on electronic commerce (LEC), Official Journal of the Republic of Serbia, Nos. 41/2009, 95/2013 and 52/2019.

means at the individual request of the recipient of the services.[12] Consequently, information society services also comprise activities which are not remunerated by those who receive them, for example free WiFi services.

LEC prescribes immunity for those intermediaries that engage in 'mere conduit', provided that the intermediary: (a) does not initiate the transmission; (b) does not select the receiver of the transmission; (c) does not select the information or documents that are being transmitted; and (d) does not exclude or modify the contents of the documents or message being transmitted.[13] This refers to the situation where the information society service provider has not produced the information or chosen the intended recipient but acts as a mere transmitter of the information. The intermediary must not filter the recipients, i.e. it must not restrict access to some but not to others. Also, the intermediary must not exercise any kind of editorial control over the information which is being transmitted. Failing to meet one of the four criteria set by the law would expose the intermediary to liability. The liability in question must be interpreted broadly so as to comprise both civil and criminal liability. Consequently, the intermediary needs to act in passive manner: it should not create the information and have knowledge of it or control over it. Transmissions that are covered by this provision include temporary and automatic storage for the sole purpose of carrying out the transmission. LEC requires the transmitter to store the data about the service user for minimum 30 days following the termination of the service provision. In particular, the service provider must store the information about IP address used to access the service in question.

The second activity to which the immunity applies is the case of a temporary storage of information (caching). Caching is defined as automatic, intermediate and temporary storage of computer data for faster access later on. Caching is a process that stores multiple copies of data or files in a temporary storage location—or cache—so they can be accessed faster. Caching ensures that users need not download information every time they access a website or application. In case of caching, 'safe harbor' is valid for those intermediaries: (a) that did not modify the information which is being transmitted; (b) that comply with conditions on access to the information; (c) that comply with rules regarding the updating of the information; (d) that do not interfere with the lawful use of technology; and (e) that act expeditiously to remove or to disable access to the information it has stored upon obtaining actual knowledge of the fact that the information at the initial source of the transmission has been removed from the network, or access to it has been disabled, or that a court or other competent authority has ordered such removal or disablement.[14] Consequently, a cached information must not be modified nor it could be stored indefinitely. The caching process must be operated automatically. Further to the 'safe harbor' rule related to caching, Serbian copyright law provides for a

[12] Art. 3 of the LEC. Certain services are explicitly excluded from the notion of information society service, such as games of chance (see Art. 2 of the LEC).

[13] Art. 16 of the LEC. Compare with Art. 12 of the ECD.

[14] Art. 17 of the LEC. Compare with Art. 13 of the ECD.

limitation to copyright in case of temporary reproduction of copyrighted works without the author's permission and without paying any remuneration, under the following conditions: (1) reproduction is transient or incidental; (2) reproduction is an integral and essential part of a technological process; (3) purpose of reproduction is to enable a transmission of data in a network between two or more persons through an intermediary, or to enable a lawful use of a copyrighted work; and (4) reproduction does not have independent economic significance.[15] By prescribing this limitation to copyright, the Serbian legislator harmonized national IP rules with the provisions of the EU InfoSoc Directive.[16]

The third and final activity to which the 'safe harbor' rule applies is hosting. Unlike mere conduits or caching, hosting represents an act of permanent storage of information, based on a contract between a provider and the user. The information is placed on the host's servers from where it is made available to the general public. In case of hosting services, the 'safe harbor' is offered to intermediaries which: (a) do not have actual knowledge of illegal activity or information; and (b) upon obtaining such knowledge or awareness, act expeditiously to remove or to disable access to the information.[17] The basic requirement for exemption of liability is therefore the hosting provider's lack of knowledge of the illegal content on its website. Therefore, proving that the hosting provider could have found out about the illegal content will not be sufficient to hold the hosting provider liable. In other words, it has to be evidenced that the hosting provider had knowledge of the illegal activities of users. However, once the right-owner informs the hosting provider of the alleged infringement, the latter must act efficiently in order to avoid being exposed to liability. An IP right owner who intends to demand compensation from the hosting provider in a civil court would have to prove that the hosting provider was aware or knew of the infringements on its platform. In a criminal court the IP right owner would have to demonstrate that the hosting provider had reliable information about the illegal content on its platform.[18] Specifically, IP right owners would have to prove that the hosting provider disregarded reliable information or an official notice stating that the site contains infringing content.

Obviously, this 'notice and take down' procedure can be abused for censorship purposes. The threat of secondary liability induces hosting providers to comply with the notice and takedown provisions, making it more difficult for speakers to post material that challenges someone who can potentially make a copyright (or other IP right) claim.[19] If a notification about the alleged infringement comes from a third

[15] Art. 48 of the LCRR.

[16] See: Art. 5, para. 1 of the Directive 2001/29/EC of the European Parliament and of the Council on the harmonisation of certain aspects of copyright and related rights in the information society, Official Journal of the European Union, No. L 167, 22.6.2001.

[17] Art. 18 of the LEC. Compare with Art. 14 of the ECD. The same conditions for imuunity are set for linking (see Art. 19 of the LEC).

[18] Karwowska (2020), p. 43.

[19] Seltzer (2010), p. 177.

party, the provider may be concerned that removing the material prematurely may expose it to action by the content poster.[20] It seems that providers are prepared to remove content at a mere notice from the affected party, since the risk of a lawsuit from the right-owner is higher than the corresponding risk of a lawsuit from the customer.[21]

In line with ECD, Serbian legislator did not impose a general obligation on information society service providers to monitor the information which they transmit or store, nor a general obligation to actively seek facts or circumstances indicating illegal activity.[22] However, if a service provider has reasonable grounds to believe that the user of its services is undertaking illegal activity, it is required to inform the competent state authority of it. Under court or administrative order, the service provider must disclose all information necessary for criminal act detection or criminal prosecution.[23] In Serbia, there are no additional rules with respect to Internet traffic monitoring, since LCRR is not yet harmonized with the EU Directive on Copyright in the Digital Single Market (DSMD).[24] At this moment, it remains unclear whether or not DSMD *de facto* introduces a monitoring obligation to platforms operators. Clearly, Article 17 of the DSMD does not explicitly oblige online content-sharing service providers to generally filter all the content uploaded onto their platforms by their users, since this would be in contradiction with the prohibition on general monitoring obligations instated by Article 17(8). However, in the absence of the rightholder's authorization, the obligation imposed onto online content-sharing service providers to make their 'best efforts' to ensure the unavailability of notified protected content can only, given the current state of technology, be discharged where such preventative verification mechanisms have been set up.[25]

2.2 *Blocking Injunctions*

The Law on Electronic Commerce (LEC) specifically allows injunctions against intermediaries in the three safe harbours (conduit, caching and hosting).[26] The Law requires information society service providers to remove illegal content within

[20] Savin (2020), p. 175.

[21] *Ibid.*

[22] Art. 20, para. 1 of the LEC. Compare with Art. 15, para. 1 of the ECD.

[23] Art. 20, paras. 2–3 of the LEC.

[24] Directive (EU) 2019/790 of the European Parliament and of the Council on copyright and related rights in the Digital Single Market and amending Directives 96/9/EC and 2001/29/EC, Official Journal of the European Union, No. L 130, 17.5.2019.

[25] Taylor (2021), p. 8. This argument is put forward by the Republic of Poland in its request for a preliminary ruling before the Court of Justice of the European Union: CJEU, case C-401/19, *Republic of Poland v European Parliament and Council of the European Union.*

[26] Art. 20, para. 5 of the LEC.

2 days following the receipt of an injunction issued by a competent authority. The request for removal of allegedly illegal content can be submitted by a third party as well, in which case the service provider can refuse to comply and transfer the request to the competent state authority.[27] By laying down 'safe harbor' rules, LEC envisages limitations on civil and criminal liability within its sphere of application, but does not influence the liability of the primary infringer nor does it prevent the introduction, by other laws, of other measures to stop the infringement. Consequently, IP laws may prescribe additional measures which can be imposed to online intermediaries. Since primary infringers of IP rights are typically hard to identify, at least in short term period, various online intermediaries are 'perfect targets' for IP right-owners in performing the civil enforcement of their rights.

The Serbian IP law has only recently introduced the explicit possibility for an IP right owner to seek an injunctive relief against online (but also any other) intermediary. The 2019 amendments to the Law on Copyright and Related Rights (LCRR),[28] as well as the 2020 Law on Trademarks (LT)[29] both allow to IP right owners to apply for injunction relief of blocking (or content removal). Thereby, Serbian IP law is being harmonized with Art. 9, para. 1 of the EU Directive on the enforcement of intellectual property rights (IPRED),[30] which regulates provisional and precautionary measures in general. However, even before the recent reform of Serbian IP rules, the courts sporadically imposed blocking injunctions on intermediaries, by extensively interpretating the rules on provisional measures. For example, the Commercial Court in Belgrade granted a preliminary injunction for alleged trademark infringement against the buy and sell online platform *korpica.rs,* which advertised the sale of counterfeited products labelled with a protected trademark "Scholl".[31] The Court granted the injunction against both the seller (advertiser) and the online platform which exhibited the advertisement. The provisional measure imposed by the Court under Art. 75 of the 2009 Law on Trademarks[32] consisted in: (1) seizure and removal from circulation of infringing products; and (2) injuction prohibiting the continuation of activities which could result in an infringement. In the subsequent trademark infringement proceedings, the same court found that both the advertiser and the intermediary infringed the trademark right and, *inter alia*,

---

[27] Art. 20, para. 6 of the LEC.

[28] Law on Copyright and Related Rights (LCRR), Official Journal of the Republic of Serbia, Nos. 104/2009, 99/2011, 119/2012, 29/2016 – Decision of the Constitutional Court and 66/2019. The unofficial translation of the consolidated text of the LCRR is available on http://www.zis.gov.rs/legal-regulations/legislation.110.html.

[29] Law on Trademarks (LT), Official Journal of the Republic of Serbia, No. 6/2020. The translation to English is not yet available.

[30] Directive 2004/48/EC of the European Parliament and of the Council on the enforcement of intellectual property rights, Official Journal of the European Communities, No. L157, 30.4.2004.

[31] Commercial Court in Belgrade, Case No. 13 P 3357/2018, 11 September 2018.

[32] Law on Trademarks, Official Journal of the Republic of Serbia, No. 104/09, 10/13 and 44/18. This law was in force until the adoption of the 2020 Law on Trademarks.

ordered the permanent removal of the infringing advertisements from the online platform.[33]

In another, somewhat specific, case *Novosti v. Mirjana Gojgolović,* the Higher Court in Belgrade ordered the removal of the entire contents of the website for alleged trademark infringement, and prohibited the further use of the domain name *vecernjenovosti.rs* by the defendant.[34] The case combined an ADR domain name dispute resolution proceedings with a court-ordered injuction. The publisher of the daily newspaper "Večernje novosti" (usually referred to as "Novosti") first initiated a domain name dispute resolution proceedings before the National Commission for Domain Name Disputes (NCDND), which acts within the auspices of the Serbian Chamber of Commerce, against Ms. Gojgolović who registered a domain name *vecernjenovosti.rs*. The claimant operated for years its domain name at the address *novosti.rs*, which represents the official web-page of the daily newspaper. The defendant illegaly used the claimant's trademark not only as part of the domain name itself, but also within the contents of the website. Under Art. 17, para. 1 of the Rules on Domain Name Dispute Resolution,[35] the Serbian Internet Domain Name Registry Foundation (RNIDS) is required to prevent the transfer of the domain name and changes to the registration data until the completion of the procedure before the NCDND. Although ADR domain name dispute resolution proceedings is very efficient (cca 60 days since the constitution of the expert panel), it does not allow for the claimant to request the website content removal while the proceedings are pending.[36] Consequently, the trademark owner requested that the Higher Court in Belgrade grants a preliminary injunction against a domain name registrant. In order to ensure that the content will be efficiently removed, the Court also ordered RNIDS to prevent the registrant from further using the infinging domain name *vecernjenovosti.rs*.

As our analysis of a rather scarce case-law of the Serbian courts related to blocking injunctions has demonstrated, the courts did not limit their measures to 'information society service providers' within the meaning of the LEC, but also imposed preliminary measures to other service providers acting as intermediaries. It is to be expected that such trend will continue, given that Art. 210, para. 2 of the LCRR, as well as Art. 95, para. 2 of the LT, now use a broader term of an 'intermediary' against which a preventive injuction may be granted. Both laws define an intermediary as any person whose services are used while infringing an IP right. This definition is in line with the Court of Justice of the European Union (CJEU) case-law, which interprets the term 'intermediary' in broad way, thereby

[33] Commercial Court in Belgrade, Case No. Posl. br. 13 P 3357/2018, 24 January 2019.

[34] Higher Court in Belgrade, Case No. 8 P 1253/18, 13 December 2018.

[35] Rules of Procedure for the Resolution of Disputes Relating to the Registration of National Internet Domain Names, Official Journal of the Republic of Serbia, No. 31/11, 24/12, 67/14, 61/16 and 74/19. The Rules are modeled upon the Uniform Domain Name Dispute-Resolution Policy (UDRP), adopted by the Internet Corporation for Assigned Names and Numbers (ICANN).

[36] For a detailed analysis of the Serbian domain names dispute resolution system see: Popović (2014), pp. 141–147; Marković and Popović (2020), pp. 315–320.

including anyone who 'provides a service capable of being used by a third party to infringe'.[37] The CJEU is of the view that 'it is not necessary to maintain a specific relationship with that or those persons',[38] which suggests that even being an indirect beneficiary of a service is sufficient.[39] This would cover also offline or not-at-distance intermediaries, such as ordinary contractors.

Under LCRR and LT, a preventive injunction may be used against the infringer and/or against the intermediary, at the claimant's discretion. Under Art. 95, para. 2 of LT, if a person makes it probable that its trademark right has been infringed, or that it shall be infringed, the court may pass a provisional measure of: (1) seizure or removal from the channels of commerce of objects infringing the right; (2) seizure or prohibition of alienation of materials and objects predominantly used in the creation of objects infringing the right and/or predominantly intended for creation or manufacture of products infringing the right; (3) prohibition of actions infringing the right or presenting serious threat that the right shall be infringed. The LT allows for all three sub-types of injuction to be granted against an intermediary as well, which could, in our view, jeopardize the right balance between effective protection of IP rights, on the one hand, and fundamental rights of online intermediaries, on the other. Indeed, the second sub-type of injuction, consisting in the seizure of objects used for the alleged infringement, seems to allow for the seizure of an online intermediary's technical equipment, which would unduly restrict its freedom to conduct a business. On the other hand, Art. 210, para. 2 of the LCRR, limits the contents of the injuction that may be granted against an intermediary to the third sub-type only (i.e. prohibition of actions infringing the copyright or presenting serious threat that the right shall be infringed). Such approach, in our view, is more adequate and should have been followed by the Serbian legislator when reforming the trademark rules.

Consequently, both LCRR and LT empower the court to order an injunction which not only requires the online intermediary to terminate ongoing infringements—'take-down' obligations—but also to prevent future infringements—'stay-down' obligations. The latter have recently been codified in EU law in the case of online content-sharing service providers (OCSSPs).[40] The rather vague wording of the relevant Serbian legal provisions ('prohibition of actions infringing an IP right'), does not seem to prevent the court from ordering an online provider to:

1. take down 'identical' copies of infringing materials—specifically, to remove information which it stores, the content of which is identical to the content of information which was previously found to be unlawful, or to block access to that information, irrespective of who requested the storage of that information; and/or

[37] CJEU, *Tommy Hilfiger Licensing LLC and Others v. Delta Center a.s.*, Case C-494/15, 7 July 2016, § 25.

[38] *Ibid*, § 23.

[39] Husovec (2017), p. 87.

[40] See Art. 17, para. 4 (c) of the DSMD.

2. take down 'equivalent' versions of infringing materials—specifically, to remove information which it stores, the content of which is equivalent to the content of information which was previously found to be unlawful, or to block access to that information, provided that the monitoring of and search for the information concerned by such an injunction are limited to information conveying a message the content of which remains essentially unchanged compared with the content which gave rise to the finding of illegality and containing the elements specified in the injunction.[41]

However, the courts should be very cautious when ordering the removal of 'equivalent' versions of content, since materials which are similar to a copyrighted work or a protected trademark need not necessarily infringe the claimant's right.[42] In EU law, the courts are indeed allowed to grant injuctions ordering an online provider to take down 'equivalent' versions of infringing materials, but (so far) only in disputes related to hate speech and not necessarily in IP-related disputes.[43]

Further to these provisional and precautionary measures, both LCRR and LT allow for the injuctions to be granted against intermediaries after the infringement has been established.[44] This is in line with Art. 11 of the IPRED, which provides that, where a court decision finding an infringement exists, it is the Member States' duty to ensure that rightholders can apply for an injunction against intermediaries used to infringe the IP right.

3 Freedom of Expression Concerns

The Serbian rules on intermediary liability, modeled upon the ECD, provide adequate protection for intermediaries who are not publishers. There is no doubt that non-active intermediaries who have not been notified on the alleged infringement can rely on the protection, and that only a notification followed by refusal to remove the infringing content can lead to liability. There are, however, two challenging areas that may generate the freedom of expression and also privacy concerns. First, the right of information, i.e. the conditions under which a right owner can learn the identity of the infringer. Second, the scope of specific filtering injuctions which may be imposed to online intermediaries.

[41] CJEU, *Eva Glawischnig-Piesczek v Facebook Ireland Limited*, Case C-18/18, 3 October 2019, § 53.

[42] For example, a similar trademark may, in principle, be registered in another class of products.

[43] Rosati (2019), p. 677.

[44] See Art. 205, para. 2 of the LCRR and Art. 92, para. 3 of the LT.

3.1 Right of Information

In order to identify the primary infringer of an IP right, a right owner would typically require the assistance from online intermediaries. Under Art. 8 of the IPRED, in the context of (civil) proceedings concerning an infringement of an intellectual property right and in response to a justified and proportionate request of the claimant, the competent judicial authorities may order that information on the origin and distribution networks of the goods or services which infringe an intellectual property right be provided by the infringer and/or any other person who, *inter alia*, was found to be providing on a commercial scale services used in infringing activities. This provision ensures not only the effective exercise of the fundamental right to intellectual property protection, but also the right to an effective remedy.

However, the personal details submitted by users for the purposes of registration to an online service are often falsified. Consequently, other types of information, such as Internet Protocols (IP address), are more valuable to IP right owners. The collection of this type of information, as well as its storage in the platform's server logs, have usually been consented to by the user in accepting the platform's general terms of service and privacy policy. Under Art. 8, para. 2 of the IPRED, the right owners may require from 'other persons' (e.g. online intermediaries) information comprising the names and addresses of the producers, manufacturers, distributors, suppliers and other previous holders of the goods or services, as well as the intended wholesalers and retailers. In several cases, the CJEU was required to define the scope of the right of information or, more specifically, what constitutes an 'address' within the meaning of Art. 8, para. 2 of the IPRED. Surprisingly, the CJEU held that an 'address' must be understood in the usual sense—as the infringer's postal address.[45] The CJEU explicitely stated that the term does not refer to the email address, telephone number or IP address. This restrictive interpretation was justified by the need to establish a 'fair balance' between the interests of rightholders, on the one hand, and the right of users to the protection of their personal data from unlawful processing, on the other.[46] Nevertheless, EU Member States are allowed to (and most of them did) implement provisions granting rightholders 'rights to receive fuller information',[47] provided that the requests are determined in each case in such a manner as to take due account of the specific characteristics of that case, including the specific features of each intellectual property right and, where appropriate, the intentional or unintentional character of the infringement.[48]

In Serbian law, the right of information is enshrined in both LEC, which concerns online infringements generally, and LCRR/LT, which are specific to infringements of IP rights. The LEC requires information society service providers to disclose all

---

[45] CJEU, *Constantin Film Verleih GmbH v YouTube LLC and Google Inc*, Case C-264/19, 9 July 2020, § 30–31.

[46] *Ibid*, § 37–38.

[47] See Art. 8, para. 3 (a) of the IPRED.

[48] See Recital 17 of the IPRED.

information necessary for criminal act detection or criminal prosecution, under court or administrative order.[49] The scope of the right of information is set broadly, so as to include 'all information' about users which is necessary for criminal investigation and subsequent proceedings. This would encompass not only user's name and postal address, but all other useful information, such as the IP address used to access the online service. With respect to infringement of IP rights, this provision may be relied upon to investigate or prosecute the following criminal acts: violation of moral right of author or performer (Art. 198 of the Criminal Code); unauthorised use of copyrighted work or subject-matter of related rights (Art. 199 of the Criminal Code); unauthorised removal or altering of electronic information on copyright or related rights (Art. 200 of the Criminal Code); patent infringement (Art. 201 of the Criminal Code); design right infringement (Art. 202 of the Criminal Code).[50] At the same time, the right of information in civil law proceedings is laid down by LCRR and LT. With respect to alleged copyright infringements, Art. 210, para. 4 of the LCRR empowers the competent court of justice to grant a preliminary injuction against intermediary, consisting in disclosure of banking, financial, business or other relevant documents and data, or in enabling access to those documents and data. The term 'other relevant documents and data' is broad enough to include users' personal information and IP address. LT lays down the identical rule with respect to preliminary injuctions in trademark infringement (civil) proceedings.[51] A preliminary injunction may also be granted for the purpose of preserving evidence in respect of the alleged infringement.[52]

Further to preliminary injunctions, the court may, at the request of an intellectual property right owner whose right was infringed, order that information on the origin and distribution networks of the goods or services which infringe an intellectual property right be provided by any other person who, *inter alia*, was found to be providing on a commercial scale services used in infringing activities.[53] Although this provision does not primarily target online intermediaries, it does not distinguish between offline and online intermediaries either.

The (overly) broad scope of the right of information in civil law proceedings, as laid down by LCRR and LT, which covers access to 'all relevant documents and data', generates privacy and freedom of expression concerns. Therefore, the Serbian courts should, when ordering (online) intermediaries to provide relevant information, take note of the CJEU interpretation of Art. 8 of the IPRED, upon which the Serbian provisions were modeled. Under the *Promusicae* ruling, IPRED did not preclude Member States from imposing an obligation to disclose personal data to private persons in order to enable them to bring civil proceedings for intellectual

[49] See Art. 20, para. 3 of the LEC.

[50] Criminal Code of the Republic of Serbia, Official Journal Nos. 85/2005, 88/2005, 107/2005, 72/2009, 111/2009, 121/2012, 104/2013, 108/2014, 94/2016 and 35/2019.

[51] See Art. 95, para. 4 of the LT.

[52] See Art. 212, para. 7 of the LCRR and Art. 99, para. 2 (3) of the LT.

[53] See Art. 213, para. 2 (3) of the LCRR and Art. 103, para. 2 (3) of the LT.

property right infringement.[54] However, in doing so, Member States are required to ensure a fair balance between the protection of an IP right and the protection of personal data. Regrettably, this decision fails to address an increasingly important question of access to retained data. Such data would include all data necessary for: (1) tracing and identifying the source of a communication; (2) identifying the destination of a communication; (3) determining the beginning, duration and end of a communication; (4) identifying the type of communication; (5) identifying users' terminal equipment; (6) identifying the location of the users' mobile terminal equipment. Hence, when determining the scope of right of information in civil law proceedings, the Serbian courts should also consider the provisions of the Law on Electronic Communications (LECOM),[55] which lays down the conditions for collection and access to retained data. Under Art. 128, para. 2 of the LECOM, the access to retained data may only be granted by court order, for the purpose of conducting criminal proceedings or the protection of security of the Republic of Serbia, in accordance with the relevant laws. Therefore, in civil law proceedings the access to retained data cannot be granted. In 2015, the Commissioner for Information of Public Importance and Personal Data Protection conducted an investigation on the treatment of retained data by Internet service providers, as a result of which several deficiencies were detected. Following its investigation, the Commissioner recommended that the security of such data be improved and that the 12 months-period during which the data must be retained[56] be shortened.[57]

When interpreting the scope of the right of information, the Serbian courts have indeed applied the principle of proportionality and, indirectly, affirmed the freedom to conduct a business: the IP-specific provisions were interpreted in light of the limitations imposed by the LEC and/or other laws regulating the provision of online (and offline) intermediary services. For example, the Commercial Court of Appeal in case *DKH Retail Limited v AKS Ekspress Kurir doo* affirmed that a trademark owner may request the issuance of a measure for securing of evidence, before the competent court, targeting specifically a provider of priority mail delivering services.[58] However, when determining the scope of such measure, which would require from an intermediary to provide information about its users, the competent court should also consider the relevant provisions of the Law on postal services (LPS).[59] Under Art.

[54] CJEU, *Productores de Música de España (Promusicae) v. Telefónica de España SAU*, Case C-275/06, 29 January 2008, § 70. For a detailed analysis of this decision see: Coudert and Werkers (2010), pp. 50–71.

[55] Law on Electronic Communications (LECOM), Official Journal of the Republic of Serbia, Nos. 44/2010, 60/2013, 62/2014 and 95/2018.

[56] Under Art. 128, para. 6 of the LECOM, an electronic communications operator may keep the retained data for 12 months after the communication has taken place.

[57] Commissioner for Information of Public Importance and Personal Data Protection, Report on the control of the implementation of the Law on personal data protection by operators of electronic communications which provide Internet access services, 30 June 2015, p. 16.

[58] Commercial Court of Appeal, Case No. 9 Pvž 202/20, 25 June 2020.

[59] Law on Postal Services (LPS), Official Journal of the Republic of Serbia, No. 77/2019.

47 of the LPS, the postal operator is obliged, upon collection of cash-on-delivery and insured items, to inspect the user's ID with a photograph and record the registration number of the identity document, in order to determine the identity of the sender and to prevent money laundering and terrorist financing and turnover of goods of unrecorded entities. The postal operator is required to keep the collected information as a business secret, to use it for the purpose for which it was collected, and to submit the information only at the request of the court or other competent authority, for the purposes of the proceedings before that authority.

3.2 *Specific Filtering Obligation*

As already explained,[60] the Serbian legislator did not impose a general obligation on information society service providers to monitor the information which they transmit or store, nor a general obligation to actively seek facts or circumstances indicating illegal activity.[61] This provision is modeled upon Art. 15, para. 1 of the ECD. The ban of imposition of general monitoring obligation is justified not just by safeguarding the freedom of expression, but also on clear grounds of a practical and economic nature: general monitoring would be technically impractical and economically unsustainable.[62] However, in accordance with Recital 47 of the ECD, these provisions would not, *prima facie*, preclude an injunction imposing 'specific' monitoring obligations:

> Member States are prevented from imposing a monitoring obligation on service providers only with respect to obligations of a general nature; this does not concern monitoring obligations in a specific case and, in particular, does not affect orders by national authorities in accordance with national legislation.

This approach was further developed by the CJEU in cases *L'Oreal eBay*[63] and *SABAM*.[64] In the former, the CJEU stated that injunctions can be issued not only to take measures to bring infringements to an end, but also to prevent further infringements. According to the CJEU, an online intermediary can be ordered to suspend the perpetrator of an IP infringement in order to prevent: (1) further infringements of that kind; (2) by the same seller; and (3) in respect of the same trademarks. However, the prevention of further infringements cannot be achieved through an active monitoring of all the data of each of the users of an online intermediary.[65] The CJEU reiterated in

---

[60] See § 2.1 of this paper.

[61] Art. 20, para. 1 of the LEC.

[62] Montero and van Enis (2011), p. 29.

[63] CJEU, *L'Oréal SA and Others v eBay International AG and Others*, Case C-324/09, 12 July 2011.

[64] CJEU, *Scarlet v. SABAM*, Case C-70/10, 24 November 2011. CJEU, *SABAM v. Netlog*, Case C-360/10, 16 February 2012.

[65] CJEU, *L'Oréal SA and Others v eBay International AG and Others*, § 141–144.

two *SABAM* cases that a requirement to install a filtering system capable of identifying specific types of content, for almost all information stored by the users, applied indiscriminately to all of them, as a preventive measure, and for unlimited period of time, amounts to a general monitoring obligation.[66]

Further to acknowledging the CJEU case-law on monitoring obligations, the Serbian courts should imperatively interpret the relevant LEC provisions in line with the decisions of the Council of Europe (CoE) and of the European Court of Human Rights (ECtHR), which the Republic of Serbia is a member of.[67] Under Art. 10 of the European Convention on Human Rights (ECHR), everyone has the right to freedom of expression. This right shall include freedom to hold opinions and to receive and impart information and ideas without interference by public authority and regardless of frontiers. Applying the guarantees under Art. 10 ECHR to online intermediaries does not raise any obstacle of principle. In a recommendation addressed to CoE Member States, the Committee of Ministers emphasized that the development of information and communication technologies and services should contribute to everyone's enjoyment of the rights guaranteed by Art. 10 ECHR, for the benefit of each individual and the democratic culture of every society.[68] The ECtHR has, on many occasions, emphasized that those who provide authors with a medium participate fully in freedom of expression and thus enjoy the guarantees offered by Art. 10 ECHR. For example, in a case concerning measures adopted by the Swiss Confederation obstructing parabolic antenna reception of televised broadcasts, the ECtHR affirmed that Art. 10 protects both the content of information and the means of transmitting and receiving it, since any restriction imposed on the means necessarily interferes with the right to receive and impart information.[69] Furthermore, the ECtHR does not exlude 'commercial speech' from the scope of Art. 10 ECHR.[70] Indeed, Art. 10 guarantees freedom of expression to everyone, without making a distinction according to the type of aim pursued (profit-making or not).

The CoE approach to the freedom of speech in digital context is best reflected in the Recommendation to Member States on measures to promote the respect for freedom of expression and information with regard to Internet filters.[71] In the said Recommendation, the CoE Committee of Ministers urged the Member States to guarantee that blocking or filtering measures are introduced only if the filtering concerns specific and clearly identifiable content, a competent national authority has

---

[66] CJEU, *Scarlet v. SABAM*, § 51.

[67] Serbia became the 45th member of the Council of Europe in April 2003.

[68] CoE Committee of Ministers, Declaration on Human Rights and the rule of law in the Information Society, 13 May 2005.

[69] ECtHR, *Autronic AG v Switzerland*, Case 12,726/87, 22 May 1990, § 47.

[70] ECtHR, *Markt Intern Verlag GmbH and Klaus Beermann v Germany*, Case 10,572/83, 20 November 1989, § 26.

[71] CoE Committee of Ministers, Recommendation CM/Rec(2008)6 on measures to promote the respect for freedom of expression and information with regard to Internet filters, 26 March 2008.

taken a decision on its illegality and the decision can be reviewed by an independent and impartial tribunal or regulatory body, in accordance with the requirements of Art. 6 ECHR.

4 Concluding Remarks

The countries aspiring to join the European Union, such as the Republic of Serbia, have set the legal framework for online intermediary liability which closely reflects the EU model. Hence, the biggest challenge for a comprehensive harmonization of national rules with the EU law lies in the proper enforcement of the rules on liability. Given that the legislative intervention of the Union in this area is primarily conducted via directives, it is the national rules that are actually being enforced in the Member States. Despite the fact that enforcement has traditionally been viewed as something very national, we are of the view that the Serbian courts should imperatively take into account decisions and argumentation models from EU Member States. The national courts should also communicate their decisions more than ever before. The Internet is global, hence the enforcement of Internet-related rules cannot be construed in a national-protective manner. This approach, which we commend, is commonly referred to as 'harmonisation through communication'.[72]

As our analysis demonstrated, the enforcement of the rules on online intermediary liability generates significant freedom of expression concerns. It is doubtful whether blocking or removal injuctions for alleged IP law infringement may be proportional, as required under Art. 10 ECHR. Given the current state of the technology, most filters do not seem suitable for determining whether a communication is authorised or infringes intellectual property rights. Therefore, even those filtering measures that are limited to specific content may be 'over-inclusive',[73] since the imposition of such measures may lead to blocking or removal of content that in no way infringes IP rights (for example, in situations covered by an exception or limitation to copyright). Unfortunately, despite all technological progress, we have not yet developed an appropriate filtering or blocking measure which would be both effective, from the owners of IP rights perspective, and protective of the freedom of expression. Clearly, this global problem should be addressed at a supra-national level.

References

Coudert F, Werkers E (2010) In the aftermath of the Promusicae case: how to strike the balance? Int J Law Inf Technol 18(1):50–71

[72]Norrgård (2012), p. 221.

[73]Montero and van Enis (2011), p. 34.

Dinwoodie GB, Dreyfuss RC, Kur A (2009) The law applicable to secondary liability in intellectual property cases. New York Univ J Int Law Polit 42:201–235

Husovec M (2017) Injunctions against intermediaries in the European Union: accountable but not liable? Cambridge University Press, Cambridge

Karwowska A (2020) Hosting provider liability for user-generated content. Przegląd Prawa Publicznego 2020(1):41–50

Marković SM, Popović DV (2020) Pravo intelektualne svojine (Intellectual Property Law), 9th edn. University of Belgrade Faculty of Law, Belgrade

Montero E, van Enis Q (2011) Enabling freedom of expression in light of filtering measures imposed on internet intermediaries. Comput Law Secur Rev 27(2011):21–35

Norrgård M (2012) The European principles of IP enforcement: harmonisation through communication? In: Ohly A (ed) Common principles of European intellectual property law. Mohr Siebeck, Tübingen, pp 203–222

Popović DV (2014) Registracija naziva internet domena i pravo žiga (registration of internet domain names and trademark law). University of Belgrade Faculty of Law, Belgrade

Popović DV (2021) Freedom of expression on social networks: an international perspective. In: Wielec M (ed) The impact of digital platforms and social media on the freedom of expression and pluralism - analysis on certain central European countries. Ferenc Mádl Institute of Comparative Law, Budapest, Hungary, pp 277–310

Rosati E (2019) Material, personal and geographic scope of online intermediaries' removal obligations beyond Glawischnig-Piesczek, C-18/18 and defamation. Eur Intellect Prop Rev 41(11): 672–682

Savin A (2020) EU Internet Law. Edward Elgar, Cheltenham

Seltzer W (2010) Free speech unmoored in Copyright's Safe Harbor: chilling effects of the DMCA on the first amendment. Harv J Law Technol 24(1):171–232

Taylor H (2021) Online Platforms: The new brokers of copyrights? An EU Perspective. Available at SSRN. https://doi.org/10.2139/ssrn.3809728

Compulsory Licensing System in Bosnia and Herzegovina: How Pandemic-Proof Is It?

Iza Razija Mešević

Contents

1 Introduction

The year 2020 has truly been unprecedented. The Covid-19 pandemic, declared as such on 11 March 2020 by the World Health Organization (hereinafter: WHO),[1] has affected not only human lives but also the economy on the global scale. Nearly every aspect of life was in some way influenced, and the existing national legislations in many areas of law fell under the scrutiny of the pandemic, for not being necessarily sufficient in the current circumstances to offer an adequate response to a number of

[1] World Health Organization (2020).

I. R. Mešević (✉)
University of Sarajevo, Faculty of Law, Sarajevo, Bosnia and Herzegovina
e-mail: ir.mesevic@pfsa.unsa.ba

D. V. Popović et al. (eds.), *Balkan Yearbook of European and International Law 2021*, Balkan Yearbook of European and International Law 2021,
https://doi.org/10.1007/978-3-030-97431-2_3

questions, some of which have never been posed before. However, the last year has also shown the importance of promoting research and innovation, supporting certain industries and their manufacturing capacities, and eliminating or reducing administrative and legal barriers for access to health technologies. Interestingly, although the whole world currently shares the same health priority, this historical event has brought to the surface some old inequalities related to access to essential health technologies and, if possible,—at affordable prices. One of the areas most certainly and heavily influenced by the new developments and closely related to the issues of access to diagnostics, medicines and vaccines indispensable to prevent, diagnose, and treat Covid-19 is Intellectual Property (hereinafter: IP or IPR). Creativity and new solutions that we strongly need in these times lie at the core of IPRs and those rights represent incentives for innovation, which is the key to long-term economic growth, enhancements in the quality of human life,[2] but at this point—also to the potential end of the pandemic.[3] However, since they are, as a rule, monopolistic in nature, the IPRs and the national IP systems require to an extent a "pandemic-adequate" update or adjustment which will result in increased efficiency of the latter, but foremost create a stronger balance between promoting and rewarding innovation on the one hand, and the high value of public health on the other. It is obvious that the public health concern and the related need for intervention within the IP systems are predominantly focused on patent law, but the trademark, copyright and design systems, as well as the protection of trade secrets and clinical trial data also play an important role.[4] However, interventions were also needed in other, supporting areas, such as government procurement, regulatory standards or tariffs, and imports. Accordingly, a number of national and regional IP offices[5] recognised the urgency of the situation early on and responded by expediting or simplifying their administration of the IP system, in particular with regard to patents and trademarks.[6] For example, the United States Patent and Trademark Office has established a

[2]Bacchus (2020).

[3]For example, the work on the Pfizer/BioNTech vaccine began in January 2020, and the first emergency use authorisation was issued by the U.S. Food and Drug Administration on 11 December of the same year. In the meantime, a number of other vaccines have been approved for emergency use in the U.S. (Moderna and Johnson & Johnson) and the EU (Moderna, Oxford-AstraZeneca and Johnson & Johnson). Some vaccines also have been approved, or the their emergency use has been authorised, in other countries (e.g. Sinopharm and Sinovac are approved in China and in emergency use in other countries), whilst a number of vaccine candidates is in large-scale efficacy tests (phase 3). See: Zimmer et al. (2021).

[4]World Trade Organization (2020), The TRIPS Agreement and COVID-19 Information Note, 2 et seq.

[5]Institute for Intellectual Property of BiH did not introduce any particular measures apart from shortening operating hours, working remotely with clients and postponing the professional examination for representatives of the protection of industrial property. Those measures ended on 22 May 2020. See: World Intellectual Property Organization (2020a). Covid-19 IP Policy Tracker. Bosnia and Herzegovina. See also: Institute for Intellectual Property (2020a) Institut za intelektualno vlasništvo BiH vraća se na redovni režim rada.

[6]World Trade Organization (2020), The TRIPS Agreement and COVID-19 Information Note, 1.

COVID-19 Prioritised Examination Pilot Program in order to accelerate the examination of COVID-19-related applications filed by small and micro enterprises, and a similar path was also taken by the Brazilian National Institute of Industrial Property for the period from 7 April 2020 to 30 June 2021.[7] Furthermore, a number of countries[8] also introduced expedited public procurement of essential products by applying emergency procedures, which involve shorter timelines and issuing direct contract awards.[9]

A particularly interesting development related to the escalated demand in medication, diagnostics and, since the end of 2020, also the vaccines, is an increased interest in the mobilisation and application, we could even say a "comeback," of a rather traditional mechanism of the national, but also international patent system—the compulsory licence. In fact, the pandemic reopened the issue of exploring the means and methods of gaining equitable access to all these health technologies and whenever possible—to affordable versions of them. The latter does not exclude relying on the "spirit of collaboration" by the patent holders and their will to issue voluntary licences for their protected products, but a number of countries justifiably also decided to put in place instruments for taking swift measures to enable access to medical products and protect public health, even if it means limiting the exclusive rights of patentees. As for the others who did not take any particular actions with regard to this, now seems to be a good time to brush the dust off of the relevant provisions on compulsory licensing in their national laws and to carefully examine them in order to see if they are pandemic-proof. In particular, if they have been unused or very rarely used in the past.

The goal of this article is to do the same with the provisions on compulsory licences set forth in the patent legislation of Bosnia and Herzegovina (hereinafter: BiH) and to explore the potential for granting such a licence for the national territory.

2 Compulsory Licences in the International Context

The term "compulsory licence" or "non-voluntary licence" is an "umbrella term"[10] for a type of limitation of exclusive rights of a patent holder, which involves different kinds of authorisations to use the patented invention on a non-voluntary basis. The latter in the sense that a licence to exploit a patented invention by a third party is not

---

[7] *Ibid*, 3.

[8] World Trade Organization, World Health Organization, World Intellectual Property Organization (2020), p. 2.

[9] On the other hand, the House of Representatives of the Parliamentary Assembly of BiH just adopted the Proposal for laws amending the Law on Public Procurement and the Law on Medicines and Medical Devices on 25 February 2021 in order to expedite and simplify the procurement of Covid-19 vaccines. See: Bosnia and Herzegovina, Parliamentary Assembly of Bosnia and Herzegovina (2021).

[10] 't Hoen (2016), p. 50.

given by the right holder on a voluntary basis (voluntary licence), but by a competent authority of a country, where the patent is granted, provided that prescribed conditions are fulfilled.[11] This term usually also refers to "government use", which represents a non-voluntary authorisation to use the invention by a government agency or a third party on behalf of the government, but also to "crown use" licences to remedy anti-competitive practices, etc.[12] Compulsory licences represent a powerful policy tool that fulfils a range of goals and objectives. They include the promotion and protection of interests of the general public in the areas of, e.g., public health or national security, striking a balance of interests between the private, monopolistic rights of patent holders on the one hand, and public interests and interests of third parties on the other, and finally, the prevention of abuse of those exclusive rights.[13]

Although compulsory licences were already regulated on the international level by the Paris Convention (Art. 5A),[14] they grew in importance with their introduction to the TRIPS Agreement (Art. 31)[15] as one of the flexibilities to patent rights. This mechanism became even more relevant during the HIV/AIDS epidemic, which represented a public health crisis, as discussions started to intensify on reducing patent barriers for access to affordable medicines in (developing and least developed) countries which did not have their own manufacturing capacities and relied solely on import of medication.[16] In 2001, the discussions resulted in the Doha Declaration,[17] the decision of the General Council of 2003 on the implementation of paragraph 6 of the Doha Declaration (so-called "Interim Waiver")[18] and the decision of the General Council of 2005 on the amendment of the TRIPS Agreement,[19] which finally entered into force on 23 January 2017[20] and introduced a special compulsory licensing system in the TRIPS Agreement (Art. 31bis).

Compulsory licences are a powerful policy tool. Sometimes even a "threat" of issuing one can influence the right holder's decision with regard to voluntary

[11] World Intellectual Property Organization (2019), p. 3.

[12] *Ibid.* See also: 't Hoen (2016), p. 50.

[13] World Intellectual Property Organization (2019), p. 4 *et seq.*

[14] Paris Convention for the Protection of Industrial Property of 20 March 1883, as revised in Brussels on 14 December 1900, in Washington on 2 June 1911, in The Hague on 6 November 1925, in London on 2 June 1934, in Lisbon on 31 October 1958, and in Stockholm on 14 July 1967, and as amended on 28 September 1979.

[15] Agreement on Trade-Related Aspects of Intellectual Property Rights. Annex 1C of the Marrakesh Agreement Establishing the World Trade Organization. Signed 15 April 1994. Entered into force on 1 January 1995.

[16] Urias and Ramani (2020), p. 368 *et seq.* See also: 't Hoen (2016), p. 8.

[17] World Trade Organization (2001). Declaration on the TRIPS Agreement and public health adopted on 14 November 2001.

[18] World Trade Organization, General Council (2003) Decision of 30 August 2003.

[19] World Trade Organization, General Council (2005) Decision of 6 December 2005.

[20] World Trade Organization (2021c). Protocol Amending the TRIPS Agreement. Done at Geneva on 6 December 2005. Entry into force: 23 January 2017.

licensing or price reduction.[21] Furthermore, compulsory licences have the effect of reducing prices of patented medication, however, they also have the (unproven) reputation of undermining R & D investments.[22] Notwithstanding the benefits, compulsory licences are not a very widely welcome instrument. Governments (of developing and least developed countries) often choose to refrain from applying this mechanism out of precaution and, perhaps, even fear of trade sanctions, "scaring away" foreign investors, creating an impression of not respecting IPRs, but also being put under scrutiny by the pharmaceutical industry.[23] However, difficult times obviously call for a change of policy (not to say desperate measures). Surprisingly, some developed countries which were previously adversaries of the actual use of TRIPS-flexibilities internationally, despite proclaiming support for the Doha Declaration on TRIPS and Public Health,[24] started to shift their attitude toward issuing compulsory licences. For example, the European Union is encouraging coordination of compulsory licensing in the EU in its new IP strategy "Making the most of the EU's innovative potential"[25] and refers to compulsory licences under TRIPS as "absolutely legitimate tools for Members in need, and as we are in the midst of this pandemic" in its Statements at the WTO General Council from December 2020.[26]

3 Covid-19 and Compulsory Licences

Since the emergence of the Covid-19 pandemic, a number of countries, including the developed ones, has made necessary legislative steps to ensure that mechanisms for expedient compulsory licensing are in place, in case a swift response is needed in order to facilitate access to COVID-19-related health technologies. Some even made actual use of this instrument.

For example, in Canada, the COVID-19 Emergency Response Act (Bill C-13) was passed into law on 25 March, prescribing that the Commissioner for Patents may allow the Canadian state to produce, sell, and exploit a patented invention in the

[21] 't Hoen (2016), p. 71. See also: World Intellectual Property Organization (2019), p. 53 *et seq.*

[22] Urias and Ramani (2020), p. 372 *et seq.* and 380. See also: Bacchus (2020).

[23] Saha (2009), p. 372. See also: 't Hoen (2016), p. 66 *et seq.* See also: World Intellectual Property Organization (2019), p. 49 *et seq.*

[24] 't Hoen (2020b) Some Surprises in the European Commission's New Intellectual Property Strategy.

[25] European Commission (2020) Communication from the Commission to the European Parliament, the Council, the European Economic and Social Committee and the Committee of the Regions: Making the most of the EU's innovative potential. An intellectual property action plan to support the EU's recovery and resilience, 12.

[26] Permanent Mission of the European Union to the World Trade Organization (2020) EU Statements at the WTO General Council, 18 December 2020.

event of a public health emergency.[27] In Hungary, the Government Decree No. 212/2020 on Public Health Compulsory Licences for Exploitation Within Hungary, which entered into force on 17 May 2020, authorised the Hungarian Intellectual Property Office to grant non-exclusive public health compulsory licences in order to satisfy domestic needs related to the health crisis.[28] France took a step beyond government-use licences and, introduced in the new law (Loi n°2020-290 d'urgence pour faire face a` l'e´pide´mie de covid-19) of 23 March 2020 Article L.3131-15 in the national health code, which authorises the Prime Minister to introduce temporary price control and launch generic products before the expiry of the patents or Supplementary Protection Certificates in case of a health crisis.[29] In Germany, the Prevention and Control of Infectious Diseases in Humans Act of 28 March 2020 authorised the Federal Ministry for Health to issue a compulsory licence in accordance with Section 13 (1) of the national Patent Act in case a national epidemic is declared by the Bundestag.[30] This provision has never been used and it allows for the circumvention of patent rights by the government or selected third parties in case of public interest or national security in order to ensure the supply of various health technologies (e.g. medicines, diagnostics and personal protection equipment).[31] Finally, in Israel, the Covid-19 crisis triggered the first ever government-use licence[32] to be issued under section 104 of the patent legislation since its introduction in 1967, which allows the state to surpass the legal requirements for a compulsory licence (e.g. consultation with the patentee and judicial review) for national defence purposes.[33]

[27] Houldsworth (2020). See also: Urias and Ramani (2020), p. 379. See also: World Trade Organization (2020), The TRIPS Agreement and COVID-19 Information Note, 9. See also: Jones Day (2020), p. 1.

[28] World Intellectual Property Organization (2020b) Hungary: Government Decree No. 212/2020 on Public Health Compulsory Licenses for Exploitation Within Hungary. However, the Decree is no longer in force since 18 June 2020. World Trade Organization (2020), The TRIPS Agreement and COVID-19 Information Note, 9.

[29] Houldsworth (2020). See also: Urias and Ramani (2020), p. 379.

[30] § 5 Epidemische Lage von nationaler Tragweite (2) 5.

[31] Houldsworth (2020). See also: World Trade Organization, World Health Organization, World Intellectual Property Organization (2020), p. 4. See also: Jones Day (2020), p. 3.

[32] It was for the generic version of the HIV/AIDS antiretroviral called Kaletra (a combination of lopinavir and ritonavir developed), which is developed by the company AbbVie, although at that time the positive effect on Covid-19 patients was not even confirmed. See: Urias and Ramani (2020), p. 379 *et seq.*

[33] Houldsworth (2020). See also: 't Hoen (2020a) Covid-19 and the comeback of compulsory licensing. See also: World Trade Organization, World Health Organization, World Intellectual Property Organization (2020), p. 4.

4 Non-voluntary Licences in Bosnia and Herzegovina

Before we take a closer look at the provision governing compulsory licensing in BiH, it is important to underline, in context of the implementation of international standards of IP protection and enforcement in the national legislation, that BiH is a party to the majority of international treaties and conventions in this field.[34] However, BiH is neither a Member State of the European Union (hereinafter: EU) nor a Member of the World Trade Organization (hereinafter: WTO). Only one more country (Serbia) from the region of Southeast Europe is not a WTO member state, which makes the status of these countries somewhat specific, also in the context of obligations arising from the TRIPS Agreement. Nevertheless, BiH is in the Stabilisation and Association[35] process with the former and has the status of an observer in the latter.[36] The consequence of these relations is that BiH has harmonised national IP laws with the level of their protection in the EU[37] up until 2010, as well as with the majority of standards set forth by the TRIPS Agreement.

The national Patent Law (hereinafter: BiH PL)[38] was adopted in 2010 and provisions on the "Limitation to the effects of a patent" are situated in Chapter II. With regard to non-voluntary licensing, the law provides for two mechanisms, stipulated in Arts. 79 (Compulsory licence) and 80 (Compulsory licence in the public interest), which are predominantly regulated within the framework of flexibilities provided in Art. 31 of the TRIPS Agreement (Other Use Without Authorisation of the Right Holder). It's important to underline that these limitations in the BiH PL are not restricted to a certain type of invention/technology, but are certainly of special interest in the context of pharmaceutical inventions for prevention, diagnostic and treatment of Covid-19.

4.1 Compulsory Licence (Art. 79)

The compulsory licence from Art. 79 of the BiH PL is issued by the Court of Bosnia and Herzegovina (hereinafter: Court of BiH) at the request of an interested party, it is non-exclusive in nature, its scope and duration are linked to the circumstances that

---

[34] The full list of international treaties that BiH is a party to is available at: Institute for Intellectual property (2020b) International Conventions and Agreements Applied in BIH.

[35] Stabilisation and Association Agreement between Bosnia and Herzegovina on one side, and the European Communities and their Member States on the other, was signed in Luxembourg on 16 June 2008 and entered into force on 1 June 2015 (hereinafter: SAA). See: Directorate for European Integration (2021) Stabilisation and Association Agreement.

[36] The negotiations on the accession to the WTO started in July 1999. See: World Trade Organization (2021d) Understanding the WTO: The Organization. Members and Observers. See also: World Trade Organization (2021a) Accessions. Bosnia and Herzegovina.

[37] See Art. 73 (3) of the SAA.

[38] Official Gazette of Bosnia and Herzegovina, no. 53, 2010.

led to its granting and it is, as a rule, non-transferable (Art. 79 (7), (8), (10) and (12)). This mechanism primarily serves the purpose of supplying the domestic market, unless it is necessary to correct anti-competitive practices determined as such in a judicial or administrative procedure (Art. 79 (9)). Finally, the patent holder is entitled to remuneration, taking into account the economic value of the licence and the need for correcting anti-competitive practices (Art. 79 (11)). Interestingly, there is no provision stating that the compulsory licence is granted on an individual, case-by-case basis. Unfortunately, the conditions that need to be fulfilled for this instrument to be invoked seem restrictive, to an extent confusing and inadequate, both in general and in particular in the light of the pandemic for a number of reasons. Furthermore, the BiH PL alone seems to be an insufficient legal basis to actually enforce this mechanism, since other related legislation is not aligned with its provisions.

Firstly, the predecessor law to the BiH PL from 2002, the Law on Industrial Property in BiH (Art. 134),[39] already provided for the mandate of the Court of BiH for issuing compulsory licences, but during the period this law was in force, no legislative updates in other areas of the law were conducted in order to make this mechanism enforceable and effective. This practice has continued since the adoption of the BiH PL. Namely, no amendment has been passed to the Law on Court of BiH extending its mandate to include granting compulsory licences. The competencies of the court are very specific and defined in a narrow manner[40] and this procedure could have potentially been assigned to its Administrative Division[41] and conducted in accordance with the Law on Administrative Procedure of BiH.[42] However, it would have been constructive and more than advisable if specific procedural rules for the granting of this licence were passed in accordance with Art. 2 of this law and necessary amendments made to the Law on Court of BiH. Frankly, since so far, an interested party never actually requested to invoke Art. 79, this deficiency was never addressed in practice. However, access to Covid-19-related health technologies might trigger the use of this instrument, and the Court of BiH would find itself very unprepared and dealing with a vague and insufficient legal basis, which might even result in failure to issue such a licence.

Secondly, in the case of Art. 79 (1)-(4), the compulsory licence instrument serves as a corrective measure[43] for the purpose of preventing patent abuse. However, in order to actually fulfil this goal, it is not designed efficiently, since such a licence can be issued if the right holder refuses to assign the right to the economic exploitation of a protected invention in BiH or imposes unreasonable conditions for such an

[39] Official Gazette of Bosnia and Herzegovina, no. 3 of 19 February 2002.

[40] Art. 8 of the Law on Court of Bosnia and Herzegovina. Official codified version. Official Gazette of Bosnia and Herzegovina, no. 49 of 22 July 2009. Correction. Official Gazette of Bosnia and Herzegovina, no. 74 of 21 September 2009. Amendments. Official Gazette of Bosnia and Herzegovina, no. 97 of 15 December 2009.

[41] Art. 10 (2) b) of the Law on Court of Bosnia and Herzegovina.

[42] Official Gazette of Bosnia and Herzegovina, no. 29 of 2002, 12 of 2004, 88 of 2007, 93 of 2009, 41 of 2013 and 53 of 2016.

[43] Cohen (1979), p. 169.

assignment without having made effective and serious preparations for the exploitation thereof in BiH (Art. 79 (1)). In other words, the potential licensee preferably needs to experience a refusal by the patent holder in order to invoke this mechanism. In case the patent holder has "made effective and serious preparations for the exploitation" of the invention in BiH, the "unreasonable conditions" for the assignment of rights seem not to be a sufficient reason for a compulsory licence to be granted (no case of abuse). Regardless of this, the sole circumstance that the right holder has made these preparations does not imply that the compulsory licence should not be granted because, e.g., the exploitation by the right holder might not be sufficient for the supply of the domestic market. Furthermore, the precondition on the part of the potential licensee is that this person had unsuccessfully attempted, within a reasonable period, to obtain an authorisation on reasonable commercial terms and conditions (Art. 79 (3)).[44] Finally, a compulsory licence may not be granted if the patent holder proves the existence of legitimate reasons justifying non-exploitation, or insufficient exploitation of the protected invention (Art. 79 (4)). Although the majority of these provisions are in line with international standards of the TRIPS Agreement and the Paris convention,[45] the issue that needs to be addressed in this context is the interpretation of the terms "effective and serious preparations for the exploitation," "unreasonable conditions," "reasonable commercial terms and conditions," "reasonable period," and "legitimate reasons justifying"[46] in light of the pandemic. Moreover, since the latter had an unprecedented and profound effect on economies around the world[47] and gave rise to the necessity for actions to be taken urgently in order to protect public health, the mentioned legal standards cannot be interpreted in the same manner as before. Accordingly, these circumstances need to be taken into account and the fulfilment of these conditions and periods for their completion assessed from the perspective of current circumstances.[48]

Thirdly, the periods that need to be upheld in order for the interested party to even be entitled to file a request for the grant of a compulsory licence, tailored in accordance with Art. 5A (4) of the Paris Convention, are completely maladjusted when it comes to the circumstance of a public health crisis and necessity to quickly access essential medication. The latter in the sense that the request can be submitted after expiration of the four-year period from the filing date of a patent application, or

[44] See wording of Art. 31 (b) of the TRIPS Agreement.

[45] Art. 5A (4).

[46] The comparable wording from Art. 5A (4) of the Paris convention already left a lot of room for different interpretations. See: Ford (2000), p. 958. In some countries, those reasons include *force majeure,* grounds beyond patent holder's control, public regulation, lack of resources etc. (See: World Intellectual Property Organization (2019), p. 30 *et seq.*). Again, it is questionable whether those justifications seem adequate for the current context of a pandemic.

[47] See: The World Bank (2020).

[48] E. g. national solutions regarding "reasonable period to obtain a voluntary licence", which speak of 3–6 months, 150, or 210 days, seem highly inadequate in the light of the pandemic. See: World Intellectual Property Organization (2019), p. 22 *et seq.*

after expiration of the three-year time limit from the date of the grant of a patent, whichever of the two time limits expires later (Art. 79 (2)). It is evident that these restrictive deadlines could potentially represent a severe obstacle in case of the need for compulsory licensing of a relatively new Covid-19-related health technology.

Finally, Art. 79 of the BiH PL does not entail any provision related to the specificities of the procedure for granting a compulsory licence, documentation that needs to be submitted, or deadlines that need to be upheld by the interested party or the Court of BiH. Also, there is no bylaw that regulates this topic. Further insufficiencies include the lack of legal remedies at the disposal of the interested party or the patent holder in case of a grant or refusal to grant a compulsory licence by the Court of BiH,[49] no obligation of the patent holder to provide the interested party (licensee) with the necessary know-how or training as in case of a voluntary licence, and no compulsory licence for export[50] or explicitly for import.

As already mentioned above,[51] BiH is not a member of the WTO or the TRIPS Agreement, although the BiH PL is mostly harmonised with its provisions. However, the latter explicitly provides in its Art. 31bis a special compulsory licence system[52] which waives the obligation of producers under Art. 31 (f) (predominantly for the supply of the domestic market) and enables Member countries with no or insufficient manufacturing capacities[53] to import affordable generic pharmaceutical products[54] manufactured under compulsory licence in other Member countries. Such exception is not provided in the BiH PL[55] and the question is—how badly do we actually need it in the current situation? In other words, in case the manufacturing capacities of the BiH pharmaceutical industry are potent enough to generate

[49] Compare to Art. 31 (i) of the TRIPS Agreement: The legal validity of any decision relating to the authorisation of such use shall be subject to judicial review or other independent review by a distinct higher authority in that Member.

[50] See also: CMS (2021) Compulsory Licensing in Bosnia and Herzegovina, paragraphs 14, 15 and 17.

[51] See Sect. 4. Compulsory licences in Bosnia and Herzegovina.

[52] Art. 31 bis (1): "The obligations of an exporting Member under Article 31(f) shall not apply with respect to the grant by it of a compulsory licence to the extent necessary for the purposes of production of a pharmaceutical product(s) and its export to an eligible importing Member(s) in accordance with the terms set out in paragraph 2 of the Annex to this Agreement". Annex to the TRIPS Agreement (2): "The terms referred to in paragraph 1 of Article 31bis are that: (a) the eligible importing Member(s) has made a notification to the Council for TRIPS, that... (ii) confirms that the eligible importing Member in question, other than a least developed country Member, has established that it has insufficient or no manufacturing capacities in the pharmaceutical sector for the product(s) in question..."

[53] It is deemed for the least-developed WTO Members that those capacities are insufficient or non-existent.

[54] The latter not only includes medicines but also vaccines and diagnostics. See: World Trade Organization (2021b), Compulsory licensing of pharmaceuticals and TRIPS.

[55] Art. 79 (9): A compulsory licence shall be authorised primarily for the purpose of supplying the domestic market, unless it is necessary to correct the practices determined in a judicial or administrative process to be uncompetitive.

pharmaceutical products necessary to prevent, diagnose and treat Covid-19 and supply not only the domestic market but also the markets of some other countries, the answer would be positive. But in order to make that conclusion, it is necessary to take a closer look at the local pharmaceutical sector in the country, which will be done later in the article.[56] However, it would be advisable to amend Art. 31 with a wording explicitly enabling the grant of a compulsory licence for the purpose of import, especially due to pandemic. Art. 79 (1) speaks of "commercial exploitation of the protected invention," which also includes import (Art. 66 (1) a); hence it can be interpreted as if the compulsory licence for import is already existent. However, particularly due to the current circumstances, the interpretation of this provision is something that should not be left to chance. Then BiH could benefit from this provision in case a pharmaceutical product enjoys patent protection on its territory and there is a generic version of it produced in a country that also allows the possibility of granting compulsory licences for the purpose of export. This would allow the local population to have access to the necessary health technologies at affordable prices.

Notwithstanding the above, the BiH PL also provides for compulsory cross-licensing in case of interdependence between two patented inventions (Art. 79 (5) et seq.),[57] in the sense that the patent holder of the first patent cannot exploit their protected invention without infringing somebody else's patent (second patent). Such a compulsory licence may be granted, provided that the first patent involves the invention of an important technological advancement, which is of considerable economic significance to the invention protected by the second patent. The second condition is that the holder of the second patent is entitled to a cross-licence under reasonable terms and conditions.

4.2 Compulsory Licence in the Public Interest (Art. 80)

In comparison to the compulsory licence from Art. 79, the compulsory licence in the public interest is regulated in a rather scarce manner and the provisions of Art. 80 leave a lot of room for interpretation of the actual intent of the lawmaker and again, there is also the issue of their enforceability in practice.

Firstly, the Court of BiH is not in charge of issuing such licences, but the Council of Ministers of BiH, which is the authority representing executive power on the state level (Art. 80 (1)). The condition for the grant of such a licence is that it is necessary due to states of emergency on the national level for the purpose of state security, protection of public interest in the field of health and nutrition, protection and improvement of the human environment, special interest in a particular branch of the economy or where it is necessary to correct practices determined in a judicial or

[56] See Sect. 6. Local manufacturing capacities.

[57] Comparable to Art. 31 (l) of the TRIPS Agreement.

administrative process to be anti-competitive (Art. 80 (1)). It is evident that, at least hypothetically, in the context of the Covid-19 pandemic, the justification of an emergency on the state level for the purpose of protection of the public interest in the field of health and nutrition, could apply. Another question is to which extent is this provision actually enforceable in practice, due to the complex state organisation of BiH.[58]

Namely, in accordance with the BiH Framework Law on the Protection and Rescue of People and Material Assets in Case of Natural and Other Disasters (Art. 13 (h)),[59] the Council of Ministers of BiH declares the incurrence and the termination of the state of natural and other disasters on the territory of BiH at the proposal of the Coordination body of BiH for Protection and Rescue, or at the request of the competent authorities of the entities (Federation of Bosnia and Herzegovina/FBiH and Republika Srpska/RS), or Brčko District BiH (hereinafter: BD BiH), which have already declared the state of disaster on their territories. There is not a single mention of the concept of "state of emergency" in the Framework Law, which is a consequence of the circumstance that the Constitution of BiH[60] does not entail a provision that allows the declaration of such a state on the national level.[61] Unlike the Constitution of BiH, the constitutions of both entities (Art. 70 in RS and Art. 9 in FBiH) allow for the declaration of a state of emergency on their respective territories.

The Council of Ministers exercised its authority from Art. 13 (h) of the Framework Law on 17 March 2020 by passing a Decision on the declaration of incurrence of the state of natural or other disasters on the territory of BiH.[62] It was based on the Decision of the Government of FBiH on the declaration of a state of disaster caused by the incurrence of the Coronavirus, the Decision of the Government of RS on the declaration of incurrence of a state of emergency and the Decision of the Mayor of BD BiH on the declaration of a state of natural disaster due to Covid-19.[63] In Art. 1 of its Decision, the Council of Ministers states that the declaration was made "due to danger of potential incurrence of an infectious disease epidemic caused by the novel Coronavirus (Covid-19)". Noticeably, only RS chose to declare a state of emergency, while FBiH opted for a state of disaster[64] in accordance with the Law on Protection and Rescue of People and Material Assets in Case of Natural and Other

[58] See: European Committee of the Regions (2021).

[59] Official Gazette of Bosnia and Herzegovina, no. 50 of 20 July 2018.

[60] For the Constitution of BiH, FBiH and RS, see: Office of the High Representative (2021).

[61] OSCE Mission to Bosnia and Herzegovina (2020), p. 15.

[62] Official Gazette of Bosnia and Herzegovina, no. 18 of 20 March 2020.

[63] See: Preamble of the Decision.

[64] OSCE Mission to Bosnia and Herzegovina (2020), p. 16.

Disasters of FBiH (Art. 24 (11)).[65] However, on 21 May 2020 in RS[66] and on 29 May 2020 in FBiH,[67] the above-mentioned decisions were repealed.[68] Although the Decision of the Council of Ministers was not formally repealed on the date the research for this article was finalised (February 2021), it is apparent that it has no legal effect, since every legal act that it is based on has been abrogated and the conditions of Art. 13 (h) of the Framework law no longer apply.

Notwithstanding all of the above—it is quite evident that Art. 80 is not enforceable in its current wording—generally and in the light of the pandemic. Additionally, there is presently no legal basis for a state of emergency, but only a state of disaster, to be declared on the national level in BiH, which is a precondition for the application of Art. 80 (1) in the first place. Furthermore, even if such a state could have been declared, it is unclear whether its termination would also invoke the application of Art. 79 (10) (the circumstances which led to the authorisation cease to exist and are unlikely to recur) to the compulsory licence in the public interest or not. As stated above, although the Decision of the Council of Ministers is formally still in force, its legal effects lasted only for a bit longer than 2 months. It is questionable whether a procedure for the approval of a compulsory licence in the public interest would even be concluded by the Council of Ministers in that period. The dilemma also brings out the issue of the procedural rules for the grant of such a compulsory licence, the documentation that would need to be submitted, the deadlines etc., which are all left unregulated in the BiH PL or any bylaw, as already elaborated in the case of a compulsory licence in accordance with art. 79.[69]

Moreover, Art. 80 (3) stipulates that the provisions of Art. 79 (3)[70] shall not apply in the cases referred to in Art. 80 (1).[71] In other words, there is no obligation to previously attempt obtaining a voluntary licence. However, the wording also implies

65 Official Gazette of the Federation of Bosnia and Herzegovina, no. 39 of 2003, no. 22 of 2006 and no. 43 of 2010.

66 Bosnia and Herzegovina, Republika Srpska, National Assembly. Decision on the termination of the state of emergency for the territory of Republika Srpska, 21 May 2020. Official Gazette of Republika Srpska, no. 48 of 2020.

67 Bosnia and Herzegovina, Federation of Bosnia and Herzegovina, Government of the Federation of Bosnia and Herzegovina. Termination of the state of disaster caused by the incurrence of the Coronavirus in FBiH is declared, 29 May 2020. Official Gazette of the Federation of Bosnia and Herzegovina, no. 34 of 3 June 2020.

68 In FBiH on 13 July 2020, the Federal Ministry of Health issued an Order on the declaration of a state of the epidemic of the infectious disease Covid-19, and on 24 July 2020, this state was also declared in BD BiH. See also: OSCE Mission to Bosnia and Herzegovina (2020), p. 15.

69 See Sect. 4.1. Compulsory licence (Art. 79).

70 A compulsory licence may be granted only if the person filing the request referred to in paragraph (2) of this Article unsuccessfully attempted, within a reasonable period of time, to obtain authorisation from the patent holder for the exploitation of the protected invention on reasonable commercial terms and conditions.

71 "... This requirement may be waived by a Member in the case of a national emergency or other circumstances of extreme urgency or in cases of public non-commercial use..." See Art. 31 (b) TRIPS Agreement.

that the mechanism from Art. 80 (1) can be invoked only at the request of an "interested party", the concept of which the BiH PL omits to define in more detail. This leads to the conclusion that the BiH PL apparently does not include in its Art. 80 a possibility of a government-use licence in the sense of non-commercial use for public purpose by the government itself or a third entity on its behalf.[72]

Additionally, this is the only provision of Art. 79 (compulsory licence) explicitly derogated by Art. 80 (compulsory licence in the public interest), which, again, leaves room for interpretation if that means that other paragraphs of Art. 79 (e.g., related to remuneration, non-transferability, non-exclusivity, justification of non-use, time periods and above-mentioned termination of licence) accordingly apply to this type of compulsory licence as well or not. The time limit for the submission of a request for the granting of a compulsory licence from Art. 79 (2) seem to be particularly problematic in case of its *mutatis mutandis* application to the licence from Art. 80. A four-year period from the filing date or a three-year time limit from the date of the grant of a patent seem completely inadequate for a state of emergency.

As in the case of compulsory licence from Art. 79, a compulsory licence in the public interest has also never been issued. Hence, there was no possibility to address the complete lack of enforceability of this provision. Unlike Art. 79, which is ambiguous and flawed, yet could be implemented, Art. 80 fails the test at the first hurdle - the precondition of a state of emergency on the national level.

5 Other Legislation Affecting Compulsory Licensing

It must not be disregarded that the pharmaceutical sector is a highly regulated industry branch. Accordingly, is not only the patent legislation that can "make or break" a compulsory licence, but also the laws governing regulatory approval for the production, distribution and import of medicines in a particular country.

In BiH, the state regulatory body responsible for authorising production, marketing and conducting quality control of medicines and medical devices, among other competencies, is the Agency for Medicines and Medical Devices (hereinafter: Agency) that was established in 2008 by the Law on Medicines and Medical Devices[73] and started its operation on 1 May 2009. One particular provision of that Law might have a great impact on the hypothetical compulsory licensing event, namely its Art. 140 (8).

[72] For characteristics of government-use licences in other countries, see: World Intellectual Property Organization (2019), p. 43 *et seq*.

[73] Arts. 3 et seq. of the Law on Medicines and Medical Devices. Official Gazette of Bosnia and Herzegovina, no. 58 of 21 July 2008.

The provision sets forth that Art. 34 (1) c)[74] of the same Law, with regard to data exclusivity, shall not be applied at least 5 years from entry of the law into force. This provision is after those 5 years and at the proposal of the director, subject to mandatory examination by the Professional Council of the Agency for Medicines and Medical Devices. In fact, the Professional Council of the Agency postponed the application of Art. 34 (1) c) with its decisions in 2013, and again in 2018, with effect until 29 July 2021.[75] However, the last decision was subject to scrutiny by the Directorate for European Integration of BiH.[76] Namely, this body informed the Agency that the latter extension is not in accordance with the SAA,[77] which entered into force on 1 June 2015, and determined 1 June 2021 as the general deadline for the harmonisation of the national legislation in this area. Furthermore, the Directorate drew attention to the fact that Art. 34 (1) c) is not harmonised with Art. 14 (11) of the Regulation of the European Parliament and of the Council of 31 March 2004 laying down Community procedures for the authorisation and supervision of medicinal products for human and veterinary use and establishing a European Medicines Agency.

Nevertheless, so far, no amendments have been made to the Law on Medicines and Medical Devices in order to harmonise Art. 34 (1) c with the EU legislation. Also, the contested decision of the Agency from 2018 has not been repealed. However, in any case and at the latest by the end of June 2021, the data exclusivity provision of the Law on Medicines and Medical Devices shall begin to apply, which is not very favourable for a potential future compulsory licensing event. Then, even if a generic manufacturer decides to invoke this mechanism, manages to overcome the obstacles of the ambiguous wording of Art. 79, and a compulsory licence is actually obtained, the data exclusivity provision could prevent the access of a generic medicine to the national market. Accordingly, in case the provisions on compulsory licenses from the BiH PL are amended in the future, this issue also needs to be addressed. The latter in the sense, that an exception to data exclusivity applies, when

[74](1) Notwithstanding the provision of Article 33 of this Law, the applicant is not obliged to submit their own results of pharmacological-toxicological or clinical trials if they prove that:... c) a medicinal product, for which an application for a marketing authorisation is submitted, is substantially similar to a medicinal product for which a marketing authorisation has already been issued in BiH, the EU or in other countries that have the same standards of quality, safety and efficacy of medicines, which is valid at least for 8 years, provided that the Agency may issue a marketing authorisation for a medicinal product with a validity date not earlier than 10 years after the issuance of the authorisation for a substantially similar medicinal product to which documentation of the applicant refers...

[75]Bosnia and Herzegovina, Agency for Medicines and Medical Devices. Odluka stručnog savjeta o odgađanju primjene ekskluzivnosti podataka. Official Gazette of Bosnia and Herzegovina, no. 57 of 6 August 2013 and Odluka stručnog savjeta o odgađanju primjene ekskluzivnosti podataka. Official Gazette of Bosnia and Herzegovina, no. 75 of 31 October 2018.

[76]Bosnia and Herzegovina, Council of Ministers. Directorate for European Integration. Obavijest o nepoštivanju odluke o postupku usklađivanja zakonodavstva Bosne i Hercegovine s pravnom tečevinom Evropske unije, no. 03-07-3-337-11/18 of 4 January 2019.

[77]See Sect. 4. Non-voluntary licences in Bosnia and Herzegovina.

compulsory license is issued, since otherwise this instrument could potentially be inoperative.

6 Local Manufacturing Capacities

The efficiency and actual enforceability of the mechanism of compulsory licences is not only dependent on the clear legislative framework but also strongly on the technological and manufacturing capacities of the local pharmaceutical sector. The latter unless the compulsory licence is issued only for import.

Unfortunately, there is not a lot of information available on the particularities and full potential of the pharmaceutical industry in BiH, in order to be able to offer a well-founded conclusion on whether its representatives would have the competence and the ability to implement a compulsory licence. On the other hand, some indicators[78] imply that the industry might be the smallest obstacle to invoking this mechanism in BiH, due to the fact that there are currently seven pharmaceutical companies in the Registry of Drug Manufacturers[79] at the Agency, thirty in the Registry of Manufacturers of Class 1 Medical Devices,[80] six of which potentially produce medical devices of relevance for Covid-19 prevention, and eight in the Registry of Manufacturers of Class 2 Medical Devices and Lower.[81]

A study on the pharmaceutical industry in BiH conducted in 2001[82] stated that BiH as a country represents a market with insufficient potential for the majority of local manufacturers. The manufacturers are, more or less successfully, joined in interest groups, like the Association of Innovative Pharmaceutical Manufacturers,[83] or the Association of Domestic Drug Manufacturers in FBiH. Sadly, the pharmaceutical industry does not enjoy the status of a strategic industry branch in BiH, although this initiative was initiated at least at the level of the Sarajevo Canton in

[78] For example, the company Bosnalijek was established in 1951 and is the oldest and largest pharmaceutical company in the country, producing predominantly generics, but also a number of original products. See: Bosnalijek (2021).

[79] Those companies are: Hemofarm d.o.o, Zada Pharmaceuticals, Amsal Pharmaceuticals, Bosnalijek, Farmavita, Natura Pharm d.o.o. and Pharmamed. See: Bosnia and Herzegovina, Agency for Medicines and Medical Devices (2020a) Registry of drug manufacturers.

[80] Bosnia and Herzegovina, Agency for Medicines and Medical Devices (2020b) Registry of manufacturers of medical devices, which have the authorisation of the Agency for producing class 1 medical devices.

[81] Bosnia and Herzegovina, Agency for Medicines and Medical Devices (2020c) Registry of manufacturers of medical devices, which have the authorisation of the Agency for producing class 2 medical devices and other lower classes of medical devices.

[82] Deutsche Gesellschaft für technische Zusammenarbeit GTZ (2001).

[83] The association of innovative pharmaceutical manufacturers UIPL includes the following companies: Sanofi, MSD, Roche, Pfizer, Novo Nordisk, Lilly, GSK, Bayer, Takeda, Boehringer Ingelheim, Abbvie and Novartis.

2015,[84] however, without success. Also, the Strategy of Development of the Sarajevo Canton 2021–2027 does not foresee a special role for the pharmaceutical industry, despite of changes in priorities caused by the pandemic.[85] Consequently, it is evident that, in spite of continuous obstacles in accessing Covid-19 medications[86] and vaccines, no lessons were learned in BiH from the pandemic in the context of the indispensability of putting an emphasis on domestic manufacturing.[87] Particularly when there is already an existent pool of local pharmaceutical companies to build on.

7 Compulsory Licensing Potential

A year into the pandemic, there is still no cure for Covid-19. However, very early on in 2020, the antiviral drug remdesivir, which is produced by the pharmaceutical company Gilead Science under the name Veklury, gained a lot of attention. It is administered intravenously[88] and represents a product originally developed for other viral diseases, including Ebola, Hepatitis C and the Marburg virus,[89] for which it showed limited results.[90] There is still scepticism, as well as reluctance with regard to the benefits of remdesivir in treating Covid-19, which was also expressed by the WHO, that recommended against the use of this drug.[91] However, the U.S. Food and Drug Administration (hereinafter: FDA) first issued an emergency authorisation for remdesivir in May last year, which was expended in August and finally became a full approval on 22 October 2020.[92] Moreover, the European Medicines Agency also issued a conditional marketing authorisation for this drug on 3 July 2020.[93]

Additionally, remdesivir is widely patented,[94] including in BiH. According to data from MedsPaL database of the Medicines Patent Pool,[95] since 2009 there have been five granted patents and two patent applications for remdesivir in favour of Gilead Sciences, Inc at the national Institute for Intellectual Property in BiH. The last

[84] Chamber of Commerce of the Sarajevo Canton (2015).

[85] Bosnia and Herzegovina, Federation of Bosnia and Herzegovina, Sarajevo Canton (2020).

[86] See Sect. 7. Compulsory licensing potential.

[87] For an opposite example in Canada, see: Bolongaro (2021).

[88] Urias and Ramani (2020), p.377 *et seq.*

[89] 't Hoen (2020), Covid-19 and the comeback of compulsory licensing.

[90] Wu et al. (2021).

[91] It is important to underline that the WHO review report did not completely rule out the use of this drug as a Covid-19 treatment, but pointed out that evidence was lacking to recommend its use. Carey (2021).

[92] Wu et al. (2021).

[93] European Medicines Agency (2020).

[94] 't Hoen (2020) Covid-19 and the comeback of compulsory licensing.

[95] MedsPaL (2021).

application was filed on 16 September 2016 and it refers to the "Methods for Treating Arenaviridae And Coronaviridae Virus Infections".[96] The existing patent protection for remdesivir could potentially also explain the current price of the treatment, which costs as much as 3120 $ in the United States for a period of five days.[97]

However, already in May 2020, Gilead Science signed voluntary licensing agreements with generic pharmaceutical manufacturers based in Egypt, India and Pakistan to manufacture remdesivir for distribution in 127 countries (nearly all low-income and lower-middle-income countries, as well as a number of upper-middle- and high-income countries) and also promised to donate the first 1.5 million doses.[98] BiH is not one of these countries. Furthermore, remesdivir is also in general not being used in the treatment of Covid-19 patients in the country, which is due to administrative failure related to the complex state structure, which resulted in the omission to participate in the Joint Purchase Agreement with the European Union,[99] but might also have a connection to the above-mentioned price. This medicine is currently not approved by the Agency for Medicines and -Medical Devices in BiH, however, there was a case of an urgent import of smaller amounts of it based on the authorisation of the Federal Ministry of Health.[100]

All things considered, it seems like remdesivir could potentially be an adequate hypothetical candidate for a compulsory licence in BiH in accordance with Art. 79. Provided that its inadequacies and ambiguities[101] could be conquered, that there is an actual political will in the country to grant one and that there is interest and capacity on the side of local pharmaceutical manufacturers. Potentially, this could be a compulsory licence for manufacturing and distribution invoked by the representative of the local pharmaceutical sector and not a licence for import. Even if the existence of a compulsory licence for import could be interpreted from Art. 79, it is highly unlikely that any of the 127 countries where the generic version of remdesivir is currently being manufactured will be willing to jeopardise the licensing agreement with Gilead Science and issue a compulsory licence for export. However, even a sole attempt to invoke Art. 79 of the BiH PL for remdesivir in BiH could have a positive policy effect[102] in the sense that BiH could be included in the Gilead licence, or this event could have an influence on the price of this medication for the local market.

[96] This means the condition of Art. 79 (2) regarding the four-year period from the filing date of a patent application or the expiration of the three-year time limit from the date of the grant of a patent could be fulfilled.

[97] Wu et al. (2021).

[98] Gilead Sciences (2020). See also: Urias and Ramani (2020), p. 380.

[99] BIRN BiH (2020).

[100] N1 BiH (2020).

[101] See Sect. 4.1 Compulsory licence (Art. 79).

[102] See Sect. 2. Compulsory licences in the international context.

8 Conclusion

In a number of countries that implemented international standards regarding compulsory licensing in their national patent legislation, the result was more than disillusioning once those provisions were put to the test of their actual enforceability. They lack clarity and instead display ambiguousness, complexity, pose restrictions and challenges to the interested parties and lack procedural rules.[103] As elaborated above, the provisions in the BiH PL are no exception to that trend. Art. 79 and particularly Art. 80 need to undergo a thorough remodelling, which also includes amendments to the related legislation (e.g., the Law on Court of BiH), in order to make this mechanism efficient.

On the other hand, mere improvement of the legislative framework related to compulsory licences is not the solution to the problem, if the manufacturing and technological capacities of the local pharmaceutical industry are insufficient. Unfortunately, the pandemic and difficult access to essential medicines and vaccines in BiH did not move the national (or entity) government(s) to direct investments in improving those capabilities.

Notwithstanding the above, it would be easy to say that the compulsory licensing system in BiH in its current state is nothing more than a dead letter even in normal circumstances, let alone in the pandemic. However, we cannot claim this with certainty, a least with regard to Art. 79, since the mechanism of compulsory licensing has never been invoked in BiH. And when would be a better time to change that circumstance then now? Not only in BiH, but also in other countries, in particular in the region of Southeast Europe. Then one issued compulsory license could potentially cause a "chain reaction" in the neighbouring countries.

In spite of the general reluctance to use this instrument due to a number of reasons elaborated above,[104] if any occurrence can trump those arguments, it is the global health crisis that we are experiencing right now. The solution to the pandemic lies inevitably in innovations in the medical field and their patent protection is indispensable in order to incentivise the research. The patent holders should, most certainly, be given the time and opportunity to issue voluntary licences. However, when and if the critical moment occurs that access to essential and protected health technologies for Covid-19 cannot be obtained in this manner, compulsory licensing must be invoked without a sense of guilt with the instruments at our hands, however flawed and ambiguous they might be. Just as exclusive rights are a part of the patent system, so is the instrument of compulsory licences, and now is definitely the time to utilise the whole complexity of that system in the fight against the pandemic.

[103] World Intellectual Property Organization (2019), p. 50.

[104] See Sect. 2. Compulsory licences in the international context.

References

Bacchus J (2020) An Unnecessary Proposal: A WTO Waiver of Intellectual Property Rights for COVID-19 Vaccines, 16 December 2020. https://www.cato.org/publications/free-trade-bulletin/unnecessary-proposal-wto-waiver-intellectual-property-rights-covid

BIRN BiH (2020) BiH se zbog tromosti administracije nije uključila u evropsku nabavku lijekova za koronavirus. Voice of America, 17 July 2020. https://ba.voanews.com/a/bih-se-zbog-tromosti-administracije-nije-ukljucila-u-evropsku-nabavku-lijekova-za-koronavirus/5506880.html

Bolongaro K (2021) Trudeau Signs Deal to Make Novavax Covid-19 Vaccine in Canada. Bloomberg, 2 February 2021. https://www.bloomberg.com/news/articles/2021-02-02/trudeau-signs-deal-to-make-novavax-covid-19-vaccine-in-canada

Bosnalijek (2021) Our history. http://www.bosnalijek.com/our-history

Bosnia and Herzegovina, Agency for Medicines and Medical Devices. Odluka stručnog savjeta o odgađanju primjene ekskluzivnosti podataka. Official Gazette of Bosnia and Herzegovina, no. 57 of 6 August 2013

Bosnia and Herzegovina, Agency for Medicines and Medical Devices. Odluka stručnog savjeta o odgađanju primjene ekskluzivnosti podataka. Official Gazette of Bosnia and Herzegovina, no. 75 of 31 October 2018

Bosnia and Herzegovina, Agency for Medicines and Medical Devices (2020a) Registry of drug manufacturers, 20 November 2020. http://www.almbih.gov.ba/_doc/proizvodjaci/rpl.pdf?5

Bosnia and Herzegovina, Agency for Medicines and Medical Devices (2020b) Registry of manufacturers of medical devices which have the authorisation of the Agency for producing medical devices of class 1. http://www.almbih.gov.ba/_doc/proizvodjaci/rpms-kl1.pdf

Bosnia and Herzegovina, Agency for Medicines and Medical Devices (2020c) Registry of manufacturers of medical devices which have the authorisation of the Agency for producing medical devices of class 2 and other lower classes of medical devices. http://www.almbih.gov.ba/_doc/proizvodjaci/rpms-kl2.pdf

Bosnia and Herzegovina, Council of Ministers. Directorate for European Integration. Obavijest o nepoštivanju odluke o postupku usklađivanja zakonodavstva Bosne i Hercegovine s pravnom tečevinom Evropske unije, no. 03-07-3-337-11/18 of 4 January 2019. https://www.dei.gov.ba/uploads/documents/rjesenje-o-pristupu-informacijama-od-21022019_1603448267.pdf

Bosnia and Herzegovina, Council of Ministers. Decision on the declaration of incurrence of the state on natural or other disasters on the territory of BiH. Official Gazette of Bosnia and Herzegovina, no. 18 of 20 March 2020

Bosnia and Herzegovina, Federation of Bosnia and Herzegovina, Federal Ministry of Health. Order on the declaration of the state of the epidemic of the infectious disease Covid-19. Official Gazette of the Federation of Bosnia and Herzegovina, no. 48 of 17 July 2020

Bosnia and Herzegovina, Federation of Bosnia and Herzegovina, Government of Federation of Bosnia and Herzegovina. Termination of the state of disaster caused by the incurrence of the Coronavirus in FBiH is declared, 29 May 2020. Official Gazette of the Federation of Bosnia and Herzegovina, no. 34 of 3 June 2020

Bosnia and Herzegovina, Federation of Bosnia and Herzegovina, Sarajevo Canton (2020) Development Strategy of the Sarajevo Canton (Strategija razvoja Kantona Sarajevo 2021-2027. Strateška platforma. Nacrt – proširena verzija), September 2020. http://zpr.ks.gov.ba/sites/zpr.ks.gov.ba/files/strategija_razvoja_ks_2021-2027._strateska_platforma_nacrt_prosirena_verzija_0.pdf

Bosnia and Herzegovina, Parliamentary assembly of Bosnia and Herzegovina. Održana 17. sjednica Predstavničkog doma, 25 February 2021. https://www.parlament.ba/Publication/Read/16574?pageId=238

Bosnia and Herzegovina, Republika Srpska National Assembly. Decision on the termination of the state of emergency for the territory of Republika Srpska, 21 May 2020. Official Gazette of Republika Srpska, no. 48 of 2020

Carey B (2021) W.H.O. Rejects Antiviral Drug Remdesivir as a Covid Treatment. New York Times, 30 January 2021. https://www.nytimes.com/2020/11/19/health/remdesivir-covid-19.html

Chamber of Commerce of the Sarajevo Canton (2015) Farmaceutskoj industriji dati status strateške industrije u Kantonu Sarajevo Inicijativa, no. 04/MK/EBK/7-84/15 of 1 December 2015. https://pksa.ba/wp-content/uploads/2018/03/Inicijativa_farmaceutska_industrija_PKKS.pdf

CMS (2021) Compulsory Licensing in Bosnia and Herzegovina, 15 February 2021. https://cms.law/en/int/expert-guides/cms-expert-guide-to-compulsory-licensing/bosnia-and-herzegovina

Cohen S (1979) Compulsory licensing of patents - the paris convention model. IDEA J Law Technol 20(2):153–190

Deutsche Gesellschaft für technische Zusammenarbeit GTZ (2001) Provedba studija za sektore s potencijalom. Kratka studija: farmaceutska industrija u Bosni i Hercegovini, nacrt, November 2001. https://www.esiweb.org/pdf/bridges/bosnia/GTZ_Farmaceutika.pdf

Directorate for European Integration (2021) Stabilisation and Association Agreement. https://www.dei.gov.ba/en/stabilization-agreement

European Commission (2020) Communication from the Commission to the European Parliament, the Council, the European Economic and Social Committee and the Committee of the Regions: Making the most of the EU's innovative potential. An intellectual property action plan to support the EU's recovery and resilience. COM(2020) 760 final, 25 November 2020. https://eur-lex.europa.eu/legal-content/EN/ALL/?uri=CELEX:52020DC0760

European Committee of the Regions (2021) Bosnia and Herzegovina - Summary. https://portal.cor.europa.eu/divisionpowers/Pages/Bosnia-Herzegovina.aspx

European Medicines Agency (2020) Update on remdesivir - EMA will evaluate new data from Solidarity trial, 20 November 2020. https://www.ema.europa.eu/en/news/update-remdesivir-ema-will-evaluate-new-data-solidarity-trial

Ford SM (2000) Compulsory licensing provisions under the TRIPs agreement: balancing pills and patents. Am Univ Int Law Rev 15(4):941–974

Gilead Sciences (2020) Voluntary Licensing Agreements for Remdesivir. https://www.gilead.com/purpose/advancing-global-health/covid-19/voluntary-licensing-agreements-for-remdesivir

Houldsworth A (2020) The key Covid-19 compulsory licensing developments so far. IAM, 7 April 2020. https://www.iam-media.com/coronavirus/the-key-covid-19-compulsory-licensing-developments-so-far

Institute for Intellectual Property (2020a) Institut za intelektualno vlasništvo BiH vraća se na redovni režim rada, 22 May 2020. https://www.ipr.gov.ba/bs/novost/10146/institut-za-intelektualno-vlasnistvo-bih-vraca-se-na-redovni-rezim-rada-

Institute for Intellectual Property (2020b) International Conventions and Agreements Applied in BIH. https://www.ipr.gov.ba/en/stranica/international-conventions-and-agreements-applied-in-bih

Jones Day (2020) Quick Reference Guide: Compulsory Patent Licensing During COVID-19 Crisis, April 2020. https://www.jonesday.com/en/insights/2020/04/quick-reference-guide-compulsory-patent-licensing-during-covid19-crisis

MedsPaL, Medicines Patent Pool (2021) 23 February 2021. https://www.medspal.org/?disease_areas%5B%5D=COVID-19&country_name%5B%5D=Bosnia+and+Herzegovina&page=1

N1 BiH (2020) Inspekcija: Favira i Remdesivir na tržištu BiH na osnovu interventnog uvoza, 4 December 2020. https://ba.n1info.com/vijesti/a492451-inspekcija-favira-i-remdesivir-na-trzistu-bih-na-osnovu-interventnog-uvoza/

Office of the High Representative (2021) Constitutions. http://www.ohr.int/laws-of-bih/constitutions-2/

OSCE Mission to Bosnia and Herzegovina (2020) Odgovor na krizu uzrokovanu pandemijom Covid-19: Analiza iz perspektive ljudskih prava i rodne ravnopravnosti. https://www.osce.org/files/f/documents/7/a/470658.pdf

Permanent Mission of the European Union to the World Trade Organization (2020) EU Statements at the WTO General Council, 18 December 2020. https://eeas.europa.eu/delegations/

world-trade-organization-wto_en/90872/EU%20Statements%20at%20the%20WTO%20General%20Council,%20on%2018%20December%202020
Saha S (2009) Patent law and TRIPS: Compulsory licensing of patents and pharmaceuticals. J Patent Trademark Office Soc 91(5):364–374
't Hoen E (2016) Private patents and public health. Changing intellectual property rules for access to medicines. https://haiweb.org/wp-content/uploads/2016/07/Private-Patents-Public-Health.pdf.
't Hoen E (2020a) Covid-19 and the comeback of compulsory licensing. Medicines Law & Policy, 23 March 2020. https://medicineslawandpolicy.org/2020/03/covid-19-and-the-come-back-of-compulsory-licensing/
't Hoen E (2020b) Some Surprises in the European Commission's New Intellectual Property Strategy, 2 December 2020. https://medicineslawandpolicy.org/2020/12/some-surprises-in-the-european-commissions-new-intellectual-property-strategy/
The Association of Innovative Pharmaceutical Manufacturers UIPL. https://uipl.ba
The World Bank (2020) The Global Economic Outlook During the COVID-19 Pandemic: A Changed World, 8 June 2020. https://www.worldbank.org/en/news/feature/2020/06/08/the-global-economic-outlook-during-the-covid-19-pandemic-a-changed-world
Urias E, Ramani SV (2020) Access to medicines after TRIPS: is compulsory licensing an effective mechanism to lower drug prices? A review of the existing evidence. J Int Bus Policy 3:367–384
World Health Organization (2020) WHO Director-General's opening remarks at the media briefing on COVID-19 - 11 March 2020, 11 March 2020. https://www.who.int/director-general/speeches/detail/who-director-general-s-opening-remarks-at-the-media-briefing-on-covid-19%2D%2D-11-march-2020
World Intellectual Property Organization (2019) Draft reference document on the exception regarding compulsory licensing, 21 May 2019. https://www.wipo.int/edocs/mdocs/scp/en/scp_30/scp_30_3-main1.pdf
World Intellectual Property Organization (2020a) Covid-19 IP Policy Tracker. Bosnia and Herzegovina, 8 May 2020. https://www.wipo.int/covid19-policy-tracker/#/covid19-policy-tracker/by-country?countryId=30
World Intellectual Property Organization (2020b) Hungary: Government Decree No. 212/2020 on Public Health Compulsory Licenses for Exploitation Within Hungary, 17 May 2020. https://www.wipo.int/news/en/wipolex/2020/article_0009.html
World Trade Organization (2001) Declaration on the TRIPS agreement and public health, adopted on 14 November 2001. https://www.wto.org/english/thewto_e/minist_e/min01_e/mindecl_trips_e.htm
World Trade Organization (2020) The TRIPS Agreement and COVID-19 Information Note, 15 October 2020. https://www.wto.org/english/tratop_e/covid19_e/trips_report_e.pdf
World Trade Organization (2021a) Accessions. Bosnia and Herzegovina. https://www.wto.org/english/thewto_e/acc_e/a1_bosnie_e.htm
World Trade Organization (2021b) Compulsory licensing of pharmaceuticals and TRIPS. https://www.wto.org/english/tratop_e/trips_e/public_health_faq_e.htm
World Trade Organization (2021c) Protocol Amending the TRIPS Agreement. Done at Geneva on 6 December 2005. Entry into force: 23 January 2017. Status of WTO Legal Instruments – 2021 edition. https://www.wto.org/english/res_e/booksp_e/sli_e/20TRIPSAmendment.pdf
World Trade Organization (2021d) Understanding the WTO: The Organization. Members and Observers. https://www.wto.org/english/thewto_e/whatis_e/tif_e/org6_e.htm#observer
World Trade Organization, General Council (2003) Decision of the General Council of 30 August 2003. Implementation of paragraph 6 of the Doha Declaration on the TRIPS Agreement and public health. https://www.wto.org/english/tratop_e/trips_e/implem_para6_e.htm

World Trade Organization, General Council (2005) Decision of 6 December 2005. Amendment of the TRIPS Agreement. https://www.wto.org/english/tratop_e/trips_e/wtl641_e.htm

World Trade Organization, World Health Organization, World Intellectual Property Organization (2020) Promoting Access to Medical Technologies and Innovation, 2nd edn. Intersections between Public Health, Intellectual Property and Trade. https://www.wto.org/english/res_e/booksp_e/extract_who-wipo-wto_2020_e.pdf

Wu KJ, Zimmer C, Corum J (2021) Coronavirus Drug and Treatment Tracker. New York Times, 11 February 2021. https://www.nytimes.com/interactive/2020/science/coronavirus-drugs-treatments.html

Zimmer C, Corum J, Wee S-L (2021) Coronavirus Vaccine Tracker. New York Times, 25 February 2021. https://www.nytimes.com/interactive/2020/science/coronavirus-vaccine-tracker.html

Damage Compensation Due to Copyright Infringement on the Internet in Serbian Law

Sanja Savčić

Contents

S. Savčić (✉)
University of Novi Sad, Faculty of Law, Novi Sad, Serbia
e-mail: s.savcic@pf.uns.ac.rs

D. V. Popović et al. (eds.), *Balkan Yearbook of European and International Law 2021*, Balkan Yearbook of European and International Law 2021,
https://doi.org/10.1007/978-3-030-97431-2_4

1 Introduction

The first intellectual creations came along with the emergence of human society. Many anthropological and sociological studies indicated that humanity itself arose out of human's ability to think creatively and to create meaningfully. In other words, intellectual creation is entwined into the very notion of the human being and society as a whole. It has always been *sine qua non* of the existence, survival and progress of every social community. However, for thousands of years, society has not made any distinction between material and intellectual goods. While laws related to material goods had their foundations already established in Roman law, and even in the period preceding it, the creations of the human remained for a long time beyond of legal regulation and any form of legal protection. The beginnings of modern copyright coincide with Gutenberg's invention of the printing press in the fifteenth century. Nevertheless, it took nearly three centuries from then for the first laws in the field of copyright to be adopted.

At the beginning of the third millennium, the results of intellectual creation have been regarded as fundamental values of a society. It is therefore, in the best interest of every modern legal system to provide the widest possible incentive to intellectual creativity. However, this is a rather complex issue. The digital revolution, the development of the global computer network and other modern technological achievements have become a top challenge to the legal thought of the third millennium. The technological development and the changes arisen out of it have been so extensive and dynamic that even the most inventive legislator cannot predict them. Therefore, legislation very often lags behind practical needs.

Similar problems exist in court practice as well. Resolving disputes in the field of intellectual property rights is a complex action and requires a serious approach. Moreover, even traditional institutes for which case law has been already established, demonstrate their weaknesses and inertia in the field of copyright.

Here, in the first place, we have in mind the problem of compensation for damages caused by copyright infringement. Namely, the IT environment has enabled the emergence of new forms of authorship and new types of exploiting author's work both in tangible and intangible form. At the same time, copyright infringement is also getting new forms. Digital picture and sound carriers together with the highly developed technology have enabled the expansion of various forms of piracy and computer crime, due to which economic losses are measured in billions of euros.

Referring to the social circumstances and the current regulations, it could be said that the theory did not respond in a proper way to the mentioned challenges of a modern society.[1] Many issues have remained unresolved, while some were not even the subject of academic discussions. In addition to this, taking into account that the use of copyrighted works, being permitted or not, is not limited territorially, it is not unusual to incorporate solutions from comparative law into these legal systems.

[1] Popović (2015), pp. 69–71.

Therefore, the adopted solutions are often contrary to the essence of the domestic legal system which makes them insufficiently clear or could lead to greater dilemmas in their implementation. This is especially the case when it comes to traditional institutes of civil law protection, such as compensation for damages, since new solutions bring confusion to the already established system of compensation law.

This article is going to examine problems arising from the application of general tort rules to specific situations when damage is caused by copyright infringement, and in particular the case when it has been done on the internet. With this regard, attention would be focused on the issue of liability and the amount of damage compensation.

2 Civil Law Protection of Copyright: In General

When an author or other copyright holder is prevented or hindered from exercising the rights recognized by the law, his primary goal is to protect his private interests, i.e. to enable him to exercise his rights in full force. This could be achieved by civil legal protection, which has two basic forms. One is direct and the other is indirect.[2]

Direct protection refers to the exclusive rights of an author,[3] while indirect protection refers to the exploitation of the object of protection including the use of unauthorized copies of that object, i.e. on the basis of unauthorized broadcasting, as well as other precisely defined procedures: unauthorized removal or modification of any electronic information on the use of rights; placing on the market, import for the purpose of placing on the market, broadcasting or informing the public without authorization, a copy of the object of copyright protection, with the knowledge that electronic information on the use of rights has been removed or unauthorized; ownership of devices or their placing on the market which exclusive purpose is to facilitate removing or disrupting the technical protection of computer programs or other types of objects of protection from unauthorized exploitation.[4]

According to the Law on Copyright and Related Rights (LCRR), in case of copyright or related rights infringement or existence of a serious threat that these rights will be infringed, a plaintiff may request in particular: determination of infringement or serious threat that the right will be infringed; prohibition of actions that represent a serious threat of violating the right, as well as a ban on repeating such or similar actions under the threat of paying an appropriate amount of money to the plaintiff; compensation for pecuniary and non-pecuniary damage; exclusion from the market, confiscation or destruction or alteration of objects used by which the rights have been violated without any compensation, including copies of objects of

[2] Marković (1999), pp. 361–379.

[3] Art. 204 of the Law on Copyright and Related Rights of Republic of Serbia (LCRR), Official Gazette of Republic of Serbia, No. 104/2009, 99/2011, 119/2012, 29/2016 and 66/2019.

[4] Art. 208 of the LCRR.

protection, their packaging, matrices, negatives, etc.; prohibition of alienation, confiscation or destruction of materials and objects that have been mainly used in creation or production of objects that violate the right without any compensation; announcing the verdict at the expense of the defendant; providing information about third parties who participated in the violation of rights.[5]

Although this normative technique does not represent a novelty, at this point it seems necessary to highlight that for the purposes of civil protection, the approach of the legislator to emphasize what could be claimed in a lawsuit seems to be quite uncommon. In comparison to the Law on Industrial Property within which the plaintiff's requests have been enlisted briefly, in LCRR this limitation of the plaintiff's disposition has been which is partially mitigated by introducing the listed claims with the determinant *especially*.[6] This formulation allows supplementing the above claims with additional ones that, in a particular case, correspond to the injury.

3 Claims for Damages for Copyright Infringement

When it comes to claiming for damages, the LCRR stipulates that general rules of the Law on Obligations are to be applied.[7] According to the general rules of the Law on Obligations, damage stands for the reduction of someone's property (real damage) or the prevention of its increase (lost profits), as well as causing physical or mental pain or fear to another person (non-pecuniary damage).

Most often, the best interest of the author (and other right's holder) is to oblige the responsible person to compensate the damage caused by the committed copyright infringement. Compensation for damages due to copyright infringement has no other purpose than the one acknowledged by the general tort law. Therefore, the goal is the injured party to acquire compensation for the property loss caused by the infringement (pecuniary damage), i.e. to provide him gratification on account of the infringement of personal rights (non-pecuniary damage). The question is whether the general rules of the Law of Obligations can meet that requirement. In these terms, we are going to answer to the questions that are relevant to the claim for damages.

---

[5] Art. 205(1) LCRR.

[6] In the Draft Law on Amendments to the Law on Copyright and Related Rights, which was presented at a public hearing in December 2013, the claims have been listed exhaustively. Precisely with the explanation of the participants in the public debate that such an approach constitutes lawsuits *numerus clausus*, the provision was corrected by introducing the determinant "especially". See: Report from the public debate on the Draft Law on Amendments to the Law on Copyright and Related Rights, p. 27.

[7] Art. 214a(2) LCRR.

3.1 Who Is Entitled to Claim Damages?

Pursuant to Art. 204a(1), lawsuit for infringement of copyrights or related rights or the existence of a serious threat that these rights will be infringed may be filed by the author, i.e. copyright holder, performer, phonogram producer, film producer, broadcasting organization, database producer, acquirer of exclusive copyright or related rights, as well as organization for the collective management of copyright and related rights. The acquirer of exclusive copyright and related rights may file a lawsuit for the infringement of copyright or related rights to the extent to which he has acquired the right to exploit it on the basis of law or contract, unless otherwise has been stipulated by the contract on assignment of rights.[8] Relevant provision does not deal exclusively subject-matter of damages. This is not unusual, since damage compensation is not *sedes materiae* of LCRR. Moreover, it is suppossed that the goal of the legislator is to remove any doubt who can initiate and conduct proceedings for copyright infringement, nevertheless we consider it quite necessary to stress that citation of actively legitimized persons is unnecessary. Namely, if we leave aside the procedural aspect and issues of participants in civil proceedings, from the aspect of substantive law, we could be satisfied with the conclusion that any subject, who has a claim against another person or persons, can be actively legitimized in civil proceedings so as his claim to be met. However, if we link the issue of infringement that the legislator explicitly envisages to persons who could be plaintiffs, we explain this normative approach by the need to define copyright disputes more precisely, so as special rules could be applied to them. Therefore, any acquirer of exclusive copyright and related rights who suffer damage caused by infringement of these rights may claim damages.

3.2 Who Could Be Obliged to Compensate the Author?

Whoever causes damage to another person is obliged to compensate it, unless he proves that the damage was not caused by his fault. Damage caused by certain objects or activities, due to which a danger of damage to the environment increases, is liable regardless of fault. Irrespective of fault, he is also liable for damage in other cases provided by law.[9]

According to the general rules, liability grounds on the infringer's fault (presumed) in fault liability or on causality (again presumed) in strict liability. Strict liability is to be provided when the damage is caused by a dangerous object or

[8] Art. 204a(2) LCRR.

[9] Art. 154 of Law on Obligation, Official Gazette of SFRY, No. 29/78, 39/85, 45/89, Official Gazette of FRY, No. 31/93, Official Gazette of Serbia and Montenegro, No. 1/2003 (LO).

dangerous activity, as well as in cases that are explicitly declared.[10] If there are no special rules on liability, it is based on the principle of fault liability.

3.3 Is It Always Possible to Apply the Rules of the Tort Law to Compensation in Copyright?

According to the relevant provision of the Law on Obligation (LO), a person who causes damage to a copyright holder is obliged to compensate it, unless he proves that the damage was not caused by his fault.[11]

The basis of liability in copyright is therefore the presumed fault of the person whose action caused the damage. In particular, a person who has undertaken an action without the permission of the right holder, which is covered by the exclusive rights of the author, is obliged to compensate the damage caused by the unauthorized exploitation. In traditional forms of exploitation of an author's work, the application of this rule is feasible without exception. However, we encounter difficulties when it comes to exploiting the author's work via internet. Namely, from the aspect of general rules, in order to succeed with his request for compensation, the damaged right holder has to prove that there is a causal link between the unauthorized use of the author's work by another person and the damage itself. It is obvious that his position in the internet environment where injury occurred is not easy at all.

In order to understand better the context in which the issue of liability for copyright infringement on the internet appears to be controversial, we will identify the entities that are usually involved in the exchange of copyrighted works through a global computer network.

3.3.1 Entities Exchanging Author's Work Via Internet

In the context of the use of the author's work, participants in the exchange of information on the internet are the copyright holder, the user of the author's work and the internet intermediary.

The interest of the author to exploit economically his own work is nowadays most easily to satisfy by publishing the work on the internet. This creates conditions for further exploitation, in the real and digital world, by collecting fees from its use, reproduction and in other ways. On the other hand, internet users, for whom the exchange of information in this way represents the dominant way of communication, download available content and continue to share it with other users. When they do

[10] Art. 154 (2)(3) LO.

[11] Art. 154(1) LO.

so without the authorization of the holder or their action is not allowed by law,[12] it is considered to be an infringement of the right, which causes damage to the holder. Finally, communication between the aforementioned entities could not take place without an internet intermediary (internet service provider, internet provider).[13]

Internet providers are not necessarily directly related to copyright infringement. When this is the case, they are certainly liable according to the general rules of liability for unauthorized copyright exploitation. This means that the general regime of civil liability is applied to them. When there is no direct responsibility of the provider, for the right holder who has been the subject of infringement via internet it is not easy to determine the entity against whom he is going to file his claim. In order to obtain compensation for the caused damage, the right holder must prove that there is a causal link between the action of a certain person and the damaging consequences that have occurred. In the internet environment, none of these relevant facts are obvious.

3.3.1.1 Liability of the Internet Provider in General

The most common problem that emerges on daily basis is when the internet provider enables the posting of illegal content and its sharing among users. In the context of this paper, this service is of high importance.

The provider did not directly commit the injury, but by performing his service he enabled the injury to incur. The responsibility of the service provider is, therefore, indirect (shared or liability for another). According to the general rules on liability, its determination grounds on the issue of conscientiousness, i.e. the question of whether the internet provider knew or could have known that copyright infringement was being committed through performing his service. In other words, the responsibility of the provider depends on the question whether he applied a fair trade principle while providing his service?

The technological environment in which data is exchanged, the amount of information transmitted via internet, as well as the speed of their flow, are only some of the circumstances that make difficult to assess conscientiousness. Consequently, it is rather difficult to distinguish situations in which it has been assumed that the provider knew or could have known about the violation of rights? This is especially important when we take into account the general absence of the rights and

[12] Under certain circumstances, for certain actions explicitly consent of the right holder is not needed. See Art. 41–58 LCRR.

[13] Therefore, it is in their interest that the flow of information between users be fast and intensive. Services, on the other hand, can be of different content, and are most often divided into three groups: simple mediation (mere conduit), caching services and hosting services. See: Radovanović (2015), pp. 83–112.

obligations of the internet service provider to supervise, i.e. control communication among users.[14]

3.3.1.2 Liability of Internet Service Provider in Serbian Law

The liability of internet intermediaries, i.e. information society service providers in the law of the Republic of Serbia is normatively regulated by the Law on Electronic Commerce (hereinafter: LEC).[15]

According to this Law, the intermediary is liable for a violation when he knew or could have known about the unauthorized actions of service users or the content of the data and did not remove or disable the access to the given data immediately upon acknowledgement of an unauthorized action or data.[16] Having in mind that internet intermediaries have got different rules in the internet communication, cited provision applies mainly to host service providers.[17]

The obligation to monitor the content stored and exchanged via internet is not prescribed. However, if there is a reasonable doubt that illegal actions or exchanging illegal content are being performed by using the service, the provider is obliged to inform the competent state authority. Disclosure of the user data, as well as content removal and disabling access to suspicious content is possible only on the basis of a court or administrative decision.[18] The latter directly complements the issue of liability for damage compensation. If we consider that fault as a condition of liability for damages, can be excluded when the intermediary proves that he did not act with intent or negligence, the crucial fact depends on what is considered to be negligence in providing services.[19]

It could be imagined that the provider would prevent further infringement by disabling access to unauthorized content or removing unauthorized content. However, such actions could violate the rights of other entities.[20] As the provider, in

[14]On April 17, 2019, the European Parliament adopted the Directive on Copyright in the Digital Single Market, which has been criticized in legal circles precisely because it leaves room for monitoring users and other forms of privacy threats. See: Directive EU 2019/790 of the European Parliament and of the Council of the 17 April 2019 on copyright and related rights in the digital single market and amending Directives 96/9/EC and 2001/29/EC, Official Journal of the European Union, L130 of 17th May 2019, also available at: https://eur-lex.europa.eu/legal-content/EN/TXT/PDF/?uri=CELEX:32019L0790&from=EN.

[15]Art. 1 of Law on Electronic Commerce (LEC), Official Gazette of Republic of Serbia, No. 41/2009, 95/2013 and 52/2019.

[16]Art. 18 LEC.

[17]This is for the reason that only host service providers has got active rule in the communication among its users. The other two, mere conduit and caching service providers, are passive intermediaries, or at least, mainly passive when provide service.

[18]Art. 20 LEC, in relation to Art. 210 LCRR.

[19]Reljanović (2016), pp. 119–134.

[20]It is, above all, about the right to freedom of expression and the right to privacy, which are the fundamental values of modern society. Therefore, there is a reason in legal circles to insist on

principle, has no obligation to supervise the exchanged content, the very notification of the existence of a breach instigates the obligation of the provider to alert the competent authorities and further to act in accordance with their decisions.

In the context of the liability for damages, the provider is considered liable when he has received notification of a possible infringement and fails to alert the competent authorities. Additionally, the provider could be considered liable even if, on the basis of an appropriate judicial or administrative act, he fails to provide information that is relevant for the detection of the person whose action directly caused the damage. In both cases, it is about the fault of the provider because he did not act with the expected care.

3.3.1.3 Liability of the Direct Perpetrator of the Copyright Infringement on the Internet for Damages

Once an entity has been identified that could have directly infringed copyright by its actions, the injured party may file a claim for damages against the person identified as the alleged perpetrator. When it comes to damages committed via internet, determining the debtor of compensation is based on the assumption of the fault of the person who has been the owner of the IP protocol. That person, ordinary, is also the person who directly undertook the infringement of copyright, which caused the damage. This presumed connection between the owner of the IP address, the act of injury and the damage caused usually corresponds to the reality.

However, according to the general rules on compensation for damages, fault, as the basis of liability, is presumed at the person whose action or neglect caused the damage.[21] The causal link between the action and the damage, as well as the damage itself, should be proven by the injured party. The starting point is the belief that the owner of the IP address has undertaken a detrimental action. Further would be explained to which extent this approach departs from the application of the general rules on liability.

Therefore in the case of an online infringement, the presumed fault is grounded on the presumed causal link. Let us remember that the presumption of causality is the basis of strict liability. In the domain of the fault liability, the plaintiff has to prove that the defendant undertook a harmful action, and his fault is presumed. Given that the basis of liability is the presumed fault of the owner or user, in compliance with the general rules, the designated debtor may be released from liability, if he proves that the damage did not occur by his fault, the copyright infringement was committed neither intentionally nor due to utter carelessness.

In the context of online infringement, it is difficult to imagine that there are circumstances that would indicate the absence of the fault. However, situations in

defining the role of the intermediary in terms of infringement of rights, because the intermediary does not have the authority to decide neither on the right, nor on infringement of it.

[21] Art. 154 (1) LO.

which the defendant did not take damaging action at all, are not inconceivable, e.g. when he was not physically able to access the internet from the given IP address. By applying the general rules, his liability is excluded. The reason for that lies not (only) in the absence of fault, but in the circumstance that excludes the causal link between the ownership of the IP address and the action taken by which the copyright infringement was committed. Therefore, if the infringer of the right was not the owner of IP address, any person could have undertaken a harmful action. The burden of proving the fault falls on the plaintiff, due to which it might happen that the legal protection regarding the caused damage would be left out.

Pursuant to LCRR, the court may order the person who committed the infringement of copyright or related rights to provide information on third parties who participated in the infringement of copyright or related rights and on their distribution channels, or to submit documents related to the infringement.[22] In terms of procedural law, persons who are required to provide information have the capacity of witnesses. LCRR explicitly provides the corresponding application of the Law on Civil Procedure.[23] Thus, a witness may refuse to answer certain questions if there are justifiable reasons for that, and especially if he would expose himself to severe indignity, significant property damage or criminal prosecution of himself or his relatives of a certain type and degree of relationship by answering those questions.[24]

Therefore, when a copyright holder has filed a lawsuit against the owner of the IP address linked to damages caused by sharing protected content via internet, and who apparently did not undertake such action, the court may order the defendant to submit data on persons related to the infringement and set an appropriate deadline

---

[22] Art. 213 LCRR. The delivery of information may also be ordered to a person who has discovered goods in distribution that infringe copyright or related rights, has provided services in trade that infringe copyright or related rights, has provided services that are used in activities that infringe copyright or related rights, or has been identified by the aforementioned persons as a person involved in the production or distribution of goods or the provision of services that infringe copyright or related rights.

[23] Art. 214a LCRR.

[24] Art. 249(1) of the Law of Civil Procedure (LCP), Official Gazette of Republic of Serbia, No. 72/2011, 55/2014 and 87/2018. In the explanation of the Proposal of the Law on Amendments to the Law on Copyright and Related Rights, in connection with the mentioned amendment, i.e. the new provision, it is stated that its introduction requires a harmonization of domestic law with Art. 8 of Directive 2004/48/EU (on the right of information) and the fundamental values of modern European society. (Predlog Zakona o izmenama i dopunama Zakona o autorskom i srodnim pravima, (eng. Proposal for Law on amadments of Law on Copyright and Related Rights), http://www.parlament.gov.rs/upload/archive/files/cir/pdf/predlozi_zakona/2019/225-19.pdf. However, the European Court in the decision *Bastei Lübbe GmbH & Co. KG* against *Michaela Strotzera*, pointed out that intrusion into family life is considered inadmissible when the copyright holder has at his disposal other means that could ensure the determination of civil liability of the owner of the internet connection. If this is not the case, special protection of the family is contrary to the aim of Directive 2001/29 and Directive 2004/48, which needs to provide the right holder with effective protection. The protection of the family is, therefore, subordinate to the protection of the author. See: Judgement of the Court (Third Chamber) of the 18th October 2018, in Case C-149/17, par. 53.

for this. In the event that the defendant does not act according to the order, the court may accept the claim and oblige the defendant to pay damages. His responsibility then does not refer to undertaking the act of injury, but to failing to provide information about the injury.

The application of the general rules on damages from the LCT is obviously not possible without certain modifications. One of them refers to the issue of assumptions about the circumstances that are relevant for the success of the dispute. While according to the general rules, the fault of a person who undertakes a detrimental action is presumed, in this case it is initially presumed which person has undertaken that action, and only then his fault. The owner of the internet connection may still be liable for damages, due to his failure to provide relevant information. If we contemplate the above rules stipulated by LCRR according to which damage can still be borne by the owner of the internet connection, regardless of the fault for the infringement, it seems that liability for damages for infringement via internet does not represent a fault liability in its pure form.[25]

3.4 Scope of the Damage (and Compensation)

In order to succeed in claiming damages, the injured party must prove the damage existence and its volume. Given that the author's work is an intangible asset, determining the amount of compensation that would compensate the injured party (for pecuniary damage) or obtain gratification (for non-pecuniary damage) is not an easy task to be performed. The reason for this lies in the fact that protected information is inexhaustible. Therefore, it is not so uncommon for unauthorized exploitation not to end in a single illegal act, but with each exchange of content the damage increases as well. This problem seems even more conspicuous when it comes to today's almost common forms of exploitation of works via internet.

Let us remind ourselves that the real damage (*damnum emergens*) involves the impairment of someone's property. It is most often reflected in destruction or damage of objects, i.e. a copy of an author's work. For example, the destruction of the first standard copy of a film certainly represents a real damage that could stand for the value invested in its creation. The lost profit (*lucrum cessans*) represents the property value which, in the ordinary course of things or circumstances of a specific case, would have been realized if there had not been a damaging action performed by the responsible person. In the above example, by destroying the first standard copy of the film, the co-authors were hindered in gaining profits that they would have acquired by having the film shown in cinemas.

The Law on Obligations prescribes two basic types of remedies in case of damages: natural restitution, and monetary compensation.

[25] Radovanović (2019), p. 57.

Natural restitution means the obligation of the responsible person to re-establish the condition that preceded the damage.[26] Naturally, the injured party will file such a claim if the nature of the damaged property indicates that the damage caused to his property or property interests can be compensated by restitution. However, if the restoration of the previous form of the property does not eliminate completely the detrimental consequences, the responsible person is obliged to compensate the rest of the damage in cash.[27] Moreover, the court will oblige the responsible person to monetary compensation for property damage even if re-establishing the previous condition is not possible, or if it does not consider necessary that the responsible person should do so,[28] but also if the injured party primarily requests a monetary compensation for the suffered damage.

Compensation for property damage in kind or monetary, aims to compensate for the loss in the property of the injured party. In this regard, the amount of money awarded for damage compensation is equivalent to the suffered damage, which by rule is determined by the market value of the object or right. However, the compensation completion does not imply a simple reinstatement of the previous condition, but the establishment of the condition in the property of the injured party, if had not been the detrimental consequences that had occured.

3.4.1 Determining the Extent of the Damage Caused by Copyright Infringement Under the General Rules of Law on Obligations

By exercising property rights, the copyright holder economically exploits the copyrighted work by collecting income from the entities to which it has assigned (or transferred) the authorization to undertake specific exploitation actions. Consequently, exercising these powers without having the permission of the copyright holder, is considered as a loss of money or an action of hindering its increase.

The LO contains only general guidelines applied by the court when measuring the amount of damages. However, the method of determining the amount of money required for full compensation of the injured party in the specific case of causing the damage, depends on the nature of the violated right or the legal interest. Hence, even before the amendments were made to the LCRR dating from 2019, which explicitly have regulated it,[29] there had been three methods of calculating the amount of monetary compensation developed in court practice: the differential method, the method of illegal profit of damage perpetrator and the method of analogy including the fee for authorization assignment/transfer.

---

[26] Art. 185(1) LO.

[27] Art. 185(2) LO.

[28] Art. 185(3) LO.

[29] Art. 206(1) LCRR.

3.4.1.1 The Differential Method

According to the general rules of tort law, the amount of monetary compensation is calculated by applying a differential method consisting of "determining and monetarily expressing the difference in the plaintiff's property that (difference) exists when comparing the condition in which his property would have been if there had been no violation, with the condition in which his property actually is after the violation of rights has taken place".[30]

The court, therefore, takes into account the benefit that the right holder would have obtained in the ordinary and predictable course of events, if the infringement had not occurred, as well as the costs of eliminating detrimental consequences, thus the calculated compensation includes total damage (real damage and lost profits).[31] Although this method suits best the purpose which should be achieved by the compensation in terms of the general rules of the law of obligations, the application of the differential method in calculating the compensation for damage caused by copyright infringement has a limited scope. Namely, the initial presumption of this method is that the author or another person to whom the infringed right was transferred or ceded, has been already economically exploiting the author's work. In that case, he suffers the loss of a certain amount of money by having the rights in his property being violated or is hindered from generating income from his work.

In case the exploitation of the author's work has not even begun, consequently the real damage and lost profits could not be reliably determined. The injured right holder could point to the fact that the violation caused indirect damage, but the responsible person would not be obliged to compensate it because there is no causal link between his illegal action and indirect detrimental consequences resulting from the copyright infringement.[32] Thus, if the author has not taken any action in order to derive economic benefit from his work, the condition of the property that preceded the infringement is equal to the one in which the property has been after the infringement occurred.

However, the fact that right holder did not obtain economic value of his work does not exclude the existence of damage, but the amount of compensation cannot be calculated by applying the differential method. The reason for this lies in the fact that the injured party cannot prove the scope of the suffered damage because the court, due to right holder's passive standpoint regarding the exercise of his rights, cannot rely on an arbitrarily determined level of distribution in which the carriers would multiply copies for sale and the price that would be achieved by their sale.

In addition to the above, the practical application of the differential method indicates another disadvantage. Namely, infringement of the author's economic rights is not usually the only cause of the detrimental consequences. In this regard, first the copyright holder in the lawsuit for damages, and only then the court when

---

[30] Marković (1999), p. 370.

[31] Art. 189, 190 LO.

[32] Bently et al. (2018), p. 1342.

deciding on the lawsuit, must unquestionably determine the extent to which the reduction of property or the absence of its increase is caused by the action of the responsible person, as well as to what extent this has been caused by other circumstances. This is rather important since by assigning the amount of money in the property of the injured party, the condition that would have existed if the injury had not occurred, has been reinstated.[33]

Since the differential method is primarily a general method, it is not sufficiently adapted to the specificities of pecuniary damage caused by copyright infringement. For these reasons, the method of illegal profit of damage perpetrator and the method of analogy including the fee for rights assignment/transfer are being much more often applied in practice.

3.4.1.2 The Method of Illegal Profit of Damage Perpetrator

Starting from the fact that the exercise of economic rights derives economic benefit from the author's work, the method of illegal profit of damage perpetrator is based on the assumption that the economic benefit that the responsible person has achieved by infringing these rights, belongs to the copyright holder.[34] Consequently, the injured party does not have to prove in what condition his patrimony would have been if the injury had not occurred, which would make his position in the dispute for damages rather easier.[35]

However, the profit made by the perpetrator is the result of investing his assets too, as well as his willingness to take a risk of not achieving economic benefits, and a number of other circumstances. Therefore, it cannot be considered that the entire amount of acquired income belongs to the damaged copyright holder only.[36] In these terms, the injured party must prove what part of the gained income can be brought into a causal link with the unauthorized use of the author's work, because the damage is compensated only to the extent that resulted from that infringement.[37]

---

[33] Marković (1999), p. 371.

[34] Marković (1999), p. 371, Bently et al. (2018), pp. 1347–1349.

[35] The plaintiff extends the lawsuit for new collections of haberdashery that are sold under the plaintiff's marked codes. It indicates that for individual numbers-pieces of the collection it has been asked for a certain amount plus 4% of the sale. According to the Supreme Court, the scope and quality of the offered evidence are relevant when assessing the merits and amount of the claim, and the first instance court will trial the merits in the repeated procedure on the merits in accordance with applicable regulations." Decision of the Supreme Court of Serbia, no. Gž-53/02 dated 6 February 2003, in the *Intermex* legal database.

[36] Marković (1999), p. 372.

[37] "The defendant, without the knowledge and approval of the plaintiffs and contrary to the accepted conditions of using a computer program, economically exploited their coauthored work - using unauthorized copies of the work (990 in total), and the first instance court correctly concluded that the plaintiffs, as co-authors, infringed the copyright, in terms of Article 172, paragraph 1, items 1 and 5 of the Law, in the amount in which the defendant gained benefits by economic exploitaton of the coauthored work of the plaintiffs in the prescribed manner", Judgment of the Court of

On the other hand, when the perpetrator did not generate income by unauthorized use of the author's work, monetary compensation for the damage suffered by consistent application of this method may be omitted. It is unquestionable, however, that the copyright holder still suffers damage that implies the lost fee for the assignment/transfer of the right to exploit the object of protection.

3.4.1.3 The Method of Analogy Including the Fee for Rights Assignment/Transfer

This method refers to calculating the amount of the usual compensation that the defendant would have paid to the plaintiff if he had exploited the object of protection in compliance with a contract on the assignment/transfer of certain property rights, and not unlawfully."[38] The copyright holder enters into a dispute for damages with an expected outcome. Having proved the violation of a specific property right, the causal link between the unlawful act of the perpetrator and the damage related to the missed compensation is indisputable.[39] Therefore, the amount of monetary compensation is easily determined because it represents the usual compensation that the author would receive.[40]

On the other hand, the usual fee is determined in practice by concluding a contract on the transfer of copyright. This, of course, depends on what type of author's work it is about, and whether it has been already economically exploited and to what extent, as well as other circumstances relevant to the decision making in this case.

The compensation calculated in this way, in fact, corresponds to the amount of a real damage suffered. Besides, if the copyright holder proves that he has failed to generate additional income by having his property rights violated, he is also entitled to compensation for lost profits. This would, for example, be the case if the author, due to the violation of his right, fails to conclude a contract on the exclusive assignment of property authorization on the basis of which he would generate higher income than the one calculated as a compensation for real damage.

Appeals in Belgrade P 113/2018 of 13.02.2019. More: Judgment of the Court of Appeals in Kragujevac, Gž 2246/10 of 19 January 2011, in the *Intermex* legal database.

[38] Marković (1999), p. 372, Bently et al. (2018), p. 1342.

[39] This method of calculating the monetary compensation is also applicable in the case of a request for return of the *condictio sine causa*, in the sense of Art. 210 LO.

[40] "Since the defendant did not try to find out who the author was before taking and publishing the photo of the plaintiff, nor he disputed that fact during the proceedings, the conclusion of the first instance court that the defendant reproduced, made public and made it available to the public without knowledge and approval, is correct. The author of the mentioned photograph is the plaintiff, as a result of which the plaintiff being the author caused pecuniary damage in the amount of royalties that he would have gained if the photo had been published with his consent, so the contrary allegations are unfounded," Judgment of the Court of Appeals in Belgrade Gž 227/13 16.04.2014, Bulletin of the Higher Court in Belgrade, no. 85, in the *Intermex* legal database, 05.02.12021.

The method of analogy including the transfer fee is the most favourable for the right holder, at least when it comes to his procedural position. Namely, given that the lost profit is often difficult to be proved, even when it exists, the compensation is essentially reduced to the real damage suffered, i.e. to the payment of royalties. However, in the case of unauthorized exploitation, the right holder missed the opportunity to condition the use of the object of protection with certain actions, to earn interest on the grounds of arrears and to perform business planning based on the expected fee confirmed by the contract, which is to be paid within certain deadlines and other benefits. As the copyright holder should not suffer the detrimental consequences of illegal actions committed by other persons, the issue intriguing the legal public is whether it is justified in these cases to determine the amount of compensation in a lump sum?[41] The current LCRR explicitly prescribes this.

3.4.2 Provisions of LCRR on Determining the Damage

In case if the committer knew or could have known that he was infringing, when determining the amount of damages, the court will take into account all the circumstances of the case, such as the negative economic consequences suffered by the injured party, including lost profits, profits made by the infringer, and, where appropriate, non-economic circumstances, such as non-pecuniary damage.[42] The court may, instead of damage compensation, when the circumstances of the case justify this, award the injured party a lump sum compensation which cannot be lower than the usual compensation he would have received for a specific form of use of the object of protection, if that use had been lawful.[43]

The drafting of the relevant provision indicates that two institutes have been established in respect of the damage suffered. One is traditional, the damages, and the other is a lump sum, which is imposed instead of damages.

The Statement of Reasons to the Law emphasizes that this provision harmonizes the legal regulations regarding the compensation of damages with the relevant provision of Art. 13 of Directive 2004/48 EC.[44] Although we cannot dispute whether this is true, from the very formulation of the relevant legal provision we can already anticipate that its application in practice is going to cause more challenges in the field of damages than it will actually solve them.

First of all, the criteria for calculating damages were applied even before the explicit normative regulation. In accordance with the principles of civil procedure,

---

[41] International Association for the Protection of Intellectual Property (AIPPI) Resolution, Q186, Punitive Damages as a contentious issue of Intellectual Property Rights, Yearbook 2005/1, p. 1, available at: https://www.aippi.fr/upload/Berlin%202005%20Q186%20187%20188/rs186english.pdf.

[42] Art. 206(1) LCRR.

[43] Art. 206(2) LCRR.

[44] Explanation of the Proposal of the Law on Amendments to the Law on Copyright and Related Rights (2019), p. 54.

the request for compensatory damages is to be found in the exclusive disposition of the injured party, thus the method of calculation as well. We do not inquire the fact that the new provision does not change anything in that respect. Therefore, depending on the circumstances of the case, the injured party will assess by himself which method is applicable when calculating the scope of the damage suffered and file a request for its compensation accordingly. What essentially intrudes the general rules, concerns, to some extent, the basis of liability, therefore the feasibility of the court to accept the plaintiff's request for damages expressed in the amount increased due to the insufficiently clear criteria, as well as the lump sum compensation.

3.4.2.1 Perception of Responsibility Under the LCRR

The first paragraph of the relevant article stipulates that lost profits and obtained illegal profits may be claimed from a perpetrator who knew or could have known that he was committing infringement. In other words, these calculation methods can be used to claim compensation for damage caused by an unscrupulous perpetrator. In tort law, it is not common to talk about conscience, i.e. negligence, since the condition of responsibility is a fault. The essential difference is that in the case of conscience, it is insisted upon the perpetrator's awareness of permissible or impermissible behaviour, while in the case of the fault, the attention is drawn to his actions: whether or not he has deviated from what was expected.[45]

3.4.2.2 Increase the Amount of the Compensation in Certain Circumstances

When determining the amount of monetary compensation, in certain cases the court should take into consideration circumstances of a non-economic nature, such as non-pecuniary damage. Although this provision has been almost literally taken over from the Directive 2004/48,[46] it seems that it has not been adequately implemented in our legal system. The reason for this can be found in the previous article. Namely, the provision of Art. 205 (1)(3) stipulates that in the event of the infringement of a copyright or a related right or due to existence of a serious threat that it is going to be

[45] According to Marija Karanikić Mirić, if the responsibility is based on a wrong procedure, and the wrong procedure is understood as a manifestation of a certain mental state, and if it is considered that mental state determined the way the perpetrator acted, then determining fault by the perpetrator's mental state represents a step in place. Therefore, the only thing that should be relevant for the court is what can be expected from a reasonable and careful person in the given circumstances. Karanikić Mirić (2009), p. 333.

[46] Directive 2004/48/EC of the European Parliament and of the Council of 29 April 2004 on the enforcement of intellectual property rights, Official Journal of the European Union, No. L 157 of 30 April 2004.

infringed, the plaintiff may claim, inter alia, compensation for pecuniary and non-pecuniary damage.[47]

The Directive 2004/48 does not explicitly emphasize the right of the holder to claim both pecuniary and non-pecuniary damage, but uses the common term *damages*. Therefore, taking non-pecuniary damage into account when measuring the amount of monetary compensation is in fact a normative formulation of the compensatory function of compensation that dominates in systems in which non-pecuniary damage, as result of copyright infringement, is not generally accepted.

Digression: Indemnification as a Function of Compensation

When multiple damages were introduced into domestic copyright by law from 2004,[48] the legislator in power offered the following explanation accompanied by the relevant provision: "it is about introducing the institute of criminal damages, which according to the experience of many countries, represents a serious sanction for violation of rights, which does not aim at restitution, but *compensation* and prevention of damage".[49]

Given that the multiple fee has been withdrawn by the latest editorial board, we consider opening a discussion on its nature or need for its introduction, redundant. However, since the aim of the provision of the Directive that our law has taken over is to provide *compensation*, we consider it necessary to refer to the meaning of this function in the legal system from which it originates, i.e. the Anglo-Saxon.

Namely, the right to compensation in the Anglo-Saxon systems is grounded on the principle of compensation for the infringement of the right.[50] This principle implies that a person who has caused damage to another person by his actions must pay a certain amount of money in order to compensate the injured party for his infringed right. In most cases, the amount of monetary compensation corresponds to the scope of the damage actually suffered. However, in some cases, compensation can be provided only if the amount of money would cause proper suffering by the perpetrator due to the committed injury.[51] Consequently several different types of monetary compensation for damage have been created, out of which some have

[47] The Directive prescribes only damage compensation, without explicit determination of "property" or "non-property". The reason for this lies in the fact that EU member countries do not have a unique approach to the issue of compensation for non-property damage due to the copyright infringement.

[48] Art. 178 Law on Copyright and Related Rights from 2004, Official Gazette of Republic of Serbia and Montenegro, No. 61/04 of 24th December 2004.

[49] *Final Report on Harmonisation of Copyright and Related Rights Law of the Serbia and Montenegro*, website of Economic and Legal Advisory Center of Serbia and Montenegro, www.plac-org.yu. Used in printed version.

[50] Christie and Meeks (1990), p. 5.

[51] Dobbs (2000), p. 3.

gained criminal characteristics due to their preventive function.[52] While doing so, we should be aware of the fact that the countries of the common law system do not, in principle, recognize monetary compensation for non-pecuniary damage, thus punitive compensation represents an effective tool in achieving the purpose of the right to reparation—compensation for the infringement. Namely, the usual sanction imposed for the infringement of moral rights is the prohibition of further performance of actions that lead to their infringement. If such injuries cause pecuniary damage, punitive damage is assigned.[53]

In our law such formulation can be problematic, having in mind that the right holder can also obtain compensation for non-pecuniary damage. Namely, if the request for compensation includes also a non-economic segment, the issue that arises refers to whether the plaintiff has thus exhausted the claim for compensation of non-pecuniary damage, as an independent one? In other words, does a request for compensation for pecuniary damage, which includes non-economic damage, impose a single compensation, which is certainly not common in our legal order?

We may find a certain similarity in the rules of the law of obligations on the compensation of affective value, when the damage is caused by a criminal act committed with intent.[54] It is, in fact, a specific compensation which, in addition to pecuniary damage, also takes into account non-pecuniary damage, i.e. mental pain that the injured party has probably suffered due to intentional destruction or damage to objects to which he has been particularly emotionally bonded.[55] Therefore, compensation of affective value is awarded only if there is non-pecuniary damage, but in connection with a damaged or destroyed object. The purpose of the part of the monetary compensation that exceeds the amount of the market value of the destroyed or damaged item corresponds to the purpose of the monetary compensation of non-pecuniary damage in general—the gratification of the injured party. However, given that the affective value is being considered only when it is determined that the damage was caused by committing intentional criminal offense (and non-pecuniary damage is not legally recognized, in terms of Article 200 LO), these rules cannot be applied to the detriment caused by copyright infringement, unless the criminal offense with intent was committed at the same time.

[52] In common law legal systems traditionally there are several kinds of strong remedies for infringement in the area of civil law, but punitive damage is the most rigorous one. Landon (1951), pp. 136–143; Bently et al. (2018), p. 1346; Meurkens (2014), pp. 28–36; Street (1962), pp. 29, 33.

[53] Laddie et al. (1998), p. 1798. Moreover, in the theory of common law legal systems, it is strongly emphasized that compensation for copyright damage should have a compensatory rather than a penal function. Therefore, increased fees, in any form, can be awarded only if the author's moral authority has been infringed, especially if the author's reputation is harmed. See Cornish and Llewelyn (2003), p. 451. In this regard, the literature points out that punitive damage in common law countries of the System has the same function as compensation for non-pecuniary damage in continental law. See Von Bar (2000), p. 127.

[54] Art. 189 LO, Radišić (2016), p. 312; Dudaš in: Pajtić et al. (2018), p. 530; Klarić and Vedriš (2014), p. 89.

[55] Nikolić (2003), p. 150.

Due to the abovementioned reasons, we believe that it would be more adequate in terms of our law if the term *non-pecuniary damage* was avoided in the relevant provision, and the term *affective value* was used instead.

3.4.2.3 Lump Sum Compensation

Lump sum compensation may be awarded instead of compensation for damages, when the circumstances of the case justify it. Let us assume that the circumstances of the case justify this when the infringement of rights (e.g. unauthorized posting of protected content on the internet) caused mass unauthorized exploitation in various forms and it is not possible to calculate the exact amount of damage suffered, or the calculation depends on very expensive procedure of proving.[56] It is more comfortable for the injured party to indicate the claim for monetary compensation in a lump sum, since he does not have to prove the scope of the damage he suffered. But, unlike the undesirable multiplied compensation that was based on more severe forms of fault, the lump sum can be awarded only when the perpetrator of the injury acted with conscience.

By using the term *instead*, the legislator enables the exclusion of the rules of tort law in the application of this provision, because the lump sum, according to the linguistic interpretation, is being awarded instead of compensation. From the set of lump sum corrective frameworks, justified circumstances and the lowest amount, it could be undoubtedly deducted that in order to award the lump sum, it is necessary that the damage has occurred. The injured party must prove the damage, but not its scope. In which way the court will assess the groundedness of the claim for compensation exceeding the minimum specified amount remains unclear, especially since this compensation can be awarded only if the perpetrator was conscientious.

3.5 *Non-Pecuniary Damage*

In respect of theory, the issue of whether awarding monetary compensation for non-pecuniary damage is justified, has been controversial for a long time.[57] On the one hand, advocates of negative theories oppose the commercialization of personality goods by insisting on the impossibility of mental pain or fear suffered to be valorised in monetary form. On the other hand, the supporters of positive theories emphasize the necessity of providing monetary gratification to a person whose moral rights have been injured and who, in that sense, has full moral justification.[58]

[56] Directive 2004/48/EC, Preamble (26).

[57] Some authors point out that monetary compensation for non-pecuniary damage was also awarded in archaic law. Such rules are contained in the Law of Table XII. Marković (1921), pp. 82,83.

[58] Nikolić (1995), pp. 123–128.

In copyright, this dilemma is deepened even more, since the moral rights of the author, which infringement causes non-pecuniary damage, are related to a specific author's work and cannot be equivalent to the goods of human personality that are covered by civil protection.

At the same time, we should not forget the fact that the very recognition of the author's moral rights in many countries took place only after the adoption of the Bern Convention.[59] In these terms, the possibility of awarding monetary compensation for suffered non-pecuniary damage to the author depends, first of all, on the standpoint of the legislator in certain legal systems regarding the moral rights of authors, but also on monetary compensation for non-pecuniary damage in general.[60]

There was no common standpoint on this issue in our literature either. Some authors completely exclude the possibility of gratifying the author for the infringement of moral rights with monetary compensation, claiming that "gratification for non-pecuniary damage in copyright can involve only public announcement of the verdict, public apology for insults and slander, etc."[61] Others justify monetary compensation for non-pecuniary damage caused by copyright infringement by civil principles.[62]

Until the enactment of the Copyright and Related Rights Act in 1998, this problem became even greater since former laws (from 1957, 1968 and 1978) had not established clear solutions. Namely, the generally allowed possibility for an author whose economic or moral right has been infringed, to demand protection of his right and compensation for damages, is provided by a provision dedicated to one of the moral rights, paternity right, and is explicitly limited to compensation for pecuniary damage. The Law dating from 1998 removes this contradiction by prescribing a right to the author to file a lawsuit for non-pecuniary damage due to infringement of his moral rights,[63] in the absence of special provisions, the general rules included in the Law on Obligations are to be applied. Such a solution has been retained to the present day.

According to the LO, monetary compensation (compensation for non-pecuniary damage) may be awarded for physical pain, mental pain due to reduced life activity, impairment, injury of reputation, honour, freedom or rights of a person, death of a close person, as well as for fear suffered.[64] If the court finds that the circumstances of the case justify it, in particular when it comes to the intensity of the pain and fear and

[59] Berne Convention for the Protection of Literary and Artistic Works, Bern 1886, as amended on September 28, 1979, available on: https://wipolex.wipo.int/en/text/283693.

[60] Radojković (1966), pp. 155–161; Klarić (1990), pp. 751–756; Krneta (1981), p. 75. The countries of the common law system in principle do not recognize the right to monetary compensation for non-pecuniary damage, especially when it comes to copyright infringement, since the author has challenged the moral rights he has in his intellectual creation. Bently et al. (2018), pp. 1346, 1347; Laddie, Prescott and Vitoria, p. 608.

[61] Spaić (1983), p. 239.

[62] Krneta (1981), p. 76.

[63] čl. 170, st. 2.

[64] Art. 200(1) LO.

their duration, it shall award fair monetary compensation, regardless of the compensation for pecuniary damage, even when it has not occurred.[65]

Having in mind the required connection between the author's moral right and his work on the grounds of which he exercises protection, it can be considered that the violation of the person's right exists in all cases of violation of the work because it represents a kind of intellectual, spiritual expression of its creator. Judicial practice shares this viewpoint too. Moreover, it cannot go unnoticed that the courts in disputes for non-pecuniary damage have not rarely recognized the author's right to non-pecuniary damage already on the basis of an acknowledged infringement, ignoring the fact that the damage (mental pain) has not been proven.[66] This neglect in the application of the general rules of obligatory relations results in the fact that the institute of compensation for non-property damage is interpreted quite extensively. Namely, given that the application of the general rules of the law of obligations is foreseen, in order to enable the author to exercise the right to compensation for non-pecuniary damage, he must prove he has suffered the mental pain due to copyright infringement in such intensity, that awarding compensation is justified.[67]

---

[65] Art. 200(1) LO.

[66] The defendants are obliged to pay the plaintiff jointly and severally the compensation for non-pecuniary damage due to the violation of the plaintiff's moral right as an author for name indication See the Judgment of the Court of Appeals in Belgrade, Gž 4328/12 of 12.12.2012. Later, the same court points out that the plaintiff, as the injured party, must prove that he suffered a detrimental consequence in the form of mental pain, as well as a causal link between the violation of his moral copyright and the violation of personality rights, as being one of the recognized forms of non-pecuniary damage. Without establishing these circumstances, the conclusion on the groundedness of the claim for compensation for non-pecuniary damage is premature. In such a situation, the conclusion of the first instance court remains unclear and unmerited and it denotes that deciding the amount of compensation for pecuniary damage took into account the significance of the damaged property and the purpose for which the compensation serves, but also that it does not favour the aspirations they are not complementary with its nature and social purpose. See the Judgment of the Court of Appeals in Belgrade, Gž no. 227/13 dated 16 April 2014. In a recent decision, the court again failed to establish the existence of damage: "From this correctly and completely established factual situation, the first instance court correctly concluded that the defendant violated the moral copyright of the plaintiff to protect the integrity of the copyright and correctly found that the defendant violated the moral copyright of the plaintiff to protect the integrity of the copyright and obliged him to compensate the plaintiff for non-pecuniary damage", See the Judgment of the Court of Appeals Gž4 66/19 of 17.07.2019 in the *Intermex* legal base, 29.01.2021. Ibid in: Judgment of the Court of Appeals in Belgrade, Gž4 47/15 of 14.10.2015, Legal Informant 11/2017, in the *Intermex* legal base, 29.01.2021, Judgment of the High Court in Novi Sad, P.9/10 of 09.02.2010; Judgment of the Court of Appeals in Novi Sad Gž. 8076/10 of 13.04.2010, in the *Intermex* legal base, 01.02.2021.

[67] Judgment of the Court of Appeals in Belgrade Gž4 44/15 of 07.10.2015. godine, Pravni informator, 5/2016, in the Intermex legal database, 29.01.2021. During the public debate on the Draft Law on Amendments to the Law on Copyright and Related Rights, it was proposed to exclude the provision regarding the application of general rules of the law of obligations with regard to compensation for damages. This intervention aimed to ease the author's position in terms of proving non-pecuniary damage, i.e. mental pain suffered as well as its intensity, on which circumstances of the request for monetary compensation for non-pecuniary damage are relevant, as well as its amount. The proposal was not adopted. See Public Hearing Report (2014), p. 27.

The assessment of the amount of monetary compensation for non-pecuniary damage is conferred to court practice, which is guided by the significance of the damaged property (reflected in the existence of a special bond between the author and his work), the goal of compensation and fairness. Besides, monetary compensation cannot favour aspirations that are incompatible with its nature and social purpose[68] (gratification of the injured party, and by no means a monetary equivalent for the injured personal property).

Finally, considering the above mentioned related to compensation for non-pecuniary damage, it remains unclear whether the plaintiff when determining the claim for compensation for pecuniary damage by taking into account the non-pecuniary damage he has suffered too, is deprived of the burden of proving mental pain and its intensity? According to the legal formulation, it seems that an affirmative answer to this question is being imposed. Consequently, this could represent the first step towards objectivization of a moral damage in copyright.[69]

3.6 Revision of the Judgement in Copyright Disputes

In the previous section, we described the challenges to the realization of the claim of the right holder for compensation of damages when damage is caused by the injury of the right. However, it seems that deviation from the general rules does not end in the domain of substantive law. Moreover, we cannot discuss only about deviation, but also about the constitution of special rules which, in some cases, disturb the established system of civil protection. According to Art. 214a (3 and 4), copyright and related rights disputes are not considered as small claims.[70] Revision is always allowed in disputes concerning infringement of copyright and related rights when they do not relate to a property claim.[71]

[68] Art 200(2) LO.

[69] Karanikić Mirić (2016), pp. 13–15.

[70] This provision was included in the valid text of the LCRR after the intervention at the public hearing, considering such a solution necessary, and having in mind the importance of copyright. In small claims procedure, relevant factual and evidentiary material is allowed only in the first instance procedure until the conclusion of the main hearing. Several cases are envisaged in which the passive conduct of the parties qualifies as a withdrawal of the lawsuit. See Art 467–479 LCP. For these reasons, there is a risk that the disputed situation will be resolved only on the basis of the evidence offered in the first instance procedure, which does not necessarily correspond to the real facts. Emphasizing the importance of the infringed right, it was suggested that disputes in the field of copyright and related rights cannot be considered as small claims, regardless of the value of the dispute. The legal text adopted this intervention made by Jelena Borovac, judge of the Supreme Court of Serbia, with the aim that the issue of a value should not be an obstacle to the protection of rights. See Report (2014), p. 34.

[71] At the same time, at the suggestion of Judge Borovac, a provision was introduced according to which revision is always allowed in disputes concerning infringement of copyright and related rights when they do not refer to a property claim. The proposer insists that a distinction must be

Without intending to go into procedural issues, and in the context of damage compensation, it seems necessary to reconsider the unlimited revision of the judgment concerning copyright and related rights' infringement. Namely, what seems to be problematic is precisely the exclusive part of the relevant provision on revision with regard to property claims, since the compensation for damages is thoroughly the property claim.

We have already indicated in the previous section that violation of a right is a harmful action to which the obligation to compensate the damage is related as well. In this regard, it might happen that, by final judgement, the request filed by the injured party of copyright or related rights for determining the infringement of the right and for monetary compensation of the damage caused in the amount lower than the one provided for the revision admissibility, is denied. If during the revision procedure the verdict was amended in the segment related to the determination of infringement, the right holder would be denied the right to compensation for damage, since he could not overturn it in this segment. It should not be overlooked that a claim for damages dominates proceedings for copyright and related rights' infringement. Moreover, due to the two-sided nature of the audit,[72] it is also conceivable that the court, acting upon the revision, may determine that there has not been any violation of the right due to which the defendant is legally obliged to pay damages. This would mean that obligation still exists, although there is no basis for liability.

Since the enactment of the Law on Amendments to the Law on Copyright and Related Rights has just recently taken place, there is still no case law in these issues.

4 Conclusion

With regard to liability for copyright infringement via internet, the discrepancy between the traditional legal framework and the requirement for the necessary modernization of the law seems to be rather prominent. Although liability for presumed fault represents a pillar of the modern tort law, it demonstrates its weaknesses in the online environment. Namely, the exercise of the author's right to damages depends essentially on the burden of proving damage in the proceedings being conducted for this purpose. Therefore, we think that by insisting on fault liability, i.e. responsibility for one's own actions, the author's right to claim for

made between disputes that are conducted due to infringement of copyright and related rights and disputes which subject refers to the payment of a certain claim based on the use of a copyright work or a subject of related law. In this regard, it could not be considered justified to allow the revision of the judgment regardless of the value of the challenged part, while in disputes due to violation of rights, ie protection of the right itself, there should be revision of the judgment, regardless of value. See Report (2014), p. 34.

[72] The bilateral nature of the audit implies that both parties may file an audit. Keča and Knežević (2017), p. 360.

damages may be endangered. When it comes to violations of the rights via internet, the legislator could shift the obligation of compensation from the perpetrator to the owner of the IP protocol.[73] To protect copyright and the right holder's interests, shifting to the strict liability rules seems to be more proper.

There are already cases in the legal system in which liability for another or special cases of liability has been explicitly prescribed. The *ratio legis* of such normative solutions lies in the circumstance that there has been usually already a special legal relationship established between the perpetrator and the responsible person, which makes this division (between the perpetrator and the responsible person) justified. At the same time, even when the issue of identifying the perpetrator is not disputable, imposing the obligation to the third party is more purposeful (from the aspect of the injured party, but also the functionality of the legal order).[74]

The application of the general rules on compensation for damages caused by copyright infringement is not as simple in other aspects related to damages. This is especially the case when it comes to compensation for pecuniary damage. This is somewhat understandable, bearing in mind that pecuniary damage refers to material goods, while copyright comprises economic and personal rights which are inseparable. If we add to that the circumstance that the use of copyrighted works in digital forms has taken on a mass character, it becomes clear that the intervention of the legislator is needed. This activity is certainly accompanied by the process of harmonization of domestic law with the law of the European Union. However, it seems that with the new wording, the legislator has taken over solutions which formulation is insufficiently comprehensible and clear to our lawyers. Therefore, the application of unclear provisions might hinder the goal set in front of the legislator, which is the effective protection of authors in case of violation their rights.

Finally, it is obvious that not all institutes of domestic obligation law have been fully exhausted, neither are they sufficiently emphasized. Here we have in mind affective value or return without a legal basis (*condition sine causa*), for example.

References

Bently L, Sherman B, Gangjee D, Johnson P (2018) Intellectual property law. Oxford University Press

Christie GC, Meeks JE (1990) Cases and materials on the law of torts. West Publishing Co., St. Paul

Cornish W, Llewelyn D (2003) Intellectual property – patents, copyright, trade marks and allied rights. Sweet & Maxwell, London

Dobbs DB (2000) The law of torts. West Group, St. Paul

Karanikić Mirić M (2009) Krivica kao osnov deliktne odgovornosti u građanskom pravu (Fault As a Basis of Liability in Civil Law). Službeni glasnik, Belgrade

Karanikić Mirić M (2013) Objektivna odgovornost (Strict Liability). Službeni glasnik, Belgrade

---

[73] Radovanović (2019), p. 60.

[74] Karanikić Mirić (2013), pp. 218, 219.

Karanikić Mirić M (2016) Non-Pecuniary Loss in Serbian Tort Law: Time for a Change in Paradigm? In: SEE | EU Cluster of Excellence in European and International Law Series of Papers. Verlag Alma Mater, Saarbrücken, available at: https://papers.ssrn.com/sol3/papers.cfm?abstract_id=3650866

Keča R, Knežević M (2017) Građansko procesno pravo (Civil Procedure). Službeni glasnik, Belgrade

Klarić P (1990) Nematerijalna šteta u nemačkom građanskom pravu (Non-Pecuniary Damage in German Civil Law). Zbornik Pravnog fakulteta u Zagrebu 40:751–776

Klarić P, Vedriš M (2014) Građansko pravo – opći dio, stvarno pravo, obvezno i nasljedno pravo (Civil Law – General Part, Property Law, Obligation Law and Inheritance Law). Narodne Novine, Zagreb

Krneta S (1981) Novčana naknada nematerijalne štete zbog povrede autorskog prava (Monetary Compensation for Non-Pecuniary Damage due to Copyright Infringement). Godišnjak Pravnog fakulteta u Sarajevu XXIX:73–88

Laddie H, Prescott M, Vitoria M (1998) The modern law of copyright and designs. Butterworths, London

Landon PA (1951) Pollock's law of torts. Stevens & Sons Limited, London

Marković Č (1921) Novčana reparacija moralne štete (Monetary Compensation of Non-pecuniary Damage). Arhiv za pravne i društvene nauke 2:81–92

Marković S (1999) Autorsko pravo i srodna prava (Copyright and Related Rights). Službeni glasnik, Belgrade

Meurkens L (2014) Punitive damages: the civil remedy in American law, lessons and caveats for continental Europe. Wolters Kluwer Business, Maastricht University

Nikolić D (1995) Građanskopravna sankcija – geneza, evolucija i savremeni pojam (Civil Remedy – Genesis, Evolution and Modern Term). Pravni fakultet Univerziteta u Novom Sadu, Novi Sad

Nikolić D (2003) Kaznena naknada štete (Punitive Damages). Coll Pap Fac Law Novi Sad 1–2: 145–156

Pajtić B, Radovanović S, Dudaš A (2018) Obligaciono pravo (Obligation Law). Pravni fakultet Univerziteta u Novom Sadu, Novi Sad

Popović D (2015) Povreda autorskog i srodnih prava na Internetu: osvrt na noviju praksu Evropskog suda pravde. In: Popović D (ed) Intelektualna svojina i Internet. Pravni fakultet Univerziteta u Beogradu, Belgrade, pp 59–83

Radišić J (2016) Obligaciono pravo – opšti deo (Obligation Law – General Part). Centar za publikacije, Pravni fakultet u Nišu

Radojković Ž (1966) Ličnopravni (moralni) elementi autorskog prava (Personal (Moral) Elements of Author's Rights). Udruženje pravnika Jugoslavije, Belgrade

Radovanović S (2015) Građanskopravna odgovornost internet posrednika za povredu autorskog prava – uporednopravni aspekt. In: Popović D (ed) Intelektualna svojina i Internet. Pravni fakultet Univerziteta u Beogradu, Belgrade, pp 83–112

Radovanović S (2019) Neka pitanja u vezi sa subjektivnom odgovornošću za naknadu štete pričinjenje povredom autorskog prava na internetu (Some questions relating to the fault liability for the compensation of damages caused by copyright infringement on the internet). Pravo i privreda 7–9:43–62

Reljanović M (2016) Odgovornost hosting provajdera za povrede prava intelektualne svojine u pravu Srbije i pravu susednih država. In: Popović D (ed) Intelektualna svojina i Internet Pravni fakultet. Univerziteta u Beogradu, Belgrade, pp 119–134

Spaić V (1983) Teorija autorskog prava i autorsko pravo u SFRJ (Theory of Copyright and Copyright in SFRY). Pravni fakultet Sveučilišta u Zagrebu, Centar za stručno usavršavanje i saradnju sa udruženim radom, RO Jugoslovenska autorska agencija, Belgrade

Street H (1962) Principles of the law of damages. Sweet & Maxwell, London

Von Bar C (2000) The common European law of torts – damage and damages, liability for and without personal misconduct, causality, and defences. C.H. Beck, Münich

The Scope of Author's Moral Right of Integrity in Serbian Law

Novak Vujičić

Contents

1 Introduction

Under copyright, as an intellectual property right, most jurisdictions grant two sets of rights: economic and moral rights. While the focus of economic rights rests on enabling authors/right holders to control the use of their copyrighted works by others and to obtain a financial reward thereof, moral rights serve a different purpose. Moral rights aim at protecting the bond between authors and their works. One of the

N. Vujičić (✉)
University of Belgrade, Faculty of Law, Belgrade, Serbia
e-mail: novak.vujicic@ius.bg.ac.rs

D. V. Popović et al. (eds.), *Balkan Yearbook of European and International Law 2021*, Balkan Yearbook of European and International Law 2021,
https://doi.org/10.1007/978-3-030-97431-2_5

essential moral rights is the right of integrity, the author's right to object to certain modifications of his/her work by others.

The right of integrity is guaranteed by the Berne Convention for the Protection of Literary and Artistic Works (Berne Convention), the central international treaty in the field of copyright protection. As such, it is widely recognized in many jurisdictions all around the world. In Article 6bis of the Berne Convention, it is foreseen that, independently of the author's economic rights, the author shall have the right: 'to object to any distortion, mutilation or other modification of, or other derogatory action concerning, the said work, which would be prejudicial to his honor or reputation'.[1] This provision has been the 'foundation' for the Berne Union member countries in prescribing the protection of the moral right of integrity to their national copyright laws. Nevertheless, the ways the right of integrity has been introduced and protected in different countries vary considerably. Whilst some countries just had provided a minimum level of protection of the right of integrity required by the Berne Convention, others went beyond those requirements.[2]

This paper analyses the moral right of integrity guaranteed in Serbian copyright law, more precisely its scope. As it will be shown in the following, there are certain ambiguities related to the scope of the protection secured to authors by the moral right of integrity in Serbian law. The objective here is to show how the scope of the right of integrity is defined, to draw attention to ambiguities implied, and provide guidelines for tackling them.

The analyzed matter can be observed in the following way. Let us imagine one hypothetical situation in Serbia in which we have an author A and a person B. Person B wants to modify the copyrighted work of author A. Author A does not approve the intended modifications. As it is said, in Serbia author A has the guaranteed moral right of integrity of his/her work. The moral right of integrity entitles the author with the sole power to decide on the integrity of the work, i.e. to modify the work by him/herself (the positive aspect of the right of integrity), as well as to prohibit the modifications of the work by others (the negative aspect of the right of integrity). Therefore, the question here is whether author A could in this situation successfully use his/her moral right of integrity against the person B and stop them from making unwanted modifications to the work.[3] At first glance, it seems that the answer is confirmatory.

However, there is a catch. The right of integrity does not (or at least should not) enable the author to object to every modification of his/her work s/he does not approve of. Certain conditions need to be met for the application of the moral right of integrity. Author A will be successful in his/her attempt only if those conditions are

---

[1] Art. 6bis of the Berne Convention for the Protection of Literary and Artistic Works (Berne Convention), Paris text, 1971.

[2] Goldstein and Hugenholtz (2010), pp. 351–353.

[3] In this hypothetical example, for reasons of simplification, we are willingly disregarding the fact that Author A in Serbia enjoys the exclusive economic right of adaptation of the work, which s/he could also use against person B.

met in this case. The said conditions define the potential scope of the protection secured to authors by the moral right of integrity in Serbia. Determining them should help us in clarifying the latter.

Hence, the principal question here is: under what conditions is an author able to activate his/her right of integrity against others who modify his/her work? In other words, under what conditions the right of integrity could be applied (will be infringed). As can be seen, the focus is on the scope of the negative aspect of the moral right of integrity. This because its positive aspect (exclusive right of the author to modify the work by him/herself) seems like a clear-cut case.

Having in mind the indicated question, the paper is structurally divided into two parts. The first part intends to specify the statutory rules and legal doctrine from which the conditions for the application of the right of integrity derive. It encompasses an analytical insight into the provision(s) of the Law on Copyright and Related Rights (LCRR)[4] by which the author's moral right of integrity is guaranteed in Serbia—the statutory 'source' of the conditions (Sect. 2). In addition to that, this part also contains general remarks on the understanding of the moral right of integrity in the legal doctrine, its 'role' and 'place' in the corpus of copyright law—the doctrinal guidelines for the conditions. Based on the findings from the first part, the second part provides a list of the standard conditions for activation of the right of integrity against a third party (Sect. 3). By analyzing the clarity and application of those conditions in practice, we should get a clearer picture of the scope of the author's moral right of integrity in Serbian law.

2 Moral Right of Integrity as Prescribed in the Serbian Law on Copyright and Related Rights

Serbian copyright law has a long tradition of the protection of the author's moral rights. Moral rights and specifically the right of integrity are continuously regulated starting from the 1929 Law on Protection of Copyright, enacted in the Kingdom of Yugoslavia.[5] The 2009 LCRR, currently in force, same as its predecessors, explicitly prescribes the author's moral right of protection of the work's integrity.[6]

[4]Law on Copyright and Related Rights (LCRR), Official Gazette of the Republic of Serbia, Nos. 104/2009, 99/2011, 119/2012, 29/2016 – Decision of the Constitutional Court and 66/2019. The unofficial translation of the consolidated text of the LCRR is available on http://www.zis.gov.rs/legal-regulations/legislation.110.html.

[5]See Art. 17 of the Law on Protection of Copyright, Kingdom of Yugoslavia, 1929 http://www.zis.gov.rs/upload/documents/pdf_sr/pdf/propisi/Zakon%20o%20zastiti%20autorskog%20prava%201930-min.pdf.

[6]It should be noted, that apart from authors, in Serbian legal system performers also enjoy the moral right of protection of integrity of their performances. However, in this paper the protection of the performers' right of integrity will be set aside. See Art. 114 of the LCRR.

According to Article 17 of the LCRR, in Subsection 4.1.4. titled 'Right of Protection of the Work's Integrity':

> Any author shall have the exclusive right to protect the integrity of their work, particularly by the following actions:
>
> (1) Opposing the alterations to their work by unauthorized persons;
> (2) Opposing the communication of their work to the public in an altered or incomplete form, taking into account the concrete technical form of communication of the work and good business practices;
> (3) Permitting their work to be adapted.[7]

This formulation of the provision, which envisages the author's right of integrity, was introduced by the 1998 LCRR in Serbian law.[8] Previous regulations (laws), effective in Serbia, had contained the general provision on the author's moral rights whose wording was less detailed. Protected moral rights had been just enumerated without any detailed clarifications:

> The author's moral rights include the right of the author to be recognized and named as the creator of the work, the right of the author to object to any distortion, mutilation, or other modification of the work, and the right of the author to object (unbecoming) usage of the work which would be prejudicial to his honor or reputation (translated by the author).[9]

In the 1998 LCRR, the legislator had opted justifiably for a different approach. That is, to name and regulate separately every protected author's moral right, including the right of protection of the work's integrity.[10] Apropos the 'newly' defined right of integrity, the legislator stated in the official explanation of the 1998 LCRR the following:

> Protection of the work's integrity is a complex concept, given that it encompasses several aspects, among which it is most important to notice the active aspect (the so-called positive prerogative) and the passive aspect (the so-called negative prerogative). The first one consists of the right of the author to alter the work by him/herself, and the second one from the right of the author to oppose the alterations to the work by others. This difference is of significance for possibilities of exercising the right by other right holders (primarily the author's heirs).
>
> Albeit, the right of adaptation is 'covered' by the exclusive economic right (Article 19, Paragraph 2), in this case it has been set apart (distinguished) particularly from the aspect of the

---

[7] Art. 17 of the LCRR.

[8] Art. 17 of Law on Copyright and Related Rights, Official Gazette of the Federal Republic of Yugoslavia, No. 24/98. Only, the wording of Point 2 is changed by the 2004 LCRR when the formulation: 'taking into account the concrete technical form of communication of the work and good business practices' was added. See Art. 17, p. 2 of Law on Copyright and Related Rights, Official Gazette of Serbia and Montenegro, No. 61/2004.

[9] See provisions in the laws on (protection of) copyright applied in the former Yugoslavia: the Law from 1978 (Art. 28), the Law from 1968 (Art. 29), and the Law from 1957 (Art. 26). Texts of these laws are available on http://www.zis.gov.rs/pravna-regulativa/%D1%85%D1%80%D0%BE%D0%BD%D0%BE%D0%BB%D0%BE%D0%B3%D0%B8%D1%98%D0%B0-%D0%BF%D1%80%D0%BE%D0%BF%D0%B8%D1%81%D0%B0.1257.html.

[10] Žarković (1998), p. 18.

> moral right of protection of the work's integrity, owing to the fact that the decision of the author to allow or prohibit the adaptation of his/her own work is based on reasons that are predominantly personal in nature (translated by the author).[11]

After the 1998 LCRR, the two new LCRR were enacted (in 2004 and 2009). Nevertheless, that had not affected the provision on the right of integrity. The provision remained practically the same, so it has been applied now uninterruptedly for more than 20 years.[12] It represents the key statutory ground for the application of the author's right of integrity in the Serbian legal system. This provision also corresponds (partly)[13] to the commitment of Serbia, as a Berne Union member, to guarantee the right of integrity under Article 6bis of the Berne Convention (quoted above).[14]

Considering that the said provision of the LCRR represents the main statutory ground for the application of the author's right of integrity in the Serbian legal system, we reasonably should expect from it to provide the answer to our central question: under what conditions the right of integrity could be activated towards others (i.e. what is the scope of the protection it provides)? Consequently, the next step here is to try to determine those conditions through the analysis of the subject provision.[15]

---

[11] Official Explanation of the 1998 LCRR (the explanation of Article 17) In: Žarković B (ed) Zakon o autorskom i srodnim pravima (Law on Copyright and Related Rights). Federal Intellectual Property Office, Belgrade, pp. 92–23.

[12] It is interesting to notice that the solution of the Serbian LCRR with regards to the wording of the provision on author's right of integrity is quite unique in comparison to the provisions of laws effective in other countries of the former Yugoslavia, even though they all share the 'heritage' of the same copyright regulations (laws). Compare Art. 17 of the LCRR with: Art. 17 of the Law on Copyright and Related Rights, Nos. 37/2011 and 53/2016, Montenegro; Art. 19 of the Law on Copyright and Related Rights, No. 63/2010, Bosnia and Herzegovina; Art. 24 of the Law on Copyright and Related Rights, Nos. 115/10, 140/10, 51/11, 147/13, 154/15 and 27/16, North Macedonia; Art. 16 of the Law on Copyright and Related Rights, Nos. 167/03, 79/07, 80/11, 125/11, 141/13, 127/14, 62/17 and 96/18, Croatia; Art. 19 of the Law on Copyright and Related Rights, Nos. 21/95 [. . .] 68/2008, 110/2013, 56/2015, 63/2016 and 59/19, Slovenia.

[13] In the LCRR the two independent moral rights are envisaged based on the moral right of integrity from Article 6bis of the Berne Convention: the right of integrity and the right to oppose unbecoming exploitation of the work. See Art. 17 and 18 of the LCRR.

[14] Of course, this commitment is not absolute. The Berne Convention binds its members to provide protection to authors and works that met the criteria of eligibility for protection, set by the Convention.

[15] Before starting with the analysis of the said provision of the LCRR, a few more remarks about the author's right of integrity in Serbia should be made here, so that we can have a broader perspective on this right. Firstly, in Serbia the author's right of integrity, as well as other moral rights, is not transferable by contract, nor can be subject to waivers. Still, the author may entrust to others the execution of the right of integrity (without a transfer) or opt not to exercise it (without a waiver). For example, the author may permit someone else to decide, whether to make alteration of the work or not. This, however, does not mean that the right of integrity has been transferred/waived. The subject legal transaction is considered as *pactum de non petendo*. Author will still enjoy (keep) his/her right of integrity, but it will be burdened by the right of another person to exercise it (Marković and Popović (2020), p. 201). Secondly, the author's right of integrity, as a moral right, is

In order to determine the conditions for the application of the right of integrity three questions should be first set upon the provision of Article 17 of the LCRR: (1) what is the object of protection?; (2) what is the substance (content) of protection, and lastly (3) are there any other (specific) limits of protection (not deriving from the object)?

2.1 *Object of Protection of the Moral Right of Integrity*

Identifying the object of protection of the moral right of integrity is an important step in determining its potential scope. It not only reveals to us what is protected but also how far the protection should extend. Figuratively speaking, the object of protection sets the 'inner boundaries' of the scope of the guaranteed protection.

By reading the title of the Subsection 4.1.4 of the LCRR ('Right of Protection of the Work's Integrity'), as well as the wording of the provision of Article 17 ('author shall have the exclusive right to protect the integrity of their work'), at first sight, it can be concluded that the object of protection here is the integrity of the author's work. That is not a wrong conclusion, but rather a simplified one. The integrity of the work is undoubtedly in the center of the protection, provided by the moral right of integrity. But the real question here is: why? Why are the authors granted the right to decide on the integrity of their works?

The LCRR does not answer this question explicitly but in an instructive way. It requires from the interpreter (of its provision) a deeper doctrinal—theoretical knowledge and understanding of copyright law and its concepts. However, a hint has been given in the official Explanation of the 1998 LCRR (quoted above). Under the latter, the author's right to control adaptations of his/her work is granted in this case (separately from author's economic rights), 'owing to the fact that the decision of the author to allow or prohibit the adaptation of his/her own work is based on reasons that are predominantly personal in nature'. This hint, considered in the context of the general common ground that moral rights protect the subjective

---

the perpetual right, and lasts even after the expiration of the author's economic rights (70 years elapse from the death of the author). After the author's death, the author's heirs, however, may exercise principally its negative aspect. Also, apart from the author's heirs, associations of authors and institutions in the fields of culture, science and art may also protect the author's right of integrity of the work (primarily upon the expiration of the author's economic rights). Moreover, upon the expiration of the author's economic rights, any person shall have the right to protect the right of integrity of the work (Popović (2016), p. 29; Art. 58, 102 and 107 of the LCRR; for more about the author's right of integrity upon author's death see: Marković (1999), pp. 242–243; Radovanović (2004), pp. 215–217; Vasić (2015), pp. 56–62). Thirdly, in the Serbian legal system, the author's right of integrity is also protected by criminal sanctions. Therefore, the infringement of the right of integrity may result not only in civil remedies, but also the criminal ones (Popović (2016), pp. 40–43; Milić (2010), pp. 885–891).

bond between authors and their works,[16] leads us to the following answer. The authors are granted the moral right to decide on the integrity of their work because alterations of the works trigger their personal ('moral') interests[17] related to the works. For instance, an author may feel the subjective personal anguish from seeing his/her work altered, in spite of what others might think about it.[18] Furthermore, a message the author wants to communicate to the public with his/her work might be changed by alterations.[19] The author cares his/her work remains whole (unchanged) for his/her contemporaries, as well as for the future generations.[20] To put it simply, the unauthorized alterations of their works by others represent a 'threat' for the authors' personal interests, hence they should enjoy a certain level of protection from them. That is the rationale behind the moral right of integrity.[21]

The object of protection of the moral right of integrity, therefore, is not the integrity of the work as itself, but rather the author's personal interests materialized in the integrity of the work, i.e. personal interests related to the preservation of the work's integrity.[22] With regards to this argument, two additional clarifications should be made.

Firstly, the fact that the moral right of integrity essentially protects the authors' personal interests linked with the integrity of their works does not mean that it cannot serve for the protection of other interests. Quite the opposite, the application of the moral right of integrity by an author can have positive implications for other interests, both non-pecuniary and economic (pecuniary), of the author,[23] other

---

[16] Radojković (1964), pp. 278–279; Goldstein and Hugenholtz (2010), p. 346; Sundara Rajan (2011), p. 9.

[17] In this paper the term 'personal interest(s)' will be used to refer to author's non-economic, non-pecuniary, intangible (personality)—'moral' interests connected with his/her work, which include honor, reputation etc. These interests stem from the personal connection that the author has with the work, as an embodiment of his/her personality. They differ from the author's economic (commercial), pecuniary interests related to the commercial exploitation of the work.

[18] Hansmann and Santilli (1997), p. 102.

[19] *Ibid.*

[20] Radojković (1966), p. 121; Radovanović (2004), pp. 216–217.

[21] See Radojković (1966), p. 121; Apart from this common interpretation, there are also other argumentative and persuasive interpretations about the object of protection of the right of integrity. See Treiger-Bar-Am (2005)—the author argue that the right of integrity protects an author's autonomy of expression.

[22] In this context see Žarković (1998), p. 18.

[23] That could be illustrated by the following hypothetical example. It is known that the moral right of integrity typically protects authors' reputational interests. Reputational interest, even though personal (non-pecuniary) by their nature, can have a strong economic character. Thus, when someone alters the work in such a way that alteration damages the author's reputation, consequences for the author could be twofold. Surely, the author's personal feelings will be affected by that. Nonetheless, the author's economic interests could be affected by the damaged reputation as well, e.g. drop in sales and/or prices of his/her other works could occur. Hence, by protecting the non-pecuniary reputational interests of authors, the moral right of integrity protects consequently his/her economic interests related to the reputation. Hansmann and Santilli (1997), pp. 104–105.

individuals (who own author's works or have copyright in them),[24] and the public at large, as well.[25] Still, the protection of those interests (especially pecuniary ones of the author and other individuals) should be viewed just as an associated effect—the implication of the moral right of integrity, and not as its core.[26] The focus of the moral right of integrity remains on the protection of the author's personal interests related to the preservation of the work's integrity. Moreover, certain interests, linked with the integrity of the work, definitely stay out of the scope of protection provided by the moral right of integrity. Those include the economic interests of the author and other copyright holders connected with the economic exploitation of the altered work. They are protected by a separate economic right—the right of adaptation. This right is prescribed in the LCRR (Article 31, Subsection 4.2.11. titled 'The Right to Adapt, Arrange or Alter the Work in Some Other Manner').[27] Yet, it should be noted that all the above-mentioned interests are commonly interconnected in practice, and it is hard to tell them apart.

Secondly, when it is said that the moral right of integrity protects the authors' personal interests linked with the integrity of their works, one logical question arises: precisely which authors' personal interests are being protected? From the LCRR (Article 17), a black-and-white answer to this question is hard to get. As already mentioned, in the LCRR it is not even explicitly prescribed that the moral right of integrity protects the authors' personal interests in general, let alone what personal interests precisely. So, what should be done in this situation, when the LCRR does not give 'clear' guidelines? There are two possible approaches.

The first one, a 'restrictive' approach, is to use standards set by the Berne Convention as guidelines for the application of the right of integrity in the Serbian legal system. The Berne Convention defines the right of integrity in terms of protection from modifications of the work 'which would be prejudicial to [the author's] honor or reputation.'[28] Thus, the author's personal interests linked with honor and reputation are identified as the interests which should be protected here. Starting from that, the right of integrity in Serbia should be applied with the aim of protecting specifically the author's honor and/or reputation (and not his/her other personal interests). This approach enjoys considerable support in the Serbian legal

---

[24] Their economic interests could be jeopardized in the case of damaging author's reputation too. *Ibid.*, p. 105.

[25] Protecting the integrity of authors' works, by the moral right of integrity, certainly is a matter of interest for the public at large. Particularly, that would be the case where the work has become an important element in the community's culture (a part of the national cultural heritage) or embodies idea—message important to the society, etc. *Ibid.*, pp. 105–107; Radojković (1966), pp. 121–122; Sundara Rajan (2011), pp. 5–6.

[26] For other opinions on this topic see for example: Hansmann and Santilli (1997), pp. 102–107; Ong (2003), pp. 297–312.

[27] Art. 31 of the LCRR ('The author shall have the exclusive right to prohibit or authorize adaptation, translation, arrangement or other alterations of his work.'); see also Žarković (1998), p. 18.

[28] Art. 6bis of the Berne Convention.

theory.[29] Also, it could be argued that this approach assures a higher level of legal certainty since the object of protection is more narrowly defined.[30] However, the issue with this approach is that it goes maybe too far from the wording of the provision of the LCRR (Article 17). Therefore, someone might argue that the Serbian legislator was aware (or at least should have been) that his definition of the moral right of integrity in Article 17 of the LCRR deviates from the language of the Berne Convention. (Perhaps) the legislator wanted to go beyond the protection stipulated in the Berne Convention? How is that, that the author's honor and reputation are not explicitly prescribed by the LCRR as the protected object(s) in the case of the right of integrity, but are in the cases of the author's moral right to oppose unbecoming exploitation of the work (Article 18), the author's right of withdrawal (Article 72), and the performer's moral rights of integrity and to oppose unbecoming exploitation of the performance (Article 114)?[31] Could that be just a coincidence?

On the other hand, the Serbian legislator has prescribed two independent moral rights on the basis of the moral right of integrity—the right 'to object to certain modifications and other derogatory actions' from the Berne Convention (Article 6bis). Those two are: (1) the right of integrity (which 'covers' objection to certain modifications), and (2) the right to oppose unbecoming exploitation of the work (that 'covers' objection to other derogatory actions).[32] For the second one, the author's honor and reputation are explicitly prescribed by the LCRR as the protected objects. Thus, considering that those two moral rights share the same 'origin', maybe it is justifiable to argue that they share the same object of protection (or not).[33]

The second approach, a 'wider' one, would be to accept that the right of integrity protects a broadest scope of the author's personal interests related to the work's integrity, including to his/her honor and reputation but not limited. That it protects the subjective bond of the author with (the integrity of) his/her work in general. A

---

[29] See Marković (1999), p. 179; Milić (2007), p. 275; Miladinović (2009), 211; Marić (2015); Marković and Popović (2020), p. 58; also Vujičić (2018), pp. 213–214.

[30] An issue with this argument is that the concepts 'honor' and 'reputation' are quite vague and subjective. That does not contribute to the legal certainty in theirs interpretation and application. In this contexts see: Aplin and Mohamed (2019), pp. 268–277.

[31] Art. 18, 72 and 114 of the LCRR.

[32] Marković (1999), pp. 176 and 182.

[33] It is interesting, that if we look into the general provision of the Yugoslav laws (quoted above) on author's moral rights, which had been in the application prior to the analyzed provision of Article 17 introduced by the 1998 LCRR, it could be also debated whether the right of integrity had been reserved for the cases of the hindrance of author's honor and reputation or not. The language of the Yugoslav laws: 'The author's moral rights include: [...], the right of the author to object to any distortion, mutilation, or other modification of the work, and the right of the author to object (unbecoming) usage of the work which would be prejudicial to his honor or reputation.' Looking strictly from the literal (grammatical) perspective, the condition 'prejudicial to [author's] honor or reputation' had been only set for the last moral right—the right of the author to object (unbecoming) usage of the work. Yet those two moral rights had been commonly observed as a one. See Radojković (1966), pp. 140–142; Janjić (1982), pp. 246–249.

rationale for this approach could be found in a literal (grammatical) interpretation of the provision of Article 17 of the LCRR. In this provision it is stated: the 'author shall have the exclusive right to protect the integrity of their work'.[34] No further conditions are imposed. This more protective approach and the consequent wider scope of the moral right of integrity, although diverge from the Berne Convention 'formula' (prejudice to the author's honor or reputation), are not uncommon among the Berne member countries.[35] Still, this approach is not without issues either. Its major downside is that it may easier (than the first approach) result in overprotection of the author's right of integrity. Such overprotection would be counter-productive (possibly absurd). It may unjustifiably impede and undermine legitimate third-party interests conflicted with the author's right of integrity and not only that. Its negative impact could also affect authors in general by unreasonably restricting their possibilities to use previously existing works for their future creations. All that seems to be wrong and non-purposeful.[36] To stop indicated negative scenario, in practice a great effort should be made (primarily by courts, but by authors too) to ensure that the right of integrity is applied reasonably. A possible abusive application of this right needs to be prevented. It should be required of authors to accept reasonable, good faith alterations of their works that are justified or necessitated.[37] The 'target' of the right of integrity should be limited to the unauthorized unreasonable alteration of the works (no matter for what approach is opted).

Which of the presented two approaches will be accepted is on the Serbian courts to decide.[38] It seems that courts have been leaning towards the second approach (see more below).

To summarize, from the aforesaid it is apparent that the object of protection of the moral right of integrity, in essence, are the author's personal interests related to the preservation of the integrity of his/her work. The question that remains open (to a

[34] Art. 17 of the LCRR.

[35] Salokannel et al. (2000), pp. 155–162; de Werra (2009), p. 269: '[. . .]such a protective approach could be legitimized by the fact that the moral right of integrity protects in fine the result of the creativity of the author in the exact way that this creativity was expressed, that is, the right of integrity makes sure that the work is and remains as the author has created it so that no one else shall have the right to change it in any manner irrespective of whether these changes improve or negatively impact on the author's honour or reputation.'; Sundara Rajan (2011), p. 74.

[36] de Werra (2009), p. 269.

[37] In Serbian law exists a general ban on the abuse of rights and it applies to the author's moral right as well. Art. 13 of the Law on Contract and Torts (LCT), Official Gazette of the SFR od Yugoslavia, Nos. 29/1978, 39/1985, 45/1989, 57/1989; final amendments Official Gazette of the Republic of Serbia, No. 18/2020. The unofficial translation of the text of the LCT (without amendments from 2003 and 2020) is available on https://www.mpravde.gov.rs/files/The%20Law%20of%20Contract%20and%20Torts_180411.pdf.

[38] Perhaps, the third 'middle ground' approach could also be implemented here. Under this approach, it would be left to courts to define more precisely the 'wider' object of the right of integrity, than prejudice to honor and reputation, on a case-by-case basis. Courts should settle certain standards over time. Still, it should be noted that case law is not a source of law in Serbia. Courts are not bound by the previous case law, yet they use it as guidelines in practice.

certain extent) is how broad the protection of the authors' personal interests should be. Whether the right of integrity should be applied beyond situations when alterations of the work are harmful to the author's honor or reputation or not? Anyhow, the protection should not go beyond the justified (reasonable) personal interest(s) of the author in each individual case. Oversensitivity of an author concerning the preservation of the integrity of his/her work should not be supported by the moral right of integrity.

2.2 *Substance of Protection of the Moral Right of Integrity*

The substance (content) of the moral right of integrity can be observed from two points of view. First, from the point of view of acts in relation to the work the author is authorized to undertake based on the right of integrity. Second, from the point of view of types of copyrighted works to which the right of integrity applies.

So, the first task here is to clarify: what acts in relation to the work the author may undertake by calling upon his/her right of integrity? In the LCRR (Article 17) it is stated broadly: 'author shall have the exclusive right to protect the integrity of their work'.[39] Additionally, three types of acts of protection of the work's integrity that the author may conduct are *exempli causa* enumerated in the LCRR. Those three are: (1) opposing the alteration of the work by unauthorized persons; (2) opposing the communication of the work to the public in an altered or incomplete form, taking into account the concrete technical form of communication of the work and good business practices, and (3) giving permission for adaptation of the work.[40] As it can be seen, the legislator leaves open the 'list' of possible acts the author can undertake towards others in order to protect the integrity of his/her work.[41] That seems like a reasonable solution, bearing in mind that the work's integrity could be affected—harmed in numerous ways.[42] The right of integrity, constructed in such a broad and instructive way in the LCRR, authorizes the author to object to a wide scope of acts of others, from the smallest alterations of the work, up to the destruction of the

---

[39] Art. 17 of the LCRR. One more clarification here would not be bad. As prof. Marković points out work is an intangible creation of an author and as itself, it does not have physical integrity. So, when spoken about the protection of the work's integrity, it does not mean the protection of its physical integrity. It means securing the work to stay the same/identical every time it is presented (manifested) in or communicated to the public. Marković (1999), p. 177.

[40] Art. 17 of the LCRR. It is beyond doubt that the fact that author has the exclusive right to protect the integrity of his/her work (negative aspect), consequently means that s/he has the exclusive right to change the integrity of the work (positive aspect of the right of integrity). Marković (1999), p. 176.

[41] Marković (1999), p. 176.

[42] Broadly speaking, it is possible to divide all acts which could result in detriment of the work's integrity into two general categories: (1) acts of inauthentic materialization of the work or physical alteration of the authentic specimen of the work (original or copy) and (2) acts of communication of the work to the public in an altered form. Marković (1999), p. 177; Miladinović (2009), p. 211.

work.[43] However, this broad definition of the right of integrity in the LCRR should not be interpreted (literally) in a way it gives the author absolute, unlimited power over the integrity of his/her work. That way of interpretation would be counter-productive—would result in overprotection. Instead, it should be interpreted by relying on the teleological method of interpretation (i.e. interpreting provisions in the light of the purpose, values, legal, social and economic goals they aim to achieve). If interpreted in that manner, it will be clear that the moral right of integrity has its limits. For instance, even though it is not precisely prescribed in the LCRR, the author cannot oppose the acts of the detriment of his/her work conducted in the private sphere of others. The right of integrity 'covers' only the acts of the detriment of work's integrity that take place or have effects in the public sphere.[44] The usage of the work in the private sphere stays out of its reach. The latter stems from the general fact that the focus of copyright protection is on the usage of works in the public sphere, and not in the private sphere.[45] Furthermore, the broadly defined substance of the right of integrity in the LCRR is limited by the object of protection of the said right—the protected personal interest of the author—as well (see above). Lastly, the author's right to protect the integrity of the work is often conflicted with the legitimate interests of others (or the community in general). Those other legitimate interests should be taken into consideration when interpreting and applying the provision of the LCRR on the moral right of integrity (see more below).

The second aspect in determining the substance of the right of integrity is to see to what types of copyrighted works the said right may be applied. The LCRR does not exclude certain types of works from the application of the right of integrity. In general, the right of integrity is granted to authors of all types of works (written, spoken, music, fine arts, films, etc.), no matter are they original or derivative works or what their forms are. Indeed, for some types of works, there are certain specific copyright limitations and exceptions that could exclude (or limit) the application of the right of integrity. But, those limitations and exceptions apply only in special situations defined by the LCRR.[46]

---

[43] Destruction of the work is not explicitly mentioned in the LCRR. Still, the common viewpoint in Serbia is that the right of integrity, under specific circumstances, would enable an author to oppose the destruction of his/her work in certain cases. Marković (1999), pp. 180–181; Miladinović (2009), p. 211; Radovanović (2004), p. 216, n. 71 (see comments on two court cases brought before Serbian courts in relation to the infringement of the right of integrity in the case of destruction of the work); Marić (2015); Vujičić (2018), pp. 217–218.

[44] Marković (1999), p. 177; Miladinović (2009), p. 211.

[45] Marković (1999), p. 177.

[46] The LCRR explicitly envisages various limitations that limit the scope of application of the right of integrity. They include suspensions of exclusive rights and right to remuneration: (1) if the work is used in the course of media reporting on the current events; (2) in the case of alteration of computer programs that are necessary to achieve its interoperability; (3) for the purpose of quotations; (4) for the purpose of parody; (5) in case of adaptation of the work for personal needs which is not intended and not available to the public, etc. See Art. 41–57 of the LCRR.

2.3 *Legitimate Conflicted Interests of Other Stakeholders as the Outer Limits of Protection of the Moral Right of Integrity*

After explaining the object and the substance of protection of the author's moral right of integrity, one of its specific characteristics should also be pointed out. This characteristic refers to the fact that application of the moral right of integrity may often conflict with the legitimate interests of other stakeholders.

There are various examples. For instance, in a situation in which the owner of a commercial building (a work of architecture protected by copyright) wants to modify it due to his legitimate business needs, s/he could find him/herself in a conflict with the author-architect. The architect could use his/her moral right of integrity to oppose the modifications of the building in a way planned by the owner. The question remains if the author should be allowed to do so? Here we have the conflict between the author's personal interests, on the one hand, and the right of property on the building, on the other one. Yet, the property right and the economic interests of the owners of the copyrighted works are not the only ones that could trigger the conflict here. If we stick to our example of the owner of a building, we could imagine that s/he needs to modify the building because of safety reasons or to meet certain statutory obligations and requirements, e.g. related to special planning, environmental protection, sectoral regulations, etc. Now we have the interests of the public at large at stake, as well. Of course, the conflict of the author who wants to exercise his/her right of integrity with the legitimate interests of other stakeholders is not reserved just for buildings and other works of architecture. It may raise concerning modifications and usage of other types of copyrighted works too. Advertising breaks made in the course of the broadcasting of cinematographic works could be considered as a violation of the right of integrity for example. In that case, the conflict between the authors' interests to protect the integrity of the cinematographic works and the legitimate economic interests of others linked to the broadcasting advertisement exists.

Another scenario includes the usage of photographs in different media for the purpose of reporting. To imbed photographs in the format in which they regularly publish content (e.g. black and white printed newspapers, limited spaces for photographs, etc.), media often have to slightly alter photographs (resize them, change their resolution, make them black-and-white, slightly crop them). An author may try to oppose this practice based on his/her moral right of integrity. Furthermore, the author's right of integrity can collide with the freedom of expression of others who are legitimately using the copyrighted work to express their thoughts, ideas, beliefs, and emotions. Overall, there a plethora of situations in which the application of the right of integrity may be conflicted with the legitimate interests of others.

These legitimate conflicted interests of other stakeholders limit the scope of protection of the moral right of integrity. Same way as the object of the protection of the moral right of integrity sets the 'inner boundaries' of the scope of the guaranteed protection, these legitimate conflicting interests of others set its 'outer boundaries (limits)'.[47] They determine where the protection should not go.

So, how they do that? The answer is: on the level of application of the right of integrity. When deciding on the protection of the moral right of integrity, the courts should ensure that this right is not exercised by authors in a way that unjustifiably impedes the legitimate conflicting interests of others.[48] To put it another way, the courts should ensure that this right is not exercised by authors in an excessive way. That exercise of it does not go too far. The principle of proportionality should be respected here. Therefore, the courts need to balance all the conflicting interests involved and to find a proper solution in each individual case. That is far from an easy task for courts. Deciding on the application of the right of integrity thus can be quite challenging.[49]

This requirement to take care of the legitimate interests of other stakeholders when deciding on the protection of the moral rights of integrity is to a certain extent acknowledged in the text of the LCRR. As mentioned, in the LCRR three examples of acts of protection of the work's integrity, which the author can conduct, are *exempli causa* enumerated. One of those acts reads: 'opposing the communication of the work to the public in an altered or incomplete form, taking into account the concrete technical form of communication of the work and good business practices'.[50] In this LCRR's formulation, it can clearly be seen that the author's right to oppose the communication of the work to the public in an altered or incomplete form is not without limits. The concrete technical form of communication of the work and good business practices (i.e. the legitimate interests of other stakeholders) should be always taken into consideration. This acknowledgment by the LCRR removes any doubt about the necessity of taking into account all involved interests when allowing the application of the moral rights of integrity. And, even though it is prescribed only for one of three *exempli causa* examples of acts of protection of the work's integrity

[47] Apart from these legitimate conflicting interests of others, the scope of the right of integrity is, as already noted, limited by the certain statutory limitations and exceptions explicitly prescribed in the LCRR. These form the 'outer limits' of the scope of the right of integrity as well, but only in specific cases. In contrast, the legitimate conflicted interests of other stakeholders have a more wide-reaching limiting effect on the scope of the right of integrity.

[48] Marković (1999), p. 177; de Werra (2009), pp. 281–283. The protection of certain interests of other stakeholders may even be more important for the general community's interests in some cases than the protection of the author's personal interest.

[49] *Ibid.*

[50] Art. 17, p. 2 of the LCRR.

in the LCRR, it seems as purposeful to apply it more broadly.[51] That is the predominant standpoint in the Serbian legal theory.[52]

3 Conditions for Application of the Moral Right of Integrity

Now after the analysis of the provision(s) of the LCRR on the moral right of integrity and remarking the correlated doctrinal—theoretical standpoints, the clearer picture of the subject right in Serbia is in front of us. Thus, we could try to give an answer to the question from the beginning: under what conditions is an author able to activate his/her right of integrity against others who modify his/her work?

Based on the aforesaid, it seems that for the activation of the right of integrity against others three conditions should be met. Those are the following three conditions: (1) the work altered without authorization should be disclosed (made available) to the public; (2) the author of the work should have justified (reasonable and acceptable) personal interest to oppose the alterations of the work, and (3) the author's interest to oppose the alterations of the work have to prevail over the involved legitimate interests of other stakeholders.[53]

These three conditions define the scope of the protection of the right of integrity in Serbia. They stem (directly or indirectly) from the LCRR and are supported by the legal doctrine. However, they need to be 'put into life' in practice primarily by courts. Hence, to better understand them, it might be useful to see how they are applied by the Serbian courts (or are they applied at all). What is the scope of the right of integrity in practice? For that reason, in the following lines, the emphasis will be on the appliance and interpretation of these conditions by the Serbian courts.[54]

---

[51] In the LCRR this requirement is also explicitly prescribed (as a limitation) in relation to the works of architecture. 'The author of the work of architecture cannot oppose to the alterations of their work if the need to make alterations came out of the circumstances involving safety risk or technical reasons.' Art. 38, para. 2; for more on this see Vujičić (2018), pp. 224–226. Additionally see statutory limitation of the economic right of adaptation of the work Art. 54a, p. 3 of the LCRR ('adaptation connected to the allowed use of the work, which is caused by the very nature or manner of use' is free).

[52] See, for instance, Marković (1999), p. 177; Radojković (1966), pp. 140–141; Janjić (1982), pp. 246–249.

[53] See Marković (1999), p. 177; Vujičić (2018), pp. 212–214. The three conditions could also be observed as the elements that constitute an infringement of the right of integrity. Additionally, it should be highlighted here, that the author in Serbia can prohibit not only the infringing acts but also the acts of others that represent a serious threat that his/her right could be infringed. This should be taken into consideration when applying the three indicated conditions. Art. 204a and 205 of the LCRR; Marković (1999), p. 179.

[54] All decisions cited in this paper are publically available in whole texts or excerpts on the websites of the courts, in the online legal databases, on the Internet or in the scholarly and professional literature. Quoted parts are translated from Serbian into English by the author of this paper.

3.1 *Unauthorized Alteration of the Work (Disclosed to the Public)*

This is the most obvious condition and the easiest one to determine in practice. It itself can be broken down into three components. First, the alteration of the work made by a third party should happen. Second, that alteration needs to be unauthorized. Third, the unauthorized alteration of the work needs to be disclosed (made available) to the public. So, these three components should be clarified here.

What alteration of the work could constitute the infringement of the moral right of integrity? The LCRR points that answer to this question should be wide-ranging to encompass from the smallest alterations of the work, up to the destruction of the work (see above). The courts in Serbia adhere to that course and interpret 'alterations' broadly. In that manner, the courts, for example, have held that the following alterations could constitute the infringement of the moral right of integrity: cropping of a photograph;[55] lowering the resolution of a photograph;[56] changing the color of a photograph;[57] converting color photographs to black and white photographs;[58] altering photograph while incorporating it in the video;[59] printing text over photograph;[60] printing text over drawings;[61] unauthentic reproduction of drawings;[62] altering and dividing contents of school textbooks;[63] making a collection of works

[55] Supreme Court of Cassation, Case No. Rev 1148/2018, Judgment of 26 February 2020; Case No. Rev 314/2017, Judgment of 1 November 2017; Case No. Rev 1824/2016, Judgment of 12 October 2017; Case No. Rev 932/2016, Judgment of 7 September 2017, all available on website of the Supreme Court of Cassation, https://www.vk.sud.rs/sr-lat/sudska-praksa—hereinafter referred as 'SCC website'; Court of Appeal in Belgrade, Case No. Gž4 159/17, Judgment of 19 October 2018; Case No. Gž4 87/17, Judgment of 30 August 2017; Case No. Gž4 26/16, Judgment of 14 March 2016, all available on website of the Court of Appeal in Belgrade, http://www.bg.ap.sud.rs/cr/—hereinafter referred as 'CAB website'; Higher Court in Belgrade, Case No. P4. 68/13, Judgment of 29 November 2013, available on website of the Journalists' Association of Serbia, https://www.uns.org.rs/sr/novinari-na-sudu/sudska-praksa/autorke.html.

[56] Court of Appeal in Belgrade, Case No. Gž4 181/16, Judgment of 19 October 2016, CAB website.

[57] Supreme Court of Cassation, Case No. Rev 1551/2019, Decision of 19 September 2019, SCC website.

[58] Court of Appeal in Belgrade, Case No. Gž4 66/19, Judgment of 17 July 2019, Paragraf Lex.

[59] Court of Appeal in Belgrade, Case No. Gž4 26/16, Judgment of 14 March 2016, CAB website.

[60] Supreme Court of Cassation, Case No. Rev 1148/2018, Judgment of 26 February 2020; Case No. Rev 1551/2019, Decision of 19 September 2019, SCC website.

[61] Supreme Court of Serbia, Case No. Gž 28/05, Judgment of 7 July 2005, SCC website;

[62] Supreme Court of Serbia, Case No. Gž 111/05, Judgment of 29 December 2005, SCC website.

[63] Court of Appeal in Belgrade, Case No. Gž4 161/17, Judgment of 9 February 2018, CAB website.

from parts and quotations of the works of one author;[64] adaptation of ballet;[65] adaptation of a novel to film;[66] destruction of mosaic built into a wall.[67]

Furthermore, the right of integrity can only be used against unauthorized alterations of the work made by others. Using it against authorized alterations would be contrary to the *bona fide* principle, and generally non-purposeful. Consequently, the question at this point is: when a third party will be authorized to freely alter the copyrighted work (to change its integrity)? First of all, the third party can be authorized to change the work based on an author's permission, explicit or implicit. The author's right of integrity (same as other moral rights), is not transferable by contract, nor can be subject to waivers in the Serbian legal system.[68] Still, the author can give permission to others to make alterations to the work (or to decide about alterations). This permission does not have a nature of a contract on transfer of the right, nor a waiver though.[69] When this permission is explicit, we have the simplest case.

On the other hand, it will be more challenging to determine the existence and especially the scope of implicit permission. A typical situation in which it could be considered that the author has given his/her implicit permission for the change of the work's integrity would be a case of authorizing a third-party to commercially use the work—to make reproductions of the work, to adapt it, to communicate it to the public, etc. Sometimes, certain types of commercial usage require alterations of the work, for instance, because of technical reasons, applied business practices, and other legitimate reasons (e.g. advertising breaks made in the course of the broadcasting of cinematographic work; changes of the original text in its translation). When allowing those types of commercial usage, the author is aware (at least should be) that his/her work will be altered. The LCRR explicitly acknowledges these situations by envisaging that the license 'of a right to exploit a work shall also mean the permit for making such changes in the work that are technically inevitable or usual for such exploitation of the work.'[70] Of course, this implicit permission is not absolute. It covers only reasonable, common alterations of the work.[71] Moreover, the third party may legally alter the work when using it based on the copyright limitations and exceptions prescribed in the LCRR, as well. In this case, even though there is no author's permission (neither explicit, nor implicit), the Law authorizes the

[64] Supreme Court of Cassation, Case No. Rev 2676/2010, Judgment of 30 June 2010, SCC website.

[65] Supreme Court of Serbia, Case No. Gž. 244/72, Judgment of 29 July 1973, quoted in Milić (2011), pp. 90–91.

[66] Supreme Court of Serbia, Case No. Gž 58/05, Decision of 23 June 2005, SCC website (note: the court here had not determined the infringement, but implicitly recognized that it is possible).

[67] Supreme Court of Serbia, Case No. Gž. 108/96, Judgment of 29 January 1997, quoted in Radovanović (2004), p. 216, f. 71.

[68] See above footnote No. 15.

[69] This permission usually should be given before the altering the work, but also the author can agree with alterations subsequently. Marković (1999), p. 177.

[70] Art. 68, para. 4 of the LCRR.

[71] For more, see Marković (1999), p. 178.

third party to use the author's work, and alter it (change its integrity) to a certain extent, if that is necessary or common for the specific type of usages covered by the copyright limitations and exceptions.[72]

Last but not least, the author will be able to effectively use the right of integrity to oppose the unauthorized alteration of his/her work only if it has been disclosed (made available) to the public. The general rule is that usage (including alteration) of works by third parties in their private sphere typically is not the concern of copyright protection.[73] The same case is with the moral right of integrity. On a regular basis, a dispute between an author and a person who has altered the work without his/her consent arises after the altered work is disclosed (made available) to the public.

3.2 Justified Personal Interest of the Author to Oppose the Alterations of the Work

The author should have justified (reasonable and acceptable) personal interest(s) to be able to oppose the alterations of his/her work based on the right of integrity. This condition derives from the object of protection of the moral right of integrity. As explained above, the object of protection of the right of integrity is not the integrity of the work itself, but the author's personal interests related to the preservation of the work's integrity. Yet, that protection is not absolute, it should not go beyond the justified personal interests of the author in each individual case. Oversensitivity of the author concerning the preservation of the integrity of his/her work should not be protected here.

It is hard to give a straight-forward answer (at least from the case law available to the author of this paper) to the question, how is this condition perceived (or is it at all) by the Serbian courts?

The main reason for that is that in the LCRR it is not explicitly prescribed that the objective of the moral right of integrity is to protect authors' personal interests. The LCRR says just that '[a]ny author shall have the exclusive right to protect the integrity of their work'. Moreover, the question, how broad the protection of the authors' personal interests should be remains open. Should the right of integrity be applied only in situations when alterations of the work are harmful to the author's honor or reputation (as certain legal scholars suggest)? Or, the protection should go beyond that, and cover the subjective bond of the author with the integrity of his/her work in general (which stems from the literal interpretation of the LCRR's provision)? Indicted is reflected in the decisions of Serbian courts.

[72] Marković (1999), pp. 178–179.

[73] The LCRR even envisages the copyright limitation that confirms this general rule: 'Free adaptation of the disclosed work of authorship is allowed when it concerns [...] adaptation of work for personal needs which is not intended and not available to the public.' Art. 54a, p. 2 of the LCRR.

It could be said that the Serbian courts tend to interpret the provision(s) of the LCRR on the right of integrity literary (grammatically). As a consequence, in certain cases for courts, it has been enough that an unauthorized act of alteration of the work had happened to determine the violation of the moral right of integrity (especially if it a result of unauthorized usage of the work). In that context, in one decision of the Court of Appeal in Belgrade, the following reasoning can be found: 'As the defendant, without the author's permission and without paying remuneration, reproduced and communicated to the public the work of the author, the photograph "_", on the two web pages, [. . .] and as he communicated the work to the public in an incomplete form, by cutting (cropping) the photograph from all sides by 1/5 of its size, and as he communicated the photograph to the public in an altered form by visibly altering it and integrating it into the video, the Court of Appeal finds that the court of the first instance had correctly and completely established facts, correctly applied the substantive law, namely the provisions of [. . .] Article 17 [provision on the right of integrity] when it had found that the defendant infringed the copyright of the plaintiff [. . .]'.[74] In the other decision, the same court similarly decided that the court of the first instance had properly determined the infringement of the right of integrity '[. . .] having in mind the fact that the defendant communicated to the public the photograph in an altered form compared to the original, since the photograph which was published on the internet page had been cut out (so that the entire feet of [. . .] cannot be seen), and in the printed edition had been cut out to a slight extent [. . .]'.[75] In the same manner, the Supreme Court of Cassation concludes: 'In the concrete case, the defendant published, without the permission of the plaintiff, as the author, the said photographs, in incomplete form, i.e. with their significant cropping on all sides [. . .], so the courts had rightfully found that in this way the moral right of the plaintiff, protected by [. . .] Article 17, item 2 [. . .] of the Law on Copyright and Related Rights had been infringed [. . .]'.[76]

In some other cases, the courts pointed out that more than just altering the work is necessary for the infringement of the right of integrity. For instance, in one of its decisions the Court of Appeal in Belgrade came to the following conclusion: '[. . .] the court of the first instance failed to determine with certainty whether the cropping down of the plaintiff's photograph resulted in infringement of the integrity of his work, as an original creation of his spirit, [. . .] which implies [. . .] that the wholeness of his work had been harmed in the contexts of the originality of his author's notion, which then led to the mutilation of the said work, and in relation to that fact the evidence in a form of expertise of the expert witness of the appropriate profession should have been presented, whereas the court does not have the expert knowledge

[74] Court of Appeal in Belgrade, Case No. Gž4 26/16, Judgment of 14 March 2016, CAB website.

[75] Court of Appeal in Belgrade, Case No. Gž. 7960/2013, Decision of 29 January 2014, Paragraf Lex.

[76] Supreme Court of Cassation, Case No. Rev 314/2017, Judgment of 1 November 2017, Paragraf Lex.

to determine that fact'.[77] It seems the court insinuated here that the originality of the work should be affected by alterations. Otherwise, there will not be an infringement of the right of integrity.[78] Also, in another case, the Court of Appeal in Belgrade determined that the infringement of the right of integrity had occurred, considering that alterations made to a photograph affected its essence, as well as the impression it leaves on viewers.[79]

Bearing in mind the indicated courts' reasoning, two things could be concluded. First, as it can be seen, the courts, for the appliance of the right of integrity, generally do not demand that alterations made to the work need to be prejudicial to the author's honor or reputation.[80] It seems, that the courts are on the standpoint that the right of integrity should provide broader protection, not limited solely to the alterations prejudicial to the author's honor or reputation. That it should protect the subjective bond of the author with the integrity of the work, as the 'spiritual expression of the author's personality',[81] in general. Second, even though the courts maybe do not recognize the condition analyzed here—'the existence of the justified author's personal interest to oppose the alterations of the work'—as a separate condition for the appliance of the right of integrity, it does not mean that they do not evaluate the justification (reasonableness) of the author's hindered personal interests in each individual case. They are doing that, at least, when they are assessing the degree of alteration(s) of the work made by a third party (which is a typical course of action in this type of case).

However, the high importance of evaluating the reasonableness of hindered author's personal interests, regarding the right of integrity, in each individual case is undeniable. It ought to ensure that the protection of the right of integrity stays in its course, that it remains purposeful and justified. Hence, the criteria for the said evaluation should be further developed in the practice of the Serbian courts. Those criteria for evaluation should include the level of work's originality, the degree of

[77] Court of Appeal in Belgrade, Case No. Gž4 940/2014, Decision of 22 April 2014, Paragraf Lex.

[78] For similar reasoning see Supreme Court of Serbia, Case No. Gž 58/05, Decision of 23 June 2005, SCC website.

[79] Court of Appeal in Belgrade, Case No. Gž4 26/2018, Judgment of 4 May 2018, Paragraf Lex.

[80] As an exception, we could mention the reasoning in the one decision of the Supreme Court of Serbia: 'Henceforth, the Supreme Court also considers that plaintiffs are authorized to file the subject lawsuit, because copyright is inheritable based on the law, and by the death of the author, his economic rights and [the taking care of] moral rights pass to the heirs (natural guardians of the memory on the deceased author and his moral interests) who can than oppose the deformation and use of the work if it results in a detriment of the author's honor and reputation, which derives from the author's right to protect the integrity of his work.' Supreme Court of Serbia, Case No. Gž. 111/05, Judgment of 29 December 2005, SCC website. See also Federal Court, Case No. Gzs. 125/90, Decision of 28 February 1991, Radovanović (2004), p. 216, f. 71.

[81] Court of Appeal in Belgrade, Case No. Gž4 161/17, Judgment of 9 February 2018, CAB website.

alteration(s) of the work, the irreversibility of made alterations,[82] the nature of work, the conditions of creation of the work, the types of use of the work, etc.[83]

Lastly, it should be noted that the courts normally in the same procedure (based on the same establishment of facts) adjudicate on the infringement of the moral right of integrity and also on pecuniary compensation for non-material damages to the author, resulting from the subject infringement. Concerning the latter, the general rules on the pecuniary compensation of non-material damages are applied.[84] Thus, the author will have the right to pecuniary compensation for the non-material damages only if proved that, as a result of the infringement of the right of integrity, s/he suffered mental anguish due to offended reputation, honor, or rights of personality.[85] In other words, the author needs to prove a high level of harm to his/her personal interests to get pecuniary compensation. Hence, these rules on pecuniary compensation for non-material damages can and should serve as an additional safeguard against the overprotection of the moral right of integrity.

3.3 Prevailing Personal Interest of the Author Over the Other Involved Legitimate Interests

Not only should the author have justified personal interest to be enabled to object to alterations of his/her work based on the right of integrity, but his/her interest should be prevailing over the other involved legitimate interests in the concrete case. This condition is an amplification of the previous one, but it does not derive from the object of protection of the analyzed right. Instead, it comes from the 'outside'. It should ensure that if there are other specific legitimate interests in conflict with the protected author's personal interests, the protection should be provided to the prevailing ones, to the ones which are of the greater importance for the society (and its functioning).

---

[82] Marković (1999), p. 180.

[83] de Werra (2009), p. 283.

[84] See Art. 200–205 of the LCT.

[85] See Court of Appeal in Belgrade, Case No. Gž. 227/2013, Judgment of 16 April 2014, Paragraf Lex (the author does not have the right to the pecuniary compensation for non-material damages in every case of the infringement of his/her moral right. S/he will be entitled to compensation only if proves that s/he had suffered mental anguish due to the infringement of the moral right.). The issue of pecuniary compensation for non-material damages in case of the infringement of the moral right is the subject of many debates in Serbia. For more about this topic see: Marković (1999), pp. 374–375; Dudaš (2006), pp. 280–286; Popesku (2016), 398–402; Milić Law Office, Subjektivna autorska prava – pojam, zaštita i ostvarivanje (Copyright – definition, protection and exercise), https://www.milic.rs/autorsko-pravo/.

As noted, this condition is recognized clearly (to a certain extent) in the LCRR (Article 17, point 2),[86] and as such has been applied by courts. An example is the decision of the Court of Appeal in Belgrade concerning the unauthorized publishing of the plaintiff's photograph on the website by the defendant, a media company. The defendant used specific software—application for posting photographs on his website which functioned in that way that it automatically would crop all photographs to a certain format. That had happened with the plaintiff's photograph as well. It had been automatically cropped in course of the process of posting on the website. The defendant brought up this argument and claimed that there had not been technical conditions for posting the plaintiff's photograph on the website as a whole. The court, however, did not accept this argument. 'Referring to Article 17, point 2 of the Law on Copyright and Related Rights and pointing out that, [. . .] the computer application for internet editions of "_" automatically crops (cuts) the photographs, so that there were no technical conditions for the defendant to communicate the photograph in a full form, and that the essence of the photograph is not impeded, nor its artistic dimension, because the plaintiff marked the photograph as "[. . .] with the raised hand", is also without influence on a different decision in this legal matter. This because, according to the findings of the court of the second instance, the essence of the subject plaintiff's photograph, and thus the impression it leaves on the observer, is not only in the natural person in the photograph ([. . .] with raised hand), but in the natural person in front or next to the historic building with a raised hand or a hand pointing towards that building, as a whole.'[87] And the building was cut from the photograph by the defendant. The court here insisted on the preservation of the essence of the subject photograph, and the impression it leaves on the observer. Nevertheless, it should be noted that the photograph, in this case, had been published without the author's consent. So, the legitimate interests of the defendant related to the technical constraints are questionable here. The author could argue, that he had not wanted to give consent for publishing to the defendant particularly having in mind the said technical constraints for publication of the photograph.

Another illustrative example includes a case brought before the Court of Appeal in Belgrade. This time a dispute arose between a media company, as the defendant, and its former employee (professional photographer), as the plaintiff. The facts of the case are the following. The defendant had published in his newspaper two altered photographs taken by his former employee. Both were the photograph of the director of the media company and were taken while the plaintiff was a defendant's employee. So the defendant was a holder of economic copyrights on two photographs and had exclusive right to communicate them to the public (even though the plaintiff disputed that). The problem arose when the defendant published those photographs in altered/incomplete form. The first one was cut in a way the room

[86] 'Opposing the communication of the work to the public in an altered or incomplete form, taking into account the concrete technical form of communication of the work and good business practices' (the wording of the limiting condition was introduced by the 2004 LCRR).

[87] Court of Appeal in Belgrade, Case No. Gž4 26/2018, Judgment of 4 May 2018, Paragraf Lex.

in which the photograph had been taken, as well as the director's trousers, were not visible. The second one was cropped and the text was written over it. Considering that the defendant was authorized to publish these photographs in its newspaper and that publishing of photographs in the newspapers sometimes requires them to be altered to a certain extent (it is in line with regular business practices), it would not be unreasonable for the court to decide in favor of the defendant. Nonetheless, here it was not the case. The court concluded that the defendant infringed the moral right of integrity by publishing the photographs 'in an incomplete form, i.e. altered, cut to a greater extent, because the space in which the photographed person [. . .] was located is not visible [. . .]'.[88] Is this conclusion justifiable? Both sides can be argued. Anyway, this shows how thin of a line it is between the infringement and the legitimate action in the case when a third party alters the copyrighted work.

Additionally, one more case should be mentioned here. It was from the period when this limiting condition ('taking into account the concrete technical form of communication of the work and good business practices') was not explicitly prescribed by the LCRR. In this case, the Higher Court in Podgorica and the Supreme Court of Montenegro dealt (based on the 1998 LCRR) with the permissibility of alteration of the public school building, as a work of architecture. The dispute arose between the heirs of the deceased author of the award-winning architectural project of the public school and its owner and constructor because two additional floors were built on top of the preexisting school building without the consent from the heirs of the original author. As the author's heirs claimed, the said alterations of the school building deviated from the author's original work and were prejudicial to his honor. Yet, both courts of the first and second instance adjudicated that in this case, the infringement of the right of integrity had not occurred, taking into account other involved legitimate interests that prevail.[89] The Supreme Court of Montenegro was on the following standpoint: 'The interests of the community often lead to a conflict of interest between the owner of the building, as an architectural work, and the author, in which case the author cannot oppose alterations or destruction of the building if the owner is forced to take such a step due to his business interests or mandatory public law regulations. The said means that the change of purpose of the building, its modernization, etc. represent valid reasons based on which the owner can alter the building and even demolish it, without infringing the author's moral right to protect the integrity of the work.'[90] Even though now in the LCRR we have explicitly prescribed limitation of the right of integrity in relation to the legitimate alterations of the work of architecture,[91] this 'older' court decision is still valuable. It

[88] Court of Appeal in Belgrade, Case No. Gž4 159/17, Judgment of 19 October 2018, CAB website. See also: Supreme Court of Serbia, Case No. Gž 28/05, Judgment of 7 July 2005, SCC website.

[89] Milić (2003), pp. 1007–1014.

[90] Supreme Court of Montenegro, Case No. Gž. 7/2002, Judgment of 19 November 2002, quoted in Milić (2003), pp. 1012–1013. It seems that the court had relied on the opinion of prof. Marković. Compare Marković (1999), p. 181.

[91] Article 38, para. 2 of the LCRR.

can serve as an example. It shows us that courts should assess whether the author's interests are prevailing over the other involved legitimate interests in each individual case of the alleged infringement of the right of integrity, even though it is not explicitly stated in the LCRR. The objective here should be to try to achieve a reasonable and acceptable balance of conflicting interests linked to the integrity of the work in each case of the alteration of the work.[92] Same as with determining the fulfillment of the previous condition (existence of justified personal interest of the author to oppose the alterations of the work), the latter is far from an easy task for courts and maybe even too burdensome, but it is necessary.

4 Concluding Remarks

The subject of this paper was the analysis of the scope of the moral right of integrity guaranteed to the authors in Serbian copyright law. The focus was on the negative aspect of the moral right of integrity (the author's right to object to certain modifications of his/her work by others). The positive aspect of the analyzed right (author's exclusive right to modify the work by him/herself) was set aside because it seemed like a clear-cut case. The analysis was conducted in two steps. Firstly, an investigative insight into the provision(s) of the LCRR, by which the author's moral right of integrity is guaranteed in Serbia, was made (with general remarks on the understanding of the moral right of integrity in the legal doctrine). Secondly, the standard conditions for activation of the right of integrity against third parties are determined and analyzed through the prism of the case law in Serbia. Those conditions define the potential scope of the protection secured to authors by the moral right of integrity in Serbia. From the analysis, the following conclusions may be drawn:

(a) The LCRR (Article 17) contains the broadly defined, instructive provision on the moral right of integrity which leaves space for flexible interpretations. While such flexibility for interpretation of the moral right of integrity is desirable, considering that the work's integrity could be affected—harmed in numerous ways, it should not be taken for granted. The subject provision of the LCRR should be interpreted so that the right of integrity achieves its objective, its purpose. The objective of the right of integrity is the protection of the justified author's personal interests related to the preservation of the work's integrity. Still, that protection should not go too far and unreasonably impede the involved legitimate interests of other stakeholders. Therefore, the provision of the LCRR

[92] In this context see the Strategy for the Development of the Media (Public Informing) System in the Republic of Serbia for the period 2020–2025 developed under the auspices of the Ministry of culture https://www.kultura.gov.rs/tekst/sr/4993/strategija-razvoja-sistema-javnog-informisanja-u-republici-srbiji-za-period-od-2020-do-2025.php. The authors of the Strategy express concern over the extensive copyright protection of photographs by courts which could affect the general interests for better media coverage.

(Article 17) on the moral right of integrity should not be interpreted by relying strictly on a literal (grammatical) method of interpretation, because it can result in overprotection (or maybe even in under protection). A teleological method of interpretation seems like the most suitable for this provision of the LCRR. This method, however, requires interpreters to have a deeper doctrinal—theoretical knowledge and understanding of copyright law and its concepts.

(b) The burden of complicated interpretation and application of the right of integrity is on the courts in Serbia. Based on the instructive provision of the LCRR they need to evaluate whether the application of the right of integrity is justifiable in each individual case of altering the copyrighted work by a third party. That is a challenging task. In this paper, a list of the standard three conditions for the application of the right of integrity against third parties is proposed. Under this list for activation of the right of integrity it is necessary that: (1) the work altered without authorization has been disclosed (made available) to the public; (2) the author of the work has justified personal interest to oppose the alterations of the work, and (3) the author's interest to oppose the alterations of the work prevail over the involved legitimate interests of other stakeholders. Nevertheless, those three conditions are also instructive, especially the last two. They are more like guidelines, than precisely defined conditions. Many questions stay open. To those questions, it cannot be answered with precision on a general level. Instead, they need to be addressed taking into consideration the specific circumstances of each individual case. Some of those questions are: (1) when the protected author's personal interest will be considered as justified; (2) which of the involved interests linked to the integrity of the work will prevail, etc. Only indications for answering these questions could be given (see above).

(c) Finally, let us go back to our first question—the scope of the moral right of integrity in Serbia? As pointed out, the LCRR leaves open the question of the potential scope of the right of integrity and threw this curveball to the courts. We should not be surprised with this 'situation', considering that the provision of the LCRR needs to be broad enough to be applicable in the different circumstances of various cases in which the works' integrity should be protected. Given that the LCRR does not say too much, when determining the scope of protection of the right of integrity the courts in Serbia should rely on boundaries set by the inherent characteristic and the nature of this right. Thus, the object of protection—the justified author's personal interests related to the preservation of the work's integrity—defines its inner boundaries. And the conflicting legitimate interests of other involved stakeholders represent its outer boundaries. As shown in the analysis, the courts have recognized to a certain extent those boundaries in their practice. Yet, it can be argued that the Serbian courts should pay (even) more attention to the assessment of the justifiability of the author's personal interest to oppose the alterations of his/her work and the prevalence of those interests over the other involved legitimate interests when adjudicating on the infringement of the right of integrity. For instance, in recent years we have frequent cases in which courts confirmed that publishing cropped photograph (s) in the newspapers or on websites represents the infringement of the moral right of integrity. Is that practice good? Does every case of publishing cropped photograph in the newspapers or on websites represent the infringement of the moral right of integrity? We are not so sure. As noted a few times throughout the paper, the courts are those who should ensure that the moral right of integrity is applied in a reasonable and acceptable manner (of course the authors can also contribute to that). The moral right of integrity is undeniably one of the most important moral rights of the author. Its protection is valuable not solely for the authors, but the whole community. However, that premise stands valid, only if the right of integrity is applied in a reasonable (non-excessive) way, so that all involved interests of various stakeholders are taken into consideration in each individual case. It should be strived to achieve a balance between them. In that way, the author's moral right of integrity will be perceived and accepted as a legitimate right (legal instrument) by all involved stakeholders—the community. And the legitimate rights are those rights that have a bright future ahead of them.

References

Aplin TF, Mohamed AS (2019) The concept of 'reputation' in the moral right of integrity. J Intell Prop Law Pract 14(4):268–277. https://doi.org/10.1093/jiplp/jpz004

de Werra J (2009) The moral right of integrity. In: Derclaye E (ed) Research handbook on the future of EU copyright. Edward Elgar, Cheltenham, pp 267–285

Dudaš A (2006) Naknada štete zbog povrede ličnih prava autora (Civil Actions for the Protection of Author's Moral Rights). Zbornik radova Pravnog fakulteta u Novom Sadu 2:263–288

Goldstein P, Hugenholtz PB (2010) International copyright: principles, law and practice, 2nd edn. Oxford University Press, New York

Hansmann H, Santilli M (1997) Authors' and Artists' moral rights: a comparative legal and economic analysis. J Legal Stud 26(1):95–143. https://doi.org/10.1086/467990

Janjić M (1982) Industrijska svojina i autorsko pravo (Industrial Property and Copyright), 2nd edn. Službeni list, Belgrade

Marić V (2015) Stručni komentar: Zaštita integriteta autorskog dela (Expert Comment: Protection of the Integrity of the Copyrighted Work). Pravni instruktor 87. Available via Paragraf Lex database. https://www.paragraf.rs/

Marković SM (1999) Autorsko pravo i srodna prava (Copyright and Related Rights). Službeni glasnik, Belgrade

Marković SM, Popović DV (2020) Pravo intelektualne svojine (Intellectual Property Law), 8ed edn. University of Belgrade Faculty of Law, Belgrade

Miladinović Z (2009) Pravo intelektualne svojine (Intellectual Property Law). University of Kragujevac Faculty of Law, Kragujevac

Milić D (2003) Prerada primerka dela arhitekture – jedna sudska presuda (Redesign of Pieces of Architecture: A Judgment of the Court). Pravni život 11:1007–1014

Milić D (2007) Moralna prava autora (Moral Rights of an Author). Pravni život 13:269–283

Milić D (2010) Autorska moralna prava autora i interpretatora i njihova krivičnopravna zaštita (Author's and performer's moral rights and their criminal law protection). Pravni život 11:883–891

Milić PD (2011) Komentar Zakona o autorskom i srodnim pravima (sa sudskom praksom) (Commentary of the Law on Copyright and Related Rights (with Case Law)). Građevinska knjiga doo, Belgrade

Ong B (2003) Why Moral Rights matter: recognizing the intrinsic value of integrity rights. Columbia J Law Arts 26(3/4):297–312

Popesku D (2016) Fotografija kao autorsko delo (Photography as a Work of Authorship). Pravo i privreda 7–9:390–403

Popović D (2016) International Encyclopaedia of laws for intellectual property law: Serbia. Kluwer Law International

Radojković Ž (1964) Lična prva i njihov odnos ličnopravnim (moralnim) elementima autorskog prava (Personal Rights and Their Relation with Personal (Moral) Elements of Copyrights). Anali Pravnog fakulteta u Beogradu 12(2–3):263–279

Radojković Ž (1966) Ličnopravni (moralni) elementi autorskog prava (Personal (Moral) Elements of Author's Rights). Savez udruženja pravnika Jugoslavije, Belgrade

Radovanović S (2004) Autorsko pravo nakon smrti autora (Copyrights Upon the Author's Death). Zbornik radova Pravnog fakulteta u Novom Sadu 2:201–224

Salokannel M, Strowel A, Derclaye E (2000) Study Contract Concerning Moral Rights in the Context of the Exploitation of Works through Digital Technology. Report to the European Commission's Internal Market Directorate-General, No ETD/99/B5-3000/E° 28 April, 2000

Sundara Rajan MT (2011) Moral rights: principles, practice and new technology. Oxford University Press, New York

Treiger-Bar-Am LK (2005) The moral right of integrity: a freedom of expression. In: Macmillan F (ed) New directions in copyright, vol 2. Edward Elgar, Cheltenham/Northampton, pp 127–158

Vasić A (2015) Pravo naslednika po osnovu moralnih ovlašćenja autora (Heirs' Rights Based on Author's Moral Rights). In: Stojanovic N, Krstic N (eds) Dvadeset godina Zakona o nasleđivanju Republike Srbije (Twenty Years of the Law on Inheritance of the Republic of Serbia). University of Niš Faculty of Law, Niš, pp 53–64

Vujičić N (2018) O preradi primerka autorskog dela arhitekture (On Modification of a Copy of Copyrighted Work of Architecture). In. Vasić R, Čučković B (eds) Identitetski preobražaj Srbije: prilozi projektu 2017 – kolektivna monografija (Identity Transformation of Serbian Law – 2017). University of Belgrade Faculty of Law, Belgrade, pp 209–228

Žarković B (1998) Reforma jugoslovenskog autorskog prava (Reform of Yugoslav Copyright Law). In: Žarković B (ed) Zakon o autorskom i srodnim pravima (Law on Copyright and Related Rights). Federal Intellectual Property Office, Belgrade, pp 5–26

Part II
European Law

Customers Protection in Insurance Distribution Directive: An Overview on Harmonization of Legislation in Bosnia and Herzegovina

Jasmina Đokić

Contents

1 Introduction

The policy of strengthening consumer protection on the insurance market is implemented over the recent years in the European Union. With desire to achieve the equal protection of all insurance customers, regardless of the type of distributor from which they obtained insurance products, EU legislator enacted the Insurance Distribution Directive in 2016. Basically, its intention was simplifying,

J. Đokić (✉)
Adriatic Insurance Ltd., International Claims Department, Sarajevo, Bosnia and Herzegovina
e-mail: jasmina.djokic@adriatic.ba

D. V. Popović et al. (eds.), *Balkan Yearbook of European and International Law 2021*, Balkan Yearbook of European and International Law 2021,
https://doi.org/10.1007/978-3-030-97431-2_6

consolidating, and expanding customer protections, focusing on the area of the disclosure of information to customers. With some exclusion, it applies to almost all persons whose activity consists of providing insurance or reinsurance distribution services to the customers. Although the Insurance Distribution Directive has brought some great novelties in statutory and supervisory provisions, in this article special attention is given to the provisions about information duties towards customers and the professional and organizational requirements stipulated for insurance distributors.

By signing the Stabilisation and Association Agreement, Bosnia and Herzegovina expressed its intention to become a country candidate for EU enlargement and willingness to make its legislation compatible with the Community *acquis*. Like other civil law branches, proposing and enacting of the insurance legislation is in the exclusive competence of the territorial units—entities: Federation of Bosnia and Herzegovina and Republic of Srpska. Process of harmonization is not uniform in the entities, and it sometimes produces unequal treatment of the customers, depending on the entity where the insurance contract is concluded. In this article, there will be shown an overview of harmonization of the respective insurance legislation in Bosnia and Herzegovina with the mentioned Insurance Distribution Directive.

2 Insurance Distribution in European Union: Definition and Background

The purpose of insurance is to reduce uncertainty and make accidental loss manageable by substituting payment of an insurance premium to a professional insurer in exchange for the assumption of the risk a large loss, and a promise to pay in the event of such a loss.

By adopting the principles of liberalization, with intention of enforcing the Single Market, in last decades of twentieth century some changes have been made about regulation of insurance selling and state control over the insurance products. By the third generation of Life and Non-life Insurance Directives,[1] the state regulation and *ex ante* approval of insurance terms and conditions as well as premium tariffs was abandoned, and the new regime of control over the insurance selling was adopted. For that purpose, there have been introduced the new protective mechanisms in form of provisions that allowed the insurance customers to make an informed decision

[1] See Council Directive 92/96/EEC of 10 November 1992 on the coordination of laws, regulations and administrative provisions relating to direct life assurance and amending Directives 79/267/EEC and 90/619/EEC (third life assurance Directive), OJ L 360, 9.12.1992, p. 1–27; and Council Directive 92/49/EEC of 18 June 1992 on the coordination of laws, regulations and administrative provisions relating to direct insurance other than life assurance and amending Directives 73/239/EEC and 88/357/EEC (third non-life insurance Directive), OJ L 228, 11/08/1992 pp. 1–23.

about insurance product and scope of cover.[2] The Third Non-Life Directive introduced just the duty to inform the customer about the applicable law and the redress procedure, and the Third Life Insurance Directive had a more detailed approach concerning the information disclosure duties. Namely, since the life insurance contract is more complex and characterized as a long-term one, this Directive enacted provisions about pre-contractual information duties as well as the duties to inform the customer during the period of insurance.[3]

In this period, one of Community legislations that also regulated the sale of insurance products was Insurance Mediation Directive (hereinafter: IMD) from 2002[4] that covered the activities of intermediaries, i.e. insurance agents and brokers. According to the IMD, intermediaries had duties to inform the prospective customers about their status and their relationship with insurer, as well as to give them advices on basis of a fair and detailed market analysis. As we see, the IMD introduced some provisions about duties to advise but this duty was not precisely explained. Besides, the IMD did not contain the provisions regarding the remuneration that the intermediary has the right to. Having in mind that the IMD was a minimum harmonization directive, it was also noticed that quality of protection that has been provided to the customers might vary from one member state to another, and that it largely depends on their national rules.[5]

3 Insurance Distribution Directive

The financial crisis of 2007–2010 directly triggered taking radical steps towards improving consumer position on the financial markets in general because it called into question an old belief in rationality of financial institutions.[6] The insurance sector was also affected by the crisis and it reflected to the rights of the policyholders. In order to amend the shortcomings of the IMD and with aim to improve the insurance market by strengthening the consumers protection, EU legislator adopted a new Insurance Distribution Directive (hereinafter: IDD)[7] as a new regulatory framework that applies on insurance companies (insurance undertakings) directly as well as the other businesses that sell insurance. The IDD entered into force in February 2016, and the implementation date was postponed to 1st July 2018.

---

[2] Filipović (2018), p. 27.

[3] Slavnić and Jovanović (2008), p. 30.

[4] See Directive 2002/92/EC of the European Parliament and of the Council of 9 December 2002 on insurance mediation, OJ L 9, 15.1.2003, pp. 3–10.

[5] Ivančević (2013), p. 239.

[6] Ostrowska (2021), p. 37.

[7] See Directive (EU) 2016/97 of the European Parliament and of the Council of 20 January 2016 on insurance distribution, OJ L 26, 2.2.2016, pp. 19–59.

The IDD was not designed to ensure the maximum harmonization of national legislation, but to provide a minimum basic legislative framework, while individual Member States remain free to maintain or adopt more strict provisions in order to protect consumers, should the specific national context justify such.[8]

The single market for insurance distribution was very limited by the IMD, and one of main objectives of the new Directive was to ensure at least minimum cross border standard to selling of insurance products.[9] Some improvements for that purpose were introduced by the IDD such as a real simplification and clarification of the FOS and FOE notification procedures.[10] Nevertheless, some authors expressed scepticism about expansion of cross border provision of services because diversity of national insurance contract laws among EU member states discourages such services.[11] Since the IDD was implemented in national legislations in late 2018, it is too early for assess the impact of new provisions on cross-border activities of insurance distributors, but having in mind the increasing of these activities in the last decade, it is visible that such scepticism is not justifiable.[12]

3.1 Definition of Distribution and Its Subjects

The IDD indicates a change in the philosophy of regulatory approach, as it applies to not only insurance intermediation services but also covers all forms of insurance distribution, including direct sales carried out by the employees in insurance companies. Instead of "concluding insurance contracts", the IDD introduced "*insurance distribution*" as a new term that is in brief defined as activities of advising on, proposing, or carrying out other work preparatory to the conclusion of contracts of insurance, of concluding such contracts, or of assisting in the administration and performance of such contracts.[13] Insurance distributor means any insurance intermediary, ancillary insurance intermediary or insurance undertaking.[14]

The regulations of IDD concern not only insurance undertakings and insurance intermediaries, but also other actors in the insurance market, such as, for example, travels agents and car rental companies, so-called "*ancillary insurance*

[8]Uzelac and Dukić Mijatović (2019), p. 10.

[9]Farrugia (2019), p. 131.

[10]Audigier (2021), p. 28.

[11]Farrugia (2019), p. 134.

[12]In its overview called "Insurance Distribution Directive – Evaluation of the Structure of Insurance Intermediaries in Europe" of 2018, EIOPA (European Insurance and Occupational Pensions Authority) analysed the cross-border activities of the intermediaries throughout EU, and found out that in period 2013–2017 was a steady increase of those activities. Text available at: https://www.eiopa.europa.eu/sites/default/files/publications/pdfs/idd_evaluation_of_intermediary_markets_0.pdf.

[13]Art. 2. par. 1. of the IDD.

[14]Art. 2. par. 1.8. of the IDD.

intermediaries", meaning the persons that distribute insurance products as a secondary activity in addition to their principal business. It also applies on such distribution channels that were not included at all in previous Directive (IMD). Such channels are for instance the persons managing websites offering the customers to directly or indirectly conclude an insurance contract.[15] Concerning those persons who operate as ancillary insurance intermediaries, the IDD introduces the exemptions based on the type of risk covered (for example, breakdown, damage to or loss of luggage), or on the amount of the premium paid (premiums of less than 600 Euro calculated proportionately on an annual basis).

From these definitions, it is obvious that scope of application of the IDD is much wider than the one of the IMD. Although the application of IDD *ratione materiae* is defined clearly, detailed definitions of subjects of insurance distribution in IDD are missing since those remain the sole competency of national civil law legislations.[16] Problems are noticed in differences between national labour legislations in interpretation of term "employee" and his relationship with "insurance undertaking."

The critics on this issue might be justifiable concerning the insurance intermediaries as well, because scope of activities and contractual relations between intermediaries and insurance companies and/or customers are mostly regulated by national civil law codifications. Furthermore, IDD does not make any difference between insurance intermediaries themselves, as in this matter a different approach of the national legislators is evident.[17] The definition of the "intermediary" or the division of this term is not contained either, and only in the preamble the IDD there is a non-exhaustive list of intermediaries, as "various types of persons or institutions, such as agents, brokers and 'bancassurance' operators, insurance undertakings, travel agents and car rental companies can distribute insurance products."[18] Another indirect mentioning of the "intermediary" is stated in the preamble and it says that the scope of Directive is similar for insurance undertakings and for insurance agents and brokers.[19]

The usual civil law distinction between insurance agents and brokers is whom they represent. Insurance agents mostly represent the seller, i.e. the insurance company. They are authorized by insurance companies to enter into agreements on their behalf. The agents are also divided into the exclusive agents, who distribute insurance products from a single insurance company, and independent agents, who offer insurance products from different companies. On the other hand, insurance brokers represent the customers. This means that buyers of insurance appoint

[15] Article 2 of the IDD.

[16] Tarasiuk and Wojno (2021), p. 143.

[17] For exemple, Law on insurance of Croatia in its adoption of IDD divided insurance intermediaries into insurance agents, brokers (both of them can be natural persons, legal entities and independent enterpreneurs) as well as anciliary intermediaries, see art. 402 of Law on Insurance (Official Gazette of Republic of Croatia, 112/18).

[18] IDD, preamble no. (5).

[19] IDD preamble no (7).

brokers.[20] The same way of regulation of these two categories is adopted in ex-Yugoslav Law on Obligations that will be discussed below.

Among all distribution channels, the IDD gives primacy to insurance intermediaries in relation to the insurance undertakings.[21] However, in practice the popularity of each selling channel varies depending on both the market and the type of insurance product. This diversity of channels makes it possible for insurers to adjust to the differing cultures, needs and preferences in individual markets. According to the figures set by Insurance Europe, a leading European organization of insurers, in non-life insurance distribution in EU Member States, agents predominated in Italy (75.3%), Poland (65%) and Germany (57.7%). Meanwhile, brokers accounted for 67% of non-life premiums in Bulgaria and 61.2% in Belgium. In contrast, Croatia had the largest proportion of non-life products sold directly (57.7%). Among the largest life insurance markets, products were mainly sold via bancassurance in Italy (75% in 2018, which is the most recent year for which a breakdown is available), in Spain (64.9%) and in France (65%), whereas in the UK life products were mainly sold by brokers (71%).[22]

Widening of the scope of IDD is evidently the consequence of need for covering of more subjects, which the IDD should be applicable to. EU legislator obviously had in mind development of modern technologies and online selling of insurance products in which borders between these categories are hardly noticeable. Therefore there have been introduced a regularly framework that contains protective regulations for all policyholders, regardless of the way that they bought the insurance product.[23]

The IDD is divided into eight chapters. Although the ones that regulate procedure of registration and organisational requirements of distributors are not less important, in this article the special attention will be paid on the provisions about information requirements and conduct of business rules that are contained in chapter 5.

3.2 Information Duties

The customers have different subjective preferences in respect to insurance, and their decision about buying an insurance product depends on their individual attitude

---

[20] Eckardt (2007), p. 6.

[21] Preamble (4) of the IDD says: *Insurance and reinsurance intermediaries play a central role in the distribution of insurance and reinsurance products in the Union.*

[22] European Insurance in Figures – 2019 data, Insurance Europe, available: https://www.insuranceeurope.eu/publications/689/european-insurance-in-figures-2019-data/download/EIF+2021.pdf.

[23] Filipović (2016), p. 103.

towards risk.[24] By the IDD, through „fair, clear and not misleading„ information,[25] the high standard of transparency is intended to be achieved. The IDD contains a detailed list of issues that a distributor has to notify the customer.[26] This legislative technique corresponds to that adopted in Directive Solvency II[27] as well as the one adopted in Principles of European Insurance Contract Law ("PEICL")[28] as generally applicable.

The IDD opted for such kind of protection of customers in a broader sense, meaning that information duties are not reserved only for consumers, but for all insurance customers.

The information duties introduced by the IDD Directive are primarily of pre-contractual nature and can be divided into the following categories:

- general information on the insurance distributor (insurance undertaking or intermediary),
- information on the insurance product, information on the complaints handling procedures,
- the out-of-court complaint and redress procedures,
- identification of the customer's demands and needs and provision of advice or recommendation.[29]

Provisions on general pre-contractual information about the insurance undertaking and about insurance product were also prescribed by the earlier Community legislation governing insurance. As is said in Chapter 2, the disclosure duty was subject of regulation of the Third Life Insurance Directive, and adopted into Solvency II as well. The last duty is some kind of novelty introduced by the IDD meaning that, in order to provide the customer with adequate information, insurance distributor has duty to obtain relevant information from him about his needs and demands.[30] Upon receipt of this information from the customer, distributor is able to provide him with "personalized recommendation" in order to allow him to make an informed decision.[31] The mentioned duty in its nature is connected to duty to advise. Duty to advise is not mandatory according to IDD since it adopted so-called soft

[24] Loaker (2015), p. 19.

[25] Art. 17. par. 1 of the IDD.

[26] Art. 20. 8 of the IDD.

[27] See Directive 2009/138/EC of the European Parliament and of the Council of 25 November 2009 on the taking-up and pursuit of the business of Insurance and Reinsurance (Solvency II), OJ L 335, 17.12.2009, p. 1–155, art. 15.

[28] Art. 2:201 of PEICL.

[29] Ostrowska (2021), p. 38.

[30] Norros (2020), p. 24.

[31] Art. 20.1. of the IDD.

variant of regulation of this issue, meaning that member states are allowed to regulate it in their own legislations.[32]

The other key change to the IMD regime includes disclosure of remuneration, meaning the duty of the insurance distributor to inform the prospective customer about the fee received in relation to the insurance contract. Insurance intermediaries must establish transparent rules governing remuneration and inform the customers about the way they work, including the information whether the remuneration is paid by the customer, how is it calculated, is it included in insurance premium, etc.). Insurance undertakings are also obliged to inform customers, in pre-contractual phase, about the remuneration received by their employees in relation to the insurance contract.[33]

3.2.1 Insurance Product Information Document (IPID)

Besides "personalized recommendation", another instrument introduced by IDD is "*The insurance product information document*"(IPID), with very detailed provisions about its form and content.[34] Although the IDD prescribes the long list of content of IPID, obviously, it was not enough and EU legislator has decided to enact the Implementing regulation with intention to set out a standardised presentation format for the IPID.[35] This regulation ensures that all insurance distributors have duty to provide the customers with standardized and consistent information document and that the customers have equal treatment regardless of the type of distribution channel. By comparing the content of the IPID introduced by the IDD and the one from Information sheet prescribed by German Ordinance on Information Requirements for Insurance Contracts[36] that was in force before implementation of IDD provisions,[37] one can find similarities, and it can be concluded that this German legislation was obviously a leading framework for regulation of the content of the IPID. Although disclosure duties by means of the IPID contribute to higher level of transparency, some authors called that the promised increase in customer protection by introducing IPID has not actually materialised. Rather, it has the potential to leave both customers and insurers confused.[38]

---

[32] For exemple, art. 6 of German Insurance Contract Act (VVG, last amended by the Act of 10 July 2020, Official Gazette I p. 1653) contains strict provisions regarding the advisory duties, that are prescribed for both intrermediaries and to insurers; see in: Murray (2007), p. 1, Wandt (2012), p. 11.

[33] Malinowska (2016), p. 95.

[34] Ćurković (2019), p. 32.

[35] See Commision Implementing Regulation (EU) 2017/1469 laying down a standardised presentation format for the insurance product information document, OJ L 209, 12.8.2017, pp. 19–23.

[36] See VVG-Informationspflichtenverordnung—VVG-InfoV of December 18, 2007 (Federal Law Gazette I p. 3004), last amended on June 9, 2021 (Federal Law Gazette I p. 1666).

[37] More about German Ordinance on Information Requirements for Insurance Contracts, see in: Petrović Tomić (2015), pp. 173–178.

[38] Kolding-Krøger et al. (2021), p. 398.

The IDD set out the more quality rules on consumers and distributors' protection, but it could be noticed that its design is still very much inspired by offline world. The IDD prescribes that the IPID should be "document on a paper or another durable medium", and the Implementing regulation prescribes not only its content but also the formal requirements such as its length and format of paper.

Nowadays, in an increasing digital environment, the mentioned paper-oriented communication between insurance distributors and their customers is a bit outdated. Insurance Europe, as the leading association that directly or indirectly represents all European insurers and reinsurers, in its Position Paper on the application of IDD[39] also stressed that COVID-19 has demonstrated the importance of further facilitating digitalisation in the insurance sector. It is proposed that future regulatory framework needs to ensure the same, fair competitive conditions for all kind of distributors, not only for insurers and intermediaries, but also for so-called *Insurtech* start-ups or new market entrants from other industries. This proposal is in line with the project strategy under the name *"Shaping Europe's Digital Future"*[40] whose general purpose is to bring a new innovative regulatory framework for digital payment assets and smart contracts. Hopefully, these activities would result in facilitation of insurance distribution through different technological means in future.

3.3 Professional and Organizational Requirements

As it was said before, the IMD was the first legislation regulating selling of insurance products by the insurance intermediaries—agents and brokers. Professional requirements set in the IMD were related only to fulfilment of duty of possessing of relevant initial knowledge about insurance products and selling activities. In other words, this obligation meant that insurance intermediaries, prior to starting their activities, had to pass the exam necessary for obtaining the license for doing their job.[41]

As the market needs have been changed, new insurance products became more sophisticated and complex. The past system of professional examination for purpose of registration was considered as inadequate and insufficient. That was the reason why the IDD sets out expanded professional, organisational and conduct of business requirements for all insurance and reinsurance distributors. These requirements are prescribed with purpose of ensuring that individuals involved in selling insurance products are competent to do so, and include obligations related to their knowledge

---

[39] Response to the EIOPA survey on application of the Insurance Distribution Directive, dated 5th February 2021, available: *https://www.insuranceeurope.eu/publications/1655/response-to-the-eiopa-survey-on-the-application-of-the-insurance-distribution-directive/download/Response+to%20the%20EIOPA%20survey%20on%20the%20application%20of%20the%20Insurance%20Distribution%20Directive.pdf.*

[40] Publication about this project was issued in February 2020, available at: https://ec.europa.eu/info/strategy/priorities-2019-2024/europe-fit-digital-age/shaping-europe-digital-future_en.

[41] Art. 3.(1) and art. 4. of the IMD.

and ability, training and development, good repute and record-keeping. The only ones that are exempt from these duties are administrative staffs that do not participate in direct selling.

General principle provides that insurance distributors must always act honestly, fairly and professionally in accordance with the best interests of their customers.[42] The purpose of adopting the duties of continuous professional training should be understood as adaptation of the insurance distributors to the market needs, i.e. recently developed insurance products and newly enacted legislation.[43] According to the IDD, Member States are required to have in place the adequate mechanisms to control effectively and assess the knowledge of all insurance distributors, based on at least 15 hours of professional training per year. As we see, the IDD introduced minimum hours of education, and some Member States implemented the same provisions in their national legislations, but some countries prescribe many more. For example, Law on insurance of Croatia adopted the IDD's provision of 15-hours of minimum annual education for licensed distributors,[44] but French *Code d' assurance* prescribes 150 hours of annual professional training.[45]

It should be noted in this regard that, for insurance intermediaries a strict administrative sanction is proposed in the event of any breach of the rules on the conduct of business. Member States must ensure that, as a minimum, the competent authorities have the power to decide that the responsible natural or legal person must cease the conduct and refrain from repeating such conduct and to withdraw the registration.

Although there is no direct link between transparency and the professionalism of insurance distributors, a high level of professional expertise is necessary to ensure the proper application of the above-mentioned transparency regulations.[46] The IDD is relatively new legislation and it was recently transposed into the national legislations of EU Member States. The time will show how these protecting mechanisms will be applicable in practice of insurance distribution and interpreted by national courts and the Court of EU.

---

[42] Art. 17.(1) of the IDD.

[43] Ćurković (2019), p. 35.

[44] Law on Insurance of Croatia, art. 422 (Official Gazette no. 112/18). The adjustment deadline of one-year is also prescribed. Completion of the education quota is counted from the date of obtaining the first license.

[45] Code d'assurance, Book V, Section 2, art. R512-8 to R512-13-1.

[46] Malinowska (2016), p. 97.

4 Legislation Applicable to Insurance Distribution in Bosnia and Herzegovina

In this chapter, it will be carried out how the insurance distribution is regulated in Bosnia and Herzegovina, as a country that intends to become an EU Member State, with special attention to implementation of analysed provisions of the IDD into the recently adopted and proposed legislations.

The present structure of governments of Bosnia and Herzegovina results of the General Framework Agreement for Peace in Bosnia and Herzegovina, so-called the Dayton Peace Agreement. The Constitution of Bosnia and Herzegovina is constituent part of Dayton Peace Agreement (Annex IV).[47] It prescribes territorial division of the state into two entities: Federation of Bosnia and Herzegovina (FB&H) and Republic of Srpska (RS).[48] Legislative competence of the entities is presumed in the main areas of civil law,[49] and the responsibilities of the state institutions of Bosnia and Herzegovina are limited on the matters exclusively set in the Constitution.[50]

Upon signing of the Stabilisation and Association Agreement (SAA)[51] with European Community and its Member States in 2008, which entered into force in 2015, Bosnia and Herzegovina expressed its willingness to ensure that its existing laws and future legislation would be *gradually* made compatible with the Community *acquis,* meaning that existing and future legislation will be properly implemented and enforced.[52]

The insurance is one of the civil law matters in which there is visible lack of mutual harmonization between the legislation of the entities, as well as the different approach of the entities' legislators towards harmonization of the existing insurance law acts with the Community law. General provisions about civil liability, types of material and non-material damage as well as the provisions on contract on insurance and are prescribed in the ex-Yugoslav Code on Obligations that has been adopted

---

[47] Dayton Peace Agreement was signed in Paris on 14 December 1995. Full text of Constitution is available at: https://peacemaker.un.org/sites/peacemaker.un.org/files/BA_951121_DaytonAgreement.pdf.

[48] During the Dayton negotiations, the consent has not been reached about the territory of the city of Brčko, so that District of Brčko became an autonomous administrative unit according to the Final Arbitration Decision of 5 March 1999.

[49] Jessel-Holst (2016), p. 139.

[50] Art. III.1. of the Constitution of Bosnia and Herzegovina.

[51] Stabilization and Association Agreement with the European Communities and their Member States, Official Gazette of BiH—International Agreements, No. 10/08).

[52] Art. 70. of the SAA.

into the legal system of Bosnia and Herzegovina.[53] It is the main source of civil law on obligations, and it remained almost unchanged from 1978.[54]

First steps towards harmonization of legislation within insurance sector were managed in 2005 by adopting the set of law acts on entity level, as *legis specialis* for insurance matters. Ones of them were the Laws on insurance[55] that contained mostly statutory regulations about insurance companies and system of supervision, with a few consumer-protection oriented provisions about information duties towards policyholders. Apart from the mentioned acts, the Laws on insurance mediation[56] were enacted as separated acts, for purpose of regulation of activities of insurance intermediaries and brokers. The third part of the mentioned set of legislature from 2005 was related to mandatory insurances in traffic,[57] with main purpose of protection of victims in traffic accidents, and harmonization with EU Motor Insurance Directives. All of these entity Laws contained very similar provisions and the notable level of harmonization with EU legislation in field of insurance has been achieved after they entered into force.

4.1 B&H Entities' Laws on Insurance

About 10 years after enactment of the mentioned Laws, the further steps towards harmonization with the *acquis* were necessary due to further development of insurance market. Besides, these legislative activities were managed as a part of continuation of EU-integration process. However, the dynamism of enacting of new legislative acts in the B&H entities is not uniform. The new Law on insurance[58] was adopted in Federation of Bosnia and Herzegovina in 2017, and in Republic of Srpska there is still in force the Law on insurance companies of 2005. On the other

[53] See Code on Obligations, Official Gazette of Socialist Federative Republic of Yugoslavia no. 29/78, 39/85, 45/89 and 57/89, In Federation of Bosnia and Herzegovina the integral text of the Code was published in Official Gazette no. 2/92, 13/93 and 13/94, and in Republic of Srpska in Official Gazzete of RS, no. 7/93 and 3/96.

[54] There were around twenty articles that were changed. More about the Yugoslav Code on Obligations and its versions that are in force in Bosnia and Herzegovina see in: Bevanda (2013), p. 123.

[55] Law on Insurance Companies in Private Insurance, Official Gazette of Federation of B&H, 24/05, Law on Insurance Companies, Official Gazette of Republika Srpska, 17/05.

[56] Law on Mediation in Private Insurance, Official Gazette of Federation of B&H, 22/05, Law on Insurance Mediation, Official Gazette of Republika Srpska, 17/05.

[57] Law of Liability Insurance for Motor Vehicles and other Provisions of Mandatory Liability Insurance of Federation of B&H, Official Gazette of FB&H, no. 24/05; the same-named act in Republic of Srpska, Official Gazette of RS, no. 17/05. These acts were replaced by the new Laws on Mandatory Insurance in Traffic that was enacted in Republic of Srpska in 2015 and in Federation of B&H in 2020.

[58] Law on insurance of Federation of Bosnia and Herzegovina, Official Gazette of FB&H, no. 23/17, 29/03/2017.

hand, as will be discussed in forthcoming chapter, the Law on mediation and representation in insurance and reinsurance was enacted in Republic of Srpska in 2017, and in Federation of B&H the respective law act of 2005 remained in force.

Meanwhile, as is presented in this article, on EU level in 2016 the IDD has been adopted. Having in mind the obligation of gradual harmonization prescribed by SAA, provisions of the IDD had to be the main source of secondary EU legislation in process of harmonization of legislation in field of insurance distribution in Bosnia and Herzegovina.

Law on insurance of Federation of B&H of 2017, among others, contains mainly statutory provisions about conditions for establishment and cessation of insurance companies, their management structure, assets requirements, financial reports and competences of supervision authority. The only provisions that regulate protection of customers are the ones about out-of-court dispute settlement and redress mechanisms that are prescribed only for consumers, as well as the provisions on information duties.

The chapter "Consumers protection" begins with definition of consumer as a natural person that has duties and rights from the insurance contract.[59] Further provisions about pre-contractual duties and duties to provide information during the period of insurance contract are probably intended to cover all customers, not only consumers.[60] These provisions say that insurers are obliged to provide all insurance contractors with the mentioned information. Broader method of interpretation of the whole chapter about consumers' protection could lead to the conclusion that these disclosure duties are applicable only to consumers. However, the linguistic interpretation leads us to conclusion that protective provisions about information duties are spread to all insurance customers. Such inadequate regulation could cause confusion in its interpretation. This confusion could be avoided if the legislator used only the term "customer", and not the "consumer". On that way, these protective regulations would cover all customers, without any room for different interpretation.

Despite the fact that the IDD has already been adopted, and that it should have been a model framework of Community law in process of harmonization, it is visible that Law on Insurance of Federation of B&H omitted one of its main provisions. It did not introduce the term "insurance distribution" at all, and it did not prescribe any provision about these activities. Besides, in the new Law on insurance, the legislator in Federation of Bosnia and Herzegovina applied legislative practice from 2005: the new Law on insurance covers only insurance undertakings, and the provisions about insurance intermediaries were reserved for a separate legislation act. In the next sub-chapter, we will see how the insurance mediation is regulated and why such separated regulation is inadequate. Separation of the legislative acts on those governing the insurance undertakings and those related to the insurance intermediaries is not practice in any legislation in SEE region. Neighbouring countries opted

[59] Art. 197 of Law on insurance of Federation of B&H.

[60] Art. 200 and 201 of Law on insurance of Federation of B&H.

for unite legislative approach, adopting the Laws on insurance with the regulations about insurance undertakings and intermediaries in the same act.[61]

In Republic of Srpska, the mentioned Law on Insurance Companies of 2005 is still in force, and some amendments and additions to the Law were adopted in period from 2006 to 2019,[62] mostly with intention to amend regulations of solvency margins, to introduce anti-money laundering provisions as well as administrative provisions about organizational structure of insurance companies. Provisions about customers' rights in process of distribution of insurance were not subject of these amendments.

4.2 Insurance Mediation in the B&H Entities' Legislations

As is said above, the insurance mediation was regulated by separate entity Laws adopted in 2005.[63] These legislations regulate registration and activities of insurance intermediaries—agents and brokers, but contain only a few provisions about duties of the intermediaries towards customers. The insurance agent is defined as legal or natural person that professionally provides insurance services in the name and on the account of one or more insurance undertakings,[64] while the insurance broker is the one who acts in the name of insurance contractor (prospective policyholder) with intention to get him in touch with the insurance undertaking.[65] There are no provisions about either pre-contractual information duties or other protective measures. It is understandable having in mind that these law acts were brought more than 15 years ago, i.e. in an early phase of development of insurance market in Bosnia and Herzegovina. In that period, the focus was on administrative regulation of the intermediaries, their registration and supervision, and consumers' protection was less important.

[61] Law on insurance of Republic of Serbia, Official Gazette no. 139/2014, 44/2021; Law on insurance of Republic of Montenegro, Official Gazette no. 78/06 to 55/16.

[62] All amendments and additions to the Law on Insurance Companies of Republic of Srpska are available at: http://www.azors.rs.ba/azors/lat/pod_akti.html.

[63] Law on Mediation in Private Insurance, Official Gazette of Federation of B&H, 22/05, Law on Insurance Mediation, Official Gazette of Republic of Srpska, 17/05.

[64] Art. 6 of Law on Mediation in Private Insurance, Official Gazette of Federation of B&H, 22/05.

[65] Art. 8 of Law on Mediation in Private Insurance, Official Gazette of Federation of B&H, 22/05.

4.2.1 Law on Insurance Mediation and Representation of Republic of Srpska

On its path towards harmonization with EU legislation, Republic of Srpska brought its new Law on insurance mediation and representation in 2017.[66] This legislation act did not introduce insurance distribution as a new term adopted by the IDD, but it stayed on the aforementioned respective Law's terminology of "insurance mediation" that is managed by insurance agents and "insurance representation" by insurance brokers. These terms suit to the terminology of national Law on obligations.[67] However, in definitions of these terms stated in the Law one can find some kind of confusion between competences of these persons and their activities themselves as well as the same ones regulated by the IDD. For example, definition of the insurance mediation is clear and there is no doubt that the insurance agents conduct activities on mediation, and that the insurance agents act on behalf of the insurers.[68] However, interpretation of the activities of the representatives leaves a room for doubt on whose behalf they act and whose interests represent. It is because the definition of representation is similar as the definition of insurance distribution from the IDD,[69] although the insurance distribution covers many more activities and participants, including the insurance companies themselves.

Besides these inconsistencies in the preliminary provisions, the Law on insurance mediation and representation of RS contains a provision that is contrary to both national Law on obligations and the IDD. It is the provision that prohibits insurance agent to get payment of the premium from the contractor. Oppositely, the Law on obligations allows insurance agent to collect premiums, if not otherwise stipulated between the agent and the insurance company.[70] The IDD does not ban the insurance intermediaries to receive payment of premium, but it prescribes some measures in order to protect the customers against the inability of insurance intermediaries to transfer the premium to the insurers.[71] Legislations of the countries in SEE region

---

[66] Law on insurance mediation and representation, Official Gazette of Republic of Srpska, no. 47/17.

[67] Law on Obligations does not contain specific provisions on insurance mediation and representation, but general provisions about mediation (art. 84–98) and contract on representation (art. 813–826) might be applicable.

[68] Art. 2 of Law on insurance mediation and representation of Republic of Srpska.

[69] Art. 2.(1) of IDD says: 'Insurance distribution' means the activities of advising on, proposing, or carrying out other work preparatory to the conclusion of contracts of insurance, of concluding such contracts, or of assisting in the administration and performance of such contracts, etc., while art. 2.e) of Law on insurance mediation and representation of Republic of Srpska defines „Insurance and reinsureance representation as getting into touch potential policyholders, or contractors and (re)-insurance undertakings, activities on work preparatory to the conclusion of contract on (re)-insurance, or of assisting in the administration and performance of such contracts concluded with representation of the insurance broker.

[70] Law on obligations, art. 906.

[71] Art. 10(6) of the IDD.

allow the insurance agents to receive the payments of premium, but they prescribe obligation to discharge the received assets to the insurers in short period.[72]

Regarding the information duties towards the customers, there are also visible inadequate transpositions of the IDD's provisions, especially the ones about insurance product. According to this Law, information sheet that agents and brokers have to provide the customers with is consisted of statutory data about their registration, their relationship with the insurance undertakings, and much other information that is more or less irrelevant for the customers. The way of communication is also prescribed: material or electronic, depending on media which is available to the customer. However, there is no provision about the duty to inform the prospective customer about the insurance product in form of the IPID or otherwise. Obviously, the legislator did not transpose the IDD's provisions regarding these issues although it is more important that they receive adequate information about the insurance product that they intend to buy than the information about administrative status of the intermediary.

Due to an unknown reason, the legislator in RS also omitted to prescribe professional and organizational requirements for the insurance agents and brokers. As we have seen in the chapter 3.3 of this paperwork, these requirements are introduced by the IDD as necessary in order to ensure a high quality of service and effective consumer protection. Insurance market's needs are being changed and it is definitely recommended to prescribe obligation of the agents and brokers to continuing professional training and development in order to maintain an adequate level of performance corresponding to the role they perform at the relevant market.

4.2.2 Draft Law on Insurance Mediation and Representation in Federation of B&H

Legislative procedure of enactment of a new Law on insurance mediation and representation in Federation of B&H is now ongoing. The draft law[73] was adopted by the Government of FB&H in 2018, and all in all, it seems to be almost a copy of the same named Law of RS. Provisions on information duties are equal to the ones from the Law of RS. Similarly, the provisions on professional development of the insurance agents and brokers were not mentioned in the proposed text. If this draft is adopted in FB&H in the forthcoming period, the interstate harmonization of law in field of insurance mediation and representation will be probably achieved.

---

[72] For example, Law on insuranceof Republic of Serbia, Official Gazette of Republic of Serbia, no. 139/2014, 44/2021, in its art. 106 prescribes that the insurance agents can collect the premium in the name and on behalf of the insurance company, but they have to transfer the paid premium amounts directly to the insurer on the same day or, at the latest, the next working day.

[73] Draft Law on Insurance Mediation and Representation in Federation of B&H, available at: https://parlamentfbih.gov.ba/dom_naroda/v2/userfiles/file/Materijali%20u%20proceduri_2018/Zakon%20o%20zastupanju%20i%20posredovanju%20bos.pdf.

Nevertheless, a gap in harmonization with the respective EU legislation will unfortunately remain.

5 Concluding Remarks

Analysis of the respective IDD provisions on disclosure duties and professional requirements of the insurance distributors carried out in this article shows that European legislator took an extensive approach to the transparency of insurance services and products. Under the IDD, transparency means more than the obligation to draft the insurance terms and conditions. By disclosure duties towards customers and professional requirements prescribed for the insurance distributors, it also established principle guiding the organisation of distribution activities and the entire insurance distribution process.

Although the IDD should have been the leading source of the Community law in process of harmonization of legislation on insurance distribution in Bosnia and Herzegovina, the entities' law-making authorities did not follow its concept of "insurance distribution" and did not adequately transpose the provisions about information duties and professional requirements that should protect the customers better. Adoption of the new Law on insurance of 2017 in FB&H was a great chance to unite the provisions applicable to insurance undertakings and insurance intermediaries into one legislative act. This united principle of regulation could be a recommendation for future legislative act in Republic of Srpska who still did not adopt the new Law on insurance. By that way, some inconsistencies between these two entity acts would be avoided and the same provisions that protect the customers would be applicable to both insurance undertakings and insurance intermediaries.

From the analysis carried out in this paper, splitting these laws into two separate acts, makes an additional confusion. It is especially significant in the situation of Bosnia and Herzegovina where it means enacting of four acts because they are in competence of the entities. If we take into consideration, that harmonization with *acquis* according to SAA was intended to be gradual, such regulation we may accept as justifiable. However, hopefully the legislators in both entities will opt for comprehensive approach in this regulation in future because it may be more appropriate and more protective towards the customers.

References

Audigier I (2021) Insurance distribution directive and cross-border activities by insurance intermediaries in the EU. In Marano P, Noussia K (eds) Insurance distribution directive, AIDA Europe research series on insurance law and regulation, pp 3–30

Bevanda M (2013) Obveznopravno uređenje u Bosni i Hercegovini. Pravni fakultet Mostar

Ćurković M (2019) Nastanak i obuhvat regulatornih odredbi o distribuciji osiguranja. Hrvatski časopis za osiguranje, pp 23–38

Eckardt M (2007) Does signaling work in markets for information services? An empirical investigation for insurance intermediaries in Germany, Thünen-Series of Applied Economic Theory, Working Paper no. 77, pp 1–38
Farrugia A (2019) The Impact of Evolving EU Regulations on Insurance Underwriting, Insurance Law and Practice – Current Trends. Future Challenges – Proceedings from 20th conference of Association of Serbian Insurers, pp 127–140
Filipović N (2016) Direktiva o distribuciji osiguranja – dalja harmonizacija jedinstvenog tržišta osiguranja. In: Reforme i novi izazovi u pravu osiguranja. Udruženje za pravo osiguranja Srbije, Beograd, pp 97–120
Filipović N (2018) Evolucija evropskih pravila o distribuciji osiguranja. Evropska revija za pravo osiguranja, Beograd, 4, pp 24–33
Ivančević K (2013) Primena Direktive o posredovanju u osiguranju i predlozi za njene izmene. In: Marano P et al (eds) Pravo osiguranja Srbije u tranziciji ka evropskom (EU) pravu osiguranja. Udruženje za pravo osiguranja Srbije, Beograd, pp 232–249
Jessel-Holst C (2016) The Reform of Private International Law Acts in South East Europe, with Particular Regard to the West Balkan Region. Anali Pravnog fakulteta u Zenici, no. 18. year 9, pp 133–145
Kolding-Krøger CB, Hansen RA, Brofeldt A (2021) The reality of the promised increase in customer protection under the insurance distribution directive. In: Marano P, Noussia K (eds) Insurance Distribution Directive, AIDA Europe Research Series on Insurance Law and Regulation, pp 395–439
Loaker LD (2015) Informed insurance choice: the insurer's pre-contractual information duties. Edward Elgar Publishing
Malinowska K (2016) Insurance transparency and protection regime under the Insurance Distribution Directive, Insurance Review. Wiadomości Ubezpieczeniowe 4:89–101
Murray C (2007) Germany: the new German Insurance Contract Law (VVG). Lloyd's Market Buletin, Ref. Y4100, pp 1–2
Norros O (2020) Insurers duty to obtain information under the IDD Directive – threat or opportunity? Juridica Int Law Rev 29:23–33
Ostrowska M (2021) Information duties stemming from the insurance distribution directive as an example of faulty application. In: Marano P, Noussia K (eds) Insurance Distribution Directive, AIDA Europe Research Series on Insurance Law and Regulation, pp 31–55
Petrović Tomić N (2015) Zaštita potrošača usluga osiguranja – analiza i predlog unapređenja regulatornog okvira. Pravni fakultet Univerziteta u Beogradu
Slavnić J, Jovanović S (2008) Obaveza davanja predugovornih informacija i informacija posle zaključenja ugovora o osiguranju potrošačima usluga osiguranja prema direktivama EU i zakonima država članica. Revija za pravo osiguranja, Beograd, pp 26–49
Tarasiuk A, Wojno B (2021) The notion of "Employee" in the IDD: a harmonized interpretation based on the EU law. In: Marano P, Noussia K (eds) Insurance Distribution Directive, AIDA Europe Research Series on Insurance Law and Regulation, pp 139–160
Uzelac O, Dukić Mijatović M (2019) Sadržina i obim obaveza tokom procesa izrade i uvođenja proizvoda osiguranja na tržište prema Direktivi EU o distribuciji osiguranja. Evropska revija za pravo osiguranja, Beograd 1:9–18
Wandt M (2012) Transparency as a general principle of insurance law. In: Transparency in insurance law. Sigorta Hukuku Türk Derneği (AIDA – Turkey), pp 9–22

The Concept of Unfair Terms in Consumer Contracts in Serbian Law: The Case of Validity of Contracting Credit Costs

Sloboda Midorović

Contents

S. Midorović (✉)
University of Novi Sad, Faculty of Law, Novi Sad, Serbia
e-mail: s.midorovic@pf.uns.ac.rs

D. V. Popović et al. (eds.), *Balkan Yearbook of European and International Law 2021*, Balkan Yearbook of European and International Law 2021,
https://doi.org/10.1007/978-3-030-97431-2_7

1 Introduction

The paper is inspired by the reasoning of the Serbian Supreme Court of Cassation (the Court) given in its recent Supplement to the legal opinion on validity of credit costs[1] (opinion).[2] This reasoning is of the interest for this paper only in so far as it refers to the concept of unfair terms in consumer contracts. In finding arguments for its opinion, the Court, *inter alia*, relied on the relevant provisions of the Serbian Consumer Protection Act,[3] Art. 4(2) of Directive 93/13/EEC on unfair terms in consumer contracts (Directive)[4] and Case C-84/19[5] of the Court of Justice of the European Union (CJEU). The aim of this paper is to subject to scrutiny these arguments, i.e. the Court's understanding of the concept of unfair contract terms. The analysis should reveal if the Court correctly conceives, or rather misconceives this concept.

The paper at no point aims at either underpinning or disavowing the Court's final stance on validity of the credit processing costs which can be summarized as follows: "The bank is not obliged to prove in particular the structure and amount of costs that are included in the total amount of credit costs, so long as the offer to conclude the credit agreement, which was accepted by the credit user, indicated the type[6] and total amount of such costs." Nevertheless, the shortcomings that will be pointed out could possibly diminish the plausibility of the Court's reasoning. At the same time this does not mean that the Court's stance is indefensible. The diverging outcomes reached by the highest courts of some closely related legal systems[7] indicate the

[1] The Legal opinion was adopted on 16 September 2021, https://www.vk.sud.rs/sr/2021 1.11.2021.

[2] On the general critique, i.e. unconstitutionality of the out-of-trial competence of the Court to unify case law by adopting abstract legal opinions, see: Knežević (2017), pp. 23–36; Knežević (2019), p. 49.

[3] The Consumer Protection Act (CPA) to which the Court refers hails from the year of 2014, Official Gazette of RS, No. 62/2014, 6/2016 (other law), 44/2018 (other law). Meanwhile, the CPA from 2014 was substituted by the new CPA, Official Gazette of RS, No. 88/2021, which already entered into force, but whose application has been postponed. For this paper, it is noteworthy to mention that provisions of CPA 2021 that govern unfair contract terms in consumer contracts (Art. 40–44) are identical in their substance to those of the CPA 2014 (Art. 41–45). The only aspect that has changed is the numbering of the relevant provisions. So, for instance, what used to be Art. 44 and 45 are now Art. 43 and 44. To avoid confusion, this paper will follow the old numbering since it was used in the reasoning of the Court.

[4] OJ L 095, 21.4.1993, pp. 29–34 amended by the Directive 2011/83/EU of the European Parliament and of the Council of 25 October 2011 on consumer rights OJ 304, 22.11.2011, pp. 64–88.

[5] Judgment of the CJEU of 3 September 2020 in Joined Cases C-84/19, C-222/19 and C-252/19, Profi Credit Polska SA v QJ (C-84/19); BW v DR (C-222/19), and QL v CG (C-252/19).

[6] The word "type" refers to the *in abstracto* naming of the costs such as credit processing costs.

[7] On diverging decisions of German *Bundesgerichtshof* and Austrian *Oberste Gerichtshof* on this matter see: Živković (2018), pp. 19–25. Reaching opposing results with regard to the same legal matter is possible given that unfairness of the specific term is to be adjudicated at the national level given that the Directive aims at minimum harmonization. This is in accordance with the CJEU stance expressed in *Freiburger Kommunalbauten GmbH Baugesellschaft & Co. KG vs. Ludger*

possibility of finding arguments to substantiate the validity of the disputed term, as well as to dismiss it as unfair. In that respect, this paper should serve as a reminder that the Court is expected to offer tenable reasoning capable of winning a wide-ranging support by the strength of its arguments, instead of opening leeway for distrust, especially when deciding on highly sensitive matters that affect numerous consumers, such as this one, and, moreover, when announcing the departure from the recent adjudicating trend among the lower instances.[8]

Prior to subjecting the Court's arguments to scrutiny, a brief overview of the judicial review of standard terms in general, and of consumer contracts in particular, will be given. To evaluate the adequacy of the Court's reference to the Directive and CJEU case law, the character of the Directive should be recalled, along with aspects in which Serbian CPA deviates from it. Another point that should be clarified prior to scrutinizing the Court's arguments touches upon the interplay between the CPA and the main source of general contract law in Serbia—the Law on Obligations[9] (LoO). This is primarily needed for elucidating the relationship between the principle of equal value of mutual obligations of the LoO, on one hand, and criterion of significant imbalance stipulated in CPA, on the other. The relationship between the CPA and the LoO appears also relevant when examining unfairness standards in B2B (business to business) contracts juxtaposed to its scrutiny in B2C (business to consumers) contracts. The examination should reveal the most evident departures of the Court from the unfairness concept in consumer contracts, followed by proposals on how to avoid them in the future.

2 Origins and Justification of the Judicial Review of Standard Terms

In its original form freedom of contract was perceived as a guarantee that the content of the contract regularly would reflect the wills of its parties. In fact, comparable bargaining positions of the contracting parties served as a warranty for the

Hofstetter and Ulrike Hofstetter, [25] (01.04.2004, C-237/02), where it was postulated that "it is for the national court to decide whether a contractual term such as that at issue in the main proceedings satisfies the requirements for it to be regarded as unfair under Article 3(1) of the Directive." The CJEU, thus, only gives guidelines on the interpretation of the unfairness standard at the EU level, whereas it is on the court of each Member State to examine the unfairness of a specific contract term against the backdrop of its national law. The fact that national courts may develop diverging unfairness standards significantly complicates conducting of the cross-border businesses. On that see: Jansen in: Jansen and Zimmermann (2018), pp. 926–927.

[8]By saying this, the author does not imply the formal binding effect of the opinion on the lower instances, since such does not exist in Serbian law. Instead, she merely indicates a broadly accepted *de facto* binding effect of abstract legal opinions on lower courts.

[9]Official Gazette of SFRY, No. 29/78, 39/85, 45/89, 57/89; Official Gazette of the FRY, No. 31/93, (Decree - during the state of war: 22/99, 23/99, 35/99, 44/99), Official Gazette of RS, No. 18/2020.

functioning of the contractual mechanism. This mechanism assumes that, during negotiations, each party seeks to protect its own interests and that, consequently, none of them would accept terms to its disadvantage. In this setting, it was understandable that courts, relying on the maxim *pacta sunt servanda*, were reluctant to exert control over the contract's content. Their role was limited to enabling the exercise of contractual rights in the event that one of the parties deviated from what it had previously freely agreed to. Therefore, the court's task was to protect the so-called formal freedom of contract. This contracting model, in fact, served as paradigm for designing general contract law rules to be found in great civil-law codifications of the nineteenth and the beginning of the twentieth century.[10]

Throughout the time, however, the circumstances have changed. Industrialization enabled massive production. To speed up production and reduce its costs, standardization of products was necessary. In addition to products, standardization has affected legal aspects of the trade too, in the sense that producers started offering their products under pre-formulated standard terms.[11] This, in return, left a party in need for such a product with the possibility to either accept unilaterally formulated terms or stay empty-handed. It was this development that announced a shift in understanding of contractual parity.

Revising old contractual patterns inevitably led to the transformation of the courts' role. Instead of refraining from reviewing the content of contracts, the courts began to examine their fairness. The ultimate goal of such control was to prevent the superior party from abusing the non-binding nature of the contract law rules at the expense of the weaker party. Namely, by relying on non-mandatory nature of contract law rules, the stronger party is in the position to impose excessive obligations on the other party, transfer risks that it would otherwise bear, exclude or limit its liability *vis a vis* the weaker party etc.[12] This has clearly shown that "negotiations at a bazaar"[13] used as a paradigmatic model for devising general rules of contract law can no longer meet the exigencies of the new forms of entering into contractual relations. Therefore, in addition to formal freedom of contract, the courts began to assess its material, i.e. substantial aspects.[14] As a result, they are expected to prevent the weaker party from being bound by unfair terms to which, in the absence of its inferiority, it would not reasonably agree.[15]

In addition to the weaker party argument,[16] the doctrine has developed further reasoning to justify judicial intervention in the content of the contract. Namely, it is often postulated that the widespread use of general terms of contract causes the

---

[10] Mäsch in: Staudinger (2019), p. 3; Gauch and Schluep (2014), p. 131.

[11] Đurđević (2001), p. 19.

[12] Đurđević (2001), pp. 96–97.

[13] Jansen in: Jansen and Zimmermann (2018), p. 969.

[14] Karanikić Mirić (2009), p. 145.

[15] Raiser (1960), p. 132; Jansen in: Jansen and Zimmermann (2018), p. 966.

[16] Karanikić Mirić (2009), p. 134.

so-called "rational ignorance",[17] or "rational apathy".[18] Indeed, it is hardly to be expected that parties acceding to the pre-formulated terms would invest time, legal expertise and, therefore, money to study them thoroughly to detect possible perils. If it is not satisfied with general terms of the supplier, the weaker party should "investigate" the general terms of supplier's competitors. But, even if it discovers unfavorable terms, the party who wants to get a product or a service will hardly have a chance to influence their substance. For this being obviously irrational, consumers are consciously prone to accept the terms without even reading them. As a consequence, the competitors generally do not compete in offering better general terms, as price is regularly shown to be the most decisive factor in choosing between comparable products or services.[19] In the literature, this phenomenon is referred to as market failure[20] which can be corrected only by the courts in their *ex post* control of standard terms.

Against this background, the modern concept of freedom of contract became inextricably linked to the court's authority to review the fairness of the contract's content.[21] Had that not been the case, freedom of contract would easily turn into its negation and, consequently, into renunciation of self-determination.[22]

3 Tackling the Issue in the EU

It was not until the second half of the 1970s that the search for the streamlined solutions to the general terms of contract became an integral part of European legal discourse.[23] Around that time some European countries, pioneered by Germany and England, adopted national acts regulating this field of law.[24] Today, all modern legal systems have a tailormade set of rules related to the general terms of contract, and often, in addition to it, a special set of provisions on consumer contracts.

Europe-wide debate on the fairness control of standard terms and the ambition to strengthen the position and confidence of consumers in the internal market have led to the adoption of the already mentioned Directive 93/13/EEC. Although its proposal provided for the control of unfairness of all standard contracts—B2C and B2B, in the final wording, the Directive provided only for the unfairness assessment of consumer contracts.[25]

---

[17] Jansen in: Jansen and Zimmermann (2018), p. 966.

[18] Mäsch in: Staudinger (2019), p. 5.

[19] Mäsch in: Staudinger (2019), p. 4, 5; Pomar (2019), p. 179.

[20] Jansen in: Jansen and Zimmermann (2018), p. 928.

[21] Hart (1989), p. 180.

[22] Gauch and Schluep (2014), p. 131.

[23] Jansen in: Jansen and Zimmermann (2018), pp. 921–923.

[24] Jansen in: Jansen and Zimmermann (2018), fn. 15, p. 922.

[25] Jansen in: Jansen and Zimmermann (2018), pp. 923–924.

A detailed examination of the Directive's provisions undoubtedly goes beyond the scope of this paper.[26] Therefore, the solutions of the Directive will be mentioned only to the extent necessary to assess the Court's reference to it. Taking this into account, it will be only mentioned that the Directive introduced the concept of unfair terms in consumer contracts, established criteria for assessing unfairness and envisaged a consequence thereto. Should national court find that a particular term is unfair, it will not be binding on the consumer. The phrase "not binding" many countries, including Serbia (Art. 41/1 CPA), have transposed as "null and void", a consequence of which is that such term is denied any legal effect. For the purpose of this paper, it is crucial to point out the minimum harmonizing character of the Directive. This implies that member states (and those having candidate status such as Serbia), when implementing Directive's solutions, can adopt or retain stricter rules, or broaden the scope of those rules in order to achieve a higher level of consumer protection at their national level. Many countries, including Serbia, have taken the advantage of this opportunity.

In its nearly three-decade-long validity, the Directive has produced a bulk of case law before the CJEU. Lately, it even seems to be gaining the importance, which is largely due to the financial and economic crisis that erupted in 2007/2008 which severely affected some countries. As expected, the crisis has worsened the purchasing power of consumers, which has made it difficult for many to settle their financial liabilities. This gave rise to numerous court proceedings against credit institutions in which various contract terms have been disputed.[27] Challenging the validity of credit processing costs is only one of them.

4 Tackling the Issue in the Republic of Serbia

As already mentioned, in the second half of the 1970s, many European countries took normative action in response to the increasing use of standard terms in contracting. Following such a trend, Serbian legislator introduced in its LoO two provisions dedicated to the general terms of standard contracts: Art. 142 that governs conditions under which such terms may be binding on the other party, and Art. 143 that is named "Nullity of some Provisions of General Terms and Conditions", whereby the latter, *inter alia*, introduced the concept of unfair terms.[28]

---

[26] In Serbian scholarship Directive's provisions have been analyzed by Karanikić Mirić (2009), pp. 128–146.

[27] Živković (2018), p. 17.

[28] According to the official translation of the LoO (The Law of Contract and Torts), translated by Dr. Đurica Krstić (1997) Jugoslovenski pregled (Yugoslav Survey), Art. 143 reads

(1) Provisions of the general terms and conditions shall be null and void if contrary to the very purpose of contract which is concluded, or to fair business usage, even after such

By explicitly regulating this subject matter, Serbian legislator recognized a distinctiveness of general terms and conditions in relation to the contracts arising out of mutual negotiations. These provisions show that Serbian legislator was indeed aware of the fact that general provisions on nullity contained in LoO could not provide a sufficient level of protection for the party who acceded to the unilaterally formulated contract terms. In other words, Serbian legislator had in mind that it would be indisputably unfair to treat these two situations—those in which there is contractual parity and those in which such parity does not exist—identically. This is why the weaker party (the one that acceeds to the standard terms) shall enjoy a higher level of protection than that generally afforded to the contracting parties who had a chance to negotiate on a comparably equal footing.

It is noteworthy that Art. 142 and 143 are not limited in their scope of application depending on the character of the acceding party. In other words, they apply regardless of whether the acceding party is a consumer or a business entity.

In addition to paying attention to the general terms and conditions, since the beginning of the twenty-first century, Serbian legislator has been providing a special set of rules dedicated exclusively to consumer protection.[29] Nevertheless, it was not before 2010 that the concept of unfair terms in consumer contracts (Art. 46–48)[30] was introduced. Regarding this concept, the CPA as of 2014 introduced minor changes compared to the CPA as of 2010 (see fn. 3). In any case, this concept was inspired by the Directive 93/13/EEC.

When governing the concept of unfair terms, the CPA 2014 provides for the consequence of nullity (Art. 43/1). In Art. 43/2, it introduces the unfairness criteria by stating that "as unfair shall be regarded each term, which contrary to the principle of good faith, causes significant imbalance in parties' rights and obligations, to the detriment of the consumer." Furthermore, in Art. 43/3, the CPA stipulates that the accompanying criteria in assessing unfairness are: "1) nature of the goods or services for which the contract was concluded; 2) circumstances attending the conclusion of the contract; 3) other terms of the same contract or another contract with which the contract is related; 4) the manner in which consent was reached on the content of the contract and the manner in which the consumer was informed of the content of the contract." Thereupon, the CPA enshrines the black (Art. 44) and grey (Art. 45) lists of unfair terms. The terms found on the black list are irrefutably regarded as unfair. This means that, should the court encounter itself with one of these terms, it would automatically deprive it of any legal effect. Conversely, if the term in question

---

general terms and conditions containing them have been approved by the competent agency.

(2) The court may deny application of specific provisions of the general terms and conditions precluding the other party to raise demurrers, or of those on the ground of which such party is left without contractual rights or loses time limits, or those which are otherwise unjust or excessively strict towards such party.

[29] The first Serbian CPA was introduced in 2002, Official Gazette of the FRY, No. 37/2002).

[30] Official Gazette of RS, No. 73/2010.

is among those on the indicative (grey) list, it is presumed to be unfair, with the possibility of their supplier to put forward arguments to rebut this presumption. However, the fact that a certain term is neither on the black nor on the gray list does not make such a term fair. Instead, the fact that the term cannot be found on any of the lists implies that the court should review its fairness based on the general criteria from Art. 43, para. 2 and 3.

For the purpose of this analysis, it is important to clarify *ratione personae* scope of application of the described concept of unfair contract terms. This is important given that Art. 4, para. 6 of the CPA states that: "[t]o the protection of financial services users, [. . .], provisions of a special act shall apply." The cited provision may be misunderstood in the sense that, under Serbian law, the CPA concept of unfair terms is not applicable to the financial services users. According to this provision, however, the CPA only indicates that *vis a vis* financial services sector, a special sub-set of rules shall apply, and not that the CPA does not apply to it at all. Subsidiary application of the CPA, with regard to its unfair terms concept, was explicitly pointed out by Financial Users Protection Act (FUPA).[31] Its Art. 41, para. 6 states that for the sake of its application "[u]nfair business practices and unfair contractual terms have the meaning established by the law governing consumer protection." Moreover, the FUPA extends the use of the CPA unfairness terms concept to the financial users other than those considered consumers under the CPA. Whereas the CPA considers the consumer only "a natural person who procures goods or services on the market for purposes not intended for his business or other commercial activity" (Art. 5, para. 1, indent 1), the FUPA extends the application of the CPA unfair terms concept to the entrepreneurs and farmers, provided that they are holders or members of a family farm (Art. 2, para. 1, indent 9).

Having said that, it can be summarized that the concept of unfair terms of the CPA applies to consumers, entrepreneurs and farmers. To the business entities other than entrepreneurs, this concept may not apply. This, however, does not mean that B2B contracts are generally excluded from the fairness assessment. Instead, this only implies that B2B consumers shall be subject to the unfairness concept provided in Art. 143 of the LoO, and not that of the CPA. This outcome is in line with the contemporary tendencies in European contract law which indicate that it is out of question that also B2B standard contracts deserve to be scrutinized on their fairness. It it, therefore, not the question of *if* but of *how*.[32] Surprisingly, this differentiation between the regimes of B2C and B2B contracts seems to be totally neglected in the Court's reasoning.

Before finally subjecting to the scrutiny the arguments of the Court, two more remarks are needed. One refers to the relationship between the CPA and the Directive, i.e. to what extent the CPA mirrors Directive's solutions. The other one touches upon the relationship between the CPA and the LoO.

---

[31] Official Gazette of RS, No. 36/2011, 139/2014.

[32] Jansen in: Jansen and Zimmermann (2018), p. 984.

Having mentioned that Directive aims at minimum harmonization, it is necessary to determine in which directions the CPA deviates from its solutions. This is needed in order to assess the appropriateness of the Court's reference to Art. 4(2) of Directive and the pertinent case law. In short, the CPA departs from the Directive's wording in three main directions. First, unlike Directive (Art. 3), the CPA does not subject standard terms and terms individually negotiated to the different regimes. Contrary to Directive's solution, the CPA subjects all contract terms to the unfairness test, regardless of whether such a term arises as a result of negotiations or is unilaterally determined (Art. 43/1 in conjunction with Art. 5, para. 1, indent 21). This solution, without a doubt, serves to strengthen the position of consumers in the Serbian market. Nevertheless, as already mentioned, "the manner in which the consent was reached on the content of the contract" shall be used as an accompanying criterion in the fairness assessment. This means that domestic courts may consider the assertion that the specific term was individually negotiated instead of being unilaterally imposed on the party. In any case, the burden of such argument shall rest on the supplier of the terms. Second, the CPA does not distinguish between core and non-core terms. In contrast to Directive (Art. 4(2)), it subjects all contract terms to the fairness scrutiny regardless of whether they govern main subject matter or ancillary terms. Moreover, the fairness test under the CPA may also relate to "the adequacy of the price and remuneration" to be paid in exchange for good or service. On the other hand, according to the Directive, main subject matter and the adequacy price/remuneration argument can be subject to fairness control only provided they fail to meet transparency criteria. Third, while Directive contains only one indicative list of unfair terms (Annex referred to Art. 3 (3)), Serbia, like many other countries, opted for introducing two lists, splitting unfair terms in the black and grey list according to their estimated ability to impair the position of consumers.

Finally, it is important to briefly turn to the interplay between the CPA and the LoO. This is particularly important for determining the relationship between the imbalance standard introduced under the LoO compared to that of the CPA. Namely, the LoO applies to the B2C contracts according to the principle of subsidiarity. This means that, when it comes to B2C contracts, the CPA has precedence in application over the LoO, so long as it contains a special set of rules. In other words, the CPA is *lex specialis* compared to the LoO which contains the rules of general law of contracts. Accordingly, provisions of the LoO shall apply to B2C contracts only in aspects not covered by the CPA.

5 Review of the Court's Arguments

After clarifying the dogmatic background of the fairness review and its current normative framework in Serbia, the analysis may now turn to examining of the Court's arguments. As mentioned above, the assessment will be confined to the parts of the reasoning related to the concept of unfair terms. This will be done by quoting or paraphrasing the relevant part of the reasoning and subsequent commenting on it.

5.1 Relationship Between the Transparency Requirement and Good Faith Principle

"Obliging a credit user to pay credit processing costs is not contrary to the principle of good faith stipulated in Art. 12 of the LoO, provided that such an obligation has been drafted in a transparent way."[33]

By stating that, the Court seems to have placed under the same umbrella two distinctive fairness assessment criteria: transparency and good faith. In this regard, it is true that non-transparent wording of the term can serve as an indicator of its unfairness.[34] Nevertheless, it cannot be assumed that a term is considered fair so long as it is drafted in simple, intelligible language. And, vice versa, the term should not be considered unfair only because it was drafted in the non-transparent manner.[35] If an easily understandable term were automatically considered fair, transparency would be envisaged by the legislator as the only criterion for the fairness review. Instead, the lawmaker provided a multi-layered fairness control. Connected therewith, it is postulated in literature that "the duty of transparency should not be misunderstood as expecting customers to actually read the standard terms included in their contracts. It cannot be argued, therefore, that the principle of transparency should replace substantive requirements of contractual justice."[36] Consequently, after finding that the term on credit processing costs meets transparency requirement, the Court should have proceeded to examine such a term in relation to the substantive fairness benchmarks: good faith and significant imbalance.

As the imbalance criterion will be dealt with later, here it will be briefly showcased how transparency requirement is to be grasped according to the CPA, followed by the CJEU understanding of the good faith requirement. The latter will be useful for Serbian courts, as the CPA does not provide any guidelines on this issue.

When it comes to transparency requirement, the CPA mentions its two aspects. Firstly, it states in Art. 41 that "[a] contractual term is binding on the consumer if it is expressed in simple, clear and understandable language [. . .]." It could, *a contrario*, be inferred that a non-transparent term shall not be binding on consumer. However, it does not necessarily mean that a non-transparent term is drafted to the detriment of the consumer. Therefore, the CPA provides in its Art. 42 a rule of interpretation known as *contra proferentem* rule. It states that "[v]ague contract terms between the consumer and the trader are interpreted in favor of the consumer." This Article implies that ambiguous terms—those susceptible to manifold interpretations—should be understood in the way that favors consumer rather than supplier. This interpretative rule is thus seen as an incentive for the supplier to avoid "bad

[33] This argument can be read on page 5 of the Court's reasoning.

[34] Commission notice (2019), p. 22.

[35] Karanikić Mirić (2009), p. 142.

[36] Jansen in: Jansen and Zimmermann (2018), p. 987.

drafting".[37] When a non-transparent term may be interpreted in multiple ways, the court shall primary ascertain if some of these meanings facilitate interests of consumers. Conversely, if a non-transparent term cannot be understood in favor of a consumer, it should not be binding on him. Nevertheless, the fairness assessment does not cease here. After "passing" the transparency test, the term should be checked according to the substantive fairness criteria, including good faith.[38]

"The idea of good faith long seemed to lack any independent normative significance beside the Directive's essential element of a significant imbalance in the parties' rights and obligations."[39] As the correlation between these two elements was not clear, the CJEU used this ambiguity to employ "innovative interpretation".[40] In doing so, the CJEU has, in the meantime, developed an autonomous meaning of the good faith element which is closely related, but independent of the meaning of significant imbalance. According to the CJEU case law, the term will be considered contrary to the principle of good faith if the supplier cannot assume that the consumer would reasonably accept such a term, if he had an opportunity to negotiate with the supplier on an equal footing.[41]

Applied to the reasoning in question, the Court should have examined whether the credit user would accept to pay the credit processing costs if he had negotiated the contract with the bank "on an equal footing".

5.2 *The Court's Reference to the Directive and the CJEU Case Law*

In trying to find support for its opinion, the Court refers in its reasoning to Art. 4(2) of the Directive and the Case C-84/19 of the CJEU. Searching for arguments in the wording of the Directive and pertinent case law is generally recommended given Serbia's status of a candidate for the EU membership. However, this only makes sense when Serbian national rules reflect the rules of the Directive in a certain aspect. Speaking of this, it has already been mentioned that the Directive has a minimal harmonizing character and that the Serbian legislator has decided to deviate from some of its solutions in order to afford a higher standard of protection to its consumers. Having this in mind, it is inconceivable why the Court refers to Art.

[37] Jansen in: Jansen and Zimmermann (2018), p. 986.

[38] Jansen in: Jansen and Zimmermann (2018), fn. 28, 989.

[39] Jansen in: Jansen and Zimmermann (2018), p. 944.

[40] Jansen in: Jansen and Zimmermann (2018), p. 939.

[41] Commission notice (2019), p. 29 with the reference to the Judgement of the CJEU of 14 March 2013 in Case C-415/11 Mohamed *Aziz v Caixa d'Estalvis de Catalunya, Tarragona i Manresa (Catalunyacaixa)*, paragraph 69: "[...] the national court must assess for those purposes whether the seller or supplier, dealing fairly and equitably with the consumer, could reasonably assume that the consumer would have agreed to such a term in individual contract negotiations."

4(2) of the Directive, when the Serbian legislator deviated from its wording in Art. 43 of the CPA. To recall, in stark contrast to the Directive, the CPA does not distinguish between core and non-core contract terms.[42] Instead, it provides for the uniform fairness control of all contract terms regardless of whether they govern main subject matter or ancillary term. Moreover, Serbian CPA does not envisage the exception to the unfairness test with regard to the terms that pertain "to the adequacy of the price and remuneration, on one hand, as against the services or goods supplied in exchange, on the other [. . .]". Therefore, the Court's reference to Art. 4(2) of the Directive should not have any significance for the Serbian consumers. The same applies to the Court's reference to the CJEU Judgment in Case C-84/19 in as much as it refers to the arguments that concern the interpretation of Art. 4(2) of the Directive.

Precisely, the Court relied in its reasoning to what the CJEU stated in the paragraph 79 of the Case C-84/19 which reads as follows: "as regards the review of 'the adequacy of the price and remuneration' on the one hand, and the good and service, on the other hand, it is settled case-law that that category of terms, whose potentially unfair nature cannot be the subject of assessment, has a reduced scope, since it concerns only the balance between the price or remuneration provided for and the services or goods to be supplied in return, that exclusion being explained by the fact that there is no objective legal scale or criterion that can provide a framework for and guide a review of that balance." This argument would have been acceptable, if the Serbian CPA had provided for such an exception to the unfairness control. Since this is not the case, the Court's reference to paragraph 79 of the Case C-84/19 simply does not reflect the extent of the unfairness review laid down by the Serbian legislator in Art. 43 of the CPA. The fact that the CPA does not provide for such a limitation of the fairness control can only serve as an indicator for the national legislator to introduce that exception in the future revision of the CPA. However, without legislative intervention, the Court is not competent to narrow the scope of unfairness control that would be contrary to the wording of the CPA.

That this deviation from the Directive's wording is in accordance with its minimum harmonizing character was confirmed by the CJEU in relation to the Polish national law (paragraph 83–85). Namely the Polish Civil Code provides in its Art. 385(1) that the exception to the examining of the adequacy of the price and remuneration as compared to the services provided in exchange pertains only to the main subject matter of the contract. This, further, means that an ancillary contract term such as the one that envisages non-interest credit costs, cannot be subject to such an exception. Accordingly, the examination of adequacy of such costs is not precluded by way of Polish law. This is so since the Polish law provides for the more stringent unfairness benchmarks compared to those stipulated in the Directive which, as already postulated, is in accordance with its minimum character.

This demonstrates that the Court's reference to the paragraph 79 of the Case C-84/19 is not appropriate since it relates to the exception to the unfairness test

---

[42] For detailed explanation of this distinction and underlying reasons see: Pomar (2019), pp. 177–194.

which is unknown to the CPA. So long as the Serbian legislator does not provide for such an exception to the unfairness control, the Court may not introduce it by way of its interpretation. Such interpretation would be to the detriment of the Serbian consumers, in that it would lower the level of protection that they should enjoy in accordance with the currently applicable CPA.

It seems that it would have been better had the Court referred to Case C-222/19 instead of Case C-84/19 (they were adjudicated jointly). Namely, the reference to the Case C-222/19 would have been more appropriate than the reference to the previous one given the normative framework of the fairness control laid down by the CPA. The Case C-222/19 handles the question that pertains to the interpretation of the Art. 3(1) of the Directive whose wording essentially corresponds to that of Art. 43(2) of the CPA.[43] In Case C-222/19, the CJEU focused itself on giving guidance to the Polish national court as to whether "a contractual term which has not been individually negotiated and which imposes on the consumer non-interest credit costs, including costs of the lender's economic activity, below a statutory maximum upper limit, may be regarded as unfair, within the meaning of Art. 3(1) (paragraph 89)." With this regard, the CJEU concluded that "Article 3(1) of Directive 93/13 must be interpreted as meaning that a contractual term relating to non-interest credit costs, which sets that cost below a statutory upper limit and which passes on, to the consumer, the costs of the lender's economic activity, is liable to cause a significant imbalance in the parties' rights and obligations arising under the contract to the detriment of the consumer, where it imposes on that consumer costs which are disproportionate to the services provided and to the amount of the loan received, which it is for the referring court to ascertain (paragraph 97)."

Since even the courts whose national law provides for a statutory upper limit within which non-interest credit cost can be contracted may review the unfairness of such a term, all the more such a control is conceivable in legal systems that do not envisage such a statutory limit. Consequently, the Court should not have satisfied itself by saying that credit processing costs had been contained in the offer to conclude the credit agreement, and, therefore, are considered valid.

Instead, the Court should have paid attention to the question of (dis)proportion between the credit processing costs paid by the credit users, on one hand, and services provided by the banks, taking into account the amount of the loan received, on the other. Only the results of such an assessment would support the substantial interests of consumers. By saying that, the author in no way implies that the outcome of such an analysis would run contrary to the Court's final stance on validity of a contractual term stipulating such costs.

[43] As already mentioned, the only difference pertains to the scope of the terms to which this unfairness control pertains. According to the CPA it is not limited to the individually negotiated terms.

5.3 *The Court's Reference to the Principle of Equal Value of Mutual Obligations*

With regard to the principle of equal value of mutual obligations set forth in Art. 15 of the LoO, the Court recalls that this principle must only be taken into account if the law prescribes consequences for its violation. The law, for instance, provides such consequences for usury contracts, *laesio enormis* etc. Therefore, in order for the term on credit processing costs to be considered contrary to this principle, it must be established that the consequences of such a violation are provided by law.

It is notorious that courts in continental Europe shall not, in principle, decide *ex aequo et bono*. Instead, they are obliged to support their decisions with legal arguments emanating from the legal institutes and rules, whereas it is a legislator's task to *a priory* "equip" courts with a set of such rules. Therefore, it is understandable why courts, as a rule, are not allowed to base their decisions on diffuse legal tenets, but merely on the concrete legal institutes through which such tenets have been concretized.[44] This is why fairness as such, especially perceived subjectively, cannot serve as a foundation for decision-making.

General legal tenet of fairness underlies one of the basic principles of civil law—the principle of equal value of mutual obligations. To exclude the possibility of its subjective application, the legislator explicitly provided that "it shall be determined by law in which cases the violation of that principle entails legal consequences." (Art. 15, para. 2 LoO). Serbian legislator had this principle in mind when regulating numerous institutes of LoO such as usury contracts (Art. 141 LoO), *laesio enormis* (Art. 139), changed circumstances (Art. 133 LoO), and many more. However, the LoO does not prevent other pieces of legislation to introduce autonomous concepts of equality. Indeed, the LoO in its Art. 15(2) states "determined by law" without limiting its application only to the cases stipulated in the LoO. In fact, if another piece of legislation is considered *lex specialis* compared to the LoO, the courts are obliged to apply provisions of such *lex specialis,* including its autonomous concept of equality. Needless to say, this is so only provided that particular case fulfills requirements (territorial, personal and temporal) for application of that *lex specialis*.

Having said this, it is striking that the Court entirely disregarded the fact that "the nullity of unfair terms in consumer contracts can be understood as a special civil sanction for violation of the principle of equal value of mutual obligations."[45] In fact, the Court at no point found suitable to bring in conjunction the *significant* imbalance criterion of Art. 43(2) CPA with Art. 15 (2) LoO. Namely, in order to afford consumers a higher standard of protection, the CPA deviates from a well-entrenched yardstick of *obvious* imbalance set out in Art. 139 and 141 of the LoO. Moreover, the CPA does not only reduce the equivalence threshold in that it dispenses from the requirement of obvious (conspicuous) imbalance of the LoO by providing the milder

[44] Perović (2007), pp. 68–69.

[45] Karanikić Mirić (2009), p. 144.

standard of *significant* imbalance. In addition to that, by way of Art. 43, the CPA liberates consumers from proving subjective elements required under usury contracts and *laesio enormis*. Hence, the assertion that charging credit processing costs could only be viewed as a violation of the equivalence principle if, for example, such stipulation meets the criteria of usury agreements, contradicts any logic of consumer protection law. Significant imbalance standard mentioned in Art. 43 CPA in fact presents the concretization of Art. 15(2) of the LoO in that it provides for the consequence of nullity of the contract term, provided that such fails to meet fairness benchmarks (transparency, goof faith and significant imbalance).

Moreover, in connection to the principle of equal value of Art. 15 LoO, the Court also states that "the breach of the principle of equivalence relates primarily to the contract as a whole and not to its individual terms."[46] In this regard, it is true that, when assessing fairness courts need to take into account "other terms of the same contract or another contract with which the contract is related (Art. 43, para. 3, indent 3)." This is because potential disadvantages a consumer may suffer from one contractual term can be balanced against the possible surpluses that consumers may experience from other contractual terms.[47] Namely, complex contracts consist of numerous stipulations, whereas from each of them derive certain rights and obligations. In such contracts, (im)balance shall be primary established within the realm of a particular stipulation, whereby the content of other terms shall serve as accompanying criterion for verifying whether the imbalance inherent to one term can be balanced against the gains from other term(s). Needless to say, the supplier shall bear the burden of arguments that the purported surplus hailing from a specific contractual term actually exists.

In fact, if the Court's argument were correct, the entire Directive 93/13/EEC would be deprived of its substantive meaning. Namely, the Directive primarily focuses on the assessment of the fairness of specific contract terms, whereby the unfairness test is, *inter alia*, based on the criterion of significant imbalance between the rights and obligations of the contracting parties arising from a particular term. Thus, it cannot be concluded that the imbalance regularly relates to the contract as a whole. If this were true, how could it be explained that the majority of the CJEU case law in this matter has been built around the unfairness of contract terms, and not the contract as a whole?

Having ascertained that the Court does not perceive correctly the significant imbalance criterion defined in the CPA, it is desirable to briefly outline what meaning the CJEU attaches to it. Indeed, in reviewing fairness, courts need to have a fulcrum in normative standards and understand the concepts underlying these standards. So, if the courts are expected to evaluate the balance between the rights and obligations arising from a particular contracting term, they need to have a framework within which such an assessment is to be executed.[48]

---

[46] Page 5 of the Court's reasoning.

[47] Krejci in: Rummel and Lukas (Hrsg) (2014), p. 270.

[48] Jansen in: Jansen and Zimmermann (2018), p. 941.

When setting this framework, the CJEU takes non-mandatory rules of national contract law as a benchmark for the balance assessment.[49] The doctrine justifies this stance in that "[j]udges have to rely on specific normative standards when determining what counts in a legal system as a fair distribution of burdens. These standards are normally to be found in non-mandatory contract law rules."[50] The starting premise therefore is that the legislator, when designing non-mandatory rules, regularly endeavors to allocate the rights and obligations between the parties in a way that corresponds to its vision of what is to be considered a balanced distribution of their rights and obligations.[51] This, however, in no way infers that each departure from such "an ideal" should be automatically deemed as causing relevant imbalance, since it is not each and every imbalance that matters. Indeed, it is the very purpose of non-mandatory rules to give leeway to the parties to better adapt the content of the contract to their needs by deviating from such rules.[52] Nevertheless, such rules, as presenting the ideal of the legislator's vision of fair distribution, can serve as a yardstick for assessing unfairness. Accordingly, it is not the task of the court to determine whether the supplier has deviated from non-mandatory rules, but how far it has deviated from them.

Having said this, it is left open what benchmark should national courts use if the national law does not offer a relevant non-mandatory (dispositive) rule. For that case, the EU Commission provides that "a significant imbalance will have to be assessed in light of other points of reference, such as *fair and equitable market practices* or a *comparison of the rights and obligations of the parties under a particular term*, taking into account the nature of the contract and other related contract terms (emphasis added by the author)." [53] Translated to the credit processing costs, the Court should have put forward arguments substantiating why it considers a bank custom (practice) of charging such costs fair and equitable.

5.4 The Court's Reference to Art. 143 of the LoO

The Court further refers to Art. 143 of the LoO[54] in an attempt to underpin its opinion, in that it construes the wording of that article as follows: "Given that the obligation of the credit user to pay the credit processing costs is an ancillary obligation from the credit agreement, the terms of the general conditions prescribing such an obligation cannot be deemed contrary to the purpose of the credit agreement,

[49] Commission notice (2019), pp. 30–31.

[50] Jansen in: Jansen and Zimmermann (2018), p. 941.

[51] Jansen in: Jansen and Zimmermann (2018), p. 942.

[52] Vukotić (2014), pp. 385–386.

[53] Commission notice (2019), p. 30.

[54] See fn. 27.

since the purpose of the agreement can be circumvented only by amending the essential elements of the credit agreement."

With regard to this argument, it shall primary be recalled that the CPA as *lex specialis* has precedence in application over the LoO when the former provides for a special set of rules. Therefore, the Court's reference to Art. 143 of the LoO can be significant only in so far B2B contracts are concerned, since B2C contracts are governed by the unfair concept contained in the CPA.

Therefore, this argument can be subject to evaluation only in so far as B2B contracts are concerned. First, this argument of the Court is not able to sustain the basic critique that pertains to the linguistic interpretation of the Art. 143 LoO. Namely, this article is entitled "Nullity of *some provisions* of the general conditions" (emphasis added by the author). So, if the Court's assertion that only essential elements of the contract could impair the contract's aim, would be true, this would mean that only the contract as a whole, and not only one or some of its clauses (terms) could be denied legal effect. Namely, if the contract would be deprived of its essential element, it would, as a rule, be declared null and void in its entirety, since it principally cannot subsist without its essential elements. The Court's interpretation thus runs contrary to the well-known maxim *utile per inutile non vitiatur.*[55] Not to mention again that the Court extracted the notion "aim of the concluded contract" from the wording of the Art. 143 LoO, neglecting its holistic meaning. It goes without saying that this "interpretative technique" is alien to the legal methodology. This, nevertheless, does not infer that contracting credit processing costs can be considered contrary to the aim of the credit agreement. This only means that the Court's argument in support of that assertion is not viable.

5.5 *The Court's Reference to the Black and Grey Lists of CPA*

"The contract term that obliges the credit user to pay the credit processing costs cannot be subsumed under any of the cases of unfair contractual terms listed in Art. 44 and 45 of the CPA. Therefore, the application of the terms of the general conditions that enable the contracting of such an obligation cannot be questioned according to the Article 143, para. 2 of LoO."

The interplay between the CPA and the LoO has already been clarified. Therefore, the comment to this argument will be confined to the Court's premise that so long as the disputed term is neither on the black nor the grey list provided in the CPA, it is considered fair. To begin with, it is important to note that the Court has applied the correct sequence of steps. Namely, when assessing fairness, it is initial task of the court to check if the challenged term is on the black or grey list. If blacklisted (Art. 44 CPA), the term will automatically be declared void. In other

[55] Tomás (2016), pp. 259–286. All the more, the aim of the Art. 4 (2) of the Directive was to limit the fairness control only to the ancillary, i.e. non-core contract terms.

words, the black list does not leave the courts any margin of appreciation when it comes to assessing the fairness of the terms set out therein. On the other hand, when the term is to be found on the grey list (Art. 45 CPA), it only allocates the burden of argument[56] to the supplier of such term, if it endeavors to overturn the presumption of its unfairness. As already underlined, the drawbacks hailing from one term could be outweighed by the surpluses of other term(s), which is on the supplier to prove.

Nevertheless, the fact that the disputed term is not given on any of the two lists in no way implies that such term is fair.[57] Had the legislator envisaged to disapprove only the terms given in the lists, it would not simultaneously provide the general unfairness test as a necessary safety net to disavow unfair clauses other than those explicitly mentioned. The insight that a certain term is not included in the two lists, therefore, only signals the court to examine this term according to the general assessment test. Moreover, if all terms that are not on the black or gray list were to be considered fair, we would not have to "scatter" human resources when deciding on their fairness, because an algorithm could do that too.

5.6 The Court's Understanding of the "Take It or Leave It" Principle

The last argument that will be briefly touched upon refers to the Court's assertion that "[a] client who considers that the offered credit processing costs are too high, may opt for concluding a credit agreement with a bank that provides lower costs or which does not charge those costs."

The unsustainability of this argument stems from everything said so far. As already pointed out, the idea underlying the fairness review is not to leave consumers at the mercy of the suppliers, but to enable them to get the products and services at the market under fair terms. It was recognized long ago that in relation to the standard contract terms there is a market failure which can only be "fixed" by the court's intervention in the content of the standard contracts. By stating that consumers should have examined the general terms and conditions of other banks and decided accordingly, the Court only revealed its misunderstanding of the law of standard terms and conditions in general and consumer law in particular. Moreover, the Court omitted to give advice to consumers on what to do if their "legal analysis" reveals that all banks charge credit processing costs. Leaving consumers in the lurch with such a statement sends them a message that their interests will not be substantially, but only nominally protected.

[56] Jansen in: Jansen and Zimmermann (2018), p. 946.

[57] Karanikić Mirić (2012), p. 224.

6 Conclusion

The paper subjects to scrutiny the reasoning of the recent Supplement to the legal opinion of the Supreme Court of Cassation of the Republic of Serbia on validity of contracting credit costs. The opinion stirred an unprecedented dissatisfaction among credit consumers, legal profession and informed public. The paper, thus, aimed at bringing some clarity to what the Court actually said. The analysis was confined to the Court's arguments that refer to the concept of unfair terms in consumer contracts. It revealed examples of misunderstanding of the normative standards that underlie this concept. This is primarily due to the misconceiving of the relationship between the Consumer Protection Act and the Law on Obligations, on one hand, and the relationship between the Serbian Consumer Protection Act and Unfair Contract Terms Directive (93/13/EEC), on the other. By offering an inconclusive argumentation in the part relating to the concept of unfair terms in consumer contracts, the reasoning cannot merit full support. Nevertheless, this is without prejudice to the Court's final stance on the validity of contracting credit costs. Indeed, the Court's stance is not indefensible, but it can hardly be defended by the given arguments. In fact, pursuant to the given reasoning, the consumers may easily gain an impression that their rights enjoy only formal, nominal protection, instead of being protected substantially. Therefore, if it sought to gain wider support on this very sensitive issue, the reasoning should have been formulated more prudently.

References

Commission notice — Guidance on the interpretation and application of Council Directive 93/13/EEC on unfair terms in consumer contracts (Text with EEA relevance) (2019) OJ C 323, 27.9.2019: 4-92

Đurđević M (2001) Ugovor po pristupu – doktorska disertacija (Accession contract – doctoral dissertation). Pravni fakultet Univerzitet u Beogradu, Beograd

Gauch P, Schluep RW (2014) Schweizerisches Obligationenrecht. Allgemeiner Teil: ohne ausservertragliches Haftpflichtrecht, Bd. 1, 10. Aufl./erg., verb. und nachgeführt von Jörg Schmid. Schulthess, Zürich [u.a.]

Hart D (1989) Zivilrechtspraxis zwischen Vertragskonsolidirung und Vertragsrechtsfortbildung, Am Beispiel der ergänzende Vetragsauslegung und der Geschäftsgrundlage. Kritische Vierteljahresschrift für Gesetzgebung und Rechtswissenschaft 4(2):179–200

Jansen N, Zimmermann R (eds) (2018) Commentaries on European contract laws. Oxford University Press, Oxford

Karanikić Mirić M (2009) Nepravične odredbe u potrošačkim ugovorima. In: Lilić S (prir.) Pravni kapacitet Srbije za evropske integracije, knjiga 4, Pravni fakultet Univerziteta u Beogradu, pp 128–146

Karanikić Mirić M (2012) Nepravične odredbe u ugovornom pravu Republike Srbije (Unfair terms in the Contract Law of the Republic of Serbia). Forum za građansko pravo za jugoistočnu Evropu: izbor radova i analiza, Druga regionalna konferencija, Skoplje, 2012. Knjiga II:218–229

Knežević SM (2017) Ujednačavanje sudske prakse u Republici Srbiji – stanje stvari i predlozi za reform (Unifying Case Law in the Republic of Serbia – Current Status and Proposals for its Reform). Projekat "Unapređenje efikasnosti pravosuđa" 12SER 01/01/121

Knežević SM (2019) Out-of-trial case law unifying in Serbia: legal tradition as requiem for the rule of law?. In: 1. International Scientific Conference "Legal Tradition and New Legal Challenges", Novi Sad Faculty of Law 3–4 October, p 49

Mäsch G (2019) J. von Staudingers Kommentar zum Bürgerlichen Gesetzbuch, §§ 305-310. Sellier-de Gruyter, Berlin

Perović S (2007) Autonomija volje i prinudni propisi (Autonomy of will and imperative norms). Pravni život 5–6:7–37

Pomar FG (2019) Core versus Non-Core terms and legal controls over consumer contract terms: (Bad) Lessons from Europe? Eur Rev Contract Law 15(2):177–194

Raiser L (1960) Vertragsfunktion und Vertragsfreiheit. In: Hundert Jahre Deutsches Rechtsleben, Festschrift zum Hundertjährigen bestehen des deutschen Juristentages 1860-1960, Ernst von Caemmerer, Ernst Friesenhahn, Richard Lange Hrsg., Band I, Verlag C.F. Müller, Karlsruhe, pp 101–134

Rummel P, Lukas M (Hrsg) (2014) ABGB, Teilband §§ 859-916 ABGB (Vertragsrecht), 4. Auflage. MANZ'sche Verlags- und Universitätsbuchhandlung, Wien

Tomás G (2016) Utile per inutile non vitiatur: can favor contractus be considered a European regula iuris? Eur Rev Contract Law 12(3):259–286

Vukotić M (2014) Kritički osvrt na pravni režim opštih uslova poslovanja u srpskom pravu (A critical review of the legal Regime of standard contract terms in Serbian law). Pravo i privreda 7–9:375–390

Živković M (2018) On legality of the loan processing fee in the Serbian law. Bankarstvo 47(2): 14–51

Part III
International Law

International Standards on Judicial Ethics and the Pitfalls of Cursory Legal Transplantation

Ana Knežević Bojović, Milica V. Matijević, and Mirjana Glintić

Contents

1 Introductory Remarks and Context

Judicial independence is an essential element of the rule of law, understood to include the elements proposed by Bingham[1] and endorsed by the European Commission for Democracy Through Law in its seminal Report on the Rule of

[1] Bingham defined eight principles of the rule of law, which are the following: (1) Accessibility of the law (that it be intelligible, clear and predictable); (2) Questions of legal right should be normally decided by law and not discretion; (3) Equality before the law; (4) Power must be exercised lawfully, fairly and reasonably; (5) Human rights must be protected; (6) Means must be provided to resolve disputes without undue cost or delay; (7) Trials must be fair, and (8) Compliance by the state with its obligations in international law as well as in national law. Bingham (2010), p. 8.

A. Knežević Bojović (✉) · M. V. Matijević · M. Glintić
Institute of Comparative Law, Belgrade, Serbia
e-mail: a.bojovic@iup.rs; m.matijevic@iup.rs; m.glintic@iup.rs

D. V. Popović et al. (eds.), *Balkan Yearbook of European and International Law 2021*, Balkan Yearbook of European and International Law 2021,
https://doi.org/10.1007/978-3-030-97431-2_8

Law.[2] The creation of a culture of judicial independence is not only within the purview of national legislators—it is considerably influenced by international law by virtue of international human rights treaties[3] and international standards developed by governmental and non-governmental organisations, as well as by academic study groups.[4] The soft-law standards developed by supranational actors, such as the UN Human Rights Committee, Consultative Council of European Judges and the Venice Commission, are being resorted to not only by national legislators and self-regulating stakeholders within the judiciary,[5] but also by supranational courts as a legal basis to sustain the principle of independence of the judiciary both in *abstracto* and *in concreto*.[6] Judicial independence is intrinsically linked to judicial integrity. The latter can be understood as the "ability of the judicial system or an individual member of the judiciary to resist corruption, while fully respecting the core values such as independence, impartiality, competence and diligence".[7]

Additionally, judicial ethics and integrity are an important staple of multifaceted international legal and institutional framework for countering corruption.[8] The codes of professional conduct for public officials, including judges, are among the key instruments in fostering a culture of judicial independence[9] and countering corruption.[10] The implementation of anti-corruption standards in the Council of Europe (CoE) countries is monitored by the Group of Countries Against Corruption (GRECO). Through its rounds of evaluation of the state of affairs in each CoE country and relevant recommendations, this body aims at the improvement of the level of compliance with the anti-corruption standards. The fourth round of GRECO evaluations was dedicated to the prevention of corruption in respect of members of parliament, judges and prosecutors, where ethical principles and rules of conduct for these categories of public officials were among the key topics. Through this round of evaluations, GRECO frequently examined the existence of a mechanism for the so-called "confidential counselling" on ethical matters, through which judges could seek guidance from their peers, in a confidential procedure, on how to correctly

---

[2] Venice Commission (2011).

[3] For instance, at the European level, the right to an independent and impartial tribunal is guaranteed by Article 6 of the European Convention on Human Rights (Convention for the Protection of Human Rights and Fundamental Freedoms), Rome, 1951.

[4] Shetreet et al. (2021).

[5] Such as judicial self-governance bodies and professional association of judges.

[6] See: paragraph 6 of the Joint concurring opinion of judges Pinto de Albuquerque and Dedov to the judgment of the European Court of Human Rights in the case of *Baka v. Hungary*, Application no. 20261/12, Judgment of Grand Chamber of 23 June 2016.

[7] https://www.unodc.org/unodc/en/corruption/judicial-integrity.html.

[8] General Assembly of United Nations, Resolution 58/4 of 31 October 2003—United Nations Convention against Corruption; Committee of Ministers of the Council of Europe, Resolution 97/24 on the twenty guiding principles for fight against corruption of 6 November 1997.

[9] Shetreet (2012).

[10] This standard was set in: Committee of Ministers of the Council of Europe, Resolution 97/24 on the twenty guiding principles for fight against corruption of 6 November 1997.

implement ethical standards in their actions.[11] Where such a mechanism did not exist, GRECO often recommended its introduction, thus underscoring its standard-setting role.[12] This effort was additionally supported in the CCJE Opinion No. 21, which deals with prevention of corruption among judges and stresses the importance of internal guidance to be provided within the judiciary itself to judges on how to behave when faced with ethical dilemmas, including the individual ethical counselling.[13] These international developments have given impetus for a number of regulatory and institutional interventions in the Council of Europe member states, some of which seem to have been informed by comparative analyses or various technical support projects funded by the EU.[14]

However, as pointed out by Shetreet, Chodosh and Helland, implementation of standards relating to judicial independence implies the need to strike a delicate balance between the established standards, on the one hand, and the recognition of particular circumstances of the given country, on the other.[15] Hence, it might be useful to look at various comparative solutions and take under advisement the lessons learned in countries that have taken the steps to practically implement the said standards. In doing so, it is of particular importance to recognise that comparative experiences provide valuable insights not only when they represent good practice examples but also in cases when they are about practices that should not be replicated. This position is not purely a practical one—academic literature provides a sound theoretical framework for discussions on whether legal solutions from one country can be successfully transferred to another and what are the limitations of such an undertaking. These various theoretical positions will be presented in the section of the paper dealing with legal transplants.

This paper takes the position that legal transplants are possible and that successful legal and institutional transplants can contribute to the positive development of not only law but of society as a whole. The authors posit that legal transplants need to be transferred to the transplanting system as a part of a comprehensive package, which is not limited only to normative and dogmatic interventions, but also entails the establishment of the necessary societal and political support that will enable the transplant to be fully functional and effective,[16] and thus compliant with the relevant international standard the implementation of which it aims to facilitate. Further, the authors note that some tendencies similar to those that have preceded the broad

[11] The legal and institutional nature of this mechanism and concrete solutions found in comparative practice will be presented in more detail further in the text.

[12] See: Esposito (2019), p. 174. Esposito outlines that the vast majority of GRECO member states received recommendations on codes of conduct, where a third of these were to adopt such codes while the rest focused on substance and implementation, including confidential counselling.

[13] Consultative Council of European Judges (2018), Opinion No. 21 "Preventing corruption among judges".

[14] See, for instance, GRECO (2017), Compliance Report RC4(2017)14 on Montenegro and GRECO (2016), Compliance Report RC4(2016)4 on Latvia.

[15] Shetreet et al. (2021).

[16] Knežević Bojović (2019), p. 407.

advocacy for the establishment of judicial councils can be identified in the process of upgrading national advisory frameworks for ethics and integrity matters for judges. Consequently, caution should be taken to avoid shortcomings that have characterised the implementation of international standards related to judicial councils when implementing those regarding judicial ethics, particularly when the relevant mechanism is introduced through a legal transplanting exercise.

That is in the paper illustrated through the analysis of the Romanian case, where the introduction of the mechanism for confidential counselling was to a great extent shaped through a joint Romanian-Dutch cooperation project initiated in 2014. The authors of the paper argue that the attempted introduction of confidential counselling in Romania was an unsuccessful legal transplant. Even though the said transplant was aimed at ensuring adherence to international soft-law standards, its lack of success can be attributed to the failure to duly understand how the judiciary functioned in the given state.

Finally, in the conclusion of the paper, the authors outline the lessons learned from the Romanian experience in finding the optimal solution for the provision of confidential counselling to judges.

2 Standards of Judicial Ethics in International Legal Framework

Ethics is not only a theoretical discipline but also a philosophical one researching morality, moral values and the criteria of morality.[17] Society increasingly demands moral excellence from a wide range of professionals, where judges, who are "the living voice of the law" (*iudex est viva vox legis),* have an additional obligation to consistently abide by ethical norms and principles not only in their work but also in their everyday life.[18] As Garoupa and Ginsbourg point out, judicial ethics is of key relevance for judicial reputation, and judges must take care of the reputation of the entire judiciary in order to maximise their individual reputations.[19] Respect by judges of ethical requirements is a duty which comes with their powers.[20]

Over the past decades, the topic of judicial ethics and integrity has been in the focus of different supranational bodies, both global and regional. Undoubtedly, the most influential document developed as a part of such efforts are the Bangalore Principles of Judicial Conduct.[21] The Bangalore Principles aim to establish a

[17] Babić (2008), pp. 35–48.

[18] Sancho (2007), pp. 117–138.

[19] Garoupa and Ginsbourg (2015), pp. 65, 188.

[20] Committee of Ministers of the Council of Europe, Recommendation 12/2010 on judges: independence, efficiency and responsibilities of 17 November 2010, para. 69.

[21] United Nations Economic and Social Council, Resolution 2006/23 Strengthening Basic Principles of Judicial Conduct of 27 July 2006.

framework for the ethical conduct of judges and thus indirectly contribute to curbing corruption.[22]

In Europe, the CoE has taken a key role in formulating judicial ethics and integrity standards, which are outlined in the CoE CM/Rec(2010)12 Recommendation on judges: independence, efficiency and responsibilities, and later confirmed in the Magna Carta of Judges adopted by the Consultative Council of European Judges (CCJE). More detailed formulations of these standards were developed by the CCJE, an advisory body of the CoE comprised of national judges. When it comes to the ethical rules for judges, the CCJE Opinion No. 3/2002 on the principles and rules governing judges' professional conduct, in particular ethics, incompatible behaviour and impartiality, is the most topical document on the subject. However, standards relating to various aspects of ethical behaviour and good professional conduct can be found in practically all opinions adopted by the CCJE. For instance, CCJE Opinion No. 21/2018 recognises the importance of not only the existence of ethical codes or codes of conduct, but also of their full operationalisation and internalisation among the judicial corps through provision of peer guidance on how to solve ethical dilemmas, including confidential counselling mechanisms, and relevant training on judicial conduct.[23]

Concurrently with the CoE, the European Network of Judicial Councils (ENCJ) has developed its Judicial Ethics Report, which was additionally endorsed in the London Declaration, in an attempt to systematise the common values inherent to judicial office, as well as the qualities and virtues that a judge needs to possess. When it comes to efforts of academic groups, the International Conference of Judicial Independence approved in 2015 the Bologna and Milan Global Code of Judicial Ethics aiming to clarify standards for the ethical conduct of judges and at setting standards applicable both to national and international judges.[24]

The standards on judicial ethics shaped by international and regional bodies can be summarised to envisage the following: in their activities, judges should be guided by principles of professional conduct; the principles should offer guidelines for judges on how to proceed thereby enabling them to overcome the challenges they are faced with as regards their independence and impartiality; the principles should be drawn up by the judges themselves and be separate from the judges' disciplinary system; it is desirable to establish in each country one or more bodies within the judiciary to advise judges who are confronted with a problem related to judicial ethics; judges should receive proper training on ethical conduct.

[22] Terhechte (2009), p. 514.

[23] Consultative Council of European Judges (2018), Opinion No. 21 "Preventing Corruption among Judges", para. 32 and 33.

[24] Bologna and Milan Global Code of Judicial Ethics is available at: https://www.icj.org/wp-content/uploads/2016/02/Bologna-and-Milan-Global-Code-of-Judicial-Ethics.pdf. An overview of key issues related to the ethics of international judges can be found in Seibert-Fohr (2014).

3 Legal Transplants and Judicial Reforms

Legal transplant is a term developed by Alan Watson in 1974,[25] which relates to the practice of development of the law through legal borrowing—transposing or transplanting of a rule or a system of rules from one country to another.[26] While Watson famously took the position that legal transplants are the most fertile source of change in law, other legal scholars—most notably, Pierre Legrand—claimed that legal transplants are logically impossible.[27] Despite Legrand's attempts at refuting the notion of legal transplant, over the past decades Watson's concept has been supported by many legal scholars, who find legal transplants not only possible but have also analysed the conditions under which legal transplants can be successful[28] and have developed their typologies. Miller, for instance, elaborates on the typology of legal transplants by identifying the four main types: (i) the cost-saving transplant; (ii) the externally-dictated transplant; (iii) the entrepreneurial transplant; and (iv) the legitimacy-generating transplant.[29] He also indicates that in practice, pure types of legal transplants are rarely found and that in many cases transplants are a mix of these four types. Berkowitz, Pistor and Richard note that one of the key factors for the success of legal transplants lies in the receptivity of the transplanting legal system,[30] while Hantrais shows that transplants are more likely to succeed in cases of shared political orientations and values of the source country and the transplanting legal system.[31] Garoupa and Ogus note that, in the case of legal transplants, particularly those that are a result of the harmonisation of legal ideas, changes may be more visible on formal than on substantive level, given that the cost of formal compliance is lower than the price of substantive changes.[32] Some authors also

[25] Watson (1974).

[26] Đorđević (2008), p. 64.

[27] Legrand (1997). See also Grbić (2019), p. 141. Another, equaly well known theory which challenges the logical possibility of a successful legal transplant was the one developed by Otto Kahn-Freund in the very same year when Watson wrote his "Legal Transplants: An Approach to Comparative Law". Kahn-Freund argued for a context-sensitive approach to legal borrowing. See Kahn-Freund (1974), pp. 1–27.

[28] A useful overview of various theoretical positions on legal transplants can be found in Reyes (2014).

[29] Miller's categorisation of different types of transplants, which is based on ample scholarly debate, could be summarised in the following way: A cost-saving transplant implies the adoption of an existing solution to regulate a new problem, in order to save time and costly experimentation. Externally-dictated transplants involve a foreign individual, entity or government who indicate the adoption of a foreign legal model. Entrepreneurial transplants involve individuals and groups who use international norms to strengthen their positions in domestic debates by advocating for and supporting the adoption of legal transplants. In the legitimacy-generating type of transplant, the prestige of a foreign model—a legal institution or a legal system—is used to generate legitimacy. See Miller (2003).

[30] Berkowitz et al. (2003), pp. 163–203.

[31] Hantrais (2009), p. 45.

[32] Garoupa and Ogus (2006), p. 358.

indicate that a successful legal transplant implies the transfer of not only norms but also of the underlying dogmatic approach, supported through adequately conducted *ex-ante* and *ex-post* regulatory impact assessment while ensuring that the transplants are transferred through a broad and inclusive social dialogue.[33]

In the judicial sector in Central and East European countries, one of the key legal transplants of legal ideas was the judicial council as a judicial self-administration body. Supported by the CoE,[34] particularly through the work of the Venice Commission,[35] as well as through a clear political push from the European Union, judicial councils emerged as a standard of judicial independence to be implemented by former communist countries on their path towards European integration.[36] Although initially acclaimed almost as a panacea for the inherited problems of the socialist model of judicial administration, which included the considerable influence of politics on the judiciary, the newly-established judicial councils of the Southern European type, once implemented in Central and East European countries, had limited practical results.[37]

More specifically, they did not considerably contribute to the independence and accountability of the judicial power, nor did they improve trust in the judiciary.[38] The reasons for this are manifold. Some authors point to the influence of the political and social heritage;[39] others to the adverse effects of the conditionality policy,[40] coupled with the fact that the pre-existing judicial culture and the specific features of the national judiciary were not duly factored in when the judicial councils were established.[41] When it comes to the judicial sector reforms, the success of legal transplants is found to be contingent on a thorough understanding of the existing judicial culture and the way in which the judiciary functions.

The above discussion is of particular importance in the context of the GRECO recommendations on judicial ethics ensuing from its 4th round of evaluations, as GRECO not only required the adoption of ethical codes or codes of conduct for judges in countries where such codes did not exist, but also called for the establishment of mechanisms for providing guidance on ethical dilemmas. In doing so,

---

[33] Breneselović (2013), p. 346; Knežević Bojović (2019), pp. 406–407.

[34] The key CoE document which referred to this standard at the time was Committee of Ministers, Recommendation 94(12) to the member states on the independence, efficiency and role of judges of 13 October 1994.

[35] The most important documents of the Venice Commission in this field are: Venice Commission (2007, 2010, 2016).

[36] Rakić Vodinelić et al. (2012), p. 15; Marković (2017), p. 209; Preshova et al. (2017), p. 13.

[37] Kosař (2018), p. 1568; Bobek and Kosař (2014); Garoupa and Ginsburg (2009), p. 58; Voermans (2003), p. 2134; Castillo-Ortiz (2019), p. 504.

[38] Kosař (2018), pp. 1602–1612; Urbániková and Šipulova (2018).

[39] Magalhães (1999), pp. 58–59.

[40] Mendelski (2015), pp. 332–333.

[41] Preshova et al. (2017), p. 24.

GRECO did not always suggest specific solutions tailored for particular countries,[42] but instead formulated general recommendations aiming at the implementation of relevant standards. This opened the doors for a wide array of country-specific solutions. The national regulators could opt for modelling their solutions on the practices of confidential counselling already existing for other categories of public servants (e.g. civil servants), or already in place within professional associations of judges, which is a particularly useful avenue since they are, as a rule, modelled on the soft-law standards mentioned above. Another option was to look at the emerging practices in national judicial systems with a reputation of fostering judicial independence and integrity, and using them as models for developing effective solutions that are in line with the international standards—an approach that would combine the cost-effective and legitimacy-generating transplant. Such exercise seems to carry the same risks as the introduction of judicial councils, if not properly matched with the judicial culture and a thorough understanding of how the judiciary functions in a given country. Since judicial ethics is intrinsically linked to the exercise of judicial powers, and given that standards on judicial ethics formulated in international soft-law instruments are primarily addressed to the members of the judicial profession and not only or not necessarily to the national legislator, the practical implementation of the ethics-related standards is even more reliant on being properly suited to the judicial system at hand.

4 Confidential Counselling on Ethical Issues for Judges

The implementation of ethical principles for judges is closely linked to the adoption of professional codes of conduct or ethical codes developed by judges themselves, which have the added value of being flexible and adaptable to the fast-changing legal and social environments.[43] The existence of a body that judges can address for additional guidance on how to ensure that their actions are in line with the codes is an important international standard in this regard. Confidential counselling, however, is a step further: it is an institutionalised, peer-to-peer mechanism, which enables judges to receive timely advisory support and guidance on their ethical dilemmas in a confidential procedure precisely in order to avoid infringement of the code.[44]

For the success of confidential counselling, it is important that the holders of judicial offices perceive this mechanism as independent, reliable and fully confidential. It is also imperative that judges are not adverted from using it for the fear that by

[42] Serbia, for instance, is an exception in that regard, as GRECO clearly indicated not only the need for confidential counselling within the judiciary to be provided for all categories of judges, but also recommended a confidential counselling mechanism to be placed outside of the official hierarchy, *i.e.* the High Judicial Council, and organised on the level of appellate courts. See GRECO (2014), Evaluation IV Report (2014) 8E on Serbia, para 131.

[43] Sremčev Ilić (2015), pp. 275–290.

[44] Mrčela (2020).

asking questions on how to act ethically they might face adverse consequences. That is particularly important in those countries where some types of violations of ethical codes constitute a disciplinary offence,[45] as is the case in Serbia,[46] France and Hungary.[47]

What the standard does not regulate in a clear way is whether the body which monitors the implementation of ethical code is at the same time the body providing confidential counselling or not. The solutions found in comparative practice are divergent and depend on several matters, such as whether judicial ethics is regulated in a systematic manner, whether the ethical code is binding on all judges or not,[48] as well as on the pre-existing judicial culture of a country. In some countries, it is ethical boards or commissions, regardless of whether they operate under the frame of judicial councils (Spain and Lithuania) or act as independent bodies (Latvia), which are in charge of monitoring the implementation of codes of ethics and adopting general positions or opinions on whether an action is in line with the code of ethics, that also provide confidential counselling.[49] However, there are some comparative examples of clear distinction between the two.

France, for example, has two bodies. The first one is the College of Ethics of the Magistrates (*Collège de déontologie des magistrats de l'ordre judiciaire*), which is mandated with providing opinions on any ethical question concerning a magistrate personally, along with examining the declarations of interest of judges. The second body is the Deontological Assistance and Monitoring Service of the Superior

[45] International standard-setting documents in this field state that a clear distinction needs to be made between the violation of ethical and professional conduct standards and disciplinary offences. Disciplinary sanctions must be reserved for serious and flagrant misconduct, not simply for failures to observe professional standards. See in particular Consultative Council of Judges (2001), Opinion No. 2 on the funding and management of the courts; Consultative Council of Judges (2010), Magna Carta of Judges, principle 18; Committee of Ministers of the Council of Europe (2010), Explanatory memorandum to the Recommendation 12/2010 on judges: independence, efficiency and responsibilities.

[46] Art. 90 of the Law on judges, Official Gazette of the Republic of Serbia, Nos. 116/2008, 58/2009 (Decision of the Constitutional Court), 104/2009, 101/2010, 8/2012 (Decision of the Constitutional Court), 121/2012, 124/2012 (Decision of the Constitutional Court), 101/2013, 111/2014 (Decision of the Constitutional Court), 117/2014, 40/2015, 63/2015 (Decision of the Constitutional Court), 106/2015, 63/2016 (Decision of the Constitutional Court), 47/2017, 76/2021.

[47] European Network of Councils of Judiciary (2015), pp. 60 *et seq.*

[48] In some countries, there are no codes of ethics or of professional conduct that all judges are bound to apply. For instance, there is no ethical code for judges in Germany, Austrian association of judges has adopted a code of ethics for judges only recently, and it is binding only on its members, see Titz (2009), p. 36. In Italy, the existing code of ethics envisages rather broad ethical principles and is generally perceived as interference on the part of the executive, see D'Alessandro et al. (2011), p. 5. Conversely, Serbia, Croatia, Slovenia and Estonia have codes of ethics that are binding on all judges, see European Network of Councils of Judiciary (2015), pp. 60 *et seq.*

[49] Such opinions or general positions are sometimes provided in a procedure where the judge addressing the relevant body can remain anonymous or in which the judge's identity remains confidential once the opinion or general position is published. For more details see Cardoso et al. (2021).

Council of Magistrates, formed as an on-call informal service that provides prompt advice and guidance to judges on ethical issues.

Similarly, Slovenia launched in 2019 a pilot project, that has reportedly yielded very good results, aimed at introducing a new body, the Advisor to the Judges on Ethics and Integrity, which should complement the work of the Commission on Ethics and Integrity.[50] Unlike the Commission on Ethics and Integrity,[51] which has the mandate to adopt opinions in principle on the conduct in breach of the Code of Judicial Ethics and issue recommendations for compliance with the rules of judicial ethics and integrity, the mandate of the Advisor to the Judges on Ethics and Integrity is limited to providing written or oral advice, information on ethical standards and professional assistance. The Advisor does not propose concrete solutions, nor does he/she issue binding decisions. The relationship between the Advisor and the judge seeking advice is regulated as a confidential relationship.[52]

The Netherlands, conversely, has a highly decentralised system for providing guidance on ethical issues to judges and prosecutors. Namely, the Netherlands reported to GRECO in 2012 that all of its courts have decided to establish their own integrity commissions, which are usually composed not only of judges but also of court staff and human resources personnel. The objective of these commissions is to promote integrity and provide advice to judges, court staff and the court board in case of ethical dilemmas, and bring coherence to the court's integrity policy. According to the available information, integrity matters are also occasionally discussed in the course of judges' appraisal, as well as through a type of peer review mechanism established among judges who work in the same court, aimed at enabling them to follow each other's work and provide constructive criticism and suggestions about each other's ethical conduct.[53]

According to the available sources, the mechanism for confidential counselling established in the Netherlands served as a model for an attempt to develop a similar mechanism in Romania. This attempt, which will now be presented in more detail, is analysed for two reasons. The relevance of the Romanian case for the present study lies in its potential to be used as a lesson-learning exercise on the subject of failed legal transplants aimed at furthering compliance with relevant international standards. Secondly, it is a paradigmatic example of the caution with which legal transplants are to be resorted to in the fields that are intrinsically linked to the

---

[50] The establishment of such a body also seems linked to the 4th round of GRECO evaluations, as, in order to comply with the recommendations of the Evaluation report, Slovenia adopted the Code of Conduct which is mandatory for all judges, established the Commission for Ethics and Integrity and adopted the Commentary to the Code of Judicial Ethics. See GRECO (2016), Evaluation Report RC4(2016)14 on Slovenia, para. 29.

[51] The Commission on Ethics and Integrity is formed in line with art. 49 Zakon o sodnem svetu (Law on Judicial Council), Official Gazette of the Republic of Slovenia, No. 23/17.

[52] Art. 1 Pravilnik o delu svetovalca sodnikom za področje etike in integritete (Rules on the work of the advisor to judges in the field of ethics and integrity), http://www.sodni-svet.si/doc/kei/pravilnik-o-delu-svetovalca-sodnikom-za-eticne-zadeve-A.pdf.

[53] GRECO (2012), Evaluation IV Report (2012) 7E on the Netherlands, para 127, 128.

exercise of judicial powers and require a high level of internalisation by the judges themselves.

5 Implementation of International Standards and a Failed Legal Transplant: The Case of Romania[54]

Ethical counselling was in Romania first introduced in its state administration bodies. With the aim to preserve and maintain the integrity of public institutions, already in 2007, the position of "ethics counsellors" was instituted in the Romanian state administration. The law envisioned that the ethics counsellors were to be chosen among the civil servants and appointed by the head of a public institution. The ethics counsellor was to be in charge of providing counselling on ethical matters and monitoring whether the behaviour of colleagues complies with the rules of code of conduct.[55]

Several years after, the Superior Council of Magistracy (SCM), as the guardian of independence and integrity of the judiciary in Romania, embarked on the same path. With the adoption of the Action Plan for the Implementation of the Justice System Integrity Strategy for 2011–2016, the SCM had envisioned the establishment of a national network of ethics counsellors as an instrument for the standardisation of ethical practices in the Romanian judiciary.[56] The same measure was repeated in the following Action Plan,[57] and in 2016 the idea was finally laid down in legally binding provisions. In its Decision No. 434, the Judicial Section of the SCM decided to introduce the institution of ethics counsellors ("consilieri de etică") in the Romanian judiciary.[58] Two in the courts of appeal and one in each basic court (Art. 1), the

[54]This analysis was informed by the research conducted by the authors in 2021 for the purpose of an "Expert analysis of the systems of confidential counselling for judges and prosecutors on ethical matters across the CoE Member States", an activity within the joint European Union/Council of Europe action "Strengthening independence and accountability of the judiciary".

[55]Art. 21 par. 1 Legea nr. 7/2004 privind Codul de conduită a funcționarilor publici (Law No. 7/2004 on the Code of Conduct for Civil Servants), Official Gazette of the Republic of Romania No. 525/2007. See Georgescu (2012).

[56]Art. 1.2 Plan de acțiune pentru implementarea Strategiei de întărire a integrității în sistemul judiciar, 2011–2016 (Action plan for the implementation of the Strategy for strengthening the integrity of the judiciary 2011–2016), https://www.csm1909.ro/13/114/Plan-de-ac%C5%A3iuni-pentru-implementarea-Strategiei-de-%C3%AEnt%C4%83rire-a-integrit%C4%83%C5%A3ii-%C3%AEn-justi%C5%A3ie,-2011-2016.

[57]Art. C.1.3 Plan de acțiune pentru implementarea Strategiei de dezvoltare a sistemului judiciar 2015–2020, (Action plan for the implementation of the Judicial System Development Strategy 2015–2020, Official Gazette of Romania, No. 311/2016.

[58]Secția pentru judecători, Consiliului Superior al Magistraturii (2016), Hotărârea nr. 434 (Decision no. 434). The Prosecutorial Section also adopted a decision in which it laid down rules on ethics counsellors: Secția pentru procurori, Consiliului Superior al Magistraturii, Hotărâre nr. 363 (Decision no. 363).

ethics counsellors were set to provide, *ex officio* or upon request, ethical counselling to judges and undertake other activities, such as organisation of trainings, round-tables and debates, aimed at preserving the integrity of judges and judicial institutions (Art. 4). In the same act, the Judicial Section of the SCM set the competences, the selection criteria, the methods of appointment and other important rules for establishing the ethics counsellors in the Romanian judiciary.

The position of ethics counsellors in the court of appeal was to be filled by judges who have at least 15 years, and in the basic courts, at least 10 years of experience of serving as a judge. A judge could have become a candidate for the position of ethics counsellor only in the court in which he/she served. Others on the list of cumulative criteria to be met by the candidates for ethics counsellors were that a judge had received the grade "very good" in all appraisal procedures to which he/she was subject before the candidature, was never subject to disciplinary sanctions, had never violated rules of the Judicial Code of Ethics, that he/she enjoyed a good professional reputation, exhibited high moral integrity and had good communication skills (Art. 2).

Decision No. 434 also provided detailed rules on the process of filling in the position of ethics counsellors. The selection procedure was to be carried out in three stages and could be summarised as follows (Art. 3). In the first stage, judges were to be invited to submit their candidacy for the position of ethics counsellors. If there were no candidates, the President of the court was to propose a candidate among the judges serving in the court who fulfilled all the requirements, upon the condition that an express consent was obtained from the candidate. Prior to the final nomination of a candidate for the position of ethics counsellor, the President of the court was to conduct confidential consultations with all judges serving in the court regarding the candidate's merits and to record the results of these consultations in a special report. Upon completing these steps, the President of the court was to propose the candidate for the position of ethics counsellor to the court's Judicial Board. In the second phase, the candidate was to undergo training provided by the National Institute of Magistracy, a body in charge of initial and in-service training of judges and prosecutors coordinated by the SCM. The completion of the selection procedure and the appointment was to be conditioned upon a positive opinion of the trainers about the candidate's participation in the training.[59] In the final, third phase, the Judicial Board of the court was to appoint a successful candidate to the position of ethics counsellor.

For a complete understanding of the system of ethical counselling that was to be introduced in the Romanian judiciary via the 2016 Decision, it is also useful to take a look at the rules that regulated the removal of a judge from the position of ethics counsellor. According to Article 6 of Decision No. 434, there could have been

[59] The exact text of the given rule was as follows: "After the completion of the training program, the judges who participated in these training sessions receive from the trainers, based on a procedure developed by the National Institute of Magistracy, the opinion "recommended"/"not recommended".

several reasons for the termination of a judge's appointment to the ethics counsellor position. These reasons concerned both his/her performance in the role of a judge and the ethics-related issues. Namely, the removal from the office was to take place if a judge had not received positive assessment ("very good") in the process of appraisal of his/her performance as a judge (a), if he/she was found to be in breach of disciplinary rules in a final decision (b), if a judge was found to be in violation of the rules of the Code of Ethics (c), and, finally, for the non-exercise or improper exercise of the competences of ethics counsellor (d).

A closer look at the provisions of Decision No. 434 shows that several of its rules had been problematic *vis-à-vis* the basic requirements of successful confidential counselling, that is, to secure that the judges perceive this mechanism as independent, reliable and fully confidential. As we see from Article 4(e), the ethics counsellors were to advise on ethical matters not only upon request but also *ex officio,* which could have meant that their role would have also included monitoring of the conduct of fellow judges. Unusual is also the solution found in the rules on the selection procedure according to which the appointment was to depend on the assessment of the quality of the candidate's attendance of the training for the position of ethics counsellor (Art. 3(b)). From the point of view of a need to ensure integrity and independence of the very institution of ethics counsellor, which is a *sine qua non* for the possibility to establish a relationship of confidence between the ethics counsellor and the fellow judges, not less problematic is the solution found in Article 6(d), according to which the mandate of ethics counsellor could be terminated for the non-exercise or improper exercise of its competences.

These and some other rules on ethics counsellors were among the reasons which have prompted the two professional associations of judges and prosecutors to request from the SCM a cancellation of its decision on the establishment of ethics counsellors and, later on, to initiate administrative proceedings against the impugned acts. In the capacity of plaintiffs, the National Union of Judges of Romania and the Association of Romanian Magistrates have raised before the Bucharest Court of Appeal a number of arguments for the annulment of Decision No. 434.[60] In the pleadings, the associations claimed that the institution of ethics counsellor jeopardised the independence and integrity of judges and violated several other fundamental principles that should guide judges in their work and asked for an immediate suspension of its execution. They have, in particular, pointed out the negative aspects of the rules which provide for *ex officio* ethical counselling (Art. 4 (e)), confidential nature of consultations to be held in the first phase of the selection procedure (Art. 3(a)), the criteria for filling in the position of ethics counsellor (Art. 3 (c) and Art. 6), the ambiguity of the rules on selection procedure (Art. 2), the possibility that ethical issues discussed during the ethical counselling were also being discussed publicly in round tables (Art. 4), and some other rules laid down in Decision No. 434. The two associations also claimed that the Judicial Section of

[60] Asociația Magistraților din România si Uniunea Națională a Judecătorilor din România (2016), Acțiune în contencios administrativ nr. 373 (Lawsuit in administrative litigation No. 373).

the SCM did not have the competences to adopt such a decision. Eventually, the plaintiffs stated that the contested decision granted the ethics counsellors the powers that could be detrimental for the independence of judges and could lead to the creation of a parallel structure within the Romanian judiciary (6). For all these reasons, a network of ethics counsellors, in the plaintiffs' words, could become a network of "informants" whose methods of work could resemble the methods used by Ceausescu's regime.

The National Union of Judges of Romania and the Association of Romanian Magistrates in the pleadings also claimed that the shortcomings of the rules contained in Decision No. 434 to a significant extent ensued from the fact that the network of ethics counsellors was modelled after the mechanism for ethical counselling existing in the Netherlands, without taking adequate account of characteristics of the Romanian judiciary.[61] The plaintiffs noted that the Judicial Section of the SCM referred in Decision No. 434 to a joint Romanian-Dutch cooperation project "Strengthening the Integrity of the Romanian Judicial System" initiated in 2014. According to the text of the Decision No. 434, the project's objective was to bring together Romanian and Dutch experts to share good practices in order to further elaborate the ethical rules and establish in Romania "an Integrity Council and a network of integrity counsellors" (4).[62] Further, the Judicial Section also quoted the GRECO's fourth-round evaluation report in which the GRECO evaluation team rather briefly mentioned the named project and welcomed the initiative (2).

In this context, it is interesting to note that in its reports GRECO has never explicitly recommended to the Romanian authorities to create a mechanism for confidential counselling as it did to some other countries.[63] It has only recommended that "the justice system be made more responsive to risks for the integrity of judges and prosecutors, in particular by (i) having the SCM and the Judicial Inspectorate play a more active role in terms of analyses, information and advice and (ii) by reinforcing the role and effectiveness of those performing managerial functions at the head of courts and public prosecution services, without impinging on the independence of judges and prosecutors".[64] Moreover, a careful analysis of the rules laid down in Decision No. 434 shows that the ethics counsellors were not conceived as a mechanism for confidential counselling in a true sense of the word since the given decision contained no rule which would ensure that the advisory role of ethics counsellor be provided in a confidential procedure. In order words, according to the relevant provisions, confidentiality was not meant to be a principal feature of the advice-giving activities of the ethics counsellors. The only reference to

[61] *Ibid.*

[62] See also Press Release on the National Conference "Strengthening the Integrity of the Judiciary" of 26 November 2015, issued by the SCM Unit for Public Information and Mass-Media Relations.

[63] See, for instance, GRECO (2015), Evaluation IV Report 2014 (8)E on Serbia; GRECO (2015a), Evaluation IV Report (2015) 1E on Armenia, GRECO (2015b), Evaluation IV Report (2015) 5E on Portugal.

[64] GRECO (2015), Evaluation IV Report (2015) 4E on Romania, para. 114.

confidentiality is made in the above-analysed rules which mandate that the consultations between the President of the court and the judges on the suitability of a candidate for the position of ethics counsellor should be conducted in a confidential manner. In that sense, one could eventually argue that the attempted introduction of ethics counsellors was aimed at setting up a mechanism for ethical counselling which is not necessarily the same with the confidential counselling, according to the international standards presented in the previous chapter.

Whether or not we can qualify it as falling within the ambit of confidential counselling, at this point of the analysis it is important to note that the idea to establish a network of ethics counsellors was never put into practice. Four months after the adoption of Decision No. 434, the Bucharest Court of Appeal decided in favour of the plaintiff, the National Union of Judges of Romania and the Association of Romanian Magistrates, and suspended its execution until the final verdict was pronounced.[65] The decision of the first instance court was upheld by the High Court of Cassation and Justice three years after.[66] The second instance court based its ruling, among else, on the finding that the adoption of the contested decision goes beyond the mandate of the Section of Judges of the SCM. The High Court of Cassation and Justice also found that Decision No. 434 unlawfully modified the rules on the incompatibility of judges for the performance of the judicial function, thus "creating the framework in which a third party to the act of justice, namely the ethics counsellor, can intervene, *ex officio*, in the judicial activity carried out by the judge - an essentially independent activity, guaranteed as such at the constitutional level" (point 5). Eventually, in Decision No. 1305 of 29th October 2020 the Judicial Section of the SCM stated the annulment of Decision No. 434 on the ethics counsellors, as ordered by the sentence of the Bucharest Court of Appeal and upheld by the High Court of Cassation and Justice in its judgment of 24 May 2019 (Art. 1).[67]

5.1 *Reflections on the Reasons for the Failed Legal Transplant*

Apart from the reasons explicitly stated in the courts' decisions, the causes of the failure of this legal transplant can also be sought in some other aspects of the process of legal transplantation. The most obvious one is the difference between the social and political milieu in which the magistrates in the Netherlands and the magistrates

---

[65] Curtea de Apel Bucureşti, Secţia a VIII-a contencios administrativ şi fiscal (2016), Sentinţa civilă nr. 3192 (Civil sentence No. 3192).

[66] Înalta Curte de Casație și Justiție, Secția de Contencios Administrativ și Fiscal (2019), Decizia nr. 2783 (Decision No. 2783).

[67] Secţia pentru judecători, Consiliului Superior al Magistraturii (2020), Hotărârea nr. 1305 (Decision No. 1305).

in Romania operate. Since 2006, Romania's progress in undertaking judicial reforms and stepping up the fight against corruption is monitored against a set of benchmarks under the EU Cooperation and Verification Mechanism.[68] After the events of 2017, when a series of attempted reforms concerning its justice system led to large public protests, Romania has been a subject of an *ad hoc* evaluation procedure under Rule 34 of the GRECO Rules of Procedure.[69] Such a situation, existing already at the time of adoption of Decision No. 434, could have warranted a more cautious approach to the idea to introduce the network of ethics counsellors, given that it concerned matters of great importance for independence and integrity of judges. That was probably one of the reasons why the two professional associations requested from the SCM to conduct a comparative analysis of mechanisms for confidential counselling found in other European countries with the judicial systems more similar to the Romanian one.[70]

Other reasons were in an indirect way addressed in the text of pleadings submitted by the National Union of Judges of Romania and the Association of Romanian Magistrates. The two associations, for instance, referred to a lack of a prior in-depth analysis of the needs and characteristics of the Romanian judiciary that should have had informed the process of legal transplantation in the first place.[71] That could be another important aspect to consider in our attempt to understand the causes of the failure of this legal transplant as the subject of the present analysis. As noted earlier, one of the conditions for successful legal transplantation is that the process is based on adequate and timely conducted assessments of broader social conditions that could be conducive or could have adverse effects on the given legal intervention, its effectiveness in achieving objectives, its interaction with other relevant existing or planned interventions, and of other issues which are commonly part of impact assessment or similar evaluation methodologies.[72] The scholarship also points that a success of a legal transplant is directly conditional upon the inclusiveness of the process of transplantation,[73] which has been confirmed in the associations' complaints that the members of the judicial profession in Romania were not adequately consulted in the phase of the conception of the legal intervention and that the Decision No. 434 did not reflect the opinion of many Romanian judges and

---

[68] Following the conclusions of the Council of Ministers (2006), No. 13339/06, the Mechanism was established by the Commission of the European Communities (2006). For the latest report, see European Commission (2021).

[69] This *ad hoc* procedure "can be triggered in exceptional circumstances, such as when GRECO receives reliable information concerning institutional reforms, legislative initiatives or procedural changes that may result in serious violations of anti-corruption standards of the Council of Europe", see GRECO (2018), Ad Hoc Report (2012)2 on Romania, para. 2. See also CJEU, C-83/19, C-127/19 and C-195/19.

[70] Asociația Magistraților din România si Uniunea Națională a Judecătorilor din România (2016), Acțiune în contencios administrative nr. 373 (Lawsuit in administrative litigation No. 373), pp. 13–14.

[71] *Ibid.*, p. 13.

[72] Noguera (2013), p. 315. See, also, Toope (2003), pp. 357–418.

[73] Knežević Bojović (2019), p. 407.

professional associations.[74] For the creation of a mechanism of confidential counselling, it is important not only that "judges should be able to seek ethical advice from a body within the judiciary", in other words, among their peers, but also that they have a major role in the elaboration of this mechanism.[75] Finally, the Romanian experience testifies to the difficulties that exist in striking a balance between universal standards related to judicial independence and judicial ethics, and the need to recognise and take into due account the particular circumstances of any given country.

6 Concluding Remarks

Over the past decades, the topic of judicial ethics and integrity has been in the focus of different supranational bodies. The Group of States against Corruption (GRECO) dedicated its fourth round of evaluations to the prevention of corruption in respect of members of parliament, judges and prosecutors. Among the key topics of these country-specific evaluations were judicial ethical principles and rules of conduct, as well as the need to strengthen judicial integrity by providing support and guidance to judges *vis-à-vis* the most suitable responses to various ethical dilemmas they encounter in their daily work and life. In its evaluations, GRECO sometimes recommended the introduction of confidential counselling on ethical issues, "an institutionalised, peer-to-peer mechanism, which enables judges to receive timely advisory support and guidance on their ethical dilemmas in a confidential procedure". Some questions about the basic features of a mechanism of confidential counselling suitable to fulfil its purpose in diverse national settings are still open and the implementation of the international soft-law standards related to counselling and guidance on ethical issues remains a challenge, particularly in cases when it takes place via legal transplantation exercise.

The efforts of Romanian judicial authorities to introduce a mechanism for ethical counselling, which was prompted by a cooperation project between the Superior Council of Magistracy and the Judicial Council of the Netherlands, provides valuable insights in this regard, given that much can be learned not only from the good practice examples but also from the practices that should not be replicated. The good practice examples could always be useful as a source of inspiration and as reference points, but not all measures for the advancement of professional ethics are suitable for each country. The Romanian experience is thus a reminder of the requirements which need not be sidestepped for a legal borrowing to have a chance to succeed and, hence, of the limits of such socio-legal intervention. In that sense, the Romanian case can serve as yet another example of the need to avoid "the desire to produce

[74] Asociația Magistraților din România si Uniunea Națională a Judecătorilor din România (2016), Acțiune în contencios administrativ nr. 373 (Lawsuit in administrative litigation No. 373), p. 13.

[75] Committee of Ministers of the Council of Europe, Recommendation 12/2010 on judges: independence, efficiency and responsibilities of 17 November 2010, ch. VIII, para. 74.

similarity (as a pure simulacrum of universality)",[76] instead of accommodating difference.

There is no doubt that the success of legal transplants undertaken as part of the judicial sector reform, regardless of the typology of the legal transplant, is conditional upon an in-depth understanding of the legal and institutional reality of a country in which it is to be introduced and on the inclusiveness of the process of developing and implementing the given legal intervention. These two requirements were evidently not met in the failed attempt of Romanian judicial authorities to introduce a mechanism for ethical counselling. As noted in the case analysis, the professional associations of judges and prosecutors complained about a lack of prior in-depth analysis of the needs and characteristics of the Romanian judiciary that should have had informed the process of legal transplantation in the first place. It appears as well that the process of transplantation in the Romanian case was not inclusive enough, given that the associations also complained that the members of the judicial profession in Romania were not sufficiently consulted.

The analysis shows that the implementation of international standards, particularly those related to judicial ethics, must not be reduced to legal transplantation through blind copy-paste acts. To point to such a finding might seem redundant given the many arguments, which have been elaborated in legal theory, against the practices of legal borrowing ignorant of the specificities of the local context. However, the case of Romania shows that such common understanding of the minimum requirements for a successful legal transplant can be easily lost in cursory attempts to comply with international standards. While it can be claimed that there is a consensus on what are the core principles and values of judicial ethics, these are formulated in international soft-law instruments and inherently entail adaptations to the relevant national legal and social frameworks. Moreover, they are primarily addressed to holders of judicial offices, which clearly ensues from the standard which states that codes of ethics should be developed by judges themselves. From this, it logically follows that the bodies in charge of providing guidance on how to act in line with ethical norms are also to be established in a process that provides for continuous and broad involvement of the members of the judicial profession. That is, undoubtedly, the best way to secure the success of confidential counselling, which in the first place needs to be perceived by the judges as independent, reliable and confidential.

References

Asociația Magistraților din România si Uniunea Națională a Judecătorilor din România (2016) Acțiune în contencios administrative nr. 373 (Lawsuit in administrative litigation No. 373), din 29.07.2016

Babić J (2008) Etika i moral. Theoria 51(2):35–48

[76]Nelken (2007), p. 39.

Berkowitz D, Pistor K, Jean-Francois R (2003) The transplant effect. Am J Comp Law 51(1): 163–203. https://doi.org/10.1016/S0014-2921(01)00196-9

Bingham T (2010) The rule of law. Penguin Books Limited, London

Bobek M, Kosař D (2014) Global solutions, local damages: a critical study in judicial councils in Central and Eastern Europe. German Law J 15(7):1257–1292. https://doi.org/10.2139/ssrn.2351299

Breneselović L (2013) O zaštiti osnovnih prava u Srbiji u svetlu loše ocene Evropske komisije – razlozi niskog stepena stvarne zaštite osnovnih prava u Republici Srbiji i neophodne mere za njeno poboljšanje (On the protection of fundamental rights in Serbia in the light of the poor assessment of the European Commission - the reasons for the low level of real protection of fundamental rights in the Republic of Serbia and the necessary measures for its improvement). Evropsko zakonodavstvo 12(43–44):335–360

Cardoso J et al (2021) Final Report with Recommendations for a System of Confidential Counselling for Judges and Prosecutors on Ethical Matters. https://rm.coe.int/hf9-confidential-counselling-eng/1680a35870

Castillo-Ortiz P (2019) The politics of implementation of the judicial council model in Europe. Eur Polit Sci Rev 11:503–520. https://doi.org/10.1017/S1755773919000298

Commission of the European Communities (2006) Decision of 13 December 2006 establishing a mechanism for cooperation and verification of progress in Romania to address specific benchmarks in the areas of judicial reform and the fight against corruption {C(2006) 6569}

Committee of Ministers of the Council of Europe (1994) Recommendation 94(12) to the member states on the independence, efficiency and role of judges of 13 October 1994, adopted at the 518th Meeting of the Ministers' Deputies

Committee of Ministers of the Council of Europe, Recommendation 12/2010 on judges: independence, efficiency and responsibilities of 17 November 2010

Committee of Ministers of the Council of Europe, Resolution 97/24 on the twenty guiding principles for fight against corruption of 6 November 1997, adopted at the 101st Meeting of the Committee of Ministers

Consultative Council of European Judges (2001) Opinion 2/2001 on the funding and management of the courts of 23 November 2001

Consultative Council of European Judges (2002) Opinion 3/2002 on the principles and rules governing judges' professional conduct, in particular ethics, incompatible behaviour and impartiality of 19 November 2002

Consultative Council of European Judges (2010) Magna Carta of Judges of 17 November 2010, adopted at the 11th Plenary Meeting of the Consultative Council of European Judges

Consultative Council of European Judges (2018) Opinion No. 21 "Preventing Corruption among Judges, adopted at the 19th Plenary Meeting of the Consultative Council of European Judges on 7 November 2018

Curtea de Apel Bucureşti, Secţia a VIII-a contencios administrativ şi fiscal (2016) Sentinţa civilă nr. 3192 (Civil sentence No. 3192) din 24 octombrie 2016

D'Alessandro L, Marini M, Mariscoti R (2011) Ethics and Discipline: The Transition from Case Law to the Codification of Disciplinary Violations in the Italian Reform of the Judicial System, Effects on Freedom of Expression and Association. https://www.ejtn.eu/Documents/Themis%202012/Written%20paper_%20Italy_1_Magistrates_Ethics_and_Deontology.pdf

Đorđević M (2008) Pravni transplanti i Srbijanski građanski zakonik iz 1844 (Legal Transplants and the Serbian Civil Code of 1844). Strani pravni život 52(1):62–84

Esposito G (2019) Judicial Integrity and Judicial Independence: Two Sides of the Same Coin. In: Pinto de Albuquerque P, Wojtyczek K (eds) Judicial power in a globalized world. Springer, New York, pp 165–177

European Commission (2021) Report on Progress in Romania under the Cooperation and Verification Mechanism {COM(2021) 370 final}, Brussels

European Network of Councils of Judiciary (2015) Report on Minimum Judicial Standards: Disciplinary Proceedings and Liability of Judges, 2014-2015. https://www.encj.eu/images/stories/pdf/GA/Hague/encj_report_minimum_standards_v_adopted_ga_june_2015.pdf

Garoupa N, Ginsbourg T (2015) Judicial reputation: a comparative theory. University of Chicago Press, Chicago

Garoupa N, Ginsburg T (2009) The comparative law and economics of judicial councils. Berkeley J Int Law 27(1):53–83. https://doi.org/10.15779/Z383S9H

Garoupa N, Ogus A (2006) A strategic interpretation of legal transplants. J Legal Stud 35(2): 339–363. https://doi.org/10.1086/505053

General Assembly of United Nations, Resolution 58/4 of 31 October 2003 - United Nations Convention against Corruption

Grbić S (2019) Pravni transplanti i razvoj prava: zaštita prava osoba s invaliditetom i Europska konvencija o ljudskim pravima (Legal Transplants and tge Development of Law: Protection of the Rights of Persons with Disability and European Convention on Human Rights). Harmonius, J Legal Soc Stud South East Europe 9:139–165

GRECO (2016), Evaluation Report RC4(2016)14 on Slovenia, adopted by GRECO at its 74th Plenary Meeting on 28 November – 2 December 2016

GRECO, *Ad hoc* Report (2018)2 on Romania (Rule 34), adopted by GRECO at its 79th Plenary Meeting on 23 March 2018

GRECO, Compliance Report RC4(2016)4 on Latvia, adopted by GRECO at its 71st Plenary Meeting on 18 March 2016

GRECO, Compliance Report RC4(2017)14 on Montenegro, adopted by GRECO at its 77th Plenary Meeting, on 18 October 2017

GRECO, Evaluation IV Report (2014) 8E on Serbia, adopted by GRECO at its 68th Plenary Meeting on 15-19 June 2015

GRECO, Evaluation IV Report (2015a) 1E on Armenia, adopted by GRECO at its 69th Plenary Meeting on 12-16 October 2015

GRECO, Evaluation IV Report (2015b) 5E on Portugal, adopted by GRECO at its 70th Plenary Meeting on 30 November – 4 December 2015

GRECO, Evaluation Report IV (2012) 7E on the Netherlands, adopted by GRECO at its 60th Plenary Meeting on 21 June 2013

GRECO, Evaluation Report RC4(2017)8 on Serbia, adopted by GRECO at its 77th Plenary Meeting on 18 October

GRECO, Evaluation Report RC4(2020)12 on Serbia, adopted by GRECO at its 86th Plenary Meeting on 29 October 2020

GRECO, Evaluation Report Rep (2015) 4E on Romania, adopted by GRECO at its 70th Plenary Meeting on 4 December 2015

Hantrais L (2009) International comparative research: theory, methods and practice. Palgrave Macmillan, New York

Înalta Curte de Casație și Justiție, Secția de Contencios Administrativ și Fiscal (2019) Decizia Nr. 2783 (Decision no. 2783) din 24 mai 2019

Joint concurring opinion of judges Pinto de Albuquerque and Dedov to the judgment of the European Court of Human Rights in the case of *Baka v. Hungary*, Application no. 20261/12, Judgment of Grand Chamber of 23 June 2016

Kahn-Freund O (1974) On use and misuse of comparative law. Mod Law Rev 37(1):1–27

Knežević Bojović A (2019) Institutional transplants in Serbia – the stories of success and failure. In: Novaković M (ed) Common law and civil law today convergence and divergence. Vernon Press, Malaga, pp 381–412

Kosař D (2018) Beyond Judicial Councils: forms, rationales and impact of judicial self-governance in Europe. German Law J 19(7):1567–1612. https://doi.org/10.1017/S2071832200023178

Legea nr. 7/2004 privind Codul de conduită a funcționarilor publici a fost publicată (Law No, 7/2004 on the Code of Conduct for Civil Servants) Official Gazette of the Republic of Romania, No. 525/2007

Legrand P (1997) The impossibility of 'legal transplants. Maastricht J Eur Comp Law 4(2): 111–124. https://doi.org/10.1177/1023263x9700400202

Magalhães P (1999) The politics of judicial reform in Eastern Europe. Comp Polit 32(1):43–62. https://doi.org/10.2307/422432

Marković Đ (2017) Nezavisnost sudstva u Republici Srbiji-Predlozi za promenu ustavnog okvira za izbor sudija i prestanak sudijske funkcije (The Independence of the Judiciary in the Republic of Serbia - Proposals for the Change of the Constitutional Framework Concerning the Election of Judges and the Termination of Judicial Office). Srpska politička misao posebno izdanje 2017: 201–228. https://doi.org/10.22182/spm.specijal2017.11

Mendelski M (2015) The EU's pathological power: the failure of external rule of law promotion in South, Eastern Europe. Southeastern Europe 39(3):318–346. https://doi.org/10.1163/18763332-03903003

Miller J (2003) A typology of legal transplants: using sociology, legal history and argentine examples to explain the transplant process. Am J Comp Law 51(4):839–885. https://doi.org/10.2307/3649131

Mrčela M (2020) Application of a Code of Conduct for Judges. United Nations Office on Drugs and Crime, https://www.unodc.org/dohadeclaration/en/news/2020/01/application-of-a-code-of-conduct-for-judges.html

Nelken D (2007) Comparative law and comparative legal studies. In: Örücü E, Nelken D (eds) Comparative law: a handbook. Bloomsbury Publishing, Bloomsbury, pp 3–42

Noguera A (2013) Impact assessment: empirical evidence. In: Larouche P, Cserne P (eds) National legal systems and globalization: new role, continuing relevance. Asser Press, The Hague, pp 311–344

Plan de acțiune pentru implementarea Strategiei de întărire a integrității în sistemul judiciar, 2011 – 2016 (Action Plan for the Implementation of the Justice System Integrity Strategy for 2011-2016), adoptata în şedința din 22 noiembrie 2011 a Plenului Consiliului Superior al Magistraturii. https://www.csm1909.ro/13/114/Plan-de-ac%C5%A3iuni-pentru-implementarea-Strategiei-de-%C3%AEnt%C4%83rire-a-integrit%C4%83%C5%A3ii-%C3%AEn-justi%C5%A3ie,-2011-2016

Plan de acțiune pentru implementarea Strategiei de dezvoltare a sistemului judiciar 2015-2020 (Action Plan for the Implementation of the Justice System Integrity Strategy for 2015-2020), Hotărârea Guvernului nr. 282/2016 privind aprobarea Planului de acțiune pentru implementarea Strategiei de dezvoltare a sistemului judiciar 2015-2020, "Monitorul Oficial al României", Partea I, nr. 311 din 22 aprilie 2016

Pravilnik o delu svetovalca sodnikom za področje etike in integritete (Rules on the work of the advisor to judges in the field of ethics and integrity). http://www.sodni-svet.si/doc/kei/pravilnik-o-delu-svetovalca-sodnikom-za-eticne-zadeve-A.pdf

Preshova D, Demjanovski I, Nechev Z (2017) The effectiveness of the 'European Model' of Judicial Independence in the Western Balkans: Judicial Councils as a Solution or a New Cause of Concern for Judicial Reforms. Centre for the Law of EU External Relations. https://www.asser.nl/media/3475/cleer17-1_web.pdf

Press Release on the National Conference "Strengthening the Integrity of the Judiciary" of 26 November 2015, issued by the SCM Unit for Public Information and Mass-Media Relations

Rakić Vodinelić V, Knežević Bojović A, Reljanović M (2012) Reforma pravosuđa u Srbiji 2008-2012. Službeni glasnik, Beograd

Reyes M (2014) The Challenges of Legal Transplants in a Globalized Context: A Case Study on 'Working' Examples. Social Science Research Network. https://papers.ssrn.com/sol3/papers.cfm?abstract_id=2530811

Sancho I (2007) Ética Judicial: el paradigma del buen Juez. Icade. Revista De La Facultad De Derecho 72:117–138

Secția pentru judecători, Consiliului Superior al Magistraturii (2016) Hotărârea nr. 434 (Decision No. 434) din 17 mai 2016

Secția pentru judecători, Consiliului Superior al Magistraturii (2020) Hotărârea nr. 1305 (Decision No. 1305) din 29 octombrie 2020

Secția pentru procurori, Consiliului Superior al Magistraturii (2016) Hotărâre nr. 363 (Decision No. 363) din 30 mai 2016

Seibert-Fohr A (2014) The multiplication of international courts and tribunals after the end of the cold war. In: Romano C, Alter K, Shany Y (eds) The Oxford handbook of international adjudication. Oxford University Press, Oxford, pp 757–778. https://doi.org/10.1093/law/9780199660681.003.0035

Shetreet S (2012) Creating a culture of judicial independence: the practical challenge and the conceptual and constitutional infrastructure. In: Shetreet S, Forsyth C (eds) The culture of judicial independence: conceptual foundations and practical challenges. Martinus Nijhoff Publisher, Leiden, pp 15–67

Shetreet S, Chodosh H, Helland E (2021) Preface. In: Shetreet S, Chodosh H, Helland E (eds) Challenged Justice: in Pursuit of Judicial independence. Martinus Nijhoff Publisher, Leiden. https://brill.com/view/book/edcoll/9789004421554/front-6.xml

Sremčev Ilić S (2015) Sudijska etika – srpski, evropski i međunarodni standardi (Judicial Ethics: Serbian, European and International Standards). Strani pravni život 59(1):275–290

Strategia pentru întărirea integrității în sistemul judiciar 2011 - 2016 (Strategy for Strengthening Integrity in Judiciary for 2011-2016), adoptate în şedinţa din 22 noiembrie 2011 a Plenului Consiliului Superior al Magistraturii

Terhechte J (2009) Judicial ethics for a global judiciary–how judicial networks create their own codes of conduct. German Law J 10(4):501–514. https://doi.org/10.1017/S2071832200001188

Titz A (2009) Über den Umgang mit richterlicher Ethik im Ausland. Deutscher Richterbund. https://www.drb.de/fileadmin/DRB/pdf/Ethik/0902_Ethik_DRiZ_Titz_Ausland_.pdf

Toope S (2003) Legal and Judicial reform through development assistance: some lessons. McGill Law J 48(3):357–418

United Nations Economic and Social Council (2006) Resolution 2006/23 Strengthening Basic Principles of Judicial Conduct {E/RES/2006/23}

Urbániková M, Šipulova K (2018) Failed expectations: does the establishment of judicial councils enhance confidence in courts? German Law J 19(7):2105–2136. https://doi.org/10.1017/S2071832200023348

Venice Commission (2007) Judicial Appointments – Report adopted by the Venice Commission at its 70th Plenary Session on 16-17 March 2007{CDL-AD(2007)028-e}

Venice Commission (2010) Report on the independence of the judicial system part I: The independence of judges adopted by the Venice Commission at its 82nd Plenary Session on 12-13 March 2010 {CDL-AD(2010)004}

Venice Commission (2011) Report on the Rule of Law adopted by the Venice Commission at its 86th Plenary Session on 25-26 March 2011 {CDL-AD(2011)003rev-e}

Venice Commission (2016) Rule of Law Checklist adopted by the Venice Commission at its 106th Plenary Session on 11-12 March 2016{CDL-AD(2016)007}

Voermans W (2003) Councils for the Judiciary in Europe: trends and models. In: Fernandez Segado F (ed) The Spanish constitution in the European constitutional context. Libreria Dykinson, Madrid, pp 21–33

Watson A (1974) Legal transplants: an approach to comparative law. University of Georgia, Edinburgh

Zakon o sodnem svetu (Law on Judicial Council) Official Gazette of the Republic of Slovenia, No 23/17

Zakon o sudijama (Law on Judges) Official Gazette of the Republic of Serbia, Nos. 116/2008, 58/2009 (Decision of the Constitutional Court), 104/2009, 101/2010, 8/2012 (Decision of the Constitutional Court), 121/2012, 124/2012 (O Decision of the Constitutional Court), 101/2013, 111/2014 (Decision of the Constitutional Court), 117/2014, 40/2015, 63/2015 (Decision of the Constitutional Court), 106/2015, 63/2016 (Decision of the Constitutional Court), 47/2017, 76/2021

Out-of-Trial Ensuring Uniform Case Law in Serbia: Socialist Legal Tradition Reloaded

Marko S. Knežević

Contents

M. S. Knežević (✉)
University of Novi Sad, Faculty of Law, Novi Sad, Serbia
e-mail: m.knezevic@pf.uns.ac.rs

D. V. Popović et al. (eds.), *Balkan Yearbook of European and International Law 2021*, Balkan Yearbook of European and International Law 2021,
https://doi.org/10.1007/978-3-030-97431-2_9

1 Introduction

1.1 Survival of Socialist Legal Tradition

During the Cold War it was from both western and eastern perspective claimed that beside common law and civil law, there is another separate legal tradition: socialist law. In the aftermath of fall of Berlin Wall, it was perceived as rather logical step to redefine positions. If there is no more socialist law and ideology, there should be no room for Socialist Legal Tradition either. As Kötz declared in 1998, "the 'socialist legal family' is dead and buried".[1] Even if transition of those legal systems was qualified as work-in-progress,[2] symbolical steps were taken. Mańko sees them in Kötz's simple disregarding of chapters on socialist law from his textbook, without writing anything else in their place,[3] what led Kühn to his thesis that "old 'Socialist Legal Family' [. . .] had seemingly been replaced by a legal black-hole".[4] In the next decade(s), positions had to be changed once again, as it was clear that such perception of mostly western scholars was oversimplified and premature. Authors having in-depth perspective, most notably Uzelac (2010), Kühn (2011) and Mańko (2013), have demonstrated that legacy of Socialist Legal Tradition, or Socialist Legal Tradition itself, have survived, and to some extent have even been reinforced. Western scholars embraced such positions. In his monumental textbook, Kischel filled the "legal black-hole" with chapter on "Eastern Europe", characterising post-Socialist legal systems as a joint group with common legacy of relicts of Socialist legal tradition, though in varying intensity.[5]

[1] Zweigert and Kötz (1998), p. v. However, in preface to original German textbook, Kötz stated that "socialist legal tradition almost disappeared from the face of the earth"; see Zweigert and Kötz (1996), p. v.

[2] Kötz stated in preface to English edition of his 3rd edition of Comparative Law that "it will take a long time to erase the traces of more than forty years of total subjection of political ideology"; see Zweigert and Kötz (1998), p. v. Perhaps Kötz realised that his earlier statement in German version was premature.

[3] Mańko (2007), p. 86; Mańko (2013), p. 1.

[4] Kühn (2011), p. 293.

[5] Kischel (2015), pp. 571 *et seqq.*

1.2 Out-of-Trial Court's Legal Opinions

One of the typical features of Socialist law was competence of mostly supreme courts to issue abstract legal opinion without any case pending before the court. In some countries such legal opinions, sometimes called resolutions, guidelines or similar, were binding for all courts, whilst in other countries they had—in formal sense—non-binding nature. It was regarded as *the* method of unification of case law, though one might call it oxymoron[6] or qualify as *contradictio in adiecto*,[7] because such activity falls out of the scope of exercising judicial power. However, described nature of such courts' activity mirrors terminology used in this paper, i.e., "out-of-trial" or "non-adjucative" concept of ensuring uniform case law.

It appears that—though to variable extent—almost all post-Socialist legal systems kept out-of-trial model of harmonisation of case law to the present time. Doctrine claims that resilience of model is just another proof of survival of Socialist Legal Tradition, if not one of the most significant.[8]

1.3 Serbian Context

Pairing two notions in the title of this paper sounds rather ambivalent from perspective of Serbian legal and political discourse. Whilst ensuring uniform case law by out-of-trial method is everyday practice of Serbian courts, the question of legal heritage of Socialism and legal culture in general has not been problematized yet. The aim of this paper is to try to fill this gap in modest way, as contemporary Serbian concept of non-adjucative case law unification will be outlined, together with all vividness and resilience of Socialist legal tradition. I argue, as my colleagues from other post-socialist countries do from the perspective of other legal systems, that present Serbian position concept is also relict of such concept. Moreover, as the title would suggests, I claim that it is enhanced beyond known boundaries.

---

[6]Galič (2017), p. 40.

[7]Knežević (2017), p. 42.

[8]For Croatia compare Uzelac (2019); Bratković (2018), p. 92; for Poland compare Mańko (2013), p. 19; for Slovenia compare Zobec and Letnar Černič (2015), pp. 141–143; in general compare Kühn (2006), pp. 23–25.

2 Historical Background

2.1 Pre-socialist Law

The beginning of modern judiciary in Serbia dates back to the middle of nineteenth century, a period of gradual liberation from Ottoman rule.[9] Landmark should be seen in forming coherent judiciary system in 1865 with Cassation Court (CC) on the top. As the title of the court suggests, French model was chosen. Its role was ensuring uniform application of law in civil and criminal matters, and that was perceived as adjucative task.[10] However, already by initial Law on Cassation Court of 1865, CC was obliged to issue opinion on law upon request of Minister of Justice. According to the amendments of 1895, CC was empowered with another non-adjucative prerogative: for ensuring its own uniform case law, plenary session was competent to render binding legal opinion for all panels. Both competences were controversial at the time. Perić argued that any non-adjucative function was inconsistent with constitutional principle of separation of powers, and especially if legal opinion was binding for all panels of CC.[11] That was also minority view in CC regarding duty to render opinion upon request of Minister of Justice.[12] However, viewpoint of majority prevailed.

Forming the new state after the WWI—i.e., Kingdom of Serbs, Croats and Slovenians, later Kingdom of Yugoslavia—couldn't be regarded as turning point, as Serbian model dating from nineteenth century was abolished only in 1929. Legal system of Kingdom of Yugoslavia was diverse and fragmentized, so in fact it was divided into six separate legal areas, with separate judiciary and separate supreme instance.[13] Law on Organization of Courts of 1929 provided unification of judiciary, with one Cassation Court, and it should be noted that it was indeed, though not completely, deeply influenced by Austrian law.[14] Cassation Court had, just as Austrian Supreme Court at that time, competence to render an "opinion" on civil legal issues upon request of state attorney, if "there was unsettled low-level case law and Cassation Court could not, with regard to its competence, decide on relevant

[9] See Rakić-Vodinelić (2012), p. 34; Poznić and Rakić-Vodinelić (2015), pp. 37 *et seqq.*

[10] Đorđević (1923), p. 167; compare also Đorđević (1924), pp. 10–11, 56–58, emphasising pure public role of CC.

[11] Perić (1898).

[12] According to Perić (1898), p. 920, it was argued that CC is was not to be considered as some form of lawyer's council which issues advisory opinions".

[13] Cassation Court in Belgrade, Department B of Cassation Court in Novi Sad, Septemviral Court in Zagreb with two departments (A and B), Supreme Court in Sarajevo, and Grand Court in Podgorica.

[14] Austrian influence wasn't just significant in field of organisation of judiciary as such, but in civil procedure as well; codes on civil procedure and enforcement were almost strict translation of Austrian codes from end of nineteenth century. Galič (2010), p. 118, sees in such approach one historical curiosity, as one war winner adopted laws of the defeated.

issue".[15] Legal opinions were not binding for lower courts, but they served, as it was stated in the doctrine, as an instruction.[16] Even though Cassation Court was never constituted, and interim measure proved to be definite as six ex-supreme courts acted only as departments of Cassation Court, *de facto* as separate courts,[17] the provisions were in force until the end of pre-WWII Yugoslavia.

2.2 Socialist Law

After the WWII, and subsequent change of state and social system, the judiciary was on the top of agenda. Along with total sovietisation of legal order, Soviet judiciary model was introduced, which despite the breach of political ties with Soviet Union in 1948 existed until the collapse of socialist Yugoslavia.[18] The role of judiciary was fundamentally changed, as court became—like every institution—authority of ruling working class[19] in formal sense, and in fact authority in hand of ruling Communist party. Apart from its traditional role, i.e., legal protection of individual rights, it had also "educational and controlling" function,[20] moreover, it was its duty to track down "social phenomena and relations". Briefly, protection of public interests was fundamental function of courts. It was as, in its purest form, consequence of newly adopted principle of unity of powers, fundamental socialist political and legal concept which was intended to replace "hypocritic burgaos principle of separation of powers".[21] Such paradigm shift had substantial effect to case law unification model. On the one side, Soviet model abolished three-instance proceedings system, which led to adopting well known Soviet non-party legal remedy: public prosecutor could lodge an appeal for protection of legality; parties had no legal remedy on disposal which would lead to Supreme Court, though as of Code of Civil Procedure

---

[15] Para. 48 § 5 No. 4 of Law on Organisation of Courts 1929. Difference between Austrian law at that time is that non-competence of Supreme Court wasn't condition for duty to respond to Minister's request; see Feldner (2001), pp. 25 *et seqq*. On the other hand, Yugoslav legislator adopted Austrian system of plenary sessions which was meant to prevent ununiform case law of the supreme instance also, concept of "*Spruchrepertorium*" and "*Judikatenbuch*". See para. 55–63 of Law on Organisation of Courts of 1929.

[16] See Culja (1936), p. 61.

[17] Compare Uzelac and Galič (2017), p. 209.

[18] Compare Uzelac and Galič (2017), p. 210.

[19] See for example, Srzentić et al. (1949), p. 6; compare one of the last textbooks on Socialist Constitutional Law as well, Fira and Pajvančić (1989), p. 118: "in constitutional institutionalisation of protection of principle of constitutionality and legality the greatest significance has judicial function, which is not any specific power, but part of unified system of power and self-management of working class and working people".

[20] See from socialist perspective e.g. Srzentić et al. (1949), pp. 39, 84 *et seqq*.

[21] Representative for all Srzentić et al. (1949), p. 7.

of 1956 it was reintroduced.[22] On the other hand, the out-of-trial legal opinions were introduced as prerogative of both republican supreme courts and Federal Supreme Court[23] as early as first law on judiciary was passed (1946). It was a prerogative on constitutional scale as of 1963.[24] As it was stated in the first Commentary of new concept, legal opinions were to be issued in order to correct noticed errors of the courts.[25]

Legal opinions were undoubtedly binding for all panels of respective courts or their department. As for binding effect *vis-à-vis* lower courts, after initial debate in legal theory[26] it was an absolutely dominant opinion that lower courts were not formally obliged to follow legal opinions of supreme courts, though in practice they acted as they were.[27]

This model functioned until collapse of Socialist Yugoslavia, though with some modifications due to the minimising adjucative competence of Federal Court. Therefore, joint sessions of delegates of republican supreme courts and Federal Court were introduced, aiming at harmonisation of application of federal law by non-adjucative means, i.e., though non-binding legal resolutions.

2.3 *Post-socialist Law*

Collapse of Socialist Yugoslavia led to significant political and legal changes, as well as to the war. Serbia became together with Montenegro part of Federal Republic of Yugoslavia (1992), new state proclaimed as democratic state based on the rule of the law. New Serbian Constitution, previously adopted in 1990, proclaimed principle of separation of powers and independence of judges. Unlike in other states of Eastern Block, or in some ex-Yugoslav states, however, transition in fact didn't take place with abandoning of Socialism as an ideology. Last decade of past century was marked by authoritarian and undemocratic regime, in which vast majority of constitutional principles served as mere declarations, most notably independence of judges. Notwithstanding that, it should be mentioned that pertaining to

[22] Parties gained well known legal remedy in Germanic legal tradition called "revizija" (*Revision*). The right of public prosecutor to lodge his own legal remedy against second instance judgement remained, as well as possibility of federal public prosecutor to lodge similar legal remedy against judgements of Supreme Court of republic.

[23] Term "Federal Supreme Court" is used as descriptive, as it has changed name on several occasions: first, it was "Supreme Court of Democratic Federal Yugoslavia" (1945–1946), then "Supreme Court of People's Federal Republic of Yugoslavia" (1946–1953), "Supreme Federal Court" (1953–1963), Supreme Court of Yugoslavia" (1963–1974) and "Federal Court".

[24] Cf. e.g. Art. 239 of Federal Constitution of 1963; Art. 422 of Constitution of Socialist Republic of Serbia 1974.

[25] Srzentić et al. (1949), p. 120.

[26] Compare Srzentić et al. (1949), p. 120 on one side, and Kamhi (1951), p. 34 on other side.

[27] Košutić (1978), p. 95.

harmonisation of case law one could mark one change on textual scale of Serbian Constitution. Instead of empowering Supreme Court with out-of-trial jurisdiction in Constitution like in Socialist period (see Sect. 2.2), in Serbian Constitution of 1990 there was just one line: "highest court in Republic of Serbia is Supreme Court of Serbia". Such—to my understanding—rather significant change remained unnoticed, so the laws on judiciary merely mirrored its predecessors: omnibus competence of plenary sessions of every court to discuss legal issues and power of Supreme Court to issue "legal opinions". Bearing this in mind, it is no surprise that even after the political changes and enacting new Constitution in 2006 subsequent to Serbia gaining its independence,[28] everything remained unchanged, except the name of highest instance: instead of Supreme Court of Serbia, from then on it was Supreme Court of Cassation (SCC).

3 Present Out-of-Trial Case Law Unification Model

3.1 Overview: Adjudicative and Non-adjudicative Case Law Unification

Unification of case law in Serbia is conceptually divided into adjucative and non-adjucative methods. Former is composed of deciding pending cases, and, as of 2004, preliminary ruling of SCC in civil matters.[29] Even though primary task of SCC in individual cases is not regarded as public role of supreme instance, one could argue contrary to some extent. Legal remedies upon which SCC decides are in some cases structured even explicitly in that sense. In civil litigation there is, although as subsidiary remedy, leave to second appeal system, whereby one of conditions is "need for case law harmonisation".[30] Extraordinary legal remedy in criminal proceeding—application for protection of legality (*zahtev za zaštitu zakonitosti*), on disposal both to public prosecutor, accused and his lawyer—is also design by same token, as it would be admissible if the substantial legal issue is significant for "correct and uniform application of law".[31]

---

[28] In 2006 Serbia became independent state once again after 88 years, as people of Montenegro voted in referendum to break away from the State Unity of Serbia and Montenegro, state that briefly replaced Federal Republic of Yugoslavia.

[29] For further reading see Bodiroga (2012), pp. 123–126; Poznić and Rakić-Vodinelić (2015), pp. 345–347; Jakšić (2017), pp. 117–119.

[30] Art. 404 § 1 of Code of Civil Procedure (CCP), Official Gazette of Republic of Serbia, Nos. 72/2011, 49/2013 (Constitutional Court Decision), 74/2013 (Constitutional Court Decision), 55/2014, 87/2018, 18/2020.

[31] Art. 486 § 2 of Code of Criminal Procedure, Official Gazette of Republic of Serbia, Nos. 72/2011, 101/2011, 121/2012, 32/2013, 45/2013, 55/2014, 35/2019, 27/2021 (Constitutional Court Decision), 62/2021 (Constitutional Court Decision).

When it comes to harmonisation of case law in present day Serbia, non-adjucative concept is perceived as primal notwithstanding said.[32] It comprises of issuing out-of-trial legal opinions by various courts, more specifically by plenary sessions of various courts. In text that follows I will first present legal framework along with some remarks on drafting history, so it would be easier to comprehend development that led to present concept. After that, the issue of legal status of legal opinions will be addressed, along with the method for ensuring compliance with legal opinions.

3.2 *Legal Framework for Non-adjudicative Jurisdiction*

Only law that regulates out-of-trial case law unification is Law on Organisation of Courts of 2008 (LOC 2008), amended more than ten times, though crucially in 2013[33] regarding the topic of this paper (LOC 2013).

Out-of-trial jurisdiction of courts is contained in part of the LOC which regulates internal structure of courts and its organisation as institution. Basic administrative parts of courts are departments formed according to subject matters (e.g. civil, labour, criminal), composed of all respective judges or panels. Competence of plenary department's session is, among others, "reviewing of legal issues"; departments of appellate courts, Commercial Appellate Court and Misdemeanour Appellate Court review questions regarding work of subordinated courts also.

On the other hand, the jurisdiction of SCC was regulated in two separate provisions in LOC 2008: one for the "adjucative jurisdiction" (ser. "*nadležnost u suđenju*"), and the other one for the non-adjucative jurisdiction ("*nadležnost izvan suđenja*"). The latter one comprised, among other matters, "determination of principal legal opinions in order to ensure uniform application of law by courts", as well as "reviewing application of law and other regulations and the work of courts". In fact, "general legal opinions" were meant to be prerogative of plenary session of SCC, and it would be obligatory for all SCC's panels (Art. 45 LOC 2008). Plenary session of one of SCC's departments could adopt "legal opinion", which would be obligatory only for panels of respective department.[34]

It is important to stress out that Draft of LOC 2008 was transferred to Venice Commission (VC) with request for an opinion, which was subsequently adopted. In relation to non-adjucative jurisdiction of SCC, VC remarked—unsurprisingly, bearing in mind long established "practice"—that it is inappropriate in regard of principle of separation of powers.

---

[32] It is worth of mentioning that non-adjucative competence of courts has its consequence on a dogmatic scale as well. Serbian notion for case law—*sudska praksa*, literary "court practice"—is broadened up to fit a model. By that token, case law is not just result of trial, i.e., legal opinions contained in judicial decisions, but out-of-trial legal opinions as well. See e.g. Ivošević (2005).

[33] Official Gazette of Republic of Serbia, No. 101/2013, hereinafter "LOC 2013".

[34] Supreme Court of Cassation has civil, criminal, and administrative departments.

> It should be made clear that the Supreme Court of Cassation provides legal views only in the framework of a specific case; otherwise this would be in breach of the principle of the separation of powers, as a court cannot make any decision outside its jurisdiction. The same comment applies to the following sentence: "reviews application of law and other regulations and the work of courts".[35]

In the same Opinion, VC also stressed out that system of adopting out-of-trial legal opinions by any court, not just SCC, "might be considered contrary to the independence of judges", notwithstanding legal nature (sole recommendations or binding guidelines).[36]

In LOC amended version of 2013, which is still in force, all provisions in principle survived, so any court department can "review legal issues"; legal opinion adopted in SCC department's session has binding effect for its panels. Yet, two changes are significant. First, the prerogative of SCC to determine principal legal opinions was abolished and replaced with new out-of-trial task: "ensuring uniform court application of law and equality of parties in court proceedings" (Art. 31 LOC 2013). Second, "joint sessions of appellate courts" were introduced, with obligation of "informing SCC on controversial legal issues important for functioning of courts in Republic of Serbia and for uniform case law" (Art. 24 § 3 LOC 2013). The first mentioned change was a direct consequence of new critiques coming from VC. In its Opinion on Draft of LOC 2013, concerns about out-of-trial jurisdiction were raised again, and with same arguments. Moreover, it was stressed that proposed introduction of joint sessions of appellate courts could be counterproductive, as it would be—combining it with non-juducative prerogatives of SCC—contrary to both principle of separation of powers and independence of judges.

> 105. Nevertheless, the Venice Commission has criticised this method, because it gives the Supreme Court of Cassation a general "rule-making" power, which can conflict with the separation of powers. The exchange of views between judges of different instances, which is provided for in the draft (the new paragraph 3 of Article 24) is as such good and could therefore be recommended. However, when it is combined with Article 31, it becomes less clear. The need to unify practice should in principle be solved by an appeals procedure that could be designed to also solve problems that usually, only or mostly, occur in different categories of small claims cases.
>
> 106. It is not clear whether the Supreme Court adopts general views outside the specific case or while exercising its competence as a court of cassation. In case of the former, this approach will conflict with the principle of the independence of the judiciary. The argument that "general legal views" are adopted with the aim of remedying the most common errors of the judicial system, which due to some reason do not end up at the level of the highest court, seems flawed. It also fails to explain why it is impossible to remedy such errors in appeal or cassation proceedings.[37]

It should be clear that Serbian legislator didn't understand rationale of this critique, or didn't want to understand it, as it has only abolished prerogative of SCC plenary session for issuing general legal opinions, and not conceptually same,

[35] CDL-AD(2008)007, § 109.

[36] CDL-AD(2008)007, § 122.

[37] CDL-AD(2013)005.

i.e., competence of plenary sessions of SCC's departments for issuing legal opinions.[38] Moreover, prerogative to determine gener legal opinions was replaced with vague competence to "ensure uniform court application of law and equality of parties in court proceedings" (Art. 31 LOC 2013). In the aftermath, this provision led to drafting a new concept by SCC, based on its non-adjucative jurisdiction.

3.3 Drafting the Enhanced Concept: Operationalization of Article 31 of Law on Organisation of Courts by Supreme Court of Cassation

Supreme Court of Cassation has embraced new fundamental out-of-trial prerogative according to Art. 31 LOC 2013. It was the President of SCC who issued "Plan of Activities of SCC for Case Law Unification" (SCC Plan) in 2014,[39] the act which stipulates not only activities of SCC—as title would suggest—but activities of all courts, i.e., judiciary. In this act it is stated that SCC shall, apart from inherent adjucative jurisdiction, adopt legal opinions when there are "long standing and profound divergences in case law as systematic problem", referencing case law of the European Court of Human Rights (ECtHR).

As other courts are concerned, it is stated that, for example, Commercial Appellate Court shall adopt annual programme for case law unification, organize annual seminars, determine legal opinions, and inform SCC thereof. Joint sessions of appellate courts according to Art. 24 § 3 LOC 2013 were interpreted as determination of legal resolutions, and informing SCC thereof; if SCC adopts it, it will have nature of legal opinion of SCC, if not, "it means that SCC will decide to the contrary in individual cases, or it will adopt its own legal opinion". Higher courts shall hold the meetings with their appellate courts and accordingly "suggest" legal issues which should be settled in manner of legal resolutions. Basic and commercial courts (exclusive first instance courts) shall be surveyed in respect of legal issues, and thereupon SCC shall determine the list of issues along with determination of court which shall prepare the report; respective SCC department shall consequently make the statement thereof.

[38] Government reasoned proposed abolishment of principal legal opinions on constitutional scale, arguing that according to Constitution courts are bind only by law, not by principal legal opinions, See Draft on Amending LOC, p. 12, http://www.parlament.gov.rs/upload/archive/files/cir/pdf/predlozi_zakona/3947-13.pdf. Government also stated that all suggestions of VC were incorporated in Draft (sic!).

[39] See https://www.vk.sud.rs/sites/default/files/attachments/PlanAktivnostiVrhovnogKasacionogSuda.pdf.

3.4 *Typology of Legal Opinions*

3.4.1 Traditional Legal Opinions

Legal opinions are adopted on one court's department session, notwithstanding court rank. Most remarkable ones are of course SCC opinions, but all other courts tend to follow the approach, most notably common appellate courts, Commercial Appellate Court and Misdemeanour Appellate Court.[40] Most of them are published online or/and in official bulletins of a respective court. Even when structure varies, because some of them are not reasoned at all,[41] the essence is same—it is always formulated as sentence which could be part of written law. When reasoning is given, it is almost never indicated what was the real cause for the department's session (e.g. is it because President of the court called it, panel, some judges etc.). Either it is merely stated "there is an issue in case law", or sometimes, "it is remarked that some low-level courts tend to apply law in erroneous manner".[42] Exceptions are rare, but they show something rather strange: in two published opinions it was stated that Ministry of Human Rights demanded their adoption,[43] and in one, unreasoned opinion, it was just added to it that it was "upon initiative of Swisslion [*scil.* private owned company]".[44] Lastly, in majority of cases the legal ground for adopting it is omitted; only in few cases SCC indicated that it is by virtue of Art. 31 LOC 2013.[45]

One subspecies of legal opinions are "legal resolutions" (*pravni zaključci*) or just "resolutions" (*zaključci*) of SCC's respective departments, obviously without of any legal grounds. It is unclear what is the very difference apart from the title, as they have same structure. One could observe that legal resolutions are more frequently unreasoned, but, as previously stated, this could not be regarded as structural difference, as some legal opinions are not reasoned either.

---

[40] Information provided on unofficial bases shows that even plenary sessions of some basic courts (first instance courts of lower level) are adopting legal opinions.

[41] E.g. Legal Opinion of SCC's Criminal Department of 28 September 2015, Bilten Vrhovnog kasacionog suda (SCC Bulletin) 1/2016, p. 237; Legal Opinion of SCC's Civil Department of 8 December 2015, Bilten Vrhovnog kasacionog suda (SCC Bulletin) 1/2016, p. 266; Legal Opinion of SCC's Civil Department of 11 June 2015, Bilten Vrhovnog kasaciong suda (SCC Bulletin) 1/2015, p. 309.

[42] E.g. Legal Opinion of SCC's Civil Department of 4 October 2010, Bilten Vrhovnog kasacionog suda (SCC Bulletin) 2010, p. 119.

[43] Legal Opinion of SCC's Civil Department of 25 March 2011, Bilten Vrhovnog kasacionog suda (SCC Bulletin) 1/2011, p. 74; see also Legal Opinion of Criminal Department of Supreme Court of Serbia of 25 November 2008, Bilten Vrhovnog suda Srbije (Bulletin of Supreme Court of Serbia) 1/2009, p. 57.

[44] Legal Opinion of SCC's Civil Department of 18 June 2015, Bilten Vrhovnog kasacionog suda (SCC Bulletin) 1/2016, p. 316.

[45] E.g. Legal Opinion of SCC's Civil Department of 3 July 2020, Bilten Vrhovnog kasacionog suda (SCC Bulletin) 1/2020, p. 33.

3.4.2 Joint Sessions of Appellate Courts' Departments and Submission for Approval to SCC

One of significant novelties in Serbian law is the concept of joint sessions of appellate courts' departments (e.g. civil, criminal, labour). Even when LOC 2013 is vague on prerogatives of joint sessions, as it states only that their task is to inform SCC on controversial legal issues important for functioning of courts in Republic of Serbia and for uniform case law, in practice it is understood as yet another model of issuing out-of-trial legal opinions.

The concept functions on the base of delegate system. Departments of each appellate court delegate members who are attending joint session. They are the ones who are voting, so theoretically they could even depart from majority of opinion of their own departments. Upon achieving necessary votes on joint session, the resolution is issued, which has the same structure as legal opinion, though it is never published with reasoning. Resolution is then submitted to SCC's relevant department for approval, following online publishing and in SCC Bulletin with indication "approved". If not, SCC publishes its own legal resolution. Key feature is that, in both alternatives, there aren't any reasons accompanied within, just a decree style legal statement.

Published material shows that joint sessions of appellate court's departments are held at least twice a year.

3.4.3 Q & A System

Lastly, legal opinions are issued by plenary sessions of various courts upon questions of lower instance judges, hence "Q & A system". Although one could hardly find legal basis in LOC for such concept, it became undoubtedly one of key features of contemporary Serbian everyday practise. Given the fact that it is not regulated by any law or bylaw, only source for assessment thereof are published materials. So, it appears that SCC, appellate courts including Commercial Appellate Court and Misdemeanour Appellate Court are exercising such competence. For the questions of all judges SCC is naturally competent. Appellate courts are competent to provide answers on questions posed by courts within their territory. As a rule, in published material it is not indicated which specific court posed a question.

The formulation of questions varies. Some questions are formulated in abstract sense, whilst some clearly indicate that a judge is trying to get an answer with regard of pending case. With regards to contents, insight in these question gives versatile picture: from those which are suitable to be answered by law students, over those appropriate, but sometimes already answered or settled in case law of SCC or Constitutional court, to those that imply real "hard cases". In vast majority of cases questions are not accompanied with standpoint of courts asking them.

As the structure of answers matters, there are also differences. Commercial Appellate Court always provide reasoning, while SCC in general tend to avoid it. If the issue at stake is already settled in case law, with answer the reference thereof is made. In other words, it seems that answer wouldn't be rejected, what sounds rather odd, bearing in mind that in official preliminary ruling system SCC declines application if the relevant legal issue is already solved in its case law.[46]

Method of Q & A should be strictly distinguished from official preliminary ruling procedure regulated in Code of Civil Procedure. Latter is integral part of pending case[47] and parties are not only informed thereof, but also in application for preliminary ruling parties' legal arguments should be included.[48] In other words, their right to be heard is guaranteed. The legal standpoint of first instance court (single judge or panel) along with summary of facts should be integral part of application too.[49] In contrast to this, the Q & A system operates on informal level, as parties have no clue that their case is in fact referred to some other body for "advisory opinions".

Published answers show that average figures are significant. For example, SCC Criminal Department rendered more than 200 answers in one year only (December 2013–December of 2014).[50] Commercial Appellate Court issues even more answers on annual basis.[51]

3.5 *Legal Nature of Legal Opinions: Nonbinding and Semi-binding Effect*

According to Serbian Constitution, sources of law are only acts enacted by parliament (Constitution and laws), bylaws and international law (both international treatises and customary law); case law and legal opinions are not in that catalogue. Independence of judges in substantial sense (in German *sachliche Richterunabhängingkeit*) is regulated by the same token.[52] However, according to Art. 43 § 3 LOC 2013, legal opinions of SCC departments are obligatory for all panels of respective department, which is *vis-à-vis* all other courts interpreted *e contrario*.[53] Notwithstanding that, some appellate courts in few published

[46] See for example SCC's Civil Department, Decision of 12 November 2019, No. 8/19, Glasnik Advokatske komore Vojvodine 4/2019, p. 483.

[47] Bodiroga (2012), p. 123, f. 97.

[48] Art. 181 § 1 CCP; see also SCC, Decision of Civil Department of 16 September 2021, No. Spp 2/21: application for preliminary ruling is inadmissible if one of parties had no opportunity to state her opinion on respective legal issue.

[49] According to SCC, if in application standpoint of court is omitted, the applications is inadmissible; see SCC, Decision of Civil Department of 2 September 2020, No. 1/20.

[50] All published in SCC Bulletin 1/2015, pp. 202–295.

[51] For example, in 2013 Commercial Appellate Court issued 247 answers, see Bulletin of Commercial Appellate Court 3/2013, pp. 9–281.

[52] See Art. 149 § 1 of Serbian Constitution.

[53] See representatively only Rakić-Vodinelić (2012), p. 129. On contrast compare Ćirić (2020), p. 78 who argues that "legal opinions should be respected", but not in sense of modern continental

judgements were considering to be bound by the opinions. For instance, Appellate Court Novi Sad (*Apelacioni sud u Novom Sadu*) in its recent judgement, after citing one SCC legal resolution—which was, it's worth mentioning, unreasoned—stated that

> this court (i.e., Appellate Court Novi Sad) is in obligation to apply cited resolution regarding unification of case law as one of the elements of right to a fair trial and as long as it is unchanged cannot depart from it.[54]

Moreover, some courts are considering that legal opinions of their plenary sessions are obligatory for their respective panels, as it is stated in document of Misdemeanour Appellate Court.[55] Last but not least, it appears that presidents of appellate courts are regarding resolutions of joint sessions of appellate courts' department (see Sect. 3.4.2) to be binding for each panel of every appellate court. As it was stated in agreements of presidents of appellate courts on organisation of joint sessions,

> the provision of law [*scil.* art 24 § 3 LOC 2013] stipulates obligation of courts that their case law shall be internally constant, as well as that case law shall be in according to case law of other three appellate courts.[56]

3.6 Method for Ensuring Compliance with "Legal Opinions"

Law on Organisation of Courts is silent on this issue, despite the fact that it stipulates that legal opinions of SCC's departments are obligatory for all respective panels. However, this question is remarkably regulated by bylaws: Rules of Order of SCC,[57] which is adopted by plenary session of SCC, and Rules of Order of Courts,[58] applicable to all other courts and issued by Minister of Justice upon opinion of President of SCC. Both acts contain same rules with regards the issue. According to

---

theory of case law as "secondary source of law" (*die Lehre von den sekundären Rechtsquellen*), but in strict binding sense. On former theory see e.g. Bydlinski (1987); Möllers (2019), pp. 80–82.

[54] Appellate Court Novi Sad, Judgement of 3 October 2019, No. Gž 3282/19, retrievable at official case law database (hereinafter "case law database"), https://www.sudskapraksa.sud.rs; see also, by the same token, Appellate Court Novi Sad, Judgement of 21 November 2013, No. Gž 3938/13, case law database.

[55] See "Programme of Case Law Department of Misdemeanour Appellate Court for 2021–2025": "legal opinion shall be deemed as obligatory", http://pkap.sud.rs/prekrsajni-apelacioni-sud-program-rada-sudske-prakse.html.

[56] See Agreement of Presidents of Appellate Courts on organisation of joint sessions of 25 December 2017, p. 2, https://www.vk.sud.rs/sites/default/files/attachments/SPORAZUM%20PREDSEDNIKA%20APELACIONIH%20SUDOVA_0.pdf; Agreement of Presidents of Appellate Courts on organisation of joint sessions of 24 February 2021, p. 2, https://www.vk.sud.rs/sites/default/files/attachments/Sporazum.pdf.

[57] Official Gazette of Republic of Serbia, Nos. 37/2010, 51/2014, 41/2016, 62/2016, 74/2018.

[58] Official Gazette of Republic of Serbia, Nos. 110/2009, 70/2011, 19/2012, 89/2013, 96/2015, 104/2015, 113/2015, 39/2016, 56/2016, 77/2016, 16/2018, 78/2018, 43/2019, 93/2019.

the rules, when one second instance or SCC panel render the judgment, it is sent for a service to the parties via Case Law Department. It is an obligation of this department, mostly consisted of judicial advisors with one judge acting as chief, to review every judgment in order to avoid departure of case law or legal opinion. If there are no remarks, service of judgment is approved; if that is not the case, service of judgement is suspended, and case is sent back to the panel in order to "deliberate once again". If panel does not change its judgement, plenary session of respective department is called to discuss the matter, and if majority is against the decision of panel, legal opinion is issued. Case is then once again sent back to the panel to reconsider it once again. If panel persist on its legal standpoint and disregard the legal opinion, "the issue is referred to plenary session of court".[59] Formal ground for such endless remittal could be found in provisions of rules, not in procedural codes or any other laws. It is stated that "the decision could be changed until it leaves the premisses of the court, but only by panel consisted of same members".[60]

Even though provisions are silent on key issue—what is the next step? when will service of judgment, if ever, occur?—one case, or maybe the only case that was made public, shows how system is really operating.

In one case before Appellate Court Kragujevac, panel of three judges unanimously decided to reject the appeal. Case law department suspended service of judgment, referencing the departure of courts' case law. As panel stayed by its decision, first, department's plenary session was called, and then courts' plenary session as well, "voting that there is departure of case law". As panel didn't want to revise its decision, the chief of Case Law Department issued new note to the panel, stating:

> With full awareness of Your independence, I am of opinion that I can not let the case with such decision go out of court's premisses, because it would mean acting contrary to voting results of plenary sessions concerning Your case.[61]

In the aftermath president of court filed a disciplinary action against members of sitting panel, because

> acceptance of such action of judges, that unanimously rendered judgment disregarding legal opinions of Civil department and plenary session of whole court, would mean undermining of authority of plenary session, as well as collegial relations, and acceptance of arbitrariness and it would give cause to the judges to disregard resolutions, statements and legal opinions of department's and plenary court's sessions, which would by all means undermine efforts being made in harmonisation of case law and diminish already achieved results.[62]

---

[59] See Art. 200 of Rules of Order of Courts; Art. 40–41 of Rules of Order of SCC.

[60] See Art. 197 of Rules of Order of Courts; Art. 32 of Rules of Order of SCC. It was already argued that such approach is unconstitutional, as it is matter of court procedure, so it must be governed by law, not bylaw; see Poznić (2009), p. 843; compare Knežević (2017), pp. 33–35.

[61] See Note of 28 November 2013, https://www.ombudsman.rs/attachments/3294_3odgovor%20zastitnik%20gradjana%20kragujevac.pdf.

[62] President of Appellate Court Kragujevac, Disciplinary Action of 24 December 2013, No. V Su-35-19/13, https://www.ombudsman.rs/attachments/3294_3odgovor%20zastitnik%20gradjana%20kragujevac.pdf.

After that, the case was taken away from the panel by act of president of court because of filed disciplinary action; one member of panel filed a legal remedy, though unsuccessful; President of SCC rejected it, repeating arguments in contested act.[63] The end of the story is unknow to the public, apart from the fact that President of Appellate Court Kragujevac has enjoyed favourable fortune in her subsequent career. In 2021 she was promoted to the SCC becoming a Justice.

Such example speaks for itself, and I will invoke it in following text. However, one remark should be made already here. Even when law passed by parliament (LOC) doesn't contain any provision which should indicate that legal opinion of any other court apart from SCC shall be binding to respective panels, the Rules of Order of Courts, bylaw issued by administrative body (sic!), prescribes method which presupposes binding effect of such legal opinions. Described example shows that it is regarded as such in everyday life of Serbian judiciary.

4 Socialist Legal Tradition as Rationale

4.1 Is This Socialist at All?

One could argue that present Serbian concept is not proof of survival of Socialist legal tradition, as clearly—although never reviled in past or present Serbian literature—pre-socialist law had the same concept.[64] Moreover, it could be perceived as something inherent to judiciary, self-understanding appendix prerogative that goes hand in hand with adjudicative jurisdiction.[65] As a matter of fact, latter would be most likely to be common answer, due to the long-lasting tradition and maybe more important, chronical lack of comparative studies on this issue on one side,[66] and messages coming from Strasbourg on the other. In two cases concerning Serbia, ECtHR emphasized out-of-trial case law unification prerogatives as something

[63] President of SCC, Decision of 17 January 2014, No. 1 Su 2 54/13-1, https://www.ombudsman.rs/attachments/3294_3odgovor%20zastitnik%20gradjana%20kragujevac.pdf.

[64] Even in comparative perspective there is broad perception that only Hungarian law provides exception, as legal opinions were present in pre-WWII law, compare Kühn (2006), p. 24: Hungary is "the only system with pre-Communist tradition of this abstract law-making". On the other hand, present Russian authors refer to out-of-trial concept as "unique component of Russian legal system", compare Esakov (2012), p. 672, f. 21.

[65] So, the words of at that time district judge Radovanov (2003), p. 181: high admissibility rates for appeal on law lead to incapacity of Supreme Court to devote "those questions that are significant" which should be settled in manner of "creating general legal opinions".

[66] It should be noted that there is lack of proper comparative research in general, which should be once again linked with extreme positivism. From that perspective, only comparative task is to simply find foreign code or other act, and to interpret it in own way, i.e., in extreme positivistic sense.

useful and effective for eliminating "profound and long lasting" divergence of case law.[67]

Nevertheless, both assumptions are false. As for comparative perspective, it is a simple truth that concept of non-adjucative jurisdiction is strange to present "western" legal systems, and especially to those that traditionally played major role in shaping Serbian law (i.e., Germanic legal systems). The story of constitutional changes in DDR after the fall of Berlin Wall seems to be paradigmatic for understanding compliance of out-of-trial legal opinions with the real concept of *Rechtsstaat*, as such model was immediately abolished with introduction of independence of judges.[68] Changes of Austrian Supreme Court in 1969 aimed, although highly controversial both in academic and in Parliament debate, for providing clear and unsuspicious concept of method of harmonisation of case law in constitutional sense.[69] Concept of grand chambers as method of harmonisation of case law of supreme instances, as typical feature of German[70] and Austrian[71] legal systems, is still unknown to Serbian mainstream discourse.[72] Lastly, standpoint of ECtHR could not be taken for granted, because it failed to see its "unbalanced and one-sided" position.[73] Even when such approach was criticized occasionally by some Serbian scholars,[74] Serbian mainstream perception of ECtHR as unquestionable authority similar—metaphorically speaking—to the Pope, makes illusion much stronger.

Present concept has its roots in sovietisation of law after WWII, as it was integral part of import package called "socialist law". There are no records that in that time adoption of Soviet model was regarded at least as some kind of legal continuity in Yugoslavia. It was fresh product that had special aim within new ideology, with capacity for shaping the legal culture. It was, by the virtue of the principle of power unity, perfect tool to control and discipline judiciary in an authoritarian manner. If certain concept was present even in pre-Socialist law, that is only evidence that some

---

[67] *Cupara vs. Serbia*, Judgment of 12 July 2016, No. 34683/08, § 36; *Živić vs. Serbia*, Judgment of 13 September 2011, No. 37204/08, § 46.

[68] See Art. 5 § 2 sentence 3 of Principles of Constitution of 17 June 1990 (*Gesetz zur Änderung und Ergänzung der Verfassung der Deutschen Demokratischen Republik – Verfassungsgrundsätze*).

[69] Government in its Draft of Law on Supreme Court argued that competence of Supreme Court to issue legal opinions upon request of Minister of Justice was contrary to the Constitution, as well as power of president of the court to suspend a service; see Regierungsvorlage GP XI. 470, pp. 5–6, https://www.parlament.gv.at/PAKT/VHG/XI/I/I_00470/imfname_308856.pdf; compare Feldner (2001), pp. 22–28, as well as Fasching (1969), pp. 137 *et seqq*., both with further references.

[70] See Schreiber (2017), marginal numbers 1–11.

[71] See Lovrek and Musger (2019), marginal numbers 52–65.

[72] Moreover, it appears that Yugoslav out-of-trial concept was identified with German model of Grand chambers, compare Košutić (1973), p. 34, f. 100; Košutić (1978), p. 87. On the contrary, for German doctrine and case law grand chambers of supreme court are without doubt bodies that perform adjucitave tasks, as they are qualified as *Spruchkörper* in sense of right to a lawful judge; see already Bundesverfassungsgericht, Decision of 11 May 1965, No. 2 BvR 259/63, NJW 1965, p. 1323 with further references; for doctrine see Leisner (1989), p. 2447.

[73] Galič (2017), p. 41, stating also that such position of ECtHR is "highly regrettable".

[74] Knežević (2017), pp. 46–48.

features of Social legal traditions are not unique. Nevertheless, it was Socialist law that provided the most coherent model.[75]

In following text, I will try to demonstrate what was suggested, based on some already carved out salient features of Socialist legal tradition by prominent scholars, most of them vested with authentic insider perspective as they are coming from states that *cum grano salis* share same heritage as Serbia.

4.2 Mainstream Rationale: Political Instrumentalization

Rapid enhancement of non-adjucative case law unification is superficially linked with recourse to right to a fair trial, most notably in judiciary itself. Case law of ECtHR was understood—purposefully or not, it is irrelevant—in an extreme manner: legal certainty and unified case law became absolute component of right to a fair trial.[76] However, despite this misinterpretation of ECtHR's doctrine, concern for parties and for their interests is in fact just a façade. The real rationale is one of political nature, not legal. Present concept is an expression of political instrumentalization, just as it was during socialist time.[77] The root of the idea of predictable case law as integral part of right to a fair trial was result of "condemnations" coming from Strasbourg, which, on the other hand, as it was stated (see Sect. 4.1), emphasized out-of-trial model as effective tool for avoiding "profound and long-lasting differences in case law". Bearing in mind said, the goal of present concept is to avoid future "condemnations" coming from Strasbourg, and that is—from Serbian mainstream perspective—one of the key leverages in process of accession of Serbia to the EU: the less cases where ECtHR found that Serbian case law is ununified, the more Serbia's negotiation capacity is increasing. It appears that statement of at that time Minister of Justice, delivered 2013 at ceremonial of 50 years of publishing SCC Bulletin, could not be more paradigmatic in that sense.

> Ultimate contribution of such Supreme Court of Cassation's function [*scil.* non-adjucative jurisdiction] should be making the trial predictable and unification of case law, *which would*

[75] See Uzelac (2019), pp. 118–119.

[76] I claim that extreme dogmatic positions are also one of the salient features of Socialist legal tradition, because in its discourse there is no room for balance of interests. As one idea would articulate, it would become dogma. On the other hand, that idea would always represent specific public (i.e., political) interest. That being said, there is close connection with extreme positivist positions in legal methodology, also one of crucial landmarks of Socialist legal tradition. For further reading on latter see Kühn (2011); Kühn (2006); Mańko (2013), p. 6; Kischel (2015), pp. 578 *et seqq.*; Emmert (2001).

[77] I refer to Uzelac's position, that purpose of unification of case law in Socialists judiciary was implementing uniform state's policy and transindividual interests, e.g. protection of objective legal order. See Uzelac (2019), p. 117 *et seqq.*

lead to reduction of cases at ECtHR and to harmonious application of human rights protection on national scale (emphasis added).[78]

On the other hand, even before amendment of LOC in 2013, clear position of Serbian political bodies could be found in that direction. As it was stated in Opinion of VC in 2013, Serbian authorities explained to VC delegation that out-of-trial mechanism aimed at preventing future applications to ECtHR.[79] That is in result also position of presidents of appellate courts regarding *de facto* only goal of model of joint sessions of appellate courts' departments.[80] In conclusion, the concept aims at achieving political goals; concern for legal certainty and human rights is, at best, a by-product.

4.3 Reminiscence of Principle of Unity of Power: Legal Aspect

Even though principle of unity of power could be regarded as a political feature that finds its expression in political instrumentalization of out-of-trial case law unification,[81] the other side of the coin, purely legal one, could be identified as well. It is indicative that this sort of out-of-trial competence of courts perfectly fits into framework of unity of power; it is designed to provide dogmatic reasoning: the essence is that entrusting the judiciary with adjudicative competence is not, by notion, contrary to granting it semi-legislative prerogatives.[82] It is also remarkable that various constitutions from Socialist era provided for it explicitly (see Sect. 2.2). It should be, however, emphasised that present Serbian Constitution, as well as its predecessor, both based on principle of separation of powers, are lacking such provisions, and with good reason. It would be rather contrary to the founding principle of Constitution,[83] going towards *contradictio in adiecto*. Lastly, that is the core of long lasting "practice" of VC, as it was stated in numerous occasions that

[78] See https://www.mpravde.gov.rs/vest/7013/vrhovni-kasacioni-sud-ima-bitnu-ulogu-u-ujednacavanju-sudske-prakse.php.

[79] See CDL-ADL(2013)005, §§ 104, 107.

[80] See Agreement of Presidents of Appellate Courts on organisation of joint sessions of 25 December 2017, p. 2, https://www.vk.sud.rs/sites/default/files/attachments/SPORAZUM%20PREDSEDNIKA%20APELACIONIH%20SUDOVA_0.pdf; Agreement of Presidents of Appellate Courts on organisation of joint sessions of 24 February 2021, p. 2, https://www.vk.sud.rs/sites/default/files/attachments/Sporazum.pdf.

[81] See Uzelac (2019), p. 117 *et seqq.*

[82] Compare Kühn (2006), p. 24: "specific instrument of unbound judicial law-making *par excellence*"; Zobec and Letnar Černič (2015), p. 142: "quasi-legislative"; Galič (2017), p. 41: "half academic and half legislative"; Stanković (1994), p. 10: "legislative".

[83] On the issue of discrepancy of abstract legal opinions with principle of separation of powers see also Bobek (2009), p. 45; Zobec and Letnar Černič (2015), p. 142; Galič (2017), pp. 40–41; Bratković (2018), p. 92; Knežević (2017), pp. 25–27; Knežević (2019), p. 49. Dika (2018) argues

issuing abstract legal opinions is, in fact, a breach of principle of separation of powers. The absence of any critical approach on this matter in Serbian discourse at any level could be rationalised also by deeply rooted theory of unity of powers. That is why introduction of coherent concept in line with Constitution, encapsulated in the motto "adjucative function of judiciary, nothing less, but nothing more as well" could not be successful.[84]

4.4 *Comprehension of Judiciary and Independence of Judges: Collectivistic Approach*

According to Uzelac, one of the key features of Socialist Legal Tradition is collectivistic approach, as it stems from ideological background which praises collective interest at account of individualistic ones. Operationalisation thereof is a concept of democratic centralism, established by Lenin at the beginning of twentieth century: formal plurality of opinions in discussion, and unity of action upon reaching the consensus. That pattern is crucial rationale behind non-adjucative case law unification concept. After the discussion, plenary session of judges reaches legal opinion, which should be then followed in future cases decided by separate panels. As it was stated in one textbook in 1986, that is in line with democratic principles and general rationale of functioning of collegial bodies.[85]

Such understanding, though without explicitly referring to the notion of democratic centralism, still shapes Serbian discourse. Well-known dogmatic dichotomy of notion of "court" in a sense of institution as such on one hand, and adjudicative body (single judge or panel) on the other hand, seems to be unconceptualized,[86] most notably by judiciary itself. It should be regarded as dominant opinion that judicial power is by Constitution given to courts as institutions, and not to the judges which form judicative bodies of specific court in every single case. The wording of Constitution indeed provides arguments for such approach, as it states, on the first place, that "courts are autonomous and independent" (Art. 142 § 1) and that "judicial power is entrusted to the courts" (Art. 143 § 1), and only after it is stated that "judges are independent in their exercise of judicial function" and that "any interference with

from perspective of Croatian Law that only constitutional issue is binding effect, not the competence itself.

[84] One of most significant and yet unrevealed relics of Socialist law is undoubtedly competence of Misdemeanour Appellate Court to "collect from first instance courts data and reports required for tracking and scrutinizing the social phenomena and relations". See Art. 100 § 6 of Law on Misdemeanours of 2013, Official Gazette of Republic of Serbia, Nos. 65/2013, 13/2016, 98/2016-98 (Decision of Constitutional Court), 91/2019.

[85] Triva et al. (1986), p. 95. On critique of such position in present day Croatia see Bratković (2018), p. 93.

[86] See however Rakić-Vodinelić (2012), p. 44; Knežević (2017), p. 14. For clear distinction of both notions in e.g. German law see Rosenberg et al. (2010), p. 101; Lüke (2011), pp. 63–64.

the judge regarding his exercise of judicial function is prohibited" (Art. 149). Such redactional approach, even if flawed[87] together with questionable methodological value of textual arguments, is sufficient to undermine the very core of principle of independence of judges, but only when one is aware of collectivistic spirit.

As a consequence thereof, in combination with reminiscence of principle of unity of power and other features, it is self-understanding for mainstream discourse that some other body, and not an adjudicative one, even when it's comprised of judges, issues legal opinions by which it interprets and develops law. The idea of both external and internal independence of judges, i.e., judicative bodies, is still underdeveloped. Bearing this in mind, it turns out that legal opinions of plenary sessions are not regarded as contrary to independence of judges, as in result, after all, it is courts, i.e., collectives, and not individuals who are vested with independence. Therefore, one shouldn't be surprised when the judges themselves regard suspending of service of their judgments by case law department justified by the alleged need to reconsider their judgment, prescribed by bylaw (see Sect. 3.6) as something normal, or even in accordance with Constitution.[88] Not even when some other judges sitting in plenary session express "serious objections" to judicative panel that made decision.[89] Example of case before Appellate Court Kragujevac (see Sect. 3.6) couldn't be more paradigmatic, and who knows what is reality behind of curtains of other courts. From perspective of basic notion of independence of judges, said should present rather textbook example of breach of Art. 149 of Serbian Constitution which stipulates so called substantive independence of judges. However, that could be possible only in absence of collectivistic approach.

4.5 *Authoritarian Spirit of the Concept*

According to Kühn, authoritative judicial discourse must be distinguished from authoritarian one. Whilst former is proprium of judicial activity, and it presupposes pluralism of opinions and the participation of all competent persons in legal decision-making,[90] later is a feature of systems operating in undemocratic surroundings, namely socialist states.

> The "right" answer is achieved through a "one-way" process and is backed entirely be threat and force. Those to whom decisions are addressed cannot participate in finding the "right"

---

[87] Knežević (2017), p. 14.

[88] For example, Vujičić (2012), p. 266, at that time judge of Appellate Court Kragujevac, and now Justice, who categorically rejects issue of constitutionality, though without of any single argument.

[89] For example, Justice Andrejević in interview to "Politika" newspaper in 2017: "As long as case doesn't leave the court premisses, it could be revised. It could be brought on department session. *If there are serious objections, it is up to the panel to once more deliberate* [emphasise added]"; https://www.politika.rs/sr/clanak/376396/Uskoro-prve-odluke-Vrhovnog-suda-o-svajcarcima.

[90] Kühn (2006), p. 20; Kühn (2011), p. 152.

answers; instead of being subjects, they are rather objects of authoritarian decision-making.[91]

Abstract legal opinions are explicit example of authoritarian legal culture, as judicial law-making of such nature is by notion one-sided process. Competent body of court delivers the opinion without having real-life case before it, thus "without listening to anyone".[92] On the contrary, proper judicial law-making as authoritative discourse includes pluralism, as the judicial decision originates from specific case and from a dialogue with parties, and between the courts of different instances.[93] Kühn argues that the continuing adherence to the out-of-trial model confirms what the post-Communist systems understand by notion of judicial law-making.[94] I claim that present day Serbian model not just verifies his thesis, but goes beyond it. As it was previously stated (Sect. 3.4.1), it is not uncommon for SCC to publish an opinion without of reasoning, showing authoritarian discourse at its best. On such occasions one could not even refer to traditional argument in favour of concept, that "legal opinion should have effect by persuasive force of authority", because in proper judicial law-making persuasive force of authority stems from reasoning of authority. Could it be possible to speak about rational discourse without giving any arguments? The fact that even Q & A system in practise of SCC operates by same virtue (see Sect. 3.4.3) only reaffirms my thesis.

4.6 Paternalistic Spirit of Concept

Paternalism *vis-à-vis* judiciary hierarchy in Socialist legal tradition is deeply conditioned by aforementioned understanding of courts' and judges' independence. Courts are not only institutions as such which preform adjudicative and non-adjucative functions, but they are also institutions based on strict hierarchical scheme, vested with controlling and educational prerogatives. In collectivistic and authoritarian way of thinking, they are nothing more than resemblance of administrative bodies. Vertical that is immanent to every judicial system which has devolutive legal remedies is regarded as something absolute. Therefore, higher courts are not only courts of higher instance, but bodies that are superior in administrative manner. In this model it is self-explaining that higher courts are controlling lower ones through abstract guidance regarding legal issues. On the top of the pyramid there is a supreme superior body with inherent prerogative to watch over all subordinated subjects. The role of president of court or even head of

[91] Kühn (2006), p. 20; Kühn (2011), p. 152.

[92] Kühn (2006), p. 25.

[93] Kühn (2006), p. 20; Kühn (2011), p. 152; Zobec and Letnar Černič (2015), p. 141.

[94] Kühn (2006), pp. 24–25. According to Maleshin (2007), p. 556, ordinary judicial decisions are not as popular in Russian legal practice as "guiding explanations" of supreme courts.

department is understood in the same way. In short, the concept is based, as Uzelac defined it, on inquisitorial paternalism.[95]

Even though mainstream Serbian discourse is obsessed with "independence of judges", it is not affected by strong and vivid life of paternalistic spirit. To the contrary, the expansion of out-of-trial activities by various courts and by various methods, as well as the fact that it is the judiciary who reinforced it, could be easily rationalized by paternalism. Present Serbian system offers numerous indications for that diagnosis. Supreme Court of Cassation took the role of an omnipotent institution which governs the judiciary and case law, but not in a classical sense through its case law. It is not a supreme court because it is last instance in pending cases, but because it is simply supreme organ of judiciary in administrative sense. Therefore, SCC considers that it is its proprium to monitor case law of all other courts and to intervene *post festum* in out-of-trial manner whenever it finds necessary, including interventions to correct "erroneous practice". Some of SCC legal opinions are even on textual level an explicit confirmation of this thesis. In at least two occasions cause for adoption of legal opinions was—from SCC's perspective—erroneous application of law by lower courts. The SCC's reaction was openly paternalistic, as it was stated at the beginning of one opinion:

> Upon collection and examination of lower instance case law in the matter of application of [...] it was noticed that some higher courts when setting aside judgments are instructing first instance courts to apply rules of non-contentious procedure, **instead of enforcement procedure** [bolded in original]. Civil Department of SCC has thus decided, notwithstanding explicit provisions of Code of Enforcement Procedure, in this manner as well, to point out to lower-level courts' noticed erroneous practice [...].[96]

Adopting and further development of Q & A System (see Sect. 3.4.3) is another example of paternalistic approach, or perhaps even the most significant one. It is designed to provide of mentorship of higher courts over lower instance judges, perfectly fitting into the pattern of authoritarian culture also. Whenever one judge has some concerns regarding any legal issue in a pending case, he could always address higher court, even SCC, for providing an unreasoned answer. The fact that a large number of judges embraced this possibility, as well as the lack of concerns in judiciary regarding the concept as such, shows that constitutional picture of autonomous and independent judicative body is mere declaration. Judges have willingly lifted their veil of independence as a result of survival of paternalistic spirit. Here lays an explanation for another typical feature of Socialist legal tradition, namely fear of (proper) decision-making.[97]

---

[95] Uzelac (2019), p. 118.

[96] Resolution of SCC's Civil Department of 13 September 2010, Bilten Vrhovnog kasacionog suda (SCC Bulletin) 2010, p. 93; similar wording in Resolution of SCC's Civil Department of 4 October 2010 also, Bilten Vrhovnog kasacionog suda (SCC Bulletin) 2010, p. 119.

[97] Kischel (2015), p. 580 claims that there is interrelation between fear of taking the responsibility for decision-making and guidance role of higher courts. On evading responsibility to pass final judgements as a guiding principle of Socialists legal tradition in general, see Uzelac (2010), pp. 383–395; Kühn (2011), pp. 204–205.

4.7 Conclusion

Present day Serbian model of case law unification is coined in all of its features on Socialist Legal Tradition. In my point of view, constitutional principles in Serbia, such as separation of powers and independence of judges, in fact both integral part of rule of law or state of law (*Rechtsstaat*), are in substance different from their western counterparts, even though their normative basis is the same. In comparative perception that sounds normal: texts of laws, including constitutions are just starting point; complex issues that form *the* context—as Kischel defines the key figure that should replace "legal culture"[98]—provide proper answers. The problem is that, in Serbian mainstream discourse, there is self-deception that what represents Serbian model of judiciary is in principle in accordance with proper rule of law, and there is only a room for improvement with regard to gaining more external independence. As a matter of fact, present model of case law unification, as paradigmatic example of functioning of judiciary, shows that one could speak rather of "requiem of rule of law".[99] Not only that all virtues of authoritarian and paternalistic understanding survived, but they have been reinforced. To my knowledge, Serbian Q & A system is unique on European scale, and that fact is not flattering.

But is there a light at the end of the tunnel? Certainty there must be. I claim that there is potential, but the journey is long and tough, because long lasting traditions must be—paraphrasing Kötz—buried. However, recent occurrences show that even such modest optimistic prognosis is far ahead.

5 Aftermath: Self-explanatory Unwillingness for Constitutional Changes

At the end, I should refer to deliberately undisclosed information. It was done so with an aim to provide clearer perspective for crucial issue—the destiny of out-of-trial case law unification concept. Sadly, it could be said that it has rather vivid life in Serbian legal system. Tough and long Serbian journey is (once gain) delayed.

Serbia is expecting constitutional changes regarding judiciary. Present system is both by West and by domestic legal community, most notably by judges' organisations, qualified as not fully in line with the principle of judicial independence. The key problem is the model of appointment of judges.[100] Nevertheless, history of

[98] Kischel (2015), p. 238 *et seqq*.

[99] Knežević (2019), p. 49.

[100] It is argued that present model gives to much of power to the other two branches of power, as two out of 11 members of High Judiciary Council are coming from legislative and government. Serbian judiciary is arguing that judges should appoint judges, and that first three-year term should be abolished.

drafting of constitutional changes shows that the role of case law and SCC was also in focus.

In the first Draft of constitutional amendments provided by the Ministry of Justice in 2018, two issues were addressed. First, as sources of law are concerned, it was stated that "method of case law unification would be regulated by law". On the other hand, it was proposed to regulate function of SCC, which should by the way change the name again, now to the previous one (Supreme Court of Serbia), so it would "guarantee uniform application of law and equality of all."

Draft was sent to VC for the opinion. The result was anything but surprising. Venice Commission once again applied its well established "practice" concerning issues as stake. It was suggested that case law status in respect of legal sources' catalogue should be changed, so the judges should be bound by law, taking into account case law, and not by abstract legal opinions. On the other hand, VC criticised proposed provision on role of SCC, as it was not indicated "how this [*scil.* ensuring uniform application of law by the courts] is to be done",[101] suggesting adding crucial words: "The Supreme Court of Serbia shall ensure uniform application of the law by the courts *through its case law*" (emphasise in original).[102]

Immediately after the VC's opinion, new Draft was prepared by the Ministry of Justice. Recommendations of VC were fully accepted, and VC expressed its satisfaction in subsequent opinion.[103] Nevertheless, it appears that this pronounced paradigm change was ephemeral phase.

After official initiation of amending procedure in Parliament, new working group was formed in June 2021. In Draft adopted in Parliament's body in September 2021, previous drafted amendments which would eventually lead towards evident unconstitutionality of out-of-trial case law unification concept, were simply omitted. Surprisingly, VC in its new Opinion adopted in October 2021 made no remarks to this, furthermore, it failed even to mention the omission of drafted amendments which were praised by VC back in 2018.[104]

As no preparatory works of Drafting working group were published—not a single word on rationale of drafted amendments of Constitution, which is rather *per se* typical feature of authoritarian culture—one could only guess what the real reason behind the Copernican twist was. In my point of view, the Socialist legal tradition acted as *spiritus movens*. In the eyes of its supporters, it would be a disaster to accept its decline after it has survived even fall of Socialism. It could also be argued by the same token that even judiciary—in reality top stakeholders, or to put it directly: judicial oligarchy—played a role. With fall of the concept SCC would lose its function of paternalistic figure and inherent political powers within.[105] That is

---

[101] CDL-AD(2018)011, § 55.

[102] CDL-AD(2018)011, § 56.

[103] CDL-AD(2018)023, § 19.

[104] See CDL-AD(2021)011.

[105] According to Uzelac (2010), p. 395, misunderstood principle of judicial independence led in post-Socialist countries to forming impenetrable barriers to substantial changes by judiciary itself.

something also undesirable for political elite, as one method of influence would simply wannish.[106] Socialist legal tradition in Serbia can, sadly, always rely on ECtHR case law in its favour, where out-of-trial methods of case law harmonisation are praised as effective tool. And by same virtue, one could put forward rather common-sense question: if such non-judicative method is a concept deeply coined by values and virtues of Socialist legal tradition, and ECtHR praises it, has Socialist legal tradition found its way into Strasbourg? The answer should be in the negative, but the issue shows how superficial approach could lead to disservice.[107] Last but not least, same goes to the twist in approach of VC. Longer than a decade Serbian legislator was criticized for having concept that is contrary to the basic principles of rule of law (see Sect. 3.2). It was also VC that invited Serbian authorities to adapt Draft of constitutional changes back in 2018, by which out-of-trial method of case law unification would be *ex constitutionis* abolished. Yet, when all that was omitted in the new Draft in 2021, which could easily end up as successful, all said in the past simply vanished. That could be, in Serbian discourse stamped by Socialist legal tradition, understood as giving a green light. Hence, "Socialist legal tradition reloaded".

References

Bobek M (2009) Quantity or quality? Reassessing the role of supreme jurisdictions in Central Europe. Am J Comp Law 57(1):33–65

Bodiroga N (2012) Novi Zakon o parničnom postupku (New code of civil procedure). Pravni fakultet Univerziteta u Beogradu, Beograd

Bratković M (2018) Revizija po dopuštenju (Second appeal by permission). Dissertation, University of Zagreb

Bydlinski F (1987) Hauptpositionen zum Richterrecht (Key positions on judge made law). Juristenzeitung 40(4):149–155

Ćirić A (2020) (Ne)efikasnost sudstva u materiji privrednih sporova ([In]Efficiency of the judiciary in the matter of commercial disputes). Pravo i privreda 3:55–80

Culja S (1936) Građansko procesno pravo Kraljevine Jugoslavije (Civil procedure of Kingdom of Yugoslavia). Geca Kon, Belgrade

Dika M (2018) O ustavnosti odredaba Zakona o sudovima o obavezatnosti pravnih shvaćanja prihvaćenih na sjednicama odjela odnosno na sjednicama svih sudaca viših sudova i o njihovoj ustavnosudskoj kontrolabilnosti (On constitutionality of judiciary act's provisions regarding binding character of legal opinions adopted at the sittings of court's departments or at plenary sittings and on the constitutional controllability thereof). In: Slakoper Z et al (eds) Liber Amicorum Aldo Radolović. Sveučilište u Rijeci Pravni fakultet, Rijeka, pp 109–123

Đorđević A (1923) Teorija građanskog sudskog postupka II (Theory of Civil Procedure II), 2nd edn. Geca Kon, Belgrade

Đorđević A (1924) Teorija građanskog sudskog postupka I (Theory of Civil Procedure I), 2nd edn. Geca Kon, Belgrade

[106] As it was previously stated and documented, some legal opinions were adopted upon request of government administrative bodies (ministries), or powerful private company; see Sect. 3.4.1.

[107] One could even speak about "kiss of death from Strasbourg".

Emmert F (2001) Independence of judges a concept often misunderstood in Central and Eastern Europe. Eur J Law Reform 3(4):405–410
Esakov G (2012) The Russian criminal jury: recent developments, practice, and current problems. Am J Comp Law 60(3):665–702
Fasching H (1969) Zur verfassungsrechtlichen Rechtfertigung der Bindung des Obersten Gerichtshofes an seine Grundsatzentscheidungen (On constitutional justification of supreme court's binding by its own general decisions). In: Fasching H, Kralik W (eds) Festschrift für Hans Schima zum 75. Geburtstag. Manz, Wien, pp 133–151
Feldner B (2001) Verstärkte Senate beim Obersten Gerichtshof (Consolidated panels of supreme court). Springer, Wien–New York
Fira A, Pajvančić M (1989) Osnove ustavnog prava (Basics of constitutional law). Forum, Novi Sad
Galič A (2010) Das Slowenische Zivilprozessrecht zwischen Transmission, Kontinuität und Transformation (Slovenian civil procedure law between transmission, continuity and transformation). Ritsumeikan Law Rev 27:117–139
Galič A (2017) The inconsistency of case law and the right to a fair trial. In: Uzelac A, Van Rhee CH (eds) Revisiting procedural human rights. Fundamentals of civil procedure and the changing face of civil justice. Intersentia, Cambridge, pp 17–51
Ivošević Z (2005) Sudska praksa pravednog suđenja (Case law of just trial). Izbor sudske prakse 13(7–8):5–9
Jakšić A (2017) Građansko procesno pravo (Civil procedure), 9th edn. Pravni fakultet Univerziteta u Beogradu, Beograd
Kamhi S (1951) Građanski sudski postupak (Civil procedure). Veselin Masleša, Sarajevo
Kischel U (2015) Rechtsvergleichung (Comparative law). C.H. Beck, München
Knežević M (2017) Ujednačavanje sudske prakse u Republici Srbiji – stanje stvari i predlozi za reformu (Unifying of case law in Republic of Serbia – current situation and reform proposals). Judicial Efficiency Project 12SER01/01/121, unpublished
Knežević M (2019) Out-of-trial case law unification in Serbia: legal tradition as requiem for the rule of law. In: Nikolić D, Midorović S, Arsenijević D (eds) International scientific conference legal tradition and new legal challenges. University of Novi Sad Faculty of Law, Novi Sad, p 49
Košutić B (1973) Sudska presuda kao izvor prava (Judgment as legal source). Univerzitet u Beogradu, Beograd
Košutić B (1978) Načelno pravno mišljenje najvišeg suda kao izvor prava (General legal opinion of the highest court as source of law). Zbornik za teoriju prava 1:83–96
Kühn Z (2006) The authoritarian legal culture at work: the passivity of parties and the interpretational statements of supreme courts. Croatian Yearb Eur Law Policy 2(2):19–26
Kühn Z (2011) The judiciary in Central and Eastern Europe. Martinus Nijhoff Publishers, Leiden–Boston
Leisner W (1989) Urteilsverfassungsbeschwerde wegen Nichtvorlage bei Abweichung. Das Bundesverfassungsgericht als Garant der "Großen Senate" (Constitutional appeal due to non-submission in the case of departure from case law. Federal constitutional court as guarantor of grand panels). Neue Juristische Wochenschrift 42(39):2446–2450
Lovrek E, Musger G (2019) Vor §§ 502 ff ZPO (Remarks ahead para. 502 et seqq. of code of civil procedure). In: Fasching H, Konecny A (eds) Kommentar zu den Zivilprozessgesetzen, Bd. IV/1, 3rd edn. Manz, Wien
Lüke W (2011) Zivilprozessrecht (Civil procedure), 10th edn. C.H. Beck, München
Maleshin D (2007) The Russian style of civil procedure. Emory Int Law Rev 21:543–562
Mańko R (2007) Is the socialist legal tradition 'dead and buried'? The continuity of certain elements of socialist legal culture in Polish civil procedure. In: Wilhelmsson T, Paunio E, Pohjolainen A (eds) Private law and the many cultures of Europe. Private law in European context series, vol 10. Kluwer Law International, Alphen aan den Rijn, pp 83–103
Mańko R (2013) Survival of the socialist legal tradition? A Polish perspective. Comp Law Rev 4(2): 1–28. http://www.comparativelawreview.unipg.it/index.php/comparative/article/view/14/12
Möllers T (2019) Juristische Methodenlehre (Legal methodology), 2nd edn. C.H. Beck, München

Perić Ž (1898) Granice sudske vlasti (Boundaries of judiciary). Branič 5:37–45, 69–85, 143–155, 213–227, 285–296, 361–374, 445–451, 740–746, 798–808, 839–862, 902–923
Poznić B (2009) Komentar Zakona o parničnom postupku (Commentary on Code of Civil Procedure). Službeni glasnik, Beograd
Poznić B, Rakić-Vodinelić V (2015) Građansko procesno pravo (Civil procedure), 17th edn. Službeni glasnik, Beograd
Radovanov A (2003) Vanredni pravni lekovi u parničnom postupku (Extraordinary legal remedies in civil procedure). Bilten Vrhovnog suda Srbije 3:180–185
Rakić-Vodinelić V (2012) Pravosudno organizaciono pravo (Judiciary organisational law), 2nd edn. Službeni glasnik, Beograd
Rosenberg L, Schwab KH, Gottwald P (2010) Zivilprozessrecht (Civil procedure), 17th edn. C.H. Beck, München
Schreiber K (2017) Commentary on paragraph 138 GVG. In: Wieczorek B, Schütze R (eds) Zivilprozessordnung und Nebengesetze, vol 13/1, 4th edn. De Gruyter, Berlin
Srzentić N, Kalember V, Radaković R (1949) Zakon o uređenju narodnih sudova, sa komentarom (People's court organisation act, with commentary). Službeni list FNRJ, Beograd
Stanković G (1994) Načelna pravna shvatanja (General legal opinions). Zbornik radova Pravnog fakulteta u Nišu 34–35:5–14
Triva S, Belajec V, Dika M (1986) Građansko parnično procesno pravo (Civil procedure), 6th edn. Narodne novine, Zagreb
Uzelac A (2010) Survival of the third tradition? Supreme Court Law Rev 49:377–396
Uzelac A (2019) Jedinstvena primjena prava u hrvatskom parničnom postupku: tradicija i suvremenost (Uniform application of law in Croatian civil procedure: tradition and modernity). In: Barbić J (ed) Novine u parničnom procesnom pravu. Hrvatska akademija znanosti i umjetnosti, Zagreb, pp 111–168
Uzelac A, Galič A (2017) Changing faces of post-socialist supreme courts: Croatia and Slovenia compared. In: Van Rhee CH, Fu Y (eds) Supreme courts in transition in China and West. Adjudication at the service of public goals. Springer, Cham, pp 207–228
Vujičić B (2012) Ujednačavanje sudske prakse u građanskoj materiji – problemi i moguća rešenja (Harmonisation of the case law in civil law matters–problems and possible solutions). Bilten Vrhovnog kasacionog suda 3:263–274
Zobec J, Letnar Černič J (2015) The remains of the authoritarian mentality within the Slovene judiciary. In: Bobek M (ed) Central European judges under the European influence: the transformative power of the EU revisited. Hart Publishing, Oxford, pp 125–148
Zweigert K, Kötz H (1996) Einführung in die Rechtsvergleichung (Introduction to comparative law), 3rd edn. Mohr Siebeck, Tübingen
Zweigert K, Kötz H (1998) Introduction to comparative law, 3rd edn. Clarendon Press, Oxford

Requirements of the Istanbul Convention in Domestic Criminal Law and Court Practice

Slađana Jovanović and Nikola Vujičić

Contents

1 Introductory Review

The Republic of Serbia has been working, since 2002, when domestic violence was incriminated and when incrimination of rape was altered, on providing for a better protection of women against violence (especially domestic and sexual violence). In fact, until March 9, 2002, when the Law on Amendments and Supplements to the

S. Jovanović (✉)
University Union, Faculty of Law, Belgrade, Serbia
e-mail: sladjana.jovanovic@pravnifakultet.rs

N. Vujičić
Institute of Criminological and Sociological Research, Belgrade, Serbia
e-mail: nikola.vujicic@iksi.ac.rs

D. V. Popović et al. (eds.), *Balkan Yearbook of European and International Law 2021*, Balkan Yearbook of European and International Law 2021,
https://doi.org/10.1007/978-3-030-97431-2_10

Criminal Law of the Republic of Serbia came into force,[1] protection from domestic violence was through implementation of some other incrimination with elements of violence, which did not stress family relations, but in court practice such cases were (too) often treated as a "private/domestic" problem, a quarrel to be resolved within the family, and even as a legitimate way of disciplining family members by "the head" of the family. Until then, rape in marriage was not even incriminated, since the offense existed only if the person (of female gender) was raped by a man she was not married to.[2] Only after 2002, domestic violence begins to be viewed as a social problem, and more attention was also paid to other forms of gender-based violence. In 2005, a set of measures was introduced into the Family Law for protection against domestic violence[3] while the Constitution[4] in its Article 15 stipulates that the state guarantees the equality of men and women, and develops the policy of equal opportunities. However, it was soon observed that these normative mechanisms of protection faced resistance in implementation, either because of their own imperfection (for instance, with regard to interpretation of the term "family member" in the criminal-legal sphere, absence of a link between the two systems of protection, family-legal and criminal-legal), or because of the still present rigid, patriarchal attitudes of those enforcing the law (police, social services, legislature) and non-coordinated activities of services called for help[5] The situation in practice was changing slowly and with difficulties, therefore, signing and then ratification of the Convention on Prevention and Combating Violence against Women and Domestic Violence (from hereon: The Istanbul Convention) was received (especially by those dealing with protection of women's human rights) with a hope and conviction that the process of positive changes would accelerate, which would contribute to a better protection of women against violence. The Republic of Serbia signed the Istanbul Convention on April 4, 2012,[6] and ratified it on November 21, 2013,[7] while amendments to the Criminal Code (explained by the necessity of harmonization with the Convention) followed in 2016, when the Law on Amendments and Supplements to the Criminal Code[8] was adopted, more precisely, when the relevant provisions came into force—on June 1, 2017. How Serbian legislator responded to the requirements of the Istanbul Convention and what is the procedure in practice are issues which shall be discussed below.

---

[1] Official Gazette of the RS, No. 10/2002.

[2] On domestic violence in Serbia before its incrimination see: Lukić and Jovanović (2001) and Nikolić-Ristanović (2002).

[3] Official Gazette of the RS, No. 18/2005.

[4] Official Gazette of the RS, No. 98/2006.

[5] About problems in Serbian judicial practice after legislative changes see: Konstantinović-Vilić and Petrušić (2004); Konstantinović-Vilić and Petrušić (2007); Petrušić and Konstantinović-Vilić (2008); Jovanović (2010).

[6] Chart of signatures and ratifications of the Treaty 210.

[7] Official Gazette of the RS - International Treaties, No. 12/2013.

[8] Official Gazette of the RS, No. 94/2016.

2 New Forms of Violence

2.1 *Female Genital Mutilation*

Female genital mutilation is a new offense in the Criminal Code of the Republic of Serbia[9] (Article 121a of the CC), which is not justified by the needs of the practice in the Republic of Serbia because such practice, as a part of tradition and customs, has not been recorded within the national framework,[10] although because of the current migrant/refugee trends it could be justified. Anyway, this incrimination was entered into the Criminal Code, "because of the necessity for harmonization with the Istanbul Convention", as the Government of the Republic of Serbia states in its explanation of the Proposals for Amendments to the Criminal Code[11] However, the review of the requirements of the Istanbul Convention with regard to this incrimination and description of the offense in the Criminal Code raises the following question—why the Convention's requirements have not been met in full? The main form of the offense is stated more generally for offenses the Istanbul Convention states in its AArticle 38 (excising, infibulating or performing any other mutilation to the whole or any part of a woman's labia majora, labia minora, or clitoris): Whoever mutilates external parts of a female's genitals shall be punished with imprisonment of one to eight years (Article 121a, paragraph 1 of the CC), which corresponds to the severity of an exceptionally hard bodily injury from AArticle 121, paragraph 2 of the Criminal Code (as well as the punishment defined for that offense), and because of the generality certain authors raise the question of what would happen if the stated injuries are light, i.e., if the injuries are in the form of a piercing or a tattoo, which would, as injuring acts, question the ratio of this incrimination.[12] However, this issue should be put aside in order to follow definitions of the Istanbul Convention which point to harder injuries, which more often are done primarily within the framework of certain customary behaviors in African and Asian countries.[13]

Thus, the aforementioned could not be considered problematic, but what is stated in the paragraph 2 of the same AArticle is very problematic and deviates from the requirements of the Istanbul Convention. We could even say that it is very contradicted to it. An additional problem is non-harmonization with national criminal-legal solutions. In fact, paragraph 2 of Article 121a of the Criminal Code defines a lighter form of the crime: if there are some particularly extenuating

[9]Official Gazette of the RS, Nos. 85/05, 88/2005, 107/2005, 72/2009, 111/2009, 121/2012, 104/2013, 108/2014, 94/2016, 35/2019.

[10]We can read of sporadic cases in newspapers. Jealous husbands did such crimes, or pimps, in order to hold women under control, or to ensure special services to clients (Blic, 7. 10. 2016. Horrible cases in Serbia: jealous husbands performed female genital mutilations), STRAVIČNI SLUČAJEVI U SRBIJI Ljubomorni muževi sakatili polne organe žena (blic.rs).

[11]The Government of the Republic of Serbia (2016), p. 20.

[12]Miladinović-Stefanović (2017), p. 234; Ćorović (2018), p. 9.

[13]UNICEF (2021).

circumstances under which the act specified in paragraph 1 of this Article has been committed, the perpetrator shall be punished with imprisonment of three months to three years (instead of with imprisonment of one to eight years which is the punishment for the basic form of the criminal offense stipulated by paragraph 1). The Convention does not provide for such an offense at all, even forbids it, taking into consideration the provision of Article 42 which states that culture, custom, religion, tradition, or so-called "honor" shall not be regarded as justification for such acts. In fact, the assumption is that Serbian legislator had in mind exactly something of the stated, since this is a practice which is known in other cultures, and that because of the fear of the unknown, sensitiveness or caution, it envisages in advance situations in which it would be justified to privilege the perpetrator, i.e., to decide on a lighter punishment. If, though, the legislator had in mind genital mutilation for medical reasons, there was no need for this paragraph, since in that case illegality would certainly be excluded because of justified medical interventions. Such act of the legislator is completely unusual also because from 2009 to this day it is more and more repressive in amending the Criminal Code, and it is especially prone to introducing of new restrictions/bans concerning mitigation of punishments, in order to make the courts to make its penal policy stricter. As for the offense from paragraph 2 of Article 121a, Criminal Code offers the option to the court to consider the existence of especially extenuating circumstances, which it does not do for other offenses, because here we can recognize a silhouette of court mitigation of punishments which the legislator especially opposes with restrictions concerning mitigation of punishments. Even if provisions on mitigation of punishments from Article 57, paragraph 5 were applied ("If the lowest statutory penalty for the criminal offense is imprisonment of up to one year, the sentence may be reduced to three months") we would come to the sentence of imprisonment of 3 months, which is the minimum defined for the offense from paragraph 2, Article 121a, which additionally leads to the conclusion that paragraph 2 is unnecessary.

Although the Istanbul Convention stresses coercing of women to submit to acts of female genital mutilation, the legislator used a more neutral, broader term ("leading") for existence of a more serious form from paragraph 3. There is even no serious offense form if the victim is underage, although data confirm that genital mutilation is most often committed on underage girls. Indeed, with a comparable offense (gender neutral)—serious bodily injury (Article 121 of the CC), a serious form exists in case an underage person is on the side of a passive subject (paragraph 6), so courts would have to appreciate such circumstances absolutely as aggravating circumstances in making of decisions about the punishment (which is in accordance with the requirement of Article 46 of the Istanbul Convention, which pays attention to aggravating circumstances not characteristic for the offense).

A more serious form of the offense from paragraph 4 implies death of women who suffered genital mutilation, and the punishment for this is from 2 to 12 years, which corresponds to the punishment defined for a serious bodily injury qualified as death (Article 121, paragraph 3 of the CC), although a more serious punishment could have been expected, bearing in mind that, for example, if domestic violence results in death of a victim, the defined penalty is from 5 to 15 years, and if the victim is underage—at least ten years (stricter punishments were defined in the last amendments to the Criminal Code in 2019,[14] but obviously this incrimination has been forgotten).

In practice, up till today there have been no criminal charges for this crime since the beginning of implementation of this incrimination[15]

2.2 *Stalking*

Stalking is also a new criminal offense (Article 138a of the CC), in the group of criminal offenses against freedoms and rights of men and citizens, for the right incrimination was needed before too, judging by experiences of nongovernmental organizations dealing with protection of women from violence, because they faced specific cases which could not have been classified as others, because the essence of this offense is in repeating of activities which disturb and threaten other people, but do not individually (each of them) present a criminal offense[16] The Government of RS also in its explanation of the proposed changes states existence of serious criminal-political arguments which justify introducing of this incrimination.[17]

Description of the act contains insufficiently defined designations, which could lead to unequal implementation of the incrimination in practice, and thus legal insecurity. In fact, the main form of the offense is as follows: Whoever over a certain period of time persistently: (1) Follows another person without permission, or undertakes other activities with the aim of getting physically closer to such a person contrary to his/her will; (2) Contrary to the will of another person attempts to establish contact with him/her directly, through a third person, or through means of communication; (3) Abuses personal data of another person, or of a person close to him/her for goods or services; purpose of ordering; (4) Threatens to assault life, body, or freedom of another person, or a person close to him/her; (5) Undertakes other similar actions in the manner that may perceptibly jeopardize personal life of the person vis-à-vis whom such activities are undertaken, shall be punished with a fine or imprisonment of up to three years.

"A certain period" of time is surely an ambiguity concerning duration of the activity, i.e., repeating of the activity or activities in time (but what period of time is the question for which practice must provide the answer). "Other actions with the aim of getting physically closer to such a person contrary to his/her will" could also be disputable. Because of the observed problems at the very beginning, and concerning the description of the offense, this incrimination was supplemented in 2019 by entering of the term "persistently", to point to the subjective dimension

[14] Official Gazette of the RS, No. 35/2019.

[15] Statistical Office of the Republic of Serbia (2018, 2019, 2020a, 2021).

[16] Jovanović (2015), p. 209.

[17] Government of the Republic of Serbia (2016), p. 25.

existing on the side of the perpetrator which makes him dangerous and additionally confirms the necessity for duration and repeating of the activity/activities. That same year definition from paragraph 1, item 3 was altered: instead of the term "offering", now there is "ordering", because it is an open issue whether this implies delivering of advertisements to someone's postal or e-mail address (which are relatively easy to obtain today) and generally obtrusive and persistent advertising of goods and services which could disturb some people, but this, although it is not acceptable from the aspect of correct business dealings, is not rare in practice does not deserve to be a criminal offense.[18] It is disputable also if the consequence of this act is a "possibility of a significant threatening of private lives of people against whom activities are undertaken", more precisely, if all the stated activities and other similar ones must be such as to significantly threaten private lives of people against whom they are undertaken, or this is required only for "other similar activities" (from paragraph 5)[19] If, however we take into consideration Article 34 of the Istanbul Convention,[20] it is clear that activities must affect other people so that they fear for their safety, and activities stated in the Istanbul Convention are threatening and terrifying ones. It would be most correct to interpret the whole context, not only individual activities, separately from each other/s, but also in total, and as for the result absolutely from the aspect of the victim, of course not relying exclusively on the subjective feeling, which is not done in the case of a comparable criminal offense of threatening of safety from Article 138 of the CC in practice).

Defined punishment for the main form corresponds to the punishment defined for the (most comparable) offense—threatening of safety, for its serious form (Article 138, para 2 of CC). This offense has two more forms:[21] the first one implies a consequence in the form of a concrete threat for life, body or health of victims or their close people, while the second form defines lethal consequence for victims or their close people. Although stalking does not have to be linked with the context of a partner relationship and its end, research shows that the most dangerous stalkers are those from the category of rejected stalkers,[22] so there is space also for thinking about introducing of forms which would accentuate that especially,[23] and if not, this circumstance must be taken into account when deciding on the sentence.

---

[18] Stojanović (2017), p. 2.

[19] Stojanović (2017), pp. 5–6.

[20] Parties shall take necessary legislative or other measures to ensure that intentional conduct of repeatedly engaging in threatening conduct directed at another person, causing her/him to fear for her/his safety, is criminalized.

[21] (2) If a danger to life, health or body of the person vis-à-vis whom the act was committed, or a person close to him/her has been caused by an act specified in paragraph 1 of this Article, the perpetrator shall be punished with imprisonment of three months to five years. (3) If, due to an act specified in paragraph 1 of this Article, death of another person, or of a person close to him/her occurred, the perpetrator shall be punished with imprisonment of one to ten years.

[22] Mullen et al. (1999), pp. 1246–1247.

[23] Criminal Law of Croatia in its Article 140, paragraph 2, stipulates that a serious form is when the victim was a close person, a person who was in intimate relationship with the perpetrator, or his

In spite of ambiguities and criticism of this incrimination, its introduction is still a step forward, bearing in mind the already mentioned needs of the practice. Difficulties concerning precise and comprehensive description of this offense exist also in the comparative law (of which witnesses the study of the European Commission from 2010), but this incrimination is still greeted as a better respond to this specific form of violence against women than is the case with implementation of other more general incriminations.[24] Results of the research on femicide in our court practice indicate that stalking was not assessed as an aggravating circumstance when deciding on the punishment, which indicates insufficient recognition of such behavior, i.e., its danger, so the new incrimination is surely welcome in this sense as well[25]

Statistical data also indicate that it is applied, but research is needed to point to its good and bad sides, and to bring about possible promotion of the description of the offense.

According to the data of the Statistical Office of the Republic of Serbia, there is a noticeable increase in the number of reports for the criminal offense of stalking, with relative uniformity in 2019 and 2020. However, it should be borne in mind that in the observed period, each year, on average, 53% of criminal charges were dismissed (in 2018, as many as 61.3%). Of the total number of dismissed criminal charges, one quarter is due to the delay in criminal prosecution. If we look at crime rates, the average rate in the number of convictions is 1, with a maximum of 1.6 in 2020 (*see Fig. 1 for details*).

When it comes to the imposed criminal sanctions (Fig. 2), the courts most often imposed a suspended sentence (68.4%). Imprisonment, as the most severe criminal sanction, was applied in 11.3% of cases, and it should be borne in mind that the courts did not impose a prison sentence of more than 12 months (most often the sentences range from 3 to 6 months). Women appear as perpetrators of this crime in 7.5% of cases.

Data on the victim of the crime were available for 157 persons and they show that in 88% of the cases the victims were women. Among the victims, only 6 people were aged 14 to 18.

As the criminal offense of endagerement of safety (Article 138 of the CC) is most similar to stalking, we took a glance at official data regarding penal policy for it. In the last observed year (2020) more prison sentences were imposed for Endagerement of safety than for stalking (18.3%; 14.5%); fines were less frequent: 11.1% : 15.4%), as well as rate suspended sentence (60.4: 62%) and same was the percentage of home custody: 8.2%[26] Adding the data about higher percentage of rejected charges due to delay in criminal prosecution in cases of stalking (22%:16%),[27] it could be

child (Criminal Law of the Republic of Croatia, Official Gazette no. 125/11, 144/12, 56/15, 61/15, 101/17, 118/18, 126/19, 84/21.

[24] European Commission (2010), p. 68.

[25] Simeunović-Patić and Jovanović (2013), p. 164.

[26] Statistical Office of the Republic of Serbia (2021), p. 8.

[27] Statistical Office of the Republic of Serbia (2019), p. 14.

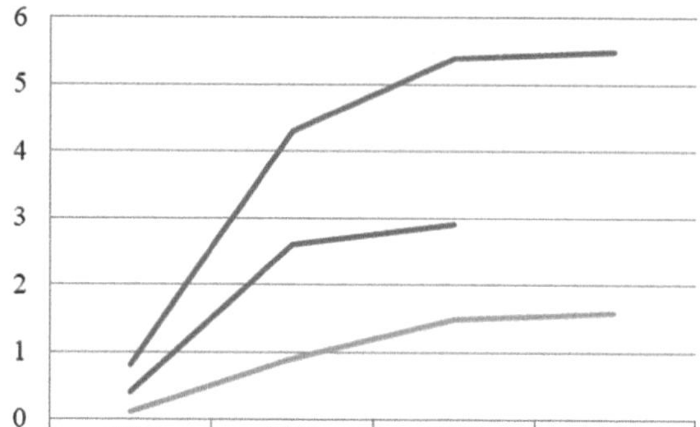

	2017	2018	2019	2020
Criminal Charges	0.8	4.3	5.4	5.5
Dismissed CC	0.4	2.6	2.9	
Conviction	0.1	0.9	1.5	1.6

Fig. 1 The crime rate of the reported criminal offenses, dismissed criminal charges and convictions for the criminal offense of stalking, in the period from 2017 to 2020 (Complete data for 2020 have not been published yet, so data on dismissed criminal charges are not available for that year.). **Source:** Made by the authors, based on data from the Statistical Office of the Republic of Serbia

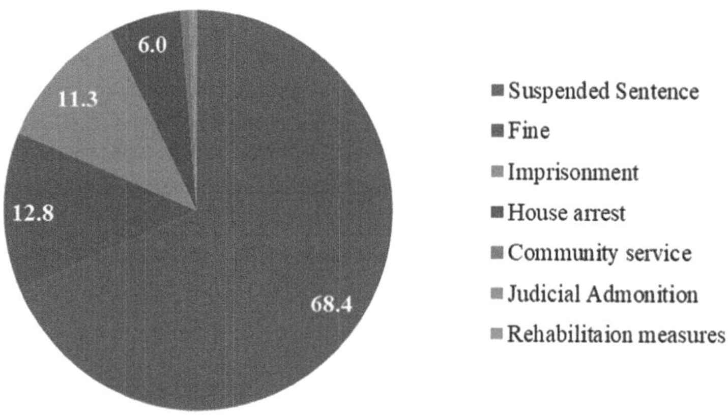

Fig. 2 The structure of the imposed criminal sanctions for the crime of stalking, in the period from 2017 to 2020. **Source:** Made by the authors, based on data from the Statistical Office of the Republic of Serbia

concluded that penal policy for stalking is more lenient than in cases of endagerement of safety.

2.3 Sexual Harassment

In defining of the offense of sexual harassment (Article 182a of the CC) an unusual nomotechnical approach was used. The offense was defined very generally: (1) Whoever sexually harasses another person shall be punished with a fine or imprisonment of up to six months, while paragraph 3 offers authentic interpretation of the legislator, i.e., the definition of sexual harassment from Article 40 of the Istanbul Convention has been taken over almost word-for-word. Thus, this crime is defined as "each instance of verbal, non-verbal or physical behavior aimed at, or that is a violation of dignity of a person in the domain of his/her sexual life, which causes fear or creates a hostile, degrading or offensive environment". Article 112 of the Criminal Code contains interpretations of certain expressions, characteristics of the criminal offense, therefore such procedure deviates from previous legal-technical proceedings. This is also indicated by the almost word-to-word translation of Article 40 of the Istanbul Convention, which does not match Serbian criminal-legal terminology (and is also not in the compatible with Serbian language). None of the criminal acts contain the activity physical behavior (what would be psychological behavior?), nor verbal and non-verbal behavior. Such definition is considered logically senseless and also senseless with regard to the language.[28]

What is the difference between non-verbal and physical behavior? The answer could be found in the Explanatory Report to the Istanbul Convention which defines non-verbal acts of sexual harassment as any expressions or communication on the part of the perpetrator that do not involve words or sounds, for example facial expressions, hand movements or symbols. Physical conduct refers to any sexual behaviour of the perpetrator and may include situations involving contact with the body of the victim.[29] Definition of sexual harassment behavior matches known forms of the criminal offense of insult (Article 170 of the CC) in practice: verbal, symbolic and real (insult)[30] However, in sexual harassment cases offensive behaviour has to violate dignity of a person in the domain of his/her sexual life, which causes fear or creates a hostile, degrading or offensive environment. As for problematic descriptions of committing of activities (in paragraph 3, Article 182a of the CC) it is not stipulated they must be activities of sexual nature, unwanted by the victim, but this has been partially compensated by the description of the consequence, which is violation of dignity of people in the sphere of sexual life, where the intention to realize that consequence is sufficient.

Prosecution for this act is undertaken upon proposal of the victim, while in implementation of the incrimination in practice a question could be raised of distinctiveness with relation to the criminal offense of prohibited sexual acts (Article 182 of the CC), but taking into consideration the nature of this act, which in essence

[28] Đorđević (2018), p. 115.

[29] CETS 210 - Explanatory Report to the Council of Europe Convention on preventing and combating violence against women and domestic violence (coe.int), p. 35.

[30] Đorđević (2017), p. 135; Đokić (2017), p. 552.

should mean affecting the body of another person (touching, kissing, hugging, etc.), in cases of sexual harassment offenses should be of another nature, with no contact with the body of another person. However, there is a problem with acts of physical behavior, so the delimitation should be primarily searched in the quality, seriousness of actions taken. Thus, more serious actions, close to the restrictively understood terms of an act equated with sexual intercours, would be considered prohibited sexual acts, and e.g. less intense touches—as sexual harassment[31] Prohibited sexual acts are done in the context of rape or other incriminated forms of sexual intercourse which is important for the distinction. It means that a perpetrator must not use coercion, helplessness of the victim or abuse the position.

The offense gets a more serious form if it is done against a juvenile (perpetrator shall be punished with imprisonment of three months to three years). In case of a more serious form of this offense the procedure is different from other incriminations from the same group of criminal offenses (against sexual freedom). In fact, in other criminal offenses there is a difference between minors (persons of 14 years of age and older) and children (under 14).[32] If the act is committed against a child, it would be justified to apply the incrimination of the Prohibited sexual acts (Article 182, paragraph 2) as more serious offense.[33]

Indeed, since Istanbul Convention does not stipulate the obligation of incriminating of this behavior, but it is possible to respond to it with other legal means, Serbia could boast with other approaches to this problem—prohibition of sexual harassment is regulated in the sphere of anti-discriminatory and labor laws.[34] We should also mention that sexual harassment was at the time stipulated as an offense (in 2003), but decriminalization[35] was soon made because this was not implemented in practice, which was linked with insufficient distinction regarding the criminal offense of an illegal sexual act. Indeed, latest research of this topic shows that sexual harassment is the most frequent form of violence against women in non-partner relationships in Serbia, but also that there is a lower rate charges in comparison to the EU, because this phenomenon is still a taboo topic within national framework.[36] Still, data of the Statistical Office of the Republic of Serbia show that the new incrimination is implemented in practice, but research of the legislative practice should determine the details concerning its implementation (especially concerning

[31] Đokić (2017), p. 553.

[32] In accordance with Article 112, para. 8–10 of the CC: a child is a person under fourteen years of age; a minor is a person of fourteen years of age or older who is not yet eighteen; a juvenile is a person who is not eighteen.

[33] Đokić (2017), p. 553.

[34] Labor Law, Official Gazette of the RS, Nos. 24/2005, 61/2005, 54/2009 (Article 21); Law on Prevention of Mobbing at Work, Official Gazette of the RS, No. 36/2010 (Article 3); Law on Banning of Discrimination, Official Gazette of the RS, No. 22/2009 (Article 12).

[35] The Law on Amendments and Supplements to the Criminal Law (Official Gazette of the RS, No 39/2003) incriminates sexual harassment, while Criminal Code from 2005 (Official Gazette of the RS, No. 85/2005) did not incriminate it.

[36] Babović and Reljanović (2020), p. 12.

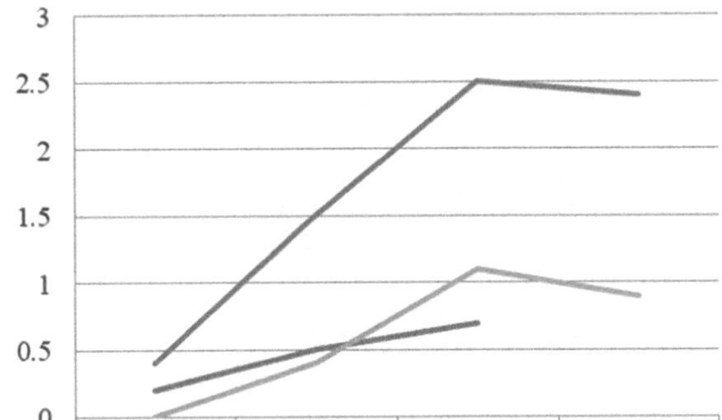

	2017	2018	2019	2020
Criminal Charges	0.4	1.5	2.5	2.4
Dismissed CC	0.2	0.5	0.7	
Conviction	0	0.4	1.1	0.9

Fig. 3 The crime rate of the reported criminal offenses, dismissed criminal charges and convictions for the criminal offense of sexual harassment, in the period from 2017 to 2020. **Source:** Made by the authors, based on data from the Statistical Office of the Republic of Serbia

uncertainity and width of the incrimination itself that may result in unnecessary overload of the criminal justice system[37]).

According to the data of the Statistical Office of the Republic of Serbia, until 2019, there was a noticeable increase in the number of reports for the crime of sexual harassment, and in that year, the maximum number was recorded (174). In 2020, there is a slight decline. On average, about 32% of criminal charges are dismissed each year. Of the total number of rejected criminal charges, 28% is due to the delay in criminal prosecution.[38] If we look at crime rates, the average rate in the number of convictions is 0.6, with a maximum of 1.1 in 2019 (*see Fig. 3 for details*).

When it comes to the imposed criminal sanctions (Fig. 4), the courts most often imposed a suspended sentence (50.9%). Imprisonment was applied in 22.7% of cases (most often the sentences are in the range of 3 to 6 months, and there is one person who was sentenced to imprisonment in the range of 3 to 5 years). In only one case, the perpetrator was a woman.

[37] Đorđević (2017), p. 136.

[38] Since the beginning of implementation of the incrimination, there has been an increase of charges: in 2017 there were 2 charges (and 2 convictions—suspended sentence); in 2018: 105 charges and 26 convictions (16 suspended sentence; 1 imprisonment, and 4 home imprisonment); in 2019: 174 charges and 75 convictions (22 imprisonments and 34 suspended sentence); in 2020: 166 charges, 60 convictions (31 suspended sentences, 14 imprisonments, 12 home imprisonments, 3 fines). From the available data for 2018 and 2019 we see that the share of unknown perpetrators in 2018 was 14%, in 2019—19%, and can contribute to the thesis (regarding the general registered number of charges) that citizens are better informed on this offense and have more courage to report it.

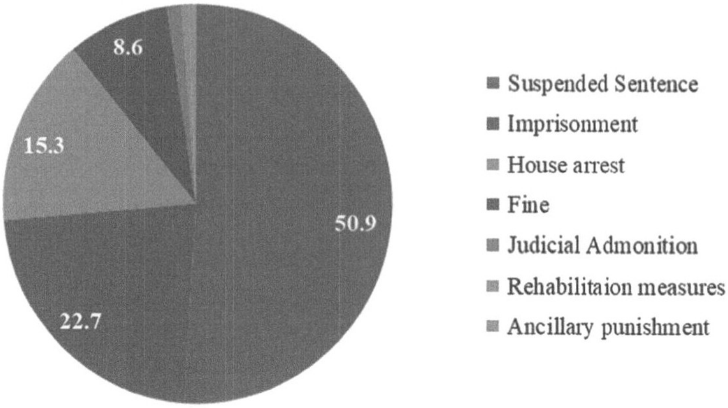

Fig. 4 The structure of the imposed criminal sanctions for the crime of sexual harassment, in the period from 2017 to 2020. **Source:** Made by the authors, based on data from the Statistical Office of the Republic of Serbia

Data on the victim of the crime were available for 104 persons and they show that in 95% of the cases the victims were women. Among the victims in 15.4% of cases were persons under 14 years of age, and in 23.1% of cases persons aged 14 to 18 years.

In the end, since we have already discussed the offense from the group of criminal offenses against sexual freedoms, we should welcome erasing of Article 186 of the Criminal Code which stipulated prosecution upon proposals of victims for offenses from Article 178 of the Criminal Code (rape) and Article 179 of the Criminal Code (sexual interscourse with a helpless person) when they were committed against spouses, as well as for the offense from Article 182, paragraph 1 of the Criminal Code (principal form of the offense of prohibited sexual acts), which is also in accordance with the requirements of the Istanbul Convention for better protection of victims of sexual violence. In accordance with that are more severe punishments for rape and other punishable rapes. Latest changes have brought about the punishment of life imprisonment for most severe forms of this act (whose consequence is death of the passive subject, or the offense was committed against a child).

2.4 *Forced Marriage*

Forced marriage (Article 187a of the CC) is regulated according to requirements of Article 37 of the Istanbul Convention. The main form of the offense is as follows: (1) Whoever uses force or threatens to coerce another person into marriage shall be punished with imprisonment of three months to three years. The second paragraph criminalizes taking people, or leading people to go abroad to get married: (2) Whoever, for the purpose of committing the offense specified in paragraph 1 of this

Article, takes a person abroad or leads him/her to go abroad for the same purpose, shall be punished with imprisonment of up to two years. However, although the Convention requires increased protection of juveniles in both cases, this is not stipulated, despite the warning data that in Serbia there is a problem of forced marriages of juveniles, usually girls, most often from the Roma community[39] (For this offense we should take into consideration that (also in the said UNICEF report) the term juvenile or child marriage often implies a relationship of two juveniles who otherwise cannot get married, or juveniles who cannot get married, because of their age, to adults. Such relationships to which children, i.e., juveniles, are forced are surely illegal, where responsibility of parents or foster parents is undoubtful, but such situations could not be classified as this offense. In such cases parents or adults in such relationships (similar to marriage) with a juvenile (under 16) would be responsible for another offense—sexual intercourse with a child, cohabiting with a minor or human trafficking. In fact, Family Law[40] (Article 23, paragraph 2) stipulates that the court may, for justified reasons, permit a minor who is sixteen, and who is physically and mentally mature to perform the rights and duties of marriage, to conclude a marriage. Thus, a serious form of the offense should be defined in accordance with that, if the incrimination title states marriage. Another option would be to enter into the description of offense a definition linked with a relationship similar to marriage, since the term marriage should not, or must not be interpreted broader, out of the framework of the norms regulated by the Family Law. However, what should be done is erasing of the provision of Article 190, paragraph 4 of CC (criminal offense of cohabiting with a minor) which abolishes perpetrators (adults in a common-law relationship with minors, i.e., parents, adopters, foster parents, who induced minors to live in a common-law relationship) in case a marriage is concluded. Existing regulations allow for making of relationships similar to marriage, before preconditions for juveniles to get married are satisfied.

Although the problem of juvenile marriages is considered a social problem with coercement in its background, even human trafficking, there have been no charges for this criminal offense up till today.

[39] UNICEF (2017) points out that in Serbia, child marriage is rare within the general population, but is very common in Roma settlement-segregated communities predominantly or exclusively occupied by ethnic Roma and commonly characterized by high levels of poverty and social exclusion—where more than half of girls (57%) are married before the age of 18 and almost one-fifth (18%) are married before the age of 15.

[40] Official Gazette, Nos. 18/2005, 72/2011, 6/2015.

3 Review of the Criminal Offense of Domestic Violence

3.1 Who Is a Family Member?

As previously said, domestic violence exists in Serbian criminal law since 2002, but the incrimination itself changed in time with regard to description of the offense and its forms, as well as concerning the stipulated punishments, which increased in severity for certain forms of the offense. Although it is not new, this offense deserves attention concerning its harmonization with the Istanbul Convention and its implementation in court practice. In fact, from the very beginning of the incrimination there has been a problem with interpretation of the constitutive designation "family member". In practice, this term is interpreted narrowly, so the legislator reacted by offering his (broader) interpretation, which today reads as follows: a family member shall also mean spouses, their children, spouses' ancestors of genuine bloodline, next of kin, cohabitating partners and their children, adopters and adoptees and foster family. A family member shall also mean brothers and sisters and their spouses, former spouses and their children and parents of former spouses if they live in same household, as well as persons who have a child together are going to have a child, although they have never lived in the same household (Article 112, paragraph 28 CC). This circle of people is different from those who would enjoy protection from domestic violence according to Article 3b of the Istanbul Convention.[41] Thus, former common-law partners are not family members even if they live in the same household (if they do not have a child together), nor their parents are (even if they are currently in a relationship). Such a solution points to the conclusion that better protection is provided for traditional marriages. Also, former spouses shall not enjoy protection, according to Article 194, if they do not live in the same household. The legislator neglects the reality, which is that the very end of a relationship (which does not have to imply the same household) brings about a large risk for women from victimization through violence, even homicide victimization, i.e., femicide[42] Results of the research done in Serbia also show that the greatest risk from victimization through murder are women who left their (most often violent) partners[43] which contributes to the thesis that women need better protection from violent partners especially after ending of a partner relationship (marriage, common-law relationship, even that which is none of them). Explanatory Report to the Istanbul Convention also points to this conclusion, in the part relating to the definition of

[41]"Domestic violence" shall mean all acts of physical, sexual, psychological or economic violence that occur within the family or domestic unit, or between former or current spouses or partners, whether or not the perpetrator shares, or has shared the same residence with the victim.

[42]Campbell (1992) and Simeunović-Patić and Jovanović (2013).

[43]Simeunović-Patić and Jovanović (2013), p. 146.

domestic violence, which stresses that "a joint residence of the victim and perpetrator is not required".[44]

The problem is also interpretation of a special form of domestic violence[45] in connection with violation of measures for protection from domestic violence set forth according to the Family Law[46] which has a broader interpretation of family members.[47] Because of disharmony in interpretation of family members in the two legal texts, the person who is not considered a family member according to criminal-legal provisions is deprived of protection according to Article 194, paragraph 5 of CC. It is possible that at the time of passing of the measure according to the rule of the Family Law persons were considered family members also according to criminal-legal provisions, but that in the meantime they ceased to be so (e.g., divorce with no child together, or former spouses do not live in the same household).

Until the said disparities are removed it would be important to point to those who apply the norms to pay attention to the cases of partner violence classified as other incriminations (with elements of violence), because in this case these are not family members in the sense of Article 112, paragraph 28 of CC in the same way they are, or should be, in cases of domestic violence, since mechanisms of power and control (over a partner) are present in both cases, risks (from victimization through serious forms of violence, even murder) are the same, and the need for a better protection of the victim (and also from secondary victimization) is the same.

3.2 *Sanctioning of Perpetrators*

According to the data of the Statistical Office of the Republic of Serbia, until 2018, there was a noticeable increase in the number of reports for the crime of domestic

---

[44]CETS 210 - Explanatory Report to the Council of Europe Convention on preventing and combating violence against women and domestic violence (coe.int), p. 8.

[45]1. spouses or former spouses; 2. children, parents and other blood relatives, and persons in in-law or adoptive relations; 3. common-law partners or former common-law partners; 4. persons who have had sexual relations during 2 years immediately preceding submission of the motion for passing of a protective measure against domestic violence (Article 200, paragraph 3 of the Family Law).

[46]Protective measures against domestic violence are: 1. issuing of a warrant for eviction from family apartment or house, regardless of the right on property or lease of an immovable; 2. issuing of a warrant for moving in the family apartment or house, regardless of the right on property or lease of an immovable; 3. restraining order; 4. banning access in the vicinity of the place of residence or work of a family member; 5. ban on further harassment of a family member; 6. mandatory treatment from alcoholism or other substance abuse; 7. mandatory psychiatric counselling or treatment; 8. other measures that may prevent commencement or continuation of domestic violence (Article 201, paragraph 2 of the Family Law).

[47]Whoever violates a measure against domestic violence imposed on them by the court in accordance with the law regulating family relations shall be punished with imprisonment of three months to three years and a fine.

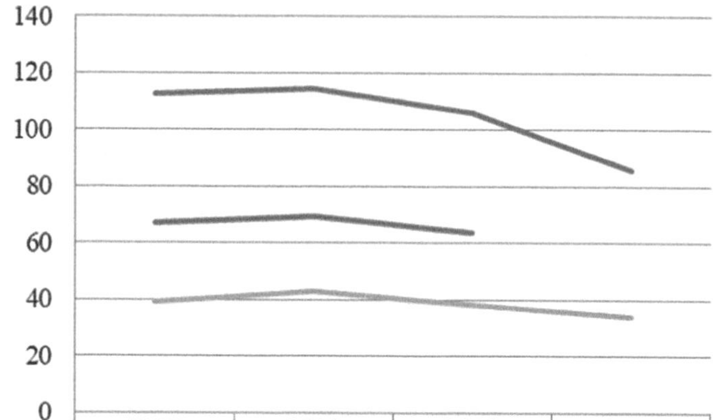

	2017	2018	2019	2020
Criminal Charges	112.8	114.6	105.8	85.9
Dismissed CC	67	69.4	63.5	
Conviction	39.3	43.1	38	33.8

Fig. 5 The crime rate of the reported criminal offenses, dismissed criminal charges and convictions for the criminal offense of domestic violence, in the period from 2017 to 2020. **Source:** Made by the authors, based on data from the Statistical Office of the Republic of Serbia

violence, and in that year, the maximum number was recorded. In the last two observed years, there has been a noticeable decline in the number of reported crimes (if we look at the first and last year, there is a decline of 23.9%). Of the total number of rejected criminal charges, 4.5% is due to the delay in criminal prosecution, which is a significantly smaller share in relation to the previously considered criminal offenses. If we look at crime rates, the average rate in the number of convictions is 38.6, with a maximum of 39.3 in 2017 (*see Fig. 5 for details*).

The next important issue are sanctions for domestic violence.[48] In Serbia suspended sentence is still the dominant sanction for domestic violence. In truth, it dominates in the structure of criminal sanctions in general, but this sentence is even more passed for domestic violence. For instance, in 2020 suspended sentence was passed for domestic violence in 64.5% cases, while in the structure of general criminal sanctions the percentage was 55.6% (Statistical Office of the Republic of Serbia, 2021: 8 and 9). Imprisonment was applied in 27% of cases (most often the sentences are up to two years and there are persons sentenced to imprisonment ranging from 10 to 15 year). See more details on Fig. 6. Women appear as perpetrators of this crime in 6.1% of cases.

[48] Istnabul Convention insists on adequate sanctions, appropriate for the severity of the act, which would defer the perpetrator from repeating of the act. The state should stipulate other measures which would ensure safety of victims, which mean supervision over perpetrators (Article 45 of the Convention).

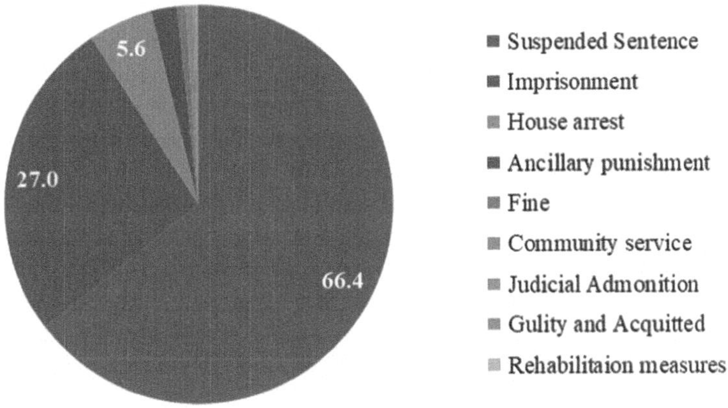

Fig. 6 The structure of the imposed criminal sanctions for the crime of domestic violence, in the period from 2017 to 2020. **Source:** Made by the authors, based on data from the Statistical Office of the Republic of Serbia

Data on the victim of the crime were available for 104 persons and they show that in 78.6% of the cases the victims were women. In contrast to the previously analyzed criminal offenses, where the participation of male persons in the total structure of victims is insignificant, in the criminal offense of domestic violence it amounts to 21.4%. Among the victims in 2.7% of cases were persons under 14 years of age, and in same percentage of cases persons aged 14 to 18 years.

However, taking into consideration the jeopardy of these acts, the risk from their repeating, intensifying, and the risk from victimization through murder, as well as provisions of the Convention which regulate supervision over perpetrators (even after they are convicted), Suspended sentence with supervision seems like a much better choice. However, there are no data on the frequency of this sentence, and knowing the limitations of capacities of parole officers, we could with certainty conclude that this number is not significant.

Of importance for sanctioning of perpetrators and special preventive effects of the main sanction is also the security measure from Article 89a (ban on approaching and communicating with the victim)[49] which was entered in the Criminal Code in 2009, but is still facing objections today. The legislator did not provide for the possibility of revoking of the Suspended sentence in case the measure is violated (which he did for other similar measures), even though Suspended sentence is the most frequent sentence. The manner of execution of the measure is also not clearly defined, nor the procedure on its voiding before expiry, if Article 89a provides for this option (while procedure is provided for other measures). Thus, the measure is not quite well

[49] The court may forbid the offender to approach the victim, forbid access to the area near where the victim lives and forbid further harassment, or further communication with the victim, if it should be reasonably believed that further exercise of such offender's actions is dangerous for the victim (Article 89a, paragraph 1).

regulated from the start, which must reflect on its implementation in practice. Its minimum duration was regulated three years later (2012), and in 2016 a separate criminal act was regulated, and thus the sanction for perpetrators who violate the measure (Violation of a Ban Laid Down in a Security Measure, 340a).[50]

As for sanctions, their choice and deciding on the punishment, the Istanbul Convention in Article 46 stressed the significance of certain circumstances which, if they are not elements of the offense, must be considered aggravating: (a) the offense was committed against a former or current spouse or partner as recognized by domestic law, by a family member, a person cohabiting with the victim or a person who abused her or his authority; (b) the offense, or related offenses, were committed repeatedly; (c) the offense was committed against a person made vulnerable by particular circumstances; (d) the offense was committed against or in the presence of a child, etc.

The latest results of research of legislative practice in the field of domestic violence and partner violence show that courts still find extenuating circumstances more (defendant's personal circumstances, youth, behavior after committing an offense, admission and repentance, the injured party did not claim indemnification and stated that this incident was "one and only", absence of earlier convictions, an "advanced age", defendant is the father of a minor child, intoxication by alcohol at the time of perpetration, factual situation related to the offense, poor financial situation).[51] Unlike extenuating circumstances, specified in a large number of explanations of judgments, aggravating circumstances are mentioned much less frequently. In a relatively large number of cases the court did not specify aggravating circumstances at all. In cases where the court established aggravating circumstances, the most common ones were: previous conviction for other criminal offenses; previous conviction for the same offense of domestic violence; conviction for violent criminal offenses; the fact that the previously imposed sentences did not correct the defendant's behavior; previous misdemeanor punishment; enhanced degree of guilt; severity of risk or damage to protected goods; defendant was intoxicated by alcohol, although he knew that alcohol made him aggressive; offense was committed against an elderly person; persistence in perpetration of the offense; violation of the restraining order; violation of suspended sentence. Interestingly, intoxication by alcohol is considered both as an extenuating and aggravating circumstance. Defendants' earlier convictions were judged differently by courts. In one case, first-instance court did not take the defendant's previous conviction as an aggravating circumstance because a lot of time had passed since the conviction, while the second-instance court, deciding on the appeal, took the defendant's previous conviction as an aggravating circumstance[52] So, the old practice of stating extenuating

---

[50] Whoever violates a ban laid down in a passed safety measure shall be fined or punished with imprisonment of up to six months.

[51] Petrušić et al. (2018), p. 136.

[52] Petrušić et al. (2018), pp. 136–137.

and aggravating circumstances by automatism[53] has continued, as well as stating more extenuating than aggravating circumstances.

Such manner of determining sentences is not characteristic solely for domestic violence, but is a universal feature of the court penal policy in Serbia. Punishments are mostly determined in the lower third of the prescribed range, close to minimum; the punishment is very often mitigated, sentencing above half of the range is rare, and the upper third of the prescribed range of the punishment is not used.[54] The results of the research of court penal policy from 2006 show the dominance of mitigating circumstances, as well as the domination of those of a personal nature—personal and family circumstances of the perpetrator, previous life of the perpetrator and posture[55] which emphasize automaticity in stating the circumstances that determine the type and measure of sanctions. Many ammendments to the Criminal Code (from 2009 onwards) are meant to compel courts to respond more sharply in determination of sanctions (at least for some acts or in relation to certain categories of perpetrators).[56]

(Any) offense committed against a child is a qualified form of offense (which is the case with domestic violence, Article 194, paragraph 3 of the CC) for which imprisonment is defined of two to ten years (which means that perpetrator cannot be sanctioned with a Suspended sentence, because of the existence of the limitation from Article 66, paragraph 2 CC concerning the duration of the stipulated punishment). However, in practice, in cases of lighter forms of violence (especially if the victim and another parent ask the public prosecutor to drop the case, ask for the perpetrator to be released from custody, etc.), this qualification appears as a problem when deciding on the punishment, so the legislature manages by changing qualifications in given cases, in order to avoid the sentence of imprisonment. The circumstance that the act was performed in the presence of a child is in our court practice most frequently (even today) not considered as aggravating (or at least in samples on which the said research was made there were no such examples, although it was determined that a child witnessed the violence[57]), while “parenthood” still appears as an extenuating circumstance (unacceptable; without determining the quality of the parenthood, which is questionable, taking into consideration the offense the perpetrator is charged for).[58] Slovenian legislature may be used as a role model, according to which a child who witnessed violence, i.e., lives in a family environment

[53] Lukić and Jovanović (2001), pp. 64–69; Konstantinović-Vilić and Petrušić (2007), pp. 85–91; Jovanović (2010), pp. 201–205; Simeunović-Patić and Jovanović (2013), pp. 112–133.

[54] Stojanović (2012), pp. 3–4.

[55] Ćirić et al. (2006), pp. 89–97.

[56] About conflict between legislator and judicial practice as well as about enhanicing repressiveness of the legislator see: Stojanović (2012, 2013).

[57] Lukić and Jovanović (2001), p. 65; Konstantinović-Vilić and Petrušić (2007), pp. 88–89; Jovanović (2010), p. 202.

[58] Simeunović-Patić and Jovanović (2013), p. 165.

characterized by violence, must be considered a victim.[59] Taking all this into consideration, it seems it is high time for courts to stop treating parenthood as an extenuating circumstance in these (and other cases, too) without previous check-up of the "quality" of parenthood. Instead of parenthood, an extenuating circumstance could (possibly) be considered existence of the obligation to support children which in one case (murder of the wife with whom the perpetrator had four juvenile children) was stressed by the Supreme Court of Serbia. In fact, the court stated that "the fact that defendant is the father of four underage children cannot present an extenuating circumstance which would be a reason for mitigation of the punishment, although the obligation for supporting of four underage children is an extenuating circumstance".[60] It could even be concluded that parenthood deserves more the treatment of an aggravating circumstance, taking into consideration the jeopardy from generational transmission of violent behaviour in family.

The latest changes in criminal legislature from 2019 touched the obviously problematic issue of recidivism, so now there are rules which order courts to mandatorily consider recidivism as an aggravating circumstance if five years have not passed from the previous conviction or served sentence, with a ban on the so-called court mitigation of the punishment (Article 55 of the CC),[61] while provisions on multiple recidivism stipulate for courts to decide on punishments even above the half of the span of stipulated punishments (Article 56).[62] Of importance for penalties for the offense of domestic violence is also provision of Article 57, paragraph 3, i.e., ban on passing a mitigated penalty to person who was previously convicted for the same, or offense of the same type (unless the court has powers of remittance from punishment, when it may reduce the penalty without limitations stipulated), as well as provision of Article 46, paragraph 2 of the CC on release on parole as an option, not a right, for those convicted for aggravated offenses of domestic violence (Article 194, para. 2–4 of the CC).

Istanbul Convention also requires assessment of the risk from lethal and repeated violence by competent bodies, within the framework of a coordinated inter-sectoral

[59] Zakon o preprečevanju nasilja v družini, "Uradni list RS", br. 16/2008.

[60] Sentence of the Supreme Court of Serbia, Kž. 744/05, fm June 30, 2005, and sentence of the District Court in Smederevo, K. 79/04, fm December 30, 2004.

[61] (1) In case the perpetrator of a criminal offense committed with premeditation was earlier convicted for a premeditated criminal offense, the court shall consider such circumstance as aggravating, unless five years have passed from the previous conviction or served sentence. (2) In case specified in paragraph 1 of this Article, the court may pronounce a punishment below the limit stipulated by the Law, or a lighter type of punishment, except when the Law states that punishment can be mitigated, or when the Law sets forth that the perpetrator may be remitted from punishment, and the court fails to do so.

[62] For a criminal offense committed with premeditation, and for which imprisonment has been defined, the court shall pronounce a punishment above the half of the range of the stipulated punishment, under the following conditions: (1) in case the perpetrator was twice convicted for criminal offenses committed with premeditation, to imprisonment of at least one year; (2) if, from the date of release of the perpetrator from serving the punishment, until committing of a new criminal offenses five years have not passed.

approach to the problem, which is also one of the Convention's requirements (Article 7 and 51). With regard to this it is important to mention the Law on Prevention of Domestic Violence which came into force on June 1, 2017, which was designed according to the so-called "Austrian model"[63] which stipulates urgent measures determined by the police after assessment of the situation and risks, while the public prosecutor may require prolongation of them, and then decide on initiating of criminal proceedings. This law does not only relate to domestic violence as a criminal offense (as defined in Article 194 of the CC), but also relates to numerous other offenses (primarily from the group of offenses against marriage and family, against sexual freedoms, and other offenses if they are a consequence of domestic violence defined by this law in Article 3, paragraph 3).[64] The circle of persons to be protected is also defined differently, broader in comparison to the criminal-legal solution, which may present a problem in subsequent proceedings with regard to implementation of the qualification of the criminal offense of domestic violence, but even if another incrimination would be applied we should expect professionals to act cautiously, to ensure effective protection of the victim before, during, and even after the trial, taking into consideration the jeopardy from domestic and partner's violence. However, implementation of this law also faces criticism relating to insufficiently coordinated cooperation of relevant actors (members of coordination groups) and insufficient inclusion of victims in the process of making of individual protection plans (Ombudsman, 2020).

What is worrying and requires research and deeper analysis is increase in the number of rejected criminal charges for domestic violence. According to data of the Statistical Office for the period from the beginning of implementation until 2019, we can see a trend of increase in the number of rejected charges. Until 2009 the share of rejected charges was below 30%, and then it began to increase, and since 2014 it has moved around 60% (in 2016 the share was the largest—64.4%, while in the last observed year it was 60%).[65] It would be necessary also to examine the practice of implementation of the institute of delaying of criminal prosecution, whose implementation experiences rejection of criminal charges if the defendant fulfills a certain obligation[66] within the defined deadline (Article 283 of the Criminal Procedure

[63] Logar (2007).

[64] Domestic violence, in the sense of this law, is an act of physical, sexual, psychological and economic violence of a perpetrator against a person with whom the perpetrator is in current or previous marriage, or common-law or partner relationship, or against a person with whom he is a first-degree blood relative, and a second-degree blood relative, or with whom he is a relative through in-laws up to the second degree, or whose he is adopter, adoptee, foster child or foster parent, or another person who he lives with, or had lived with in the same household.

[65] Statistical Office of the Republic of Serbia (2020b).

[66] (1) to rectify detrimental consequences caused by the commission of the criminal offense, or indemnify the damage caused; (2) to pay a certain amount of money to the account allocated for payment of public revenues, used for humanitarian or other public purposes; (3) to perform certain community service or humanitarian work; (4) to pay supporting obligations which have fallen due; (5) to submit to alcohol or drug treatment program; (6) to submit to psycho-social treatment for the

Code),[67] because statistical data show that this is one of the reasons for rejection of criminal charges. It should be checked if prosecutors' opportunities are also applied in cases of so-called "real repentance". (Article 284, paragraph 3 of the Criminal Procedur Code) when the public prosecutor assesses that prosecution is not practical (and rejects the criminal charge). These institutes cannot be assessed as most appropriate responds to domestic violence, so it is necessary to determine in which cases and with which explanations they are applied. Also, taking into consideration that data show sanctioning with home imprisonment in cases of domestic violence, we should determine if this choice of imprisonment is in accordance with the law, bearing in mind that it was established that there are cases where courts decided for this kind of imprisonment contrary to Article 45, paragraph 3 of the CC, which forbids implementation of home imprisonment in cases where person convicted for criminal offense against marriage and family lives in the same household with the victim.[68] In 2020 this type of imprisonment was declared in 138 cases.[69]

4 Concluding Remarks

Serbia has undoubtedly invested a lot of effort in the field of protection of women from violence, which was confirmed by GREVIO's report,[70] but many solutions are more of a declarative nature, it seems coerced (under pressure of international obligations and the EU integration processes) and because of creating an image of fulfillment of requirements for joining the EU, designed without real understanding and insufficiently harmonized with the existing national and international requirements (more precisely, with requirements of the Istanbul Convention). Thus, each new incrimination faces certain criticism from the very start. Non-harmonization is evident concerning the compliance of the new provisions with Istanbul Convention itself, but also concerning the issue of harmonization of the new incriminations with the existing (similar, comparable) criminal law solutions.

Of course, a special problem is implementation of new solutions in practice, which could have been expected, when we know that implementation of the long existing incrimination—domestic violence—and practical solutions, which is supposed to provide protection to victims, is still subjected to criticism. Among the reasons for persisting difficulties in practices (besides vagueness of the

---

purpose of eliminating the causes of violent conduct; (7) to fulfill obligations determined by the final court decision, or observe restrictions determined by the final court decision.

[67] Official Gazette of RS, Nos. 72/2011, 101/2011, 121/2012, 32/2013, 45/2013, 55/2014, 35/2019, 27/2021- Constitutional Court Decision, 62/2021- Constitutional Court Decision.

[68] Mrvić-Petrović and Jovanović (2015), p. 46.

[69] Statistical Office of the Republic of Serbia (2021), p. 9.

[70] GREVIO (2020), p. 63.

incriminations themselves) are lack of understanding of the serious nature of these forms of violence, their trivialisation in the media and in public sphere.

The best illustration of the said is the problem of femicides occurring after victimization by domestic violence being reported to authorities, but not responded to in a timely and adequate manner. The number of murdered women in the context of domestic violence is not part of the official statistics yet (despite Istanbul Convention stipulates collection of data on various forms of violence (Article 11)), so data on femicides (based on information from media) can be followed up just from the reports of Women against Violence Network. These reports (2010–2020)[71] show that about 30 women are killed annually in the context of domestic violence, despite many of previous violent incidents were reported to the authorities. For example, in 2020—at least 26 women are killed in family/partner violence context, suggesting that approximately every 8th reported case of murder in 2020 was a femicide.[72]

An older research on femicides show that 10.5% of all homicides are intimate partner homicides (whose victims are women predominantly).[73] Recently conducted research on femicides in judicial practice in Serbia shed more light on this phenomenon: more than 74 per cent of femicides take place in a family or intimate partner context and 49.3 per cent are killings of spouses or out-of-wedlock intimate partner.[74]These acts are marked with particular brutality, and more than half of them (50.7 per cent) are classified as aggravated murders. Nevertheless, in only 10 per cent of cases, the perpetrator received a maximum sentence of 40 years[75] Here we should also mention that murder of a family member who was previously abused is a form of a homicide, which can again be interpreted in the context of how much the state is interested in offering better responds to domestic violence and threaten perpetrators with the most severe penalty (life imprisonment), but this incrimination is almost not at all implemented in practice because of problems in its interpretation.[76]

References

Babović M, Reljanović M (2020) Sexual harassment in Serbia. OSCE, Belgrade

Campbell JC (1992) If I can' t have you, no one can: power and control in homicide of female partners. In: Radford J, Russell DEH (eds) Femicide: the politics of woman killing. Twayne, New York, pp 99–113

[71] Mreža Žene protiv nasilja, Femicid u Srbiji - Mreža Žene protiv nasilja (zeneprotivnasilja.net).

[72] According to official data there were 201 reported cases of murders and aggravated murders in 2020. Statistical Office of the Republic of Serbia (2021), p. 3.

[73] Simeunović-Patić and Jovanović (2013), p. 19.

[74] Konstantinović-Vilić et al. (2019), p. 350.

[75] Konstantinović-Vilić et al. (2019), pp. 353–354.

[76] Đorđević (2005), p. 151; Konstantinović-Vilić et al. (2019), p. 353; Jovanović (2021), p. 159.

Ćirić J, Đorđević Đ, Sepi R (2006) Kaznena politika sudova u Srbiji (Penal policy of courts in Serbia). Centar za mir i razvoj demokratije, Beograd

Ćorović E (2018) Krivično delo sakaćenja ženskog polnog organa iz čl. 121a Krivičnog zakonika Srbije (The criminal offense of female genital mutilation contained in Article 121a of the criminal code of the Republic of Serbia). Naučne publikacije Državnog univerziteta u Novom Pazaru, Serija B: Društvene & humanističke nauke 1(1):4–13

Đokić I (2017) Kriminalnopolitička opravdanost inkiminisanja polnog uznemiravanja u Republici Srbiji (The justification of criminalizing sexual harassment in the Republic of Serbia). Crimen 8(3):539–558

Đorđević Đ (2005) Novi oblici teških ubistava u predlogu Krivičnog zakonika (New forms of first degree murders in the draft criminal code). Pravni život 54(9):135–154

Đorđević Đ (2017) Nove inkriminacije i njihova usklađenost sa ostalim odredbama Krivičnog zakonika Srbije (New incriminations and their compliance with other criminal provisions of Serbian criminal code). In: Bejatović S (ed) Reformski procesi i poglavlje 23 (godinu dana posle) – Krivičnopravni aspekti (Reform processes and Chapter 23 (one year after) – criminal law aspects). Srpsko udruženje za krivičnopravnu teoriju i praksu, Intermex, Beograd, pp 129–139

Đorđević Đ (2018) Polno uznemiravanje (Sexual harassment). In: Ignjatović Đ (ed) Kaznena reakcija u Srbiji, VIII deo (Penal reaction in Serbia, Part VIII). Pravni fakultet Univerziteta u Beogradu, Beograd, pp 113–122

European Commission (2010) Feasibility study to assess the possibilities, opportunities and needs to standardise national legislation on violence against women, violence against children and sexual orientation violence. Publications Office of the European Union, Luxembourg

GREVIO (2020) Baseline evaluation report on legislative and other measures giving effect to the provisions of the Council of Europe convention on preventing and combating violence against women and domestic violence (Istanbul Convention) Serbia. Final report on Serbia (coe.int)

Jovanović S (2010) Pravna zaštita od nasilja u porodici (Legal protection from domestic violence). Institut za kriminološka i sociološka istraživanja, Beograd

Jovanović S (2015) Proganjanje u svetlu postojećih inkriminacija i međunarodnopravnih zahteva (Stalking in light of existing incriminations and international law requirements). In: Kolarić D (ed) Suprotstavljanje savremenim oblicima kriminaliteta – analiza stanja, evropski standardi i mere za unapređenje, tom I (Action against modern forms of crime – state of play analysis, European standards and measures for improvment). Kriminalističko-policijska akademija i Fondacija "Hans Zajdel", Beograd, pp 207–216

Jovanović S (2021) Criminal law protection of right to life in Serbia. In: Pavlović Z (ed) Yearbook human rights protection, right to life. Provincial Protector of Citizens – Ombudsman, Institute of Criminological and Sociological Research in Belgrade, Novi Sad, pp 147–163

Konstantinović-Vilić S, Petrušić N (2004) Krivično delo nasilja u porodici: pravna praksa u Republici Srbiji (Criminal offense of domestic violence: legal practice in the Republic of Serbia). Ženski istraživački centar za edukaciju i komunikaciju, Niš

Konstantinović-Vilić S, Petrušić N (2007) Krivično delo nasilja u porodici: aktuelna pravosudna praksa u Beogradu i Nišu (Criminal offense of domestic violence: actual judicial practice in Belgrade and Niš). Autonomni ženski centar, Ženski istraživački centar za edukaciju i komunikaciju, Beograd

Konstantinović-Vilić S, Petrušić N, Beker K (2019) Društveni i institucionalni odgovor na femicid u Srbiji (I deo) (Societal and institutional response to femicide in Serbia (Part I)). Pančevo, FemPlatz

Logar R (2007) Austrijski model intervencije u slučajevima nasilja u porodici (Austrian model of intervention in domestic violence cases). Autonomni ženski centar, Beograd

Lukić M, Jovanović S (2001) Nasilje u porodici: nasilje u prisustvu vlasti (Domestic violence: violence in the presence of the authorities). Institut za kriminološka i sociološka istraživanja, Beograd

Miladinović-Stefanović D (2017) Istanbulska konvencija i krivičnopravna zaštita žena od nasilja u Republici Srbiji (Istanbul convention and criminal law protection of women from violence in the Republic of Serbia). Zbornik radova Pravnog fakulteta u Nišu 76:231–252

Mreža Žene protiv nasilja, Femicid u Srbiji 2010-2020 (Femicide in Serbia 2010-2020). Femicid u Srbiji - Mreža Žene protiv nasilja (zeneprotivnasilja.net)

Mrvić-Petrović N, Jovanović S (2015) Preporuke za unapređenje primene alternativnih krivičnih sankcija i mera restorativne pravde (Reccommendations for imrovment of the application of alternative criminal sanctions and restorative justice measures). In: Nikolić N (ed) Promocija alternativnih krivičnih sankcija i mera restorativne pravde (Promotion of the alternative criminal sanctions and restorative justice measures). Fondacija Cenatar za Demokratiju, Viktimološko društvo Srbije, Beograd, pp 42–54

Mullen E, Pathé M, Purcell R, Stuart GW (1999) Study of stalkers. Am J Psychiatry 156(8): 1244–1249

Nikolić-Ristanović V (2002) Porodično nasilje u Srbiji (Domestic violence in Serbia). Viktimološko društvo Srbije, Prometej, Beograd

Petrušić N, Konstantinović-Vilić S (2008) Porodičnopravna zaštita od nasilja u porodici u praksi sudova u Beogradu (Family law protection from domestic violence in judicial practice in Belgrade). Autonomni ženski centar, Ženski istraživački centar za edukaciju i komunikaciju, Beograd

Petrušić N, Žunić N, Vilić V (2018) The criminal offense of domestic violence in judicial practice: new trends and challenges. OSCE, Belgrade. 424799.pdf (osce.org)

Republički zavod za statistiku (2018) Punoletni učinioci krivičnih dela u Republici Srbiji, 2017. (Adult Perpetrators of Criminal Offenses in the Republic of Serbia 2017) Bilten 643. Beograd

Republički zavod za statistiku (2019) Punoletni učinioci krivičnih dela u Republici Srbiji., 2018. (Adult Perpetrators of Criminal Offenses in the Republic of Serbia 2028) Bilten 653. Beograd

Republički zavod za statistiku (2020a) Punoletni učinioci krivičnih dela u Republici Srbiji, 2019. (Adult Perpetrators of Criminal Offenses in the Republic of Serbia 2029). Bilten 665. Beograd

Republički zavod za statistiku (2020b) Prijavljena punoletna lica za nasilje u porodici (Adult Persons Reported for Domestic Violence) Pretraga diseminacione baze (stat.gov.rs)

Republički zavod za statistiku (2021) Punoletni učinioci krivičnih dela u Republici Srbiji, 2020. (Adult Perpetrators of Criminal Offenses in the Republic of Serbia 2020) Saopštenje 195, 14 July 2021. G20211195.pdf (stat.gov.rs)

Simeunović-Patić B, Jovanović S (2013) Žene žrtve ubistva u partnerskom odnosu (Women victims of murder in intimate partner relation). Institut za kriminološka i sociološka istraživanja, Beograd

Stojanović Z (2012) Kaznena politika u Srbiji: konflikt između zakonodavca i sudske prakse (Sentencing policy in Serbia: conflict between legislator and judicial practice). In: Ignjatović Đ (ed) Kaznena Reakcija u Srbiji (Penal reaction in Serbia). Pravni fakultet Univerziteta u Beogradu, Beograd, pp 1–17

Stojanović Z (2013) Da li je Srbiji potrebna reforma krivičnog zakonodavstva? (Does Serbia need reform of the criminal law?). Crimen 4(2):119–143

Stojanović Z (2017) Proganjanje – novo krivično delo u Krivičnom zakoniku Srbije (Stalking – new criminal offense in the criminal code of the Republic of Serbia). In: Ignjatović Đ (ed) Kaznena reakcija u Srbiji (Penal reaction in Serbia). Pravni fakultet Univerziteta u Beogradu, Beograd, pp 1–10

UNICEF (2017) Child marriage in Serbia. Microsoft Word - Child Marriage in Serbia version1 (unicef.org)

UNICEF (2021) Female Genital Mutilation. Female Genital Mutilation (FGM) Statistics - UNICEF Data

Vlada Republike Srbije (2016) Predlog Zakona o izmenama i dopunama Krivičnog zakonika sa obrazloženjem (Draft Law on Ammendmens to Criminal Code with Explanatory Report) PREDLOG ZAKONA O IZMENAMA I DOPUNAMA KRIVIČNOG ZAKONIKA - Tekst propisa (paragraf.rs)

Zaštitnik građana (2020) Poseban izveštaj o radu grupa za koordinaciju i saradnju na području Grada Beograda (Special Report on Activities of the Groups for Coordination and Cooperation in Belgrade). Poseban izvestaj zastitnika gradjana.pdf (ombudsman.rs)

Blockchain as the Catalyst in the Shift from Closed to Open Limited Liability Companies: The Case of Greyp Bikes

Jasmina Mutabžija

Contents

1 Introduction

A limited liability company, as the most common form of incorporation of small and medium enterprises, has been historically praised as the staple of economy in most EU member states.[1] It has regularly been recognized for its advantages of being a flexible and cost-effective way of doing business, which allows the members of the company to have elasticity in structuring the company management, while typically

This paper is funded by the University of Rijeka within the project UNIRI-drustv-18-214 "Efficient Regulation of Digital Market to Boost Innovation in ICT Sector".

[1] See, for example, European Commission (2019).

J. Mutabžija (✉)
University College PAR, Rijeka, Croatia
e-mail: jasmina.mutabzija@par.hr

D. V. Popović et al. (eds.), *Balkan Yearbook of European and International Law 2021*, Balkan Yearbook of European and International Law 2021,
https://doi.org/10.1007/978-3-030-97431-2_11

not being personally responsible for business debts and liabilities.[2] However, unlike in the case of joint stock companies, the transfer of shares in limited liability companies is, in many EU member states, subject to a relatively lengthy and costly procedure and riddled with hurdles.[3] Their transfer can include several formalities, such as the obligation to conclude the share transfer agreement in the form of a notarial deed, necessarily involving the participation of a notary.[4] In addition to that, to be effective vis-à-vis third parties, the transfer usually must be registered in the relevant company register.[5] Another prominent obstacle, very often prescribed by corporate laws of EU member states, is the fact that they cannot be expressed in the form of securities *i.e.* they cannot be incorporated in financial instruments to facilitate their circulation.[6] Consequently, there is no secondary market for the shares in limited liability companies, which causes difficulties in relation to finding prospective buyers, to disclosing the relevant information about the related business, as well as to estimating the value and negotiating the price of the share to be sold. Regardless of the fact that shares can still be transferred on a contractual basis from one person to another, the shares in limited liability companies are virtually immobilized due to the described limitations and formalities. This is one of the reasons why limited liability companies are usually held by only a few individuals, who as a rule know each other personally,[7] whereas none or only an insignificant number of shares are held by outsiders.[8]

Because they are flexible and require lower share capital, limited liability companies are a popular corporate form for early-stage start-ups *i.e.* new companies that are developing an innovative product or service. However, the afore described immobility of the shares can start causing problems for such start-ups at the moment when their development activities begin to require larger investments, which cannot be financed by the founders themselves. Such start-ups do not have the opportunity to raise investment capital by easily offering and selling their shares to the public at large, unlike businesses incorporated in the more expensive and more complicated form of joint stock companies. Therefore, the lack of openness to the financial markets may prevent businesses operating as limited liability companies from seizing their full growth potential, especially in cases where their transformation into joint stock companies would be seen as too risky, for example, if they would not yet be ready to operate on such a large scale. With a few notable exceptions such as

---

[2] See, for example, Čulinović Herc (2018), p. 47.

[3] See Kalls (2004), pp. 348–360.

[4] See, for example, Article 412 paragraph 2 of the Croatian Company Act (Zakon o trgovačkim društvima) OG no. 111/93, 34/99, 121/99, 52/00, 118/03, 107/07, 146/08, 137/09, 125/11, 152/11, 111/12, 68/13, 110/15, 40/19 (hereinafter: the Croatian Company Act).

[5] See, for example, Article 411 paragraph 1 of the Croatian Company Act.

[6] See, for example, Article 385 paragraph 1 of the Croatian Company Act.

[7] Čulinović Herc (2018), p. 62.

[8] Such companies are in legal literature called closed, closely-held, unlisted or private companies. Čulinović Herc (2018), p. 47. See also Kalls (2004).

Italy,[9] the law-makers in EU member states have largely not actively attempted to solve this problem. And, as is usually the case, the market, not willing to wait for the law-makers to catch-up, tried to find its own solutions by working around the legal obstacles, *inter alia*, through the use of technology.

One of the practices that has appeared in recent years, as a form of equity crowdfunding[10] aiming to simplify the process of raising investment capital for limited liability companies, is the tokenization of shares or rights associated with shares in limited liability companies, with the help of blockchain technology.[11] Since legal literature related to the use of blockchain in the context of closed (closely-held, unlisted, private) companies, in particular, limited liability companies is scarce,[12] this paper endeavors to be a contribution in the process of filling that void. Its main aim is to show how use of blockchain technology in this context facilitates the move from private to more open limited liability companies in Europe. The paper thus commences by explaining the concept of tokenization and identifying three of the legal models of tokenizing shares in limited liability companies in Europe, and continues in a form of a study of the recent case of tokenization of shares held in Croatian limited liability company Greyp Bikes, offering an analysis of several different aspects of the case.

---

[9]When crowdfunding began to take momentum, in order to facilitate the development of the secondary market for shares in Italian limited liability companies (hereinafter: S.R.L.s), the Italian legislator introduced the so-called alternative regime of transferring shares in 2012, first only for the so-called innovative start-ups, then in 2015 for innovative small and medium enterprises, and as of 2017 for all other SMEs. In accordance with this regime, shares in SMEs operating in the form of a limited liability company can be subject to a public offering as financial instruments, including through crowdfunding platforms. Policaro (2019), pp. 247–250.

[10]For more on the types of crowdfunding see, for example, Kunda (2016).

[11]A blockchain is a decentralized, censorship-resistant database. Unlike traditional database records that are being kept on one server, blockchain records are kept on thousands of computers (nodes) which makes it close to impossible to manipulate them. Each transaction that happens on a blockchain is validated in a process called mining, by network participants called miners. Miners use their computer resources to solve cryptographic (mathematical) tasks in order to verify the validity of a transaction. The task consists of encrypting the transaction by transforming the transaction information into a string of characters, with as many zeros as possible. Once a miner has created such a string the miner broadcasts it to the rest of the network. Now the network decrypts the encrypted information, by taking the string apart and thereby confirming the transaction information. As a reward, the miner automatically receives crypto coins. Neufund (2019). For more on blockchain technology see, for example, Warburg (2019).

[12]The legal literature about the use of blockchain in the context of corporate law has so far focused on the legal status of the so-called decentralized autonomous organizations (hereinafter: DAO) and the problems related to the corporate governance of public (listed) companies. For discussions about blockchain in the context of DAOs and corporate governance in listed companies, see, for example, Hassan and De Filippi (2021), Meng and Xing (2021), Nielsen (2019), Kondova and Barba (2019), Enriques and Zetzsche (2019), Kaal (2019), Magnier and Barban (2018), Lafarre and Van der Elst (2018), Lafarre and Van der Elst (2018), Chohan (2017) and Yermack (2017).

2 What Is Tokenization?

In the context of blockchain technology, a token (sometimes also referred to as the crypto-asset) is a digital representation of an asset on a blockchain. Via tokens, any asset can be replicated in digital form and virtually divided into as many parts as is deemed necessary. Tokens are issued and managed through smart contracts[13] deployed on a blockchain, of which Ethereum[14] is most commonly used. Unless they are purposefully made non-transferable on the protocol level of the underlying blockchain, tokens can be transferred peer-to-peer from one party to another without an intermediary, by a mere interaction with the smart contract. Since tokens represent a value, the transfer from one party to another will most likely involve an exchange for another value, such as a payment in fiat or crypto-currency. Depending on the type of value they represent, they are classified into three types: utility tokens, payment tokens and security or investment tokens.[15] A utility token is a digital representation of a right to access the existing or future product or service.[16] Payment tokens are also known as crypto-currencies, amongst which bitcoin and ether are perhaps the most known.[17] They are used as alternative means of payment for goods or services. Security tokens, sometimes also referred to as investment tokens due to their investment dimension, are digital representations of ownership or other rights over certain assets, such as precious metals, real-estate, debts, equity and similar. Tokens representing shares or rights associated with shares in limited

---

[13] Smart contracts are computer programs or transaction protocols stored on a blockchain, which run when predefined conditions are fulfilled. They are usually utilized to automate the execution of contractual terms or to record certain events and actions relevant for the fulfillment of the contract, so that the parties to the contract can be certain of the outcome without the need to use various intermediaries and without wasting valuable time. Even though their name suggests this, smart contracts are not used only to execute contracts or other legal actions. They can also be used, for example, to automate processes, triggering each subsequent step once the requirements are fulfilled. They are based on if-then statements which are built into the computer code on a blockchain. Once the predefined conditions have been met, the computer network will execute the programmed actions, which can, for example, consist of executing a payment toward someone, sending notifications and similar. After a transaction has been completed, it is permanently recorded on the blockchain, so it cannot be subsequently modified or altered. Even though smart contracts may increase efficiency and accuracy, trust amongst parties, security and savings, they are subject to certain limitations. Because the parties must define their relationship in detail in the terms of if-then logic, objectively and specifically, foreseeing all possible exceptions, smart contracts have a limited scope of application and cannot be used for contractual situations involving more subjective criteria, as well as all other situations that cannot be expressed in the terms of if-then logic. For more about the technical aspects of smart contracts, see, for example, Hewa (2021). For more about the legal aspects of smart contracts, see, for example, Levi and Lipton (2018).

[14] Rodeck and Curry (2021).

[15] European Banking Authority (2019), p. 7; European Commission (2020), p. 5. For more on the legal aspects of tokens, see, for example, Token Alliance (2021).

[16] For example, Filecoin has managed to raise 257 million US dollars through the sale of tokens representing the right to access a decentralized cloud platform for data storage. See Higgins (2017).

[17] For more on crypto-currencies see, for example, Lewis (2018).

liability companies, which are of primary interest for this paper, are a type of security tokens, which are often called equity tokens.[18] Studies have also named hybrid tokens as the fourth category of tokens, which have features of more than one of the three specific categories listed above and, hence, enable their use for more than one purpose.[19]

The process in which tokens are created and attached to the value they represent is called tokenization. Therefore, tokenization of shares in a limited liability company can be defined as a process of creating digital representations of shares or (more often) rights associated with shares in the limited liability company, in the form of cryptographically generated tokens. There are two aspects to this process: technical and legal. The technical aspect consists of programming tokens that represent shares or rights associated with shares, with the help of smart contracts that run on a blockchain. Smart contracts are used for generating and transferring such equity tokens directly to the investors' crypto-wallets, in exchange for payment in fiat or crypto-currency. The legal aspect consists of creating a legal model by which the share or a right associated with a share in a limited liability company, such as the right to receive dividends or the right to vote regarding business decisions which are to be made by the company, is legally attached to the token, enabling the token holder to exercise these rights and get the same or similar level of legal protection as a traditional shareholder. The following section of this paper discusses the legal aspect of tokenization in more detail.

After tokenizing its shares, the limited liability company can subsequently offer such equity tokens for a primary market sale through a subtype of a security token offering (hereinafter: STO),[20] which is usually dubbed equity token offering (hereinafter: ETO). Once the investors purchase the tokens directly from the limited liability company that issued them, the tokens are, in principle, subsequently freely

[18] A detailed discussion on whether equity tokens fall under the definition of transferable securities and the conditions under which security token offerings may be conducted is outside of the scope of this paper. It suffices to note the difficulties related to the attempt to classify and establish legal supervision over crypto-assets as a financial instrument under the under the Directive 2014/65/EU of the European Parliament and the Council of 15 May 2015 on markets in financial instruments and amending Directive 2002/92/EC and Directive 2011/61/EU (recast), OJ L 173, 12.6.2014, pp. 349–496 (hereinafter: MiFID II Directive), including those relevant to the assessment of their features in particular cases, uneven implementation of the notion of "transferable security" in different EU member states, and confusion as to the interpretation and the application of the provisions of the MiFID II Directive in relation to crypto-assets. See European Commission (2020), p. 12. Assuming that tokenized shares of limited liability companies are considered transferable securities pursuant to the MiFID II Directive, this would, *inter alia*, mean that their issuance is subject to the supervision of financial market supervision authorities, and that equity token offerings are subject to the obligation to publish a prospectus under Regulation (EU) 2017/1129 of the European Parliament and of the Council of 14 June 2017 on the prospectus to be published when securities are offered to the public or admitted to trading on a regulated market, and repealing Directive 2003/71/EC, OJ L 168, 30.6.2017, p. 12–8, (hereinafter: the Prospectus Regulation).

[19] European Commission (2020), p. 5.

[20] For more on security token offerings see, for example, Lambert et al. (2021).

transferable from one investor to another. In other words, they can be traded peer-to-peer or (in theory) on a secondary market for security tokens,[21] without the participation of real-world intermediaries such as notaries. This widens the pool of prospective investors into the limited liability company, giving them more flexibility, because they can exit the company easily, saving on costs and time compared to the traditional transfer of shares in limited liability companies.

3 Legal Models of Tokenizing Shares in European Limited Liability Companies

The real challenge of tokenization of assets lies not in the technical, but in the legal aspect. Therefore, finding and implementing a legal model that would securely link the token with the real-world asset it represents so as to put the token holder in the position to successfully assert and enforce its claims related to the asset, is at the core of tokenization.[22] In the case the assets to be tokenized are shares or rights associated with shares in a limited liability company, the chosen legal model depends primarily on the corporate laws of the country in which the limited liability company is registered and in which the tokenization is carried out.[23] Whereas several European countries, such as Switzerland,[24] Lichtenstein[25] and Malta,[26] have recognized the potential of blockchain and enacted laws by which they have, *inter alia*, regulated transactions related to tokenized shares or rights associated with shares in limited liability companies, most European countries have not (yet) modernized their corporate laws to take blockchain into account. In the latter countries, lawyers, consequently, need to adopt a creative approach in setting-up viable legal schemes that would reconcile the use of blockchain technology in transactions related to shares in limited liability companies with the "old" corporate law rules, which envisage the participation of notaries and entries into company registers, effectively disabling the possibility to tokenize and easily transfer an actual share in a limited liability company directly to the token holder.

Unsurprisingly, avoiding these two formal requirements is the gist of all legal models that have been used in practice so far. The method by which this is achieved is common to all the models, regardless of the country in which they originated: a

---

[21] One has to bear in mind that, even though sporadic trading is present, a stable secondary market for tokenized shares in limited liability companies still does not exist.

[22] Völkel and Hollman (2020).

[23] However, even if a legal system is not favorable in relation to tokenization, in many cases the choice of law clause may be agreed in the attempt to take advantage of a more favorable legal system. The extent to which such a clause may have legal effect is a different question.

[24] For an overview of the new Swiss laws regarding blockchain see, for example, Gesley (2021).

[25] For an overview of the new Lichtenstein laws regarding blockchain see, Gesley (2019).

[26] For an overview of the new Maltese laws regarding blockchain see, Feikert-Ahalt (2018).

share (or shares) in the limited liability company that is to be tokenized is legally transferred to an intermediary, who is then entered into the company register as the formal shareholder of the company. This intermediary has the purpose to act as a bridge between the real-world "off-chain" equity and the tokens that represent this equity "on-chain". Who this intermediary is and what are its contractual obligations, however, varies according to the observed country and what is allowed by its corporate law. The text below offers concise description of legal models based on three types of intermediaries that have, *inter alia*, been used in practice so far.

3.1 Foundation

Foundations are fully-autonomous and self-owning corporate entities, without any share capital or shareholders. One form of foundation, the Dutch *Stichting Administratiekantoor* (hereinafter: STAK) is among the most popular foundations globally, due to the fact that it can be founded for an unusually wide scope of purposes, one of which is the administration of private assets, such as shares in the Dutch version of a limited liability company—the *besloten vennootschap* (hereinafter: B.V.).[27] Importantly, a STAK can be founded for the purpose of being solely a holding foundation, in which case it is a tax transparent vehicle. In other words, it is not subject to corporate income tax or VAT, because simply holding investments in the Netherlands is not classified as a business activity.[28] The STAK foundation was used several times in the last couple of years in the tokenization of B.V. shares, to avoid the participation of notaries in the transfer of B.V. shares to token holders and between token holders.

The tokenization of B.V. shares using the STAK as an intermediary is structured as follows. At the outset, a STAK is incorporated and registered at the Netherlands Chamber of Commerce and the administrating of the shares of a particular B.V. is stated as its main activity. Once incorporated, three agreements have to be concluded between the members (the shareholders) of the B.V. and the STAK. First, a trust-like agreement is concluded stipulating that all or some shares in the B.V. will be transferred to the STAK to administer them for the benefit of the transferor and that the STAK will simultaneously issue the so-called depository receipts for the shares it will hold.[29] A second agreement is the administration agreement, which stipulates the terms and conditions under which the STAK will administrate the shares it will hold. This agreement, *inter alia*, regulates the relationship between the

[27] Foundations are regulated in the Netherlands by the Civil Code of the Netherlands, Book 2, Articles Title 2.6 Foundations (Articles 285–307), Title 2.6 Foundations (Articles 285–307), available in the English language at: http://www.dutchcivillaw.com/civilcodegeneral.htm. For more on foundations in the Netherlands, see, for example, Koele (2016). For more about foundations as shareholders in companies see, for example, Braut Filipović (2020).

[28] Thompson (2020).

[29] Morris (2014).

STAK and the depositary receipt holders. Importantly, it can be customized for each particular purpose since there are no legal constraints or requirements to be met, apart from the general provisions in the Dutch contract law.[30] Finally, the share transfer agreement is concluded between the shareholders and the STAK in the form of a notarial deed. The purpose of this agreement is to transfer the legal title to the shares to the STAK, making the STAK a full-fledged member of the company, which is as such entered into the Dutch company register—the *Handelsregister*.

The depositary receipts issued by the STAK certify the value of the B.V. shares they pertain to, and, embody the right to receive dividends. In most cases, the voting rights associated with the shares will remain with the STAK, which is managed by at least one director. However, depositary receipts can also embody voting rights,[31] making them just as useful as the original shares. Therefore, a STAK has legal rights in the shares and is registered as a formal shareholder in the Dutch company register and in the share register of the B.V., but the holders of economic rights in the shares are the holders of depositary receipts. STAK has the legal obligation to maintain a register of depositary receipt holders and record all transactions related to the depository receipts. Importantly, the depositary receipts may be transferred to other persons without a notarial deed. This means that the depositary receipts can legally be issued and transferred as tokens, and that B.V. shares to which these receipts pertain to can be indirectly transferred as tokens as well. In this respect, it must be emphasized that the conditions under which the STAK will tokenize the depositary receipts, as well as all the issues related to voting rights, profit rights and the obligations of the holders of (tokenized) depository receipts, have to be determined in detail in the afore-stated administration agreement. One of the B.V.s that has utilized the STAK legal model of tokenizing its shares is Ockel Computers B.V. In the beginning of 2019, this limited liability company conducted an ETO through the tokenization platform Liquith.io, which resulted in 200 investors, who became indirect shareholders as holders of tokenized depository receipts.[32]

3.2 *Lawyer as a Trustee*

A partially similar model to the one described in the previous section has emerged in Austria. Austrian law does not envisage common-law-like trusts or STAK-like foundations that would allow the separation of legal and beneficiary ownership, but it is possible to set up a *Treuhand*, which could be translated to English as a

---

[30] Morris (2014).

[31] Infloat & Watson Law (2019), p. 5.

[32] For more information see the official web page of the Ockel Computers ETO: https://www.ockel.investments/. For the record of transactions related to the Ockel token and the current number of token holders see Etherscan, a search engine for transactions on the Ethereum blockchain https://etherscan.io/token/0x96cbc8bf2474bb28dc54e4137aae091880ff4893#balances.

trusteeship. This is not a legal entity, but a contractual relationship in which the *Treuhänder* (trustee) is authorized to exercise rights over property in its own name, on the basis of and in accordance with a binding fiduciary agreement with the *Treugeber* (settlor). It is not expressly regulated by any legislation, but is based on the contract law principle of autonomy of will and is delimited by case-law and doctrine.[33] *Treuhand* is a very common feature of the Austrian economy and is often provided as a service of Austrian attorneys, being particularly common in the case of real estate purchase contracts.[34] As a *Treuhänder*, an attorney plays a key role in the legal transaction by, for example, securing contractually agreed payments *vis-à-vis* the other party until conditions set out in the agreement have been met. In the case of a real-estate purchase agreement, the attorney keeps the purchase price deposited to his account by the buyer of the property and releases it to the seller only after the title to the property has been registered in the land register to the buyer's name.[35] Many other *Treuhand* arrangements are possible and are used in Austria, and most recently one such arrangement has appeared as a legal model of tokenizing shares in the Austrian limited liability company—*Gesellschaft mit beschränkter Haftung* (hereinafter: GmbH).[36]

This legal model uses the so-called efforts obligations to circumvent the formal requirement prescribed by Austrian company law, under which an agreement on the transfer of shares in the Austrian GmbH (and even a mere offer of such share transfer) must be in the form of a notarial deed to be valid. Efforts obligations are promises by a person to obtain performance from a third party, which can be transferred without any formalities. Therefore, instead of tokenizing the GmbH shares directly, what is tokenized in this model is a commitment to transfer a share in the GmbH, together with the efforts obligation concerning the profit and, if necessary, a commitment to co-determination rights.[37] The GmbH promises to expend its own efforts to get its formal shareholder (as a third party) to perform for the benefit of equity token holders. For example, it promises that profits distributed to the formal shareholder will be passed on to equity token holders and/or that the token holder will obtain a formal share in the GmbH by way of a share transfer or capital increase, if certain conditions are met. The problem is that promises made at the expense of third parties cannot effectively bind these third parties without their consent. However, the GmbH's promise would not have weight towards the investors interested in buying the equity tokens, unless it was able to guarantee that the formal shareholder will actually fulfill what was promised, even if it did not wish to do so. In order to alleviate this problem, a share in the GmbH which is to be tokenized is first transferred to a lawyer as the *Treuhänder*, who becomes a formal

[33] Gvelesiani (2015), p. 135.

[34] The Financial Action Task Force (2016), p. 30.

[35] The Financial Action Task Force (2016), p. 30.

[36] The transfer of shares in the Austrian GmbH is also subject to the formal requirement of concluding the transfer agreement in the form of a notarial deed. See, for example, Kulnigg (2019).

[37] Völkel and Hollman (2020), p. 9.

shareholder of the company and takes over the tokenization of the share he/she was entrusted with. In this way, the lawyer as the *Treuhänder* steps in between the GmbH and the equity token holders, with the purpose of guaranteeing the shareholder position to the equity token holder *i.e.* in order to ensure that the promises made are fulfilled after a corresponding request by the GmbH. Typically, this has to be implemented in the articles of association of the GmbH, whereas the duties of the lawyer as the trustee must be clearly set out in the *Treuhand* agreement. This trustee shareholder model is used in practice by the Austrian tokenization platform simplytokenized.com.[38]

3.3 Special Purpose Vehicle

The legal model that is, perhaps, most widely applicable for tokenizing shares in limited liability companies in Europe is the special purpose vehicle (hereinafter: SPV) model. Generally speaking, an SPV is a subsidiary company or an orphan company that is formed to undertake a specific business purpose or activity, such as asset securitization, participation in a joint venture, execution of property deals, or isolation of the parent's company assets, operations or risks, in which case it is called a bankruptcy remote entity.[39] In the context of ETOs, an SPV is a company that is formed with the purpose to represent equity token holders as a single entry in the share register of the limited liability company conducting the ETO or in the relevant country's company register in which the company conducting the ETO is registered. The relationship between the SPV and the limited liability company conducting the ETO *i.e.* the company that issues the equity tokens and receives the financial benefits of the ETO, is regulated by the so-called investment and shareholder's agreement.[40] Based on this agreement and once the ETO is successfully completed, the SPV becomes a formal shareholder of the limited liability company that has conducted the ETO in exchange for the transfer of funds raised through the ETO. The contents of this agreement may vary depending on the applicable law, but it typically has to be concluded in the form a notarial deed, allowing the SPV to be entered into the relevant country's company register as the formal shareholder.

It must be emphasized that following the successful ETO, the equity token holders, in principle, do not gain the status of formal shareholders in the SPV nor in the limited liability company that conducted the ETO, because this would also

[38] See https://www.simplytokenized.com/the-token-gmbh/. The legal model was created by the Viennese law office Stadler Stadler Völkel, Attorneys at Law. See Völkel and Hollman (2020).

[39] For more about special purpose vehicles in the context of securitization see, for example, Gorton and Souleles (2007).

[40] For more about this agreement in practice see infra 4.2.

require the participation of notaries, which is intended to be avoided.[41] Instead, the relationship between the equity token holders and the SPV is governed by a partnership agreement, which is concluded in accordance with the applicable law.[42] The function of this agreement is the assignment of limited shareholder rights arising from the SPV's share in the limited liability company that conducted the ETO to the equity token holders, such as the right to participate in the profit, the right to vote and the right to be informed—such assigned rights are what is tokenized under this model. It also regulates the manner in which the equity token holders will exercise those rights *i.e.* the manner in which the SPV will execute the will of the token holders in relation to the limited liability company that conducted the ETO. A version of the SPV legal model of tokenization was used in practice by the German tokenization platform Neufund and was used, among other examples, in the ETO of Croatia's Greyp Bikes d.o.o., which will be discussed in detail in the next section of this paper.[43]

4 Equity Token Offering of Croatia's Greyp Bikes d.o.o.

One of the first cases in which the SPV model of tokenizing shares in a limited liability company was used in practice, and perhaps the most famous of all, is the ETO conducted at the end of 2019 by the Croatian limited liability company Greyp Bikes d.o.o. (hereinafter: Greyp Bikes).[44] The tokenization was entrusted to the German platform Neufund, which operates on Ethereum blockchain and was structured as follows.

[41] However, there are also examples to the contrary. In the Tokenomica ETO, which was conducted at the end of 2019 by an Estonian limited liability company Tokenomica OÜ, the investors that have purchased Tokenomica tokens were formally registered as shareholders of the SPV Nominee TKN OÜ. For a description of this ETO see Tokenomica (2020).

[42] For more about this agreement in practice see infra 4.2. For more on third party participation in the share of a member of a limited liability company on the basis of a partnership agreement under Croatian law see Barbić (2013), pp. 144–146.

[43] In mid-2020, the Neufund platform suspended further equity token offerings stating that it does no longer wish to operate in a "grey zone" and accusing the German Federal Financial Authority (BaFin) of not taking responsibility to regulate or to ban innovative activities. Foxles (2020). The platform will continue to maintain all issued equity tokens, crypto-wallets and post-investment activities and is still available at: https://platform.neufund.org/.

[44] The majority shareholder in the company at the time of the ETO was the renown Croatian entrepreneur Mate Rimac, who is also the founder of Rimac Automobili. The total share capital being 27,000.00 HRK at the time of the ETO, Mate Rimac held a share with nominal value of 11,700.00 HRK, or a 42.09% share in the company.

4.1 Establishment of the Special Purpose Vehicle

In preparation for the ETO, Greyp Bikes, as the only shareholder, established the subsidiary company Smart Zero UG (hereinafter: Smart Zero), a German version of the simple limited liability company. The Articles of Association of Smart Zero state the following: "Object of business of the company is the acquisition, the holding, the administration and the commercialization of its own assets, particularly, but not limited to, shareholdings in other commercial enterprises as well as all related business activities, in its own name and for its own account and not for third parties and excluding any activities requiring permission according to the German Banking Act (KWG) or Capital Investment Act (KAGB)",[45] whereas the Investment Memorandum states that the purpose of Smart Zero is to "take over the shares in the Issuer in order to pass on the resulting rights to investors [. . .]. In particular, [Smart Zero] will transfer rights to participate in the profits of the Issuer and (in a limited and indirect manner) to exercise voting rights".[46] In relation to the equity tokens, the Investment Memorandum clarifies that the tokens themselves do not directly represent shares in Greyp Bikes, but "equity-like" rights, which will be exercised by the token holders through Smart Zero.[47]

4.2 Legal Relationships Between Greyp Bikes, Smart Zero and Greyp Token Holders

The legal relationships between Greyp Bikes, Smart Zero and the investors were structured as follows. The one-off event in which the issuer (Greyp Bikes) created the tokens and the investors purchased tokens was regulated by the Acquisition and Reservation Agreements.[48] These tripartite agreements were signed on-chain between Smart Zero, each individual investor that has purchased the so-called Greyp token/s, thus becoming a Greyp token holder, and Greyp Bikes, as a third-party beneficiary and obligor. Furthermore, via the Token Holder Agreements, which were concluded also between Smart Zero, each individual Greyp token holder and Greyp Bikes, as a third-party beneficiary and obligor, Smart Zero has transferred and assigned the limited shareholder rights obtained through the Investment and Shareholder Agreement, to the investors *i.e.* Greyp token holders. The function of the Token Holder Agreements was, in addition to transferring limited member rights arising from the share Smart Zero holds in Greyp Bikes to Greyp token holders, to

---

[45] Article 2 of the Articles of Association of SMART ZERO UG of 2 September 2019. The Articles of Association are available with the author.

[46] Greyp Bikes (2019), p. 11.

[47] Greyp Bikes (2019), pp. 8 and 11.

[48] The Acquisition and Reservation Agreement is available at: https://platform.neufund.org/eto/view/LI/1eb004fd-c44d-4bed-9e76-0e0858649587.

regulate the manner in which Greyp token holders would exercise those rights. By concluding these agreements, Greyp token holders did not become formal shareholders in Greyp Bikes or in Smart Zero, but they were given the right to participate in the profit, the right to vote and the right to be informed in relation to Greyp Bikes operations, in proportion to the share Smart Zero holds in Greyp Bikes and further in proportion to the number of Greyp tokens they have purchased.[49] Token Holder Agreements were also signed on-chain. It is important to emphasize that Greyp Bikes was a party and the signatory of the afore-mentioned agreements to guarantee that the Greyp token holders have direct legal claims against Greyp Bikes as the token issuer.

Considering that it was subject to notarization, the only agreement which was signed off-chain was the Investment and Shareholder Agreement. This agreement was concluded between Smart Zero and other shareholders of Greyp Bikes after the successfully completed Greyp equity token offering. Its function was to transfer the funds raised from investors through the sale of Greyp tokens to Greyp Bikes, and the acquisition of a corresponding share in Greyp Bikes by Smart Zero, in exchange for those funds. Concerning the size of the share obtained by Smart Zero in this process, the proclaimed goal of Greyp Bikes' ETO was to raise at least 971,223.02 EUR and at the most 4,760,897.21 EUR. The entire process was envisaged so that, after the ETO would be successfully completed and based on the afore-mentioned Investment and Shareholder Agreement, Smart Zero would obtain a share in Greyp Bikes that would have the size in the range from 2.15% to 10.79%, depending on the amount of capital raised from the investors. In order to implement this, it was also envisaged that Greyp Bikes would, following the successful completion of the ETO, *i.e.* after the amount of raised funds would be known, increase its share capital correspondingly, in order to enable Smart Zero to formally become a member of the company.[50] In the end, a total of 1,442,180.77 EUR was raised in the ETO and the equity tokens, dubbed Greyp Tokens (GRP), were purchased by as many as 1,017 investors from 34 countries, paying in EUR or in ether.[51] As the result of the completed ETO, the share capital of Greyp Bikes was increased by 1,100.00 HRK to 28,900.00 HRK, and Smart Zero obtained a 3.8% share in Greyp Bikes. Smart Zero was also entered in the Croatian company register as the formal shareholder of Greyp Bikes.

---

[49] See Greyp Bikes (2019), pp. 11–12.

[50] See Greyp Bikes (2019), *Investment Memorandum*.

[51] See the Greyp ETO statistics at: https://platform.neufund.org/eto/view/LI/1eb004fd-c44d-4bed-9e76-0e0858649587/stats.

4.3 Flaws in Implementation

Even though the Greyp token holders were, in fact, allowed to vote on the issues related to business operations of Greyp Bikes following the completed ETO, it is questionable whether they were legally entitled to exercise the right to vote and the right to participate in the profits of Greyp Bikes based on the implemented version of the SPV legal model. Namely, Greyp Bikes is a Croatian company and not a German one, unlike Smart Zero, which was used as the SPV in the ETO, and Fifth Force GmbH, which runs the Neufund platform and which organized the tokenization. However, the implemented legal model failed to consider the Croatian Company Act, which governs the establishment, organization, termination, changes in the legal status of companies, as well as subsidiary and affiliate companies in Croatia. The provisions being of particular relevance to this case are contained in Articles 418, 474 and 475 of the Act.

The cause of the problem lies in the fact that Smart Zero UG was established by Greyp Bikes as a 100% shareholder. After the ETO was completed, however, the Greyp token holders did not become formal shareholders in Smart Zero instead of Greyp Bikes. On the contrary, Smart Zero's ownership structure remained unchanged, with Greyp Bikes still holding a 100% share. Smart Zero, in turn, obtained a 3.8% share in Greyp Bikes. This means that, according to Article 475 of the Company Act, Greyp Bikes is considered a parent company and Smart Zero is considered its subsidiary.[52] However, Article 474 paragraph (4) of the Company Act prescribes that the shares held by a subsidiary are legally considered to be shares held by the parent company. Therefore, the share Smart Zero holds in Greyp Bikes is considered by the Company Act to be a share held by Greyp Bikes itself, as it is the parent company. In other words, in the tokenization process, Greyp Bikes ended up acquiring a share that is legally considered its own share. The problem is that, according to Article 418, paragraph 3 of the Company Act, the rights and obligations stemming from a company's own shares cannot be exercised. This means that, pursuant to the Croatian Company Act, Smart Zero and, consequently the Greyp token holders through its partnership with Smart Zero, cannot participate in the profit of Greyp Bikes or vote, which is what Greyp tokens were supposed to guarantee. The entire problem could have been avoided if Smart Zero was not established by Greyp Bikes, but some other unrelated third party, such as if established as an orphan company.[53] In that case, Article 474, paragraph 4 would not

[52] Jurić (2002).

[53] A version of an SPV tokenization model was also used in the afore-mentioned Tokenomica ETO. The SPV Nominee TKN OÜ was established by the natural person who was also the founder and shareholder of Tokenomica OÜ. After the ETO, the token holders also became formal shareholders of Nominee TKN OÜ. See the information about Nominee TKN OÜ in the Estonian e-business register, available at: https://ariregister.rik.ee/eng/company/14781834/Nominee-TKN-O%C3%9C?search_id=04f0825&pos=1&active_tab=register.

apply, and the legal construction as a whole would have been sustainable and compliant with the Croatian company law.

Even though the discussion about equity tokens from a securities point of view is beyond the scope of this paper, it is worth mentioning that the Greyp Bikes ETO has caused reactions of financial market supervision authorities. Exactly when it was beginning to gain momentum, the German Federal Financial Authority (BaFin) reacted issuing a statement that there is "cause to believe that the German public is being offered securities in the form of Greyp tokens".[54] In its statement, BaFin warned that Greyp Bikes, in accordance with Article 3, paragraph 1 of the Prospectus Regulation, had the obligation to publish a prospectus for its offering and that it is not obvious that an exception to this obligation applied in the case at hand. Namely, BaFin was of the opinion that the requirements prescribed by Article 3, paragraph 2 of the German Securities Prospectus Act (*Wertpapierprospektgesetz*, hereinafter: WpPG) for offering securities for sale without a prospectus in the case the total value of the offering is less than 8 million EUR, were not met because an information sheet about the securities offering was not submitted to BaFin, whereas it had to be submitted and published as well.[55]

4.4 Greyp Bikes Trade Sale

At the end of August 2021, the management of Smart Zero asked the Greyp token holders to vote on the possibility of selling Smart Zero's share in Greyp Bikes until 31 December 2021 at the latest, for a minimum price of 1,78 million EUR. At the time, it was announced in the media that the shareholders of Greyp Bikes are negotiating with three major investors with the aim to ensure the capital for further growth of the company.[56] Greyp token holders were called to vote for the proposal to sell, because one of those investors was interested in purchasing a majority share in Greyp Bikes, including Smart Zero's share *i.e.* the share in Greyp Bikes controlled by the Greyp token holders.[57] At the beginning of September, it was announced that the proposal has passed, allowing the possibility for a new investor to take over the 3.8% share Smart Zero holds in Greyp Bikes.[58] Finally, on 19 November 2021, it was revealed that the deal was made with the industry giant Porsche to take over the

[54] BaFin (2021).

[55] BaFin (2021). In that regard, the representatives of Greyp Bikes d.o.o. were of the opinion that the business plan of the company that was published on the Neufund platform was enough for the investors to decide whether to invest or not, and that the prospectus was not necessary if the investment value was less than 5 million EUR. Knez (2019). The author was not able to find the information on the outcome of the disagreement.

[56] Ivezić (2019) Rimac isplaćuje.

[57] Ivezić (2019) Rimac isplaćuje.

[58] Ivezić (2021b) Prva tvrtka.

majority share in Greyp Bikes, *inter alia*, buying out the Greyp token holders represented by Smart Zero.[59]

As of 22 November 2021, which is the date of the finalization of the exit transaction, Greyp tokens will no longer represent ownership in Greyp Bikes, whereas the token holders who had possession of Greyp tokens on the said date will receive a portion of the proceeds generated by the sale to Porsche, which is for each Greyp token holder calculated in proportion to the amount of Greyp tokens it owns and the proceeds.[60] Interestingly, the Greyp tokens will not be erased or transferred back to Greyp Bikes' crypto-wallet, but will remain on the token holders' crypto-wallets without any shareholder rights associated to them.[61] In other words, the tokens will continue to exist from a technical point of view, but the legal link to the shareholder rights in Greyp Bikes will be severed. Therefore, a transfer of tokens to another person that would take place after the date of the finalization of the exit transaction *i.e.* following the payout to the Greyp token holders, would still be possible from a technical point of view, but it would not result in the transfer of any token holder rights or future right to the payment of proceeds, and such disclosure would have to be made to any prospective buyer.[62] This somewhat peculiar scheme in which the tokens continue to technically exist might have to do with the transaction fees on the Ethereum blockchain, which are currently prohibitively high.[63] These fees are also the reason why Neufund has decided not to distribute the payouts on-chain, but off-chain, instead sending the wire transfer to a bank account linked to the token holder's Neufund account.[64]

5 Conclusion

The blockchain phenomenon has undoubtedly opened up many growth opportunities for small and medium-sized enterprises operating in the form of limited liability companies. Even though these companies are traditionally characterized by a very

---

[59] Ivezić (2021a) Porsche preuzeo.

[60] Neufund (2021a) Greyp Bikes exit FAQ.

[61] Neufund (2021a), Greyp Bikes exit FAQ.

[62] Neufund (2021a), Greyp Bikes exit FAQ.

[63] Users of Ethereum blockchain solutions have to pay a fee for each transaction, such as an interaction with a smart contract. This fee fluctuates depending on activity and the complexity of the transaction. More elaborate transactions, such as claiming or transferring tokens, can become more expensive, as they require more resources from the Ethereum blockchain network. For more on Ethereum transaction fees see, for example, Coen (2020). To illustrate, on 14 November 2021, the average transaction fee on Ethereum amounted to 6.514 USD. See https://ycharts.com/indicators/ethereum_average_transaction_fee.

[64] According to Neufund, this was decided to enable the Neufand users to "truly benefit from the exit proceeds", because many of the "users are struggling to cover the high costs and execute the needed transactions". Neufund (2021a), Greyp Bikes exit FAQ.

small number of mutually connected members and the illiquidity of their shares, which is due to the formalities attached to their transfer, the tokenization of shares and the offering of the resulting equity tokens to the public at large via ETOs, under the auspices of technological platforms running on blockchain networks, may lead to a complete paradigm shift. Obviously, even before the emergence and popularization of blockchain, the laws in many European countries have supported legal models of indirect transfer of shares and rights associated with shares in limited liability companies, without the transfer of formal membership in the limited liability company, several of which have been described in this paper. Blockchain, however, has enabled the application of such models on a massive scale, tremendously broadening the pool of prospective investors and allowing faster, cheaper and simpler fundraising due to its inherent technological features.

The case of Greyp Bikes, regardless of the hiccups in the implementation of the tokenization scheme, has shown that private limited liability companies can, in fact, successfully utilize blockchain-fueled equity token public offerings, simultaneously lowering the entry barriers for small investors. In the process, Greyp Bikes has become an atypical limited liability company with more than a thousand indirect shareholders from 34 countries in the world. The recent exit event symbolizes the closure of the full circle of investment for this company, from the stage of fundraising, in which 1.4 million was raised, to the stage of exit, in which 1.7 million EUR will be distributed to the Greyp token holders by the industry giant Porsche.[65] Importantly, unlike the formal shareholders in traditional limited liability companies, the Greyp token holders will exit the company upon payout easily, without formalities such as the participation of notaries. It is also not insignificant that all this was achieved in relation to a limited liability company that does not originate in Silicon Valley or some other internationally renowned technological hub, but a relatively small economy and a bureaucratic system, which speaks volumes about the potential of blockchain. Against this backdrop, it must be pointed out that the development of the market for equity tokens is at its earliest stages and there is still a long way to go. However, if the practice of tokenization takes roots and spreads, and if the European law-makers start taking more active roles in simplifying the process of raising investment capital for limited liability companies, especially taking blockchain into account, we might see a significant shift from private to public limited liability companies in the near future.

References

BaFin (2021) Greyp Bikes d.o.o.: Öffentliches Angebot ohne Prospekt. Available at: https://www.bafin.de/SharedDocs/Veroeffentlichungen/DE/Verbrauchermitteilung/weitere/2019/meldung_191028_Greyp_Bikes.html

[65] See also the statement of Neufund's founder Zoe Adamovitz. Neufund (2021b) Ground breaking Exit.

Barbić J (2013) Pravo društava (Knjiga druga; Društva kapitala). Organizator, Zagreb

Braut Filipović M (2020) Zaklada kao (većinski) član trgovačkog društva. Pravni vjesnik 36(3–4): 247–268

Chohan UW (2017) The decentralized autonomous organization and governance issues. Discussion Paper Series: Notes on the 21st Century. Available at: https://doi.org/10.2139/ssrn.3082055

Coen E (2020) Understanding Ethereum transaction fees: what is Ethereum gas? Cryptotesters. Available at https://cryptotesters.com/blog/ethereum-gas

Čulinović Herc E et al (2018) Pravno uređenje odnosa članova u zatvorenim (closely held) društvima na primjeru hrvatskog društva s ograničenom odgovornošću. Zbornik Pravnog fakulteta Sveučilišta u Rijeci 39(1):45–90

Enriques L, Zetzsche LE (2019) Corporate Technologies and the Tech Nirvana Fallacy. European Corporate Governance Institute (ECGI) - Law Working Paper No. 457/2019. Available at: https://papers.ssrn.com/sol3/Delivery.cfm/SSRN_ID3565921_code1688367.pdf?abstractid=3392321&mirid=1

European Banking Authority (2019) Report with advice for the European Commission on crypto-assets, 9 January 2019. Available at: https://www.eba.europa.eu/sites/default/documents/files/documents/10180/2545547/67493daa-85a8-4429-aa91-e9a5ed880684/EBA%20Report%20on%20crypto%20assets.pdf

European Commission (2019) Annual Report on European SMEs 2018/2019 - Research & Development and Innovation by SMEs. Luxembourg. Accessible at: https://op.europa.eu/en/publication-detail/-/publication/cadb8188-35b4-11ea-ba6e-01aa75ed71a1/language-en

European Commission (2020) Commission Staff Working Document, Impact Assessment, Accompanying the document Proposal for a Regulation of the European Parliament and of the Council on Markets in Crypto-assets and amending Directive (EU) 2019/1937. Brussels, 24.9.2020, SWD(2020) 380 final. Accessible at: https://eur-lex.europa.eu/LexUriServ/LexUriServ.do?uri=SWD:2020:0380:FIN:EN:PDF

Feikert-Ahalt C (2018) Malta: government passes three laws to encourage blockchain technology. Library of Congress. Available at: https://www.loc.gov/item/global-legal-monitor/2018-08-31/malta-government-passes-three-laws-to-encourage-blockchain-technology/

Foxles W (2020) Germany's Neufund shuts down security token platform, saying BaFin failed to act. CoinDesk. Available at: https://www.coindesk.com/policy/2020/06/22/germanys-neufund-shuts-down-security-token-platform-saying-bafin-failed-to-act/

Gesley J (2019) Liechtenstein: parliament adopts blockchain act. Library of Congress. Available at: https://www.loc.gov/item/global-legal-monitor/2019-10-30/liechtenstein-parliament-adopts-blockchain-act/

Gesley J (2021) Switzerland: new amending law adapts several acts to developments in distributed ledger technology. Available at: https://www.loc.gov/item/global-legal-monitor/2021-03-03/switzerland-new-amending-law-adapts-several-acts-to-developments-in-distributed-ledger-technology/

Gorton GB, Souleles SN (2007) Special purpose vehicles and securitization. In: Carey M, Stulz Rene M (eds) The risks of financial institutions. University of Chicago Press, pp 549–602

Greyp Bikes (2019) Investment memorandum. Available at: https://platform.neufund.org/eto/view/LI/1eb004fd-c44d-4bed-9e76-0e0858649587

Gvelesiani I (2015) German 'Treuhand' vis-a-vis Austrian 'Treuhand'. Eur Sci J. April 2015: 133–138

Hassan S, De Filippi P (2021) Decentralized autonomous organization. Internet Policy Rev 10(2): 1–10

Hewa TM et al (2021) Survey on blockchain-based smart contracts: technical aspects and future research. IEEE Access 9:87643–87662

Higgins S (2017) $257 million: Filecoin breaks all-time record for ICO funding. CoinDesk. Available at: https://www.coindesk.com/markets/2017/09/07/257-million-filecoin-breaks-all-time-record-for-ico-funding/

Infloat & Watson Law (2019) Tokenizing SME equity: an introduction to the legal classification and the technological implications for issuing security tokens in the Netherlands and the EEA. Available at: https://watsonlaw.nl/wp-content/uploads/2019/03/Watson_Law_Infloat-STO-Tokenizing-SME-Equity.pdf

Ivezić B (2019) Rimac isplaćuje vlasnike Greyp tokena, mali ulagači kritični prema načinu na koji se radi otkup. Jutarnji list. Available at: https://novac.jutarnji.hr/novac/aktualno/rimac-isplacuje-vlasnike-greyp-tokena-mali-ulagaci-kriticni-prema-nacinu-na-koji-se-radi-otkup-15097054

Ivezić B (2021a) Porsche preuzeo većinski udio u Greyp Bikesu Mate Rimca za više od 100 milijuna kuna. Jutarnji list. Available at: https://novac.jutarnji.hr/novac/aktualno/porsche-preuzeo-vecinski-udio-u-greyp-bikesu-mate-rimca-za-vise-od-100-milijuna-kuna-15122295

Ivezić B (2021b) Prva tvrtka Mate Rimca koja bi mogla dobiti novog vlasnika: 'Razgovara se s tri ulagača'. Jutarnji list. Available at: https://novac.jutarnji.hr/novac/aktualno/prva-tvrtka-mate-rimca-koja-bi-mogla-dobiti-novog-vlasnika-razgovara-se-s-tri-ulagaca-15100143

Jurić D (2002) Odgovornost vladajućeg društva za obveze ovisnog društva u hrvatskom i usporednom pravu. Zbornik Pravnog fakulteta Sveučilišta u Rijeci 23(2):507–541

Kaal WA (2019) Blockchain solutions for agency problems in corporate governance. In: Balachandran KR (ed) Economic information to facilitate decision making. World Scientific Publishers. Available at: https://ssrn.com/abstract=3373393

Kalls S (2004) The transfer of shares of private companies. Eur Company Financ Law Rev 1(3): 340–367

Knez J (2019) Rimac dobio po prstima u Njemačkoj, kazna ne bi trebala biti visoka. Lider. Available at: https://lider.media/poslovna-scena/kompanije/rimac-dobio-po-prstima-u-njemackoj-kazna-ne-bi-trebala-biti-visoka-128848

Koele IA (2016) The Dutch private foundation in comparison with trusts: for the same purpose but rather different. Trusts Trust 22(1):140–145

Kondova G, Barba R (2019) Governance of decentralized autonomous organizations. J Mod Account Audit 15(8):406–411

Kulnigg T (2019) Smart contracts: too smart for Austrian civil law?. Schonherr. Available at: https://www.schoenherr.eu/content/smart-contracts-too-smart-for-austrian-civil-law/

Kunda I (2016) Jurisdiction and applicable law in crowdfunding. In: Primorac Ž et al (eds) Economic and social development - 16th international scientific conference on economic and social development – "the legal challenges of modern world". Split, pp 253–263

Lafarre A, Van der Elst C (2018) Blockchain technology for corporate governance and shareholder activism. ECGI Working Paper Series in Law - Working paper no. 390/2018. Available at: http://ssrn.com/abstract_id=3135209

Lambert T et al (2021) Security token offerings. Small Business Economics. Available at: https://rdcu.be/cBKR2

Levi SD, Lipton AB (2018) An introduction to smart contracts and their potential and inherent limitations. Harvard Law School Forum on Corporate Governance. Available at: https://corpgov.law.harvard.edu/2018/05/26/an-introduction-to-smart-contracts-and-their-potential-and-inherent-limitations/

Lewis A (2018) The basics of bitcoins and blockchains: an introduction to cryptocurrencies and the technology that powers them (Cryptography, Crypto Trading, Digital Assets, NFT). Mango

Magnier V, Barban P (2018) The potential impact of blockchains on corporate governance: a survey on shareholders' rights in the digital era. IagnierInterEULawEast: J Int Eur Law Econ Mark Integr 5(2):189–226

Meng L, Xing S (2021) Research on the application of blockchain technology in the field of corporate governance. E3S Web Conf. 275(01064). Available at: https://www.e3s-conferences.org/articles/e3sconf/pdf/2021/51/e3sconf_eilcd2021_01064.pdf

Morris M (2014) Dutch STAK in scope of CRS. Available at: http://www.the-best-of-both-worlds.com/dutch-stak.html

Neufund (2019) What is blockchain? Available at: https://support.neufund.org/support/solutions/articles/36000130549-what-is-blockchain-

Neufund (2021a) Greyp Bikes exit FAQ. Available at: https://blog.neufund.org/greyp-bikes-exit-faq-f101fa643d87

Neufund (2021b) Ground breaking Exit: Greyp Bikes will be acquired by Porsche. Available at: https://blog.neufund.org/ground-breaking-exit-greyp-bikes-will-be-acquired-by-porsche-29510e128ac3

Nielsen T (2019) Cryptocorporations: a proposal for legitimizing decentralized autonomous organizations. Utah Law Rev 2019(5):1105–1029

Policaro GA (2019) Equity crowdfunding e s.r.l. aperte. Un cambio di paradigma nel nostro ordinamento. Il dirritto dell'economia 65(100):243–266

Rodeck D, Curry B (2021) What is Ethereum and how does it work?. Forbes. Available at: https://www.forbes.com/advisor/investing/what-is-ethereum-ether/

The Financial Action Task Force (2016) Anti-money laundering and counter-terrorist financing measures (Austria - Mutual Evaluation Report). FATF, Paris

Thompson C (2020) Dutch STAK foundations – an overview. Forsters. Available at: https://www.forsters.co.uk/news/blog/dutch-stak-foundations-overview

Token Alliance (2021) Legal landscapes governing digital tokens in the European Union. Available at: https://4actl02jlq5u2o7ouq1ymaad-wpengine.netdna-ssl.com/wp-content/uploads/2021/05/Legal-Landscapes-Governing-Digital-Tokens-in-the-European-Union.pdf

Tokenomica (2020) How to conduct a successful offering of tokenized equity in the EU: sharing our personal experience. Available at: https://blog.tokenomica.com/how-to-conduct-a-successful-offering-of-tokenized-equity-in-the-eu-sharing-our-personal-experience/

Völkel O, Hollman BW (2020) Every success story needs a beginning - tokenization in Austria, Stadler Völkel, Attorneys at Law. Available at https://www.svlaw.at/tokenize-the-world

Warburg B et al (2019) Basics of blockchain: a guide for building literacy in the economics, technology, and business of blockchain. Animal Ventures

Yermack D (2017) Corporate governance and blockchains. Rev Finance 21(1):7–31

The manufacturer's authorised representative in the EU is Springer
Nature Customer Service Centre GmbH, Europaplatz 3, 69115 Heidelberg,
Germany. If you have any concerns regarding our products, please
contact ProductSafety@springernature.com

Printed and bound by CPI Group (UK) Ltd, Croydon, CR0 4YY
22/09/2026
02220991-0019